DEATH WAITED IN THE GARAGE

The moment Ernie Brendel turned off the ignition and stepped out of the Toyota, his fate was sealed. Standing between his car and his wife's Audi, Ernie looked up to see a man in a black ninja mask holding a loaded crossbow pointed in his direction.

There was no time even for a "Who are you!" when the first arrow was released at point-blank range. Ernie shouted in shock and searing pain.

The force of it! It was so powerful, it could devastate a bear.

The arrow went right through the front side of Ernie's huge barrel-shaped chest, tore through flesh, and exited through his back. It crashed into the garage wall behind him with a heavy, dull thud.

Ernie realized he was going to die. His unknown assailant was loading the crossbow again, pulling back the drawstring and inserting another arrow. Ernie turned and tried to escape the lethal weapon aimed again in his direction.

The trigger was released. This time the arrow hit Ernie in the buttock. He fell face forward, the weight of his own body propelling him to the ground with a crashing thud. When he fell, his jaw hit the ground first, breaking and loosening his teeth. The floor was beginning to be covered with blood.

Seething with pain and panic, Ernie pulled himself up, grasping the handle of the Audi's door on the passenger side.

The man with the crossbow had reloaded and was now standing between the two cars facing him. Hanging on to the side of the car, Ernie faced him long enough to take the last arrow in the chest, dead center. It went through his aorta and stuck in his backbone. . . .

SHATTERED INNOCENCE, SHATTERED DREAMS

SUSAN HIGHTOWER and MARY RYZUK

PINNACLE BOOKS
KENSINGTON PUBLISHING CORP.

PINNACLE BOOKS are published by

Kensington Publishing Corp.
850 Third Avenue
New York, NY 10022

Pinnacle and the P logo Reg. U.S. Pat. & TM Off.

First Printing: November, 1995

Printed in the United States of America

Contents

PART I - Missing

PART II - Life with Chris

PART III - Ernie

PART IV - Murder

PART V - The Trial

PART I
Missing

Prologue

It was a high-profile, media-drenched disappearance of an entire family.

The people of the town of Barrington, Rhode Island, were stunned when fifty-three-year-old Ernest Brendel, his forty-six-year-old wife Alice, and their eight-year-old daughter Emily, vanished without a trace but with many indications leading to the conclusion that violence had played an integral part in the mystery.

This was not the sort of thing that occurred in Barrington or to people like the Brendels. Ernest and Alice were both Brown University graduates. He was a patent attorney with sufficient private financial resources to permit him to retire from a prestigious New York law firm in 1972 and work out of his home as—in his words—an "intellectual property lawyer" and part-time investor in the stock market. Quiet and reserved, Alice was a librarian at the Rockefeller Library at Brown University, well liked by associates who enjoyed her professionalism and her subtle sense of humor. Little Emily was a charming only child who had arrived late in life to her parents and was, in many respects, the center of their universe.

On September 22, 1991, the Brendel family was reported missing.

When Susan Hightower heard about it, she had no idea what had happened to the Brendels. Her estranged husband, Christopher, had a business relationship with Ernie, as well as one of friendship. From the time the two men first met, Chris had been very enthusiastic about their association.

Susan didn't know the details, but recently something had gone sour between the two men. Something to do with stocks and investments.

Now this shocking news. The entire family gone. Missing without a trace.

Although worried, family, friends, and neighbors were hopeful that the Brendels would turn up unharmed and with a reasonable explanation. But, somehow, Susan knew that Christopher had something to do with their disappearance.

What had happened to Ernie and Alice and Emily?

Susan thought of the time she and Chris had taken Emily to New Hampshire on a vacation with them along with their own two sons, Mitchell,[1] seven, and Paul,[1] five. That vacation seemed like such a long time ago—so much had happened since then—but it was really only last summer.

---

[1]To protect the children, these are pseudonyms.

Chapter 1

A Family Disappears

Monday—September 23, 1991

Susan Slicker Hightower, a thirty-year-old brunette with a bright personality, an active intellect, a pretty face, and an attractive young figure, was secretary to the Reverend Joseph T. Dye, pastor of the 275-year-old Barrington Congregational Church, which offered Protestant United Church of Christ services. "The White Church," a beautiful landmark building, was situated next to the Barrington River, and even with the austerity of its simple New England architectural lines, the surrounding setting was soft, its atmosphere warm and protective. It was a beautiful haven in which to work.

When Susan was summoned to the Barrington Police Station on the morning of September 23, 1991, at approximately 10:30 A.M. she was comfortably dressed in a simple skirt and a blouse, suitable for her job at the church. Now she wished she had put on a sweater to mitigate the sudden chill that ran up her spine. She knew it had something to do with Chris. She hated to think along those lines, but there had been much in their personal relationship that justified her thoughts.

Many marriages suffer the emotional violence that had been at the core of the Hightower union, but few wives are forced to face the nightmare of who and what Christopher Jemire Hightower proved to be.

Only four days earlier, Susan had filed a divorce complaint accompanied by a restraining order against her husband of nine years. She had loved him, married him, and borne him two sons. Now she had to keep him away from her and their boys. He had threatened to kill her more than once. The last time, this past Thursday, the nineteenth, in the offices of the "White Church," where they had married, was particularly convincing, and she had believed him.

Her wedding had been the afternoon of July 10, 1982, and she had looked stunning in her white bridal gown.

Susan: *The wedding day I was nervous. There were a lot of people who didn't like him. Even my best friends. I still don't think my parents were that crazy about him. He had very few friends and he didn't make friends easily.*

I remember being really nervous the week or two before the wedding day, Was I doing the right thing or not?

But I was in love.

I wrote it off to prewedding jitters.

. . .

Still, I was terribly anxious about it.

It had been a hot steamy day. Waiting for the start of the cere-mony, with beads of perspiration rolling down her back, Susan had stood in the rear of the church on the arm of her father, Dr. Clyde Slicker. He was a gentle, soft-spoken man, who, through-out her life, had always been there when she needed him. They were not in the habit of speaking about the confrontational as-pects of their lives, and he was supportive and comforting as usual. The tension she had been experiencing, and even the op-pressive heat, had seemed to dissipate the moment she heard the organ music begin.

Susan had deeply believed that Chris was everything she could have hoped for: bright, intelligent, educated, attentive, romantic, interesting. At thirty-two, he had been married once before and had two children, but it had mattered little to her. Anyone could make a mistake. He had been too young—and his first wife hadn't understood his need to go on with his advance studies in medicine. He had dreams of finding a cure for hypertension. Although only twenty, Susan understood. If anyone could do it, he could.

A reception for about 150 people had been held in the Assembly Hall next door to the church. Susan's entire family had been present, though none of Chris's family had come. The reception had been finger food, champagne, cake and ice cream shaped into delicious little flowers.

Susan had been on top of the world, pleased with everything. Her sense of unease and her prewedding jitters disappeared. It was a day full of love, and family, and joy, and all the anticipation of a bright future. She was so sure they would have a beautiful marriage. Certainly their relationship prior to their wedding had been full, not only of bright promises, but of fun as well.

Who could have known it would end with Susan hiding in the locked administrative office of the church in which they had married, in fear for her life.

"I'm not going to kill you myself," he had said to her the night before, laying bare the full extent of the deterioration of their marriage. "I've paid someone five thousand dollars to do it and an extra thousand to make it look like an accident. And if your parents try to interfere between me and the boys, I'll have them killed, too."

That latest threat made her decision.

She had gone straight to family court to get a restraining order and then filed divorce papers. She left the house in the Jeep Cherokee at 8:30 A.M. Instead of going to work, she met her lawyer at court at 9:00 A.M. Merely filing the papers was an unnerving ordeal. His threats made her believe she was risking her life to do this. She knew statistically, at the time of a final breakup when a man felt certain of losing control, his ego needed to maintain the relationship and a woman was in the greatest physical danger from an abusive husband. Susan shuddered at the memory of his words, for although he terrified her with the threat of death at the hands of an unknown assailant, it was the cold, menacing look in his eyes when he said it that had convinced her. If given the right opportunity, Chris was capable of escalating to physical abuse the pattern of psychological and emotional abuse he had used to control her throughout their nine years together.

Attorney Mary Ciresi had the papers ready.

Susan: *I remember thinking when I finally made the decision to file for divorce that I was risking my life by doing that. Physically risking my life.*

When Chris and his first wife divorced, he had made the conscious decision to give up his two daughters because he wanted to go to medical school and he would not be able to take care of them. He had been willing then, but he wasn't going to "make that mistake again."

She believed he would never let her have Mitchell and Paul.

Susan: *When I got to that point in August of 1991 that I knew I had to get out of that marriage, I was certain that, not only was I risking my life, but I was also risking losing my children. Still, I was determined. Death threat or not, I was going to file for divorce and I was going to keep my children as well.*

It was done.
She had signed the papers.
It had been the most terrifying moment of Susan's life.
But she had done it.
She had to be free of this man, regardless of the cost, but the strength and determination she had summoned to get to this point were not without severe cost to her peace of mind.

Before she returned to work to face the rest of the day, Susan went to a friend's house for lunch, talk, comfort, and support, reliving the anxiety of family court, the need to finally assert herself, the painful end of a dream, the man she had loved, now feared to the point of needing official protection and help to keep him away. She needed her friend. The pain of divorce for herself and for her children was bad enough, but to have the dream end with such terror and intimidation was a factor she could never have imagined.

Susan barely ate her lunch and left her friend behind to go to work. It was 1:00 P.M. and she was alone again. Talk had helped just so much; unburdening helped, but the fear remained.

She slowly drove the Jeep Cherokee around the church parking lot several times to make sure his car was not there. She finally stopped in front of the church to park in her usual spot.

Her mother Mary Lou's Caprice Classic station wagon pulled up next to her. It was the car Chris used. He was there.

Keeping her door locked, she partially rolled down the window and looked at him. "What do you want?"

"Where have you been?" he demanded.

"I've been out," she answered, trying to cover up her nervousness. He was looking agitated again, and she didn't know what he was up to.

"Are you going back to work?"

"Yes. Aren't you going home to take care of the kids?" she said, trying to deflect more questions about where she had been. If he knew she had just filed for divorce and a restraining order . . . "That's what you're supposed to be doing," she added.

"Yes, but I want to know where you've been!"

"I'm not going to tell you. I've been out. Anything else?"

"No."

"What do you want?"

"Nothing."

"Are you leaving?"

"I've been following you," he challenged. "I know you didn't go to work. I know you went somewhere else. I've been following you."

Then he pulled out of the parking lot with a jerking screech of wheels.

He drove off down the lot and made the turn back onto the main road to go home. Had he really been following her? Had he seen her go to family court? Probably not. He would have confronted her with it, then and there, if he had.

When she was sure he had gone, she unlocked the door and got out of the car. She hurried into the empty building, knowing the ministers were out to lunch. She had to leave the outside door unlocked because other people would need to get in and out, but she immediately locked her office from within. She found herself wishing the door was not half-glass. It had never mattered before, but the partitioned door offered little privacy and little safety.

She got on the phone and called her father.

"Dad, I did it," she said breathlessly. "I filed the papers, I got the restraining order. They'll serve him with all the papers to-morrow."

"Okay," the professor said with resignation. It had been com-ing.

"I'll give you more details when I get home."

"Okay, Sue."

"Dad, where are the kids?" she asked quickly. "He was sup-posed to be taking care of them but he's been here . . ."

Suddenly she stopped mid-sentence. She looked up and saw him through the glass partition.

"Dad," she said quietly, her heart pounding, "I have to go. He's standing outside my office."

Worry crept into Clyde's voice, "Are you all right?"

"Yes," she said with a calm she did not feel.

Chris was dressed normally, in jeans and a button-down cotton plaid shirt, but his eyes were not normal. Bulging out, and she could tell by the deepening red of his face that he was barely in control of his anger.

She put the phone down, never once taking her eyes off Chris. It flashed through her mind that she was alone in the building. She could not let him know how terrified she was. Summoning up as much courage as she could, she called forcefully through the locked door, "What do you want?"

"You let me in!" he demanded, jiggling the doorknob.

"You tell me what you want from that side of the door," she insisted.

"Either you let me in or I'll break this door down."

He was clicking his jaw rapidly. She knew only too well that was a sign of great anxiety. The more aggravated and distressed he was, the faster and harder he clicked his jaw.

Again she internally lamented that the door wasn't very strong.

Once, it easily had been broken in by a burglar. It could never hold back Chris. Not when he was so furious with her.

Susan: *What am I going to do? His teeth are clomping. The whole bit, and I'm in this building absolutely alone. I've got to go someplace where someone can hear me scream if something happens and being in this building alone with him is not going to do it.*

Making a sudden decision to remove herself from the vulnerable spot she was in, she grabbed her keys to the office and pushed out past him before he had a chance to react. She hurried down the stairs, with him following closely behind, until they were outside standing at the bottom of the steps between the church and the education building, where her office was located. Now, at least, she was where she could see the traffic. Her mind continued to race ahead, trying to form a plan; her adrenaline was pumping. Every muscle in her body was primed for flight. If something were to happen, she could, at least, run toward the cars for help. She would have a fighting chance of not being hurt.

"I want to know where you've been," he demanded.

"I told you," she said. "I was out."

"Where were you!" he insisted.

"It's none of your business." She probably should not have sounded so confrontational in the face of his fury, but she was determined to change her own pattern of behavior with him. No more subservience to his demands; no more apologies for her life. But despite the boldness of her stand, she was terrified.

"Until we're divorced, you're still my wife . . ." he fumed. ". . . and I have every right to know absolutely everything you're doing."

"I've been out and I don't need to tell you where I've been."

He became more agitated. "I have the right!" he insisted, stepping forward, forcing her to back away, hoping he could not see how afraid he was making her, how his intimidation was actually working. "You're still my wife and until we're divorced I have the right to know where you've been and what you've been doing all the time."

He kept repeating the same phrase over and over, and she kept insisting, almost surprised at her own courage in the face of such intimidation, "I've been out." "I'm back." "It's none of your business." But by now Susan was physically shaking and had no idea how she was going to get rid of him.

Her younger sister, Kathy, had been on her lunch hour and stopped to pick up some flowers to bring to Sue. When she drove through the parking lot and came around the corner, she saw her sister and brother-in-law standing outside the church. She realized they had seen her, and was sorry she had intruded, not knowing how bad things had become between them. *They look like they're into something deep,* she thought.

Kathy got out of her car and walked half the distance between them. Something about their demeanor made her stop.

"It's okay, Kathy," Chris called to her. "You can come on."

Kathy walked up to them and sensed the high tension between them.

Susan was so relieved to see her sister, she gave her a big hug. "I brought you flowers . . ."

Chris looked at Susan with the terrible cold stare even Kathy had come to know so well. "I'm only going to ask you one more time. Where were you?"

Sue's voice was barely controlled as she said, "I was out and I'm going to ask you now to please leave."

He turned abruptly, stepped into the station wagon, and left.

"You have the best timing I've ever seen," she said to her sister, shaking almost uncontrollably.

"Let's go inside."

"I was really worried that he was going to do something to me."

"Come on," Kathy urged gently.

They went back to the office, and Sue, opened up. She told Kathy everything that had happened, including how he had thrown a glass against the fireplace in their family room at home.

Susan collapsed in a chair and started to cry. She was terrified of what he seemed to be capable of and that she was going to bear the brunt of it because, as he coldly told her, she had "ruined his life."

Kathy was sad but not surprised. Their family had always taken the institution of marriage very seriously, and she knew Susan and Chris had tried to work things out several times over the previous years with the help of counseling. Things always seemed to get better for a short while, then the problems would return. Kathy was sure Susan had tried very hard to make things work.

"I'll stay with you until someone comes back from lunch," Kathy said quietly, then handed her sister the three roses she had brought.

"Happy birthday," Kathy said softly.

One rose for each decade. Susan had almost forgotten, today, September 19, 1991, was her thirtieth birthday.

To all outward appearances, the rest of the work day was normal except that Susan could not shake her anxiety.

At least one of the ministers was present for the remainder of the day, but she kept her office door locked. No one objected.

Susan did not know what Chris was up to. All she knew was that his look was terrifying. The confrontation in the parking lot turned out to be the last face-to-face encounter of their marriage. Since then, even having been presented with the restraining order and having been personally escorted by a constable and four Barrington policemen from her parents' home, where they had lived, Chris's presence in and out of her activities had haunted her entire weekend. On Saturday, September 21, Chris violated the restraining order by going to their son's soccer game. The fact that Chris had been his coach was no excuse; the police were called and he was asked to leave the game. Yesterday, Rev. Joseph Dye, afraid that Chris might come to the church during morning worship to confront Susan, had requested that a patrolman be stationed outside the sanctuary. Having once served in the capacity of counselor to the troubled marriage, he knew the extent of the tension between Susan and Chris. He was also aware that the situation had escalated, not only to divorce, but to the possibility of violence. During the services that Sunday, they were unaware that Chris had driven Ernest Brendel's car to the door of the church but continued on after seeing the patrol car stationed outside.

On Monday morning, September 23, the police asked Susan to come to the station to answer a few questions.

Questions about what? The restraining order? The children?

The tension had continued throughout the weekend even though Chris was physically out of the house.

Susan had been very nervous all morning, a residual effect of their last meeting in the parking lot. She knew he was enraged, defensively bitter, and that he would place the blame for their broken marriage completely on her.

Her father had been present when the papers were served and had told her Chris looked as though he had spent the night in the woods.

She wondered where he could have gone after their confrontation. It had poured all night. He was showering when the officers arrived to serve him the divorce papers and the restraining order. The judge had ordered the backup personnel, believing Mr. Hightower could become violent when he found out what his wife had done.

Susan: *There were extra police officers when they came to serve the restraining order.*
Because of the loaded guns.

Susan could imagine the rage seething through him as he was escorted off the premises on foot, carrying his personal effects in nothing more substantial than a brown paper bag. He didn't even have a car, as he'd always used her mother's.

* * *

Chris could be anywhere in the area. She certainly had no desire to see him at this stage in the legal proceedings she had set in motion. At work, she was constantly on her guard. Would he come back to the church? Was he going to wait until he could confront her alone again now that he knew what she had done? She could barely sit still that morning when she arrived at work. Getting up. Sitting down. Moving around the office. Checking on things. It was mostly make-work activity to keep herself moving since sitting still had become impossible.

Fortunately, many people came in and out of the office. In addition to the unusual activity, a computer specialist had come to service her computer system. She was thankful for his presence, feeling mildly protected by his proximity.

A staff meeting was called at approximately 10:00 A.M. Present were two ministers, one of the church custodians, and one of the church musicians. Although Susan felt safer behind closed doors surrounded by people she knew and trusted, she could not focus on the meeting, and could not remember afterward what it was about.

They were just getting started when a knock at the door made Susan jump.

It was only Lynne Githens, a familiar face. But when she said to Susan, "I need you to come down to the police station to answer a few questions," Susan realized Lynne had come this morning, not as a member of the church, but in her official capacity as a part-time assistant at the Barrington Police Department.

The police request to interrogate her did not help the jagged edge of nerves she was suffering, but at that point, after the tense, uncomfortable morning she had spent, Susan felt, "Well, it must have something to do with Chris. I'll do whatever I have to do."

Rev. Joseph T. Dye, her friend and pastor, nodded his okay.

"We'll go in my van," Lynne said.

Susan trusted Lynne to get her to the police station safely, despite the new ambiguous ingredient added to an already-perplexing situation. Safety was still uppermost in her thoughts.

"Who are we talking to?" she asked as they drove toward the center of town in Lynne's van.

Lynne looked at her and said, "These are the real good guys."

"Like the FBI?" Susan asked half-jokingly.

But Lynne would not say any more.

To her surprise, Susan had guessed correctly.

Susan: *I felt safe because I had men with guns around me. I was terrified of Chris at this point. I thought when I was in that police station I couldn't be anyplace safer, 'cause I had spent the whole morning edgy. I knew he had a crossbow. I saw the box in the car on Friday.*

Dressed casually in sports jackets, ties, and pants, the two who were waiting to question her at the Barrington Police Station were pleasant young men from the Federal Bureau of Investigation.

Susan was clueless as to the reason for their interest in her. But she had been right about one thing; their questions were all about Chris.

"Can you tell us about his daily patterns . . . ?"

She was unaware that she was answering questions that related to the missing family.

"Do you know where he is now?"

"No."

Even surrounded by the police, she was still hypervigilant. It couldn't be about her family. He couldn't have done anything to them already. She knew where her kids were; they were in school. Her mother was in Ohio because her sister-in-law had died. Her father was busy running errands, such as going to the post office to have their mail stopped while they were gone, and trying to get plane reservations to go to Ohio for the funeral. So she knew her family was all right. Susan was more worried about herself.

"Where does he usually go?"

"The only friend he has is Ernie Brendel. He might be there."

"What was he wearing when you last saw him?"

At the soccer game she had seen him in a pair of navy blue

pants. "Looked like Dickies work pants, a long-sleeve blue button-down shirt and . . . I couldn't tell what was on his feet . . ."

"What does he usually do?"

Her head was reeling. Had Chris been caught doing something
illegal with money?

"What was his state of mind?"

Embezzling with the stocks. Blackmail. Something to do with
money. Stolen money.

"What was going on in his business?"

He had always joked that if he ever ran out of money, he'd rob
a bank. And now that he had been literally thrown out of her
parents' house, he had, to her knowledge, nothing left. *He has
to be desperate for money,* she thought, her mind racing through
the questions.

"How much money did he have on him? . . ."

He had no home anymore, no place to go . . . no transporta-
tion . . . no anything. She knew eviction from his business office
was imminent because of a series of bounced checks he'd given
his landlord.

"Does he have any distinguishing marks?"

He was about to get subpoenaed into court because he was in
arrears in child support payments to his first wife.

Height . . . weight . . . hair color . . . eyes . . . scars . . .

Another thought flashed through her mind. Maybe it was
about the guns. Only this past Friday, the twentieth, after the
confrontation at the church with Chris, Susan had asked her
friend, Diane Hutton, who also worked part-time at the Barrington Police Department, to remove the guns Chris had stored
at home. When they were brought to the police station, the
sergeant found that the barrel of one shotgun had been sawed
off, and the .22 rifle, bought for their seven-year-old son
Mitchell, was loaded.

"We'll need some recent photos of him."

She couldn't imagine why they wanted a picture. It was as
though they were searching for him. As though he were a fugitive.

"I take it you're looking for him?" she asked.

They wouldn't tell her.

Confused as she was, another side of her was thinking that if anything was going to keep her safe from this man, she had to go along with whatever they asked her. She trusted them to take care of her and keep her from being harmed by him. It was a blind trust, but she felt she had no choice. She knew only that she needed to feel safe and that her children needed to be safe, and, perhaps, the only way to do that was to go along with whatever they wanted. Throughout the entire period of questioning, they never told her what the reason was behind the interrogation.

She answered all the questions to the best of her knowledge.

She was in the police station with the FBI until about noon. Then they took her back to the Barrington Congregational Church. To her surprise, they wanted to look through the wastepaper baskets at the church offices. She watched as they pulled some things out of the wastepaper basket next to the Xerox machine, but she did not know what.

Rev. Rose Amodeo, an associate minister, told her Chris had been at the Xerox machine at the church yesterday afternoon after Sunday worship was over and the building was deserted. As a Sunday school teacher and the soccer coach for the church youth team, he still had a key.

He had been there. . . . She wasn't safe.

"Can I go back to work now?" she asked, but the FBI agents were not finished. They wanted to take her home and desperation was beginning to overwhelm her. What was going on? Why all the mystery?

"I have to leave with them," she apologized to Rev. Joseph Dye and the others at the staff meeting. "They want to take me home to look for some things."

"What?"

"I don't know."

"Susan, what's it all about?"

The frustration of not knowing what it was all about was gnawing at her as she was forced to answer, "I really don't know, Joe."

* * *

The authorities drove her home to the Jones Circle house she, Chris, and the boys had been living in with her parents. Clyde was home and willingly gave his permission.

"What is it?" he asked his daughter.

"I don't know what's going on," she told him truthfully. "Chris is in the middle of something. They're looking for him."

"What for?"

"I don't know."

They searched through the basement, rummaged through the closet where he had kept the loaded guns, examined each of the family cars, and scoured the garage. Clyde discovered that the hand shovel in the garage was newly caked with earth and mud.

"When was the last time this shovel was used?"

"Not since the summer . . . I can't remember actually."

"This looks like it has been used recently."

Clyde nodded. He had to admit that it did.

Meanwhile, Susan was thinking about how to get her older son Mitchell home from school.

Two of Kathy's friends had been baby-sitting at home with the younger boy, Paul, and helping out around the house while her mother was in Ohio. Clyde had been busy with errands all day. Susan was afraid Chris might try to get to Mitchell. One of the girls offered, "We can walk down to the school to get him." But the police didn't like that idea. There was always the possibility of an angry confrontation should Chris show up at the school. The police suggested, instead, that they go to the school to bring the child home in their squad car.

Now it was Susan's turn to protest. "I don't want to frighten him. No," she said.

They spent some time trying to figure out how to get Mitchell home from school. Suggestions were going back and forth until there was a knock at the door. It was a uniformed police officer.

Susan heard him say to the agent who had answered the door, "They've got him."

The tension level in the room dropped noticeably. Susan actually could see the shoulders of the police and FBI relax.

"Well, this shouldn't be an issue anymore about how to get your son home," one of the agents said to her. "Your son can just come home from school now as usual."

"What's happened?"

"He's in custody."

"Chris?"

"Yes."

"Are you telling me my husband has been arrested?"

"Yes."

"On what charge?"

They still would not reveal to her why Chris had been taken into custody. She realized it didn't matter. At least now she knew where he was. He could not get at her himself. There might be someone else out there, but, she reasoned quickly, he couldn't have hired the assassin he had threatened her with. He had no money, only debts. No place even to borrow. The only person who might have loaned him money was Ernie Brendel.

The mystery only intensified when the police came back to the house at 8:00 P.M. for a second round of questioning.

Corporal Gerald A. Prendergast from the state police was middle-aged, with a bulldog, beaten-up face. He looked tough, as though he had been through and seen a lot in the line of duty. His associate, Stephen J. Lynch, was about thirty, with classic American good looks. Light brown, blondish hair, but not quite blond enough for a California guy, Susan thought. She would come to know that he always wore a red windbreaker jacket, making him easy to identify anywhere, even on television.

Prendergast and Lynch were just as secretive about what had happened as the FBI had been that morning, but despite the continued puzzle and confusion, Susan felt comfortable with them. They treated her well. They remained from eight o'clock to past eleven-thirty, again going over everything that had been discussed with her and Clyde during the daytime session.

There were times she was desperately tired of answering what seemed to be the same questions over and over. Strain was beginning to show. Several times Susan broke down and began to cry in the middle of the intense sessions. They let her take a break and get something to drink. She tried to apologize—it was just too overwhelming—but apologies weren't necessary. They waited quietly, patiently, until she could pull herself together again.

There were moments when the frustration was almost unendurable. "If you could just tell me what this is all about . . ."

"We just need you to answer what we ask you as honestly as you can."

"But it's the most frustrating thing not knowing."

"We know," they answered gently. "In time," they promised.

Then it was her father's turn to answer questions.

Chris had been served Friday morning with the restraining order. "I was here," Clyde told them. "I had no classes that morning. I wanted to make sure that things went the way they were supposed to. I was to give Sue a call at her office as soon as Chris came in so that she could let the constable know that he could come and serve. Things became complicated when Chris didn't come home the previous night."

"He didn't come home on Thursday night?"

"No. He came home Friday morning."

"What time was that?"

"About ten-fifteen."

"Was it unusual for him to stay out all night?"

"Very. And when he finally did come home, he looked like he had been playing rugby in the mud."

The professor noticed the glance that passed between the policemen.

"What else?"

"Well . . . his glasses were askew and bent. He was trying to fix them . . . straighten them out. And there was mud in his hair and on his clothing. It was nippy and rainy that night. He had gone out around seven-thirty and as he left he said, 'I might be home late tonight or I'll be back tomorrow morning.' " The professor shook his head slowly at the memory. "He had come home wet and muddied from his hair to his shoes."

They wanted to know what clothes Chris had been wearing that night. Did Susan have them? What did he do minute by minute when he came home Friday morning. Muddied? Did he look as though he had been digging?

Clyde told them how he had been present when Chris was served with the divorce papers and the restraining order. "That was the last time I saw him."

"What was his attitude?"

"Uptight. Very agitated. As though he had been betrayed. One thing, though," Clyde added. "When he came home Friday morning . . . he did something unusual, something that he never did."

"What was that?"

"He washed his muddy clothes. He stuck them all in the washing machine in the laundry room and washed them. He had never done anything like that before."

At 11:00 P.M. Sue needed another break. It had been three hours of intensive, repetitious questioning—always looking for the forgotten detail, an important moment suddenly remembered, a critical particular previously unnoticed—and she was exhausted. The quest for specifics was relentless. When one of the policemen got up to make a phone call, she went into the kitchen to get a glass of water and to splash some water on her face to try to clear her head.

Kathy's friends were still there. Thank goodness the two girls had stayed on. They had prepared dinner, cleaned up, and put the children to bed. Now, in the comfortable family room adjacent to the kitchen, the girls had the television turned on to the eleven o'clock news.

Sue walked out from the kitchen to the family room just in time to catch the last part of the lead story. She saw a reporter standing in front of an old wide-clapboard white house. There was something familiar about it. . . .

It looked like the Brendel home on Middle Highway!

". . . Middle Highway . . ." the reporter was saying.

It *was* the Brendel home.

But what was it doing on the news?

It had a yellow police tape stretched tautly across the driveway, blocking off the front of the property. She had seen that kind of tape often enough in films and television to recognize what it was. It was the kind of tape used to delineate the perimeter of a crime scene. The reporter was saying something about the disappearance of the Brendel family in Barrington.

All of them. Ernie, Alice, and Emily. People whom Susan knew!

Her reaction to the story of their disappearance was not one of shock. It was the integration of everything she had been going through with the FBI and the police all day. The Brendels—friends, neighbors, and business associate—were gone, and Susan, with a dreadful moment of awareness, softly exclaimed, "Oh my God . . ."

The police officer who was on the phone in the kitchen behind her heard her and said into the mouthpiece, "She knows."

Chris had done something to the Brendels. The police still would not clarify any of the details, or what Chris's actual involvement was, but she knew that much—he had done something to them.

By now, she was pretty numb. She had been through a great deal of frustration and personal speculation before the TV announcement brought the mystery into focus. An uncomfortable suspicion suddenly flashed into her mind.

Susan: *I knew he was a part of this. I knew he had done something very serious and my guess was—minimally—that he had kidnapped them and probably had done something even more serious than that.*

It would not have surprised her if he had. She was *that* certain that he was capable of it, and the certainty of her feeling was also a shock.

Her dad didn't believe that Chris could be involved. "We've lived with the man," Clyde Slicker said to Susan. "I can't believe that any man we've been so closely associated with could do something like that. Somebody else did it."

Susan was spared the need to answer her father by the ringing of the telephone.

It was the Reverend Joseph T. Dye.

"There's a big problem here in Barrington," the pastor said to Clyde. "There is a family missing."

"We know, Joe," the professor answered. "We just heard."

"And . . ." The pastor hesitated.

"What?"

"There's a possibility that maybe Chris is involved with this."

So Joe'd heard that, too. Clyde didn't know how to respond. He did not want to believe it. He glanced at Susan, whose eyes were still glued to the TV screen even though the anchorman had gone on to another story.

"I already have the airplane tickets," Clyde said into the phone.

"When are you leaving?"

"In the morning."

Susan's mother, Mary Lou, had been in Ohio for the past two weeks with Clyde's sister, who had been suffering through the last days of a terminal illness. "Last night Mary Lou called me around nine o'clock and said things were looking bad. Then she called back about nine-thirty to ten to tell me my sister died."

"I'm sorry . . ."

"So I've been running around all day today making arrangements to take everyone with me to Ohio. I want everyone with me."

"That's probably a good thing," the minister said. "There's going to be a lot of press around here because there are three people missing," he repeated, "and since they think Chris had something to do with it, they're bound to come after Sue."

Clyde still didn't want to believe it. He asked the minister to take them to the airport in the morning.

With the secrecy ended, Susan talked with her father about her continued fears regarding Chris's threats. Unlikely as it might be, Chris *did* tell her he had hired someone to kill them. . . .

Repeating to the police the story of her last meeting with Chris, she asked, "Do you think we're safe in this house tonight?"

"We don't know," they answered honestly.

Susan dialed the Reverend Joseph T. Dye's number to ask him if they could spend the night with him and his wife. "Since you're going to take us to the airport tomorrow anyway . . ."

He sensed her panic. "Yes, certainly. Of course." The offer was genuine and heartfelt.

Hurrying now through a pervasive sense of urgency, they had to leave the dog with some friends; they would take care of him and take him to the kennel in the morning.

"Where's the cat?"

They searched.

"I can't find him."

A cloud of fear and uncertainty influenced their hurried preparations to leave, making their decisions instantaneous and irrevocable.

"We'll have to leave him outside. He'll be okay. . . ."

"The neighbors will take care of him."

Susan and Clyde packed the rest of the clothes. The children were awakened. Susan pulled the sleepy Mitchell and Paul out of bed in their pajamas.

Cups with lukewarm coffee still in them were left on the kitchen table. They abandoned the house, locking it up. The coffee cups would wait until they returned.

The children were placed in the car, wrapped in blankets. They were confused, but Susan simply told them, "We need to move, we're going to spend the night at the Dyes' and then we'll be ready to go to Ohio in the morning."

They accepted their mother's explanation as the police escorted them over to the other side of Barrington.

When they finally retired for the night at the Dyes', after the long whispered conversations speculating about what could have happened to the Brendels and if Chris could really be involved, Susan remained awake the rest of the night. She listened to every sound, trying to accept the horror of all that was happening, and while she lay in terror, translating the normal night-creaking sounds of a house to those of an assassin breaking and entering in the middle of the night, she realized that she would now spend her life running and hiding. She had a new understanding of what it must have been like to be a Jew in Nazi Germany, to perceive danger everywhere, to run and hide from everything, to lose control over one's own safety.

When 6:00 A.M. came, she was still wide-awake. They left for Ohio for the funeral.

Afterward, by phone, Joseph Dye convinced them that coming home might not be a good idea at this time; the town was in a complete uproar, and with Chris adamantly uncommunicative with the police, the press would never leave Sue alone once they knew she was back in town.

When Susan and her family returned to Barrington a full week later, they realized Joe was right; the search for the missing family had indeed made Barrington a nightmare.

The running didn't stop. Susan decided to take the boys and leave Barrington. Her aunt and uncle took them to their home in Manchester, while Clyde and Mary Lou went back to Jones Circle to pick up clothing before leaving Barrington themselves for their summer home in New Hampshire.

After a couple of days, Susan called her parents to please come pick up Mitchell and Paul. She found she was too edgy to deal with the boys, and she didn't want to take it out on them. Clyde and Mary Lou came immediately to take them.

Once the boys were gone, Susan spent the rest of the week by herself in the home of her aunt and uncle, thinking about the Brendels, thinking about the divorce, but mostly, thinking about the man she had married.

* * *

Christopher Jemire Hightower was an upstanding man of the community. He had been a Wright State University Ph.D. candidate in biomedical science before becoming an investment advisor and a broker in commodity futures. He attended the Barrington Congregational Church regularly with his wife, Susan, their two young sons, Mitchell and Paul, and his in-laws, Dr. and Mrs. Slicker, with whom they lived. He taught Sunday school, coached the Barrington boys' soccer team, served regularly as a trusted confidant of adolescents with problems, and worked enthusiastically and productively on many church committees.

That was the facade people saw. That was what they believed.

Chapter 2

A Bizarre Story

Guilford, Connecticut—The Night Before

It was five o'clock on a crisp Sunday evening, September 22, 1991. From a high of sixty-nine degrees, the temperature had slipped to fifty-six.

When Christopher Hightower took the Brendel car and drove to Ernie Brendel's sister's house in Connecticut, no one, including the police, was aware that the family had disappeared.

When Christine Scriabine answered her door that evening, she had no idea it was going to be the start of a nightmare that would not end for twenty months, when, just prior to his sentencing in

June, 1993, she could finally tell the killer, face-to-face, what she thought of him.

A bit stocky, with short-cropped curly hair and a round, pleasant face, Christine was an historian at the Museum of Political Life in Hartford, Connecticut. Her tall, gray-haired husband, Alexander, was a physician and pharmacologist who spoke with a thick Eastern European accent. Well educated and comfortably in the middle of life, the Scriabines were looking forward to a pleasant evening of intelligent discourse with their four dinner guests. The guests had already arrived and were sitting in the living room with predinner cocktails.

Christine had been about to serve a lobster dinner and still had much to do when she went to answer the front doorbell.

She did not recognize the man who stood on the threshold. He was bearded, fortyish, slightly balding, and professorial in appearance.

"Yes?"

"Mrs. Scriabine? Christine Scriabine?"

The man noticed she bore a strong family resemblance to her brother, Ernest Brendel.

"Yes," she answered.

"I'm Christopher Hightower." Despite an intense gaze behind wire-rimmed eyeglasses, he had a soft, pleasant voice. "A friend of your brother Ernie." He quickly showed her a Rolodex file card with her name and address written on it in her brother's handwriting.

"Oh yes," she said, seeing Ernie's red Toyota Camry, or one that looked just like it, parked outside.

"I have to talk to you," the man said. "I've just driven from Barrington, Rhode Island." There was an undercurrent of urgency in the man's voice as he glanced past her towards the interior of the house.

"Is something wrong?"

"May I come in?" he asked.

"I'm afraid I can only spare you about ten minutes in the library," she said.

"It will take more than ten minutes."

"I have dinner guests."

He immediately pulled back. The urgency was clouded over with what seemed to be a moment of intense thought.

"Is it about Ernie?"

"I'll come back later. What time?"

She hesitated. "Well, my guests will be gone by eight."

His face broke into an ingratiating smile. She could see the crease of long dimples beneath the beard. "I'll come back at eight."

She watched him retreat to the Camry. He seemed charming, but that *was* Ernie's car. She wondered what he was doing with it. Since he had just driven all the way from Rhode Island, what was he going to do for three hours while he waited until eight o'clock?

Christine thought the incident odd. She told her husband and her guests about Christopher Hightower's unexpected visit. They, too, thought it odd but dismissed it when beckoned by the pleasant aroma of dinner.

They had forgotten about the man until later, when the Scriabines escorted their four guests to the front door and found him waiting on the doorstep. Dr. and Mrs. Scriabine didn't know they would spend the most nerve-racking hours of their lives with this stranger listening to the most frighteningly bizarre story they had ever heard.

"Look," Christopher said, pulling a dark leather wallet out of his pocket and handing it to the tall, grey-haired man.

The doctor opened it. The identification within confirmed it belonged to Ernest.

"Here," Chris said, taking two rings out of his pocket and handing them to Christine. "Do you recognize them?"

She held them in the palm of her hand. They belonged to her sister-in-law Alice.

"What's this all about?" Alexander asked.

"It's not good," Christopher said. "I have very bad news."

He proceeded to tell Alexander and Christine that his own wife, Susan, and his two young sons had been kidnapped.

"Kidnapped?"

"That's not all," Hightower continued. "They were taken with your brother, Ernie, his wife, and his daughter."

"Emily?"

"Yes."

She was only eight . . .

"And I've been contacted by the kidnappers, who are demanding $300,000 for their safe return."

"Three hundred thous . . ."

Hightower assured them he could come up with $225,000 if they could raise the remaining $75,000.

For the next five and a half hours, he elaborated on the story that his family and the Brendels had been kidnapped by the Mafia.

He looked at them nervously, as he grated his teeth together in a sharp cracking sound. He could tell they were deeply shocked as well as incredulous.

"I know it sounds weird," he insisted urgently, "but it's the truth. Saturday . . . late Saturday, when I got home from work . . . about six-thirty . . . I discovered that my wife and two sons were missing," he explained. "I had no idea where they were. Then, about eleven-thirty, I got a call from a man who said they had my family and he wanted $300,000 to get them back."

"They?"

"The mob. You see, I'm an investment broker, and somehow, these men are linked to people who had given me money to invest."

"What people?"

"I didn't know it at the time, but they were connected with the mob. As soon as I found out, I dropped their account, of course, but now they want money."

Alex and Christine were deafeningly quiet.

"Since then," the man continued in the weight of their silence, "the mobsters have been tapping my phone and trying to extort money. They even threatened my family. So, of course . . . I believed the telephone call. About the kidnapping, I mean."

It sounded like a very bad movie.

"Why would anyone want to kidnap my brother?" Christine asked. "Ernie doesn't have that kind of money."

"I don't know," Christopher said nervously. "Except, maybe they think Ernie is a partner in my business."

"Is he?"

"No. He put up some money when I started out, but, no, he's not a partner. He's a good friend."

"I see," the doctor said. But he didn't see.

"I'll need help."

"We'll call the police."

"No," Hightower said quickly. "That's too dangerous. I need you to help with the money."

"The money?"

"The ransom. I need you to contribute $75,000 of the ransom money. Ernie said you would do it."

"Ernie said what?"

"Well, actually, Alice did."

"Why don't you tell us the whole story."

They sat, he on the edge of his seat, they warily listening.

"The kidnappers agreed to exchange the hostages for the cash in downtown Providence on Tuesday," he said.

"How?" Christine demanded.

"They'll drop the hostages off in a van and be carrying walkie-talkies."

"They told you they would be carrying walkie-talkies?" Alexander asked incredulously.

Christopher nodded.

"Why would they tell you something like that?"

"I don't know."

By this time, suspicion had crowded out the edge of nerves for Christine. Either the story the man was telling was a total con, or he was telling the truth, and the lives of six people were in their hands, or the man was a liar and he had kidnapped them himself.

Chris could sense their growing skepticism as his story sagged under the weight of its own melodramatic complexity.

To prove his story, he took them outside to the driveway to show them the interior of Ernie's Toyota. To their horror, the backseat was splattered with blood. When he opened the trunk for them, they could see that it, too, was full of blood. They were stunned by the overwhelming stench that assaulted their nostrils the moment he lifted the trunk lid; the intensity was sickening. It appeared to have been strewn with baking soda in an ineffective attempt to disguise the smell. Jugs of muriatic acid were pushed over to one side of the trunk. Now Christine was terrified. Where was her brother? And Alice? And little Emily? She couldn't remember the last time she spoke to them . . . not too long ago, but, at the moment, she couldn't remember exactly when.

"Where did all this blood come from?" Alexander asked.

"They hit Ernie," Chris said quickly. "They broke his jaw." But he hastened to assure them that was all Ernie had suffered at the hands of his abductors.

The doctor knew it was impossible for a broken jaw to cause so much bleeding. The Toyota showed evidence of far greater violence. This amount of blood could only have been caused by severe physical trauma. Instead of convincing them, suspicions of foul play were now uppermost. All of his talk of the Mafia, hostages, ransom, and kidnapping rang hollow. Even if any of it were true, why would the perpetrators permit Hightower to drive away in a car that evidenced so much violence?

The Scriabines wanted him to leave the car with them. They offered to let him drive another car back to Rhode Island.

"Another car?"

The Scriabines pointed to a car standing in their driveway. It belonged to Ernie and Christine's eighty-year-old mother, Jolene, who had recently moved from her condominium into a rest home and had left her car with her daughter.

Hightower agreed. There was little else for him to do. As long as they went along with his ransom request, he was willing to leave behind the Toyota.

But, adding to the tensions of the night, the Scriabines were unable to start Mrs. Brendel's car. They went inside the house again and called AAA for road assistance.

While they waited for the mechanic to arrive, Christine asked Hightower, "Would you mind if I took some samples of the blood in the trunk?"

His jaw clicked, an obviously nervous reaction to the request. "I don't know why," he said, "but no, I don't mind."

She got some cotton balls from the medicine cabinet in her bathroom and a plastic deli container from her kitchen. She went back out into the cool night and took the samples she wanted by dabbing several cotton balls at the soaked interior of the trunk. The blood was still sticky; it had been spilled recently. It absorbed easily into the cotton balls, which she secured in the deli container.

Back in the living room, she said she wanted to photograph Hightower.

He blinked. He didn't like the idea, but he didn't hesitate. "Yes, of course."

Alexander snapped Hightower's photo as he sat awkwardly posed in the middle of their living room.

"I'll even leave you my American Express card," Hightower offered helpfully.

Alexander hesitated, not understanding the necessity for such a move.

"To prove I've been here," Chris explained.

It was illogical, but they took the card.

Christine asked him to repeat his story into a tape recorder, saying it was to make sure they remembered every detail, but actually to get it in his own words.

Chris agreed, but Alexander was unable to operate either of the two recording machines they owned.

"We'll put it on my computer," Christine said quickly.

Hightower repeated the entire story one more time while Christine's fingers flew over the keyboard of her computer, recording his long, harrowing tale of kidnapping, huge ransom demands, Mafia types, phone tapping, and beatings, frighteningly substantiated by the graphic evidence of a blood-soaked car.

This time, during the account, he stated that the men from the Mafia were masked.

But he had said they had called him on the telephone. How did he know they were masked?

"That's what Alice said." He had a ready answer for everything.

"You spoke to her?"

"They let her talk on the phone. She said you would be able to come up with the money for Ernie."

They remained noncommittal.

From the living room window, they could see the flashing lights of the AAA service truck. They went outside to meet the mechanic but he could not start the car either. Hightower would have to return to Rhode Island in Ernie's Toyota.

"It's okay," he assured them, scribbling his telephone number for them on a scrap of paper so they could reach him when they raised the ransom money. He left his work and home numbers, even though he had just been escorted from his home two days earlier by the Barrington police. He had no choice; they were the only two telephone numbers he had.

It was one-thirty in the morning when Hightower left the Scriabines.

Almost five and a half hours had passed since he had first entered their home. "Promise me two things," he said before leaving.

"Anything."

"That you'll raise the money and that you won't call the FBI."

"No, of course not."

"Their lives are in danger if you do, you know," he warned.

"Yes, we know."

"All of them. So, if you call . . ."

"We won't."

He smiled at them gratefully.

They watched him get into Ernie's red car and drive away into the darkness.

When the car had disappeared, Christine and Alexander looked at each other.

"Do you believe him?"

"No." Alexander said without hesitation. "I'm calling Ernie." Christine stood by his side as he dialed the Rhode Island number. There was no answer.

"They should be there at this hour," Christine insisted.

It was late. Maybe they simply weren't answering their phone. The answering machine finally clicked in.

"Hello. You have reached . . ." came Ernie's familiar voice.

"We're out right now. If you wish to leave a message, please wait for the beep."

"I'm calling to see how you are," Alexander said into the machine before hanging up. "Now what?"

"Call the police."

"But if that man is telling the truth . . ."

The question hung heavily between them for several moments as they pondered the potential consequences of a genuine kidnapping by the Mafia. But reason prevailed over fear. Suspecting an extortion attempt as well as foul play, Christine said, "There are too many holes in his story. He's not telling the truth. I'd stake my life on it."

"And theirs?"

Ernie was in trouble. But she was certain the trouble didn't come from the Mafia. She glanced at the deli container full of cotton balls dabbed with blood. Shakily, she dialed the telephone.

It was 1:50 A.M., only twenty minutes since the man had departed. The Scriabines never discussed how to raise the $75,000 ransom money he had asked for. They knew there were no masked kidnappers from the Mafia involved.

The officer on the other end of the line answered her call.

They had contacted their local police.

The police contacted the FBI.

Chapter 3

Missing

Barrington, Rhode Island

By 2:30 A.M. the Guilford, Connecticut, police had contacted their counterparts in Barrington to tell them there may have been a serious crime committed in Barrington, suggesting they check on a family by the name of Brendel.

By 2:45 A.M. Barrington Patrolman John C. Alfred, who was working the midnight to eight shift, was called back to the station.

"Kidnapped? The Brendels?"

"Ernest and Alice Brendel."

"What's the address."

"All we have, right now, is their telephone number."

Patrolman Alfred checked the Polk's reverse telephone directory for the address.

It was precisely 3:05 A.M. when Patrolman Alfred and Patrolman John C. Medici arrived at the darkened two-story colonial-style house on Middle Highway. The house appeared deserted, a normal appearance for the middle of the night. The Brendel family was probably asleep.

They climbed the wide porch steps and Patrolman Alfred knocked on the front door loudly enough to wake up the family. Somewhere in the distance a dog howled, but no one responded to the knocking. It appeared no one was at home. Alfred turned to leave, but something caught his eye. The railing leading up to the front porch had been severely damaged, appearing as though the steps recently had been struck hard by something. He did not like the look of it, despite the possibility that it could have been done by a car backing out of the garage at a bad angle.

He knocked on the door again. Still no response.

The Connecticut police had strongly suggested the possibility of foul play. Officer Medici decided to break the lock on the Brendel garage. Inside the barnlike structure, they could see that an Audi, the other Brendel family car, was parked inside.

"Look," Medici said, calling attention to dark stains on the garage floor next to the Audi.

"What is it?"

"I don't know," he said. It looked like bloodstains. "But I want to get into that house."

They had to break the front door to gain entry.

Once within, they noticed that a tiny light was flashing on the burglar alarm box in the entrance hallway.

They quickly sensed the house was deserted and started to search the premises.

Downstairs, Early American chairs and hardwood furniture set atop a series of deeply colored Persian rugs testified to the simple but comfortable lifestyle of the Brendels. In the cheerful kitchen, there were signs of a child's presence; colorful crayon drawings were taped on the front of the refrigerator door. Nearby, the September 21 edition of the *New York Times* was spread out on the kitchen table. A few cups and utensils were lying at the bottom of the dry kitchen sink. A mug full of cold dark coffee stood nearby. The bottom of the coffeepot on the stove was baked with dried coffee.

The officers noticed that the beige phone in the dining room next to a Rolodex file that was open to the letter S was missing its connecting cord.

They went upstairs. The bedrooms were empty. One bedroom at the rear of the house obviously belonged to a little girl. It had an assortment of dolls lined up along the top of the dresser. A colorful handmade afghan was draped neatly over the foot of a child's bed that had obviously not been slept in.

They discovered that the cords of both the upstairs phones were missing also. Medici and Alfred looked at each other. Why would all the receivers be disconnected from the bases of the phones if not to prevent someone from using them?

And where were the Brendels?

Certain that they had entered a crime scene, they took care not to contaminate anything.

Medici radioed the chief of the Barrington police from his car. "Chief," he said, "we have some problems here."

Guilford, Connecticut—4:00 A.M.

FBI Special Agent Ralph A. Di Fonzo, Jr., arrived at the Scriabine home in Guilford at almost four in the morning. He had come in response to the call from the Guilford police confirming that the Brendel family was missing.

He listened to the Scriabines' bizarre story about their unexpected visitor, and Di Fonzo gathered as evidence the plastic container with bloodied cotton balls, a computer printout of Hightower's story, the piece of paper on which he had scribbled his telephone numbers, and the film from the camera. With the help of Christine's memory, Di Fonzo carefully drew a diagram of the interior of her brother's car showing the placement of the objects in the trunk, including the jugs of muriatic acid.

Two hours later, Di Fonzo returned to his office in New Haven. He called his FBI counterparts in Providence, alerting them that Hightower was last seen driving a Toyota Camry that belonged to the missing Ernest Brendel and gave them the plate number.

Di Fonzo looked down at the scrap of paper with Hightower's telephone numbers.

The FBI and the local police wanted to find Christopher Hightower very badly, and issued an all-points on him.

Barrington, Rhode Island— 1:40 P.M. on Monday— "You've Got Nothing on Me."

Within one day of the disappearance of the Brendels, Christopher Hightower's facade as one of Barrington's most upstanding residents was about to crack.

FBI Agent Jack W. McGraw, Sr., was riding with Barrington Police Sergent Lazarro in an unmarked car when he spotted the red Toyota Camry.

"That's it," he said. "Ernest Brendel's car."

The Camry was stopped at a red light on County Road near the Barrington Shopping Center. Hightower had been at The Citizens Bank located in the center, trying to cash some checks that he would later claim had been given to him by Ernie Brendel, as well as trying to have wired in from Chicago what was left of an account of his own. He had been going in and out of the bank all morning checking to see if it had come in yet.

Sergeant Lazzaro pulled up next to the Camry.

The man in the driver's seat fit the description they had been given. He was so preoccupied with his own thoughts, he didn't notice them staring intently at him.

Lazzaro turned on his siren.

The man appeared startled as he turned to look at them.

Lazzaro flicked off the siren and motioned him to pull over.

The man nodded and pulled over into the empty parking lot of St. John's Episcopal Church, which was situated next to the center.

"Is your name Hightower?"

"You've got nothing on me," Hightower said defensively as he stepped out of the car. He made no move to escape. In fact, he was very cooperative. "I know why I've been stopped," he said, proceeding to tell them he wanted to help in the investigation of the disappearance of the Brendel family.

Searching through the car, McGraw and Lazarro found a bizarre array: massive bloodstains, four human teeth in the trunk, a huge, lethal-looking Bear Devastator crossbow next to a torn portion of an empty bag of lime.

When ordered to empty his pockets, Hightower immediately complied.

He was carrying $1500 in cash, an American Express card, a Sears credit card, and a Discover credit card, all of which belonged to Ernest Brendel.

Hightower was handcuffed and had his rights read to him.

"Do you want to call your attorney?"

"No, of course not."

A call was made to have the Toyota picked up by the Barrington police as Hightower was placed in the cruiser and driven to the police station.

Lazzaro began the questioning, during which time he repeatedly informed Hightower of his rights and repeatedly asked him if he wanted a lawyer.

"I don't need an attorney. I want to help in the investigation," Hightower said with sincerity. "I'll do whatever I can."

"I understand you told Dr. and Mrs. Scriabine that your own wife and two sons had been kidnapped as well."

"Yes."

"Why did you tell them such a thing?"

"I didn't want the Scriabines to think they were alone," he said lamely. "I have to tell you something else," he offered. "I exaggerated the amount of ransom the kidnappers asked for."

"I'm listening."

"They only demanded $200,000."

"You told them $300,000."

"Yes."

"Why?"

"I have some money problems," he admitted.

"That's quite a weapon we found in the car," Lazzaro said, referring to the crossbow. "Is it yours?"

"Yes."

"You bought it?"

"Yes."

"When?"

"A couple of . . . uh . . . weeks ago."

"Why did you buy it?"

"I just wanted it," he said.

Five and a half hours of questioning later, Lazzaro ended his interview, and Hightower was brought up to a second story office within the police station. Assistant Detective Commander, Lt. Richard H. Hurst, a twenty-one-year veteran of the state police, took over the questioning. Hightower was claiming harassment and stubbornly beginning to dig his heels in. He adamantly stuck to his story.

When his watch and eyeglasses were confiscated and he was locked up in the isolation of a holding cell with a charge of "Suspicion of extortion" hanging over his head, Hightower finally asked for an attorney.

* * *

Hightower, on the advice of his attorney, refused to speak to the whereabouts of the Brendel family other than to say they had been kidnapped and he had been selected as a go-between in the kidnappers' attempts to obtain a huge ransom.

Fourteen hours after the arrest, Sergeant Lazzaro, who had been assigned to watch him in his cell, told him the police had received a tip about suspicious-looking muddy tire tracks at Boxwood Court, a new housing development.

"I'm going to be heading up there."

"Sarge, you're wasting your time," Hightower volunteered. "They're not buried there."

"How do you know?"

He didn't respond, but Lazzaro noted that he had used the word "buried."

The Search for the Brendels Begins

Even in the middle of family grief over the death of Clyde's sister, Susan and her parents kept in contact with Joseph T. Dye during their stay in Ohio. When she heard the full story Chris had told the police, she could not believe the gaps in his wild account. What could he have been thinking of? Did he think everyone would be as gullible as she had been when she had first met him at the age of nineteen?

He had no money to pay his share of the ransom, as he had told the Scriabines he would do. He told police the kidnappers had asked for only $200,000, but he'd raised the amount to $300,000 when he spoke to the Scriabines in order to "settle some personal financial matters." According to his logic, it did not make sense that he had asked them for only $75,000.

He claimed he had been threatened by the Mafia and was forced to carry guns for self-protection, but gave no reason as to why or under what circumstances such a threat would have been made. Susan had a sense of *déjà vu* when she heard that part of his account to the police. He had used a similar Mafia story earlier when "borrowing" money from her younger sister, Kathy.

Since Susan had told Chris she wanted a divorce, he had been threatening her and her family with "elimination." She was convinced he'd meant to carry out his threats. Fearful for their lives, she was grateful for his apprehension by the police. Her parents could not believe the bizarre story Chris had concocted for the Scriabines, but Susan did.

Although she was not surprised at his arrest, she was, nonetheless, devastated. She thought of their sons, Mitchell and Paul, and of all the terrible things they were going to hear about their father.

The entire story only acted to solidify Susan's original instincts regarding the Brendels' disappearance. What had Chris done with them?

Although the search for the Brendels continued, as the days passed, hope was fading that they would be found alive.

"Have we got an identification yet on the blood type that was found in the car?"

"Type O."

"What is Ernest Brendel's blood type?"

"Type O."

They looked at Christopher Hightower seated at the table in front of them.

The evidence in the Toyota suggested that at least one person had suffered severe trauma. More and more it looked as though that person was Ernest Brendel, the missing man.

"Are you going to tell us how the bloodstains got in the back of the car?"

"I don't know. It's not my car. I just borrowed it."

There was no way Chris could give an adequate explanation

for the bloodstains or for the four human teeth that were found there.

His lawyer was portraying him as heroic in his "desperate attempts" to help bring about the safe return of the Brendels.

The Search

At 10:15 A.M. a full-fledged investigation by FBI agents and the Barrington police was in progress. SA Jack McGraw was on the scene at the Brendel home on Middle Highway overseeing 20 agents from the Providence FBI. Crowds gathered as the site took on the appearance of a crime scene. News reporters were on hand.

Friends and neighbors were stunned that someone of Hightower's high standing in the community had been arrested. Most were skeptical of his involvement in the case until some of the details surrounding his arrest were released, revealing the holes in Hightower's story, most conspicuously, that Susan and his two sons had never been kidnapped. When one of the four teeth found in the car was identified as Ernest Brendel's, the community skepticism changed to community pleas for Hightower's cooperation in the search. The disappearance of Ernest, Alice, and Emily moved the distraught Barrington residents as little else had before.

Officials investigating the case were stumped. Although there were those who believed the family had been kidnapped and would be found alive, there were others who believed there had been a killing. The frustrating part was that while they were certain they had the killer, they had no victims.

Hightower would not talk. The man being held on extortion charges continued to sullenly stand mute.

* * *

The extensive search continued around the clock. The Slickers now all believed Chris was involved.

Mary Lou Slicker: *Clyde's sister died the Sunday night Chris went to Connecticut and I was dealing with a distraught mother-in-law, and a sister-in-law who died practically in my arms, at least under my care, and the fact that my mother-in-law only wanted Clyde to arrive for the funeral—not his whole family, which included two small boys. It wasn't till the Wednesday after Chris's arrest and the funeral of Clyde's sister that the facts began to sink in! It was a horrible week and series of events.*

Kathy Slicker: *With all the odd things that had been happening over the prior weeks, I did believe he was involved with the Brendels' disappearance. There was too much coincidence backed up with proof. When I heard of the threats he'd made to us, that only made my belief stronger.*

Clyde did not want to believe it, but as the search progressed, he, too, was forced to believe that his son-in-law had done something terrible.

Susan could not escape. The FBI followed her to New Hampshire.

Crying and overwrought, she could barely go on with the incessant questions. What more could she tell them? All she could think of was, "Why the child? Why Emily?" They had children of their own. Chris had always shown a great liking for children. He had worked so well with them at the church. Even the teenagers came to him for advice and counseling.

The police told Susan they had discovered that Chris had a family Hit List. All their names were on it, listed for "elimination," as well as others who had offended Chris, including the landlord who had evicted him from his office for nonpayment of rent and his ex-wife. . . . She realized how close they had come to sharing the Brendels' fate. She was convinced he had killed them.

The question remained why a man of Hightower's background would brutally slaughter an entire family.

PART II

Life with Chris

A History of Emotional Violence and Abuse

Chapter 4

Falling in Love

She was sure he had done it.
Her husband.
How could she be so disloyal?
And yet, every atom of her being tormented her, certain that
he had done something terrible.
As she watched the anguished search taking place for the
missing family, her mind rewound to the beginning.

At the Newport Creamery—Summer of 1980

Susan Elizabeth Slicker and Christopher Jemire Hightower met at the Newport Creamery, a restaurant in the Swansea Mall in Massachusetts early in the summer of 1980. He was the assistant manager; she was working a summer job as a waitress. Susan was beautiful, vivacious and almost nineteen years old. Chris was thirty-one, intelligent, worldly, and a man of many charms.

When Susan first met Chris he appeared to be a very competent assistant store manager. He was interested in the people he was serving as well as those working for him. Things had to be done the "right way," but that made for a well-run establishment.

It started out with a simple, "Oh, hi, I remember you . . ."

The very first time she met him, she had been waitressing at the Creamery in Bristol, having worked there every summer since she was sixteen. As an assistant manager, Chris had filled in one time for someone who was sick. He had made no impression on Susan.

She didn't see him again until she applied to go back to work at the Creamery. She was in her freshman year at Wittenberg University in Ohio. When she came home during the Christmas holidays, she saw him a second time. She had a six-week break between Thanksgiving and the new year, and as business always increased at the Creamery during the holidays and she was already trained, she was hired on the spot. Always looking to earn a little extra pocket money, she was eager to go back to work. Instead of Bristol, she was placed in the Newport Creamery, where Chris was the assistant manager.

"Oh, hi, I remember you . . ."

Chris was one of her bosses. Working for him on a daily basis, she didn't like him at first, considering him a class-A pain in the neck. He was very insistent on things being done in certain ways. There was only one way to do a task and that was the way it had to be done. At first, Susan assumed he was adhering to company policy, but when she saw other waitresses rolling their eyes behind his back, she realized the demands were his; all the bills had to be placed in the same direction in the cash drawers; all the duties had to be performed in a very particular order; each utensil had to be polished a certain way—*his* way—and if it was not, he would get very annoyed with the offender and make that person do it over again. He treated Susan the same way he treated the others, and if he told her to redo something, she readily complied. Susan ignored all the little signs of rigidity and the need to control in his personality since his anger was never directed at her. In her own laughingly self-deprecatory assessment, she was too much of a goody two-shoes to resist. She did what she was supposed to do and stayed out of trouble.

When she left after the Christmas break to return to school, there had not been any major contact between them. Her romantic feelings were focused on the college boyfriend she had left behind in Ohio.

* * *

When she returned to work at the Newport Creamery during the summer break between her freshman and sophomore years, Chris was still there and still pretty much a pain in the neck. She didn't think much about him then, either.

"Oh hi, I remember you . . ."

Her college boyfriend was still very much on Susan's mind. He lived in the Springfield, Ohio, area near school. She had seen his family a great deal and, while his parents liked her, the young man's attention to her was always a wavering one. His lack of commitment only served to solidify her interest.

Susan: *I'm still not quite sure why. I guess what I had gotten into my brain as I grew up was that I was supposed to find a boyfriend during college, and get married after graduation, and have children.*

The expectations had been subtly ingrained into her psyche. That was what her mother had done. Nothing wrong with that. Mom was a good role model.

Subconsciously, Susan was insecure about her ability to be on her own, even though at school, far away from home, she did very well. She had a major in psychology with a minor in sociology and although she was learning much about human behavior in the academically programmed textbook environment of college, she, herself, was still quite unworldly. She knew it. Her hometown of Barrington was a very protected society. There were no racial problems simply because no other races lived in town. It was primarily a monied town, with affluent, mid- to upper-middle-class families. There were no homeless people, and very little disrepair in cars or buildings. Eighty to ninety percent of Barrington's high school graduates continued on to college. Few went to trade school, or thought of working for the police department or their father's local business. As an adult, Susan would be able to see the subtleties of her hometown that would characterize it as a much more heterogeneous society than originally perceived, but as a teenager in college, everything appeared uniform and safe.

Susan: *I didn't have a lot of knowledge of what was really out there when I left home. . . .*

She was youthfully naive at that point in her life, and by the time she returned home on her first summer break, she was terribly unhappy.

Her mother watched as she waited expectantly every day for the mail to come—waiting for the promised letters from her college boyfriend. And every day, the letdown as no letter came. Her daily disappointment was heartbreaking to watch.

Sue's security level dropped. Maybe it was her. Maybe it was her fault. Maybe she was too heavy. Maybe she wasn't pretty enough. Smart enough. Something. She never really saw herself clearly as others saw her, a lovely young girl with jet black hair, a bubbly personality, and a ready, captivating smile. If her boyfriend was not writing to her, the blame had to be hers. She must have done something wrong.

During school breaks, she lived at home with her parents on Chantilly Drive in Barrington, a quiet family neighborhood off New Meadow Road. Her father, Dr. Clyde Slicker, was a gentle, caring, highly acclaimed professor of Education at Rhode Island College in Providence. Her mother, Mary Lou, was an energetic, loving, maternal woman, who had a bachelor's degree in Education from Oberlin College in Ohio, where she and Clyde had met. Mary Lou had taught kindergarten and second grade before she stopped to raise her two daughters, Susan and Kathy. As a family, they exhibited solid family background, good breeding, and unostentatious affluence.

But Sue did not see herself as others saw her. With her own tender age insecurities, she never realized that she was perceived as an excellent catch.

* * *

At work at the Newport Creamery that summer, Susan was surprised when she would catch her boss looking at her. The man, who was looked upon as a bit of a martinet by the other girls, was singling her out. Chris even began to banter with her every time they passed one another, encouraging her to participate in the subtly enticing badinage. It was fun. The beginning stages of a relationship. She found herself looking forward to seeing him and to the verbal exchanges they shared during working hours.

He was older. He was funny. He was very charming. And he was attentive at a time when she was vulnerable, feeling unwanted.

Susan: *He seemed to know an awful lot about the world, and I didn't know much of anything about it. . . .*

He'd been to all kinds of places, she thought. The man knew a little bit about a lot of things: restaurants, race cars, photography, dog training, camping, pharmaceuticals, foreign countries—so many different things, all of which gave him, in her eyes, an exotic persona. He also knew something about medicine from his days in the navy as a medical assistant. His undergraduate degree from the University of Rhode Island was in zoology. He had gone from undergraduate school to working in some kind of sales position for Riker Pharmaceuticals, a subsidiary of the 3M Company.

To the young, wide-eyed beauty, all these attributes and accomplishments were fascinating. Here was this sophisticate who knew so much more about everything than she and was much more mature than the boys she knew in college, and he was paying all this attention to *her*. He made her feel good about how she looked, how she acted, what she did, even what she said and thought. And, excitingly, she found herself physically attracted to him.

Still, there were a few minor questions that came to mind. She found herself wondering why an educated, degreed, sophisticated, traveled man like Chris was working at the Creamery. And why he was still only an assistant manager. It was a bit odd.

"I hated working for Riker," he explained, "being in a position of selling to doctors who were always putting you off. Looking down at you. Especially since what I've always wanted was to study medicine myself."

The Creamery had promised they would pay for school. He could work in the management program, go to school . . . some other kind of business classes . . . and become a full-time manager. But he found he couldn't handle all of it. Although he tended toward excuses, there was an edge of bitter recrimination at how it wasn't working out to his satisfaction. Sue could understand the difficulty of dealing with all of it at the same time, especially with management's hours at the Creamery. The job had held forth a great promise, but it was difficult to work the job full-time and keep up with all the schoolwork as well.

Besides, the business classes didn't really interest him. His real love had always been medicine. After the navy, he claimed he wanted to go on to study medicine. He even picked a specialty. Obstetrics. His claim was that he wanted to bring babies into the world. "So much of the medicine I saw in the navy was guys coming back from Vietnam, and they were ugly cases." He wanted something that was positive about medicine and, as he told Susan, bringing new life into the world was it.

It took half the summer before the budding romance escalated to the point of becoming impossible to deny.

The biggest problem was that he was a married man.

Once again Chris explained. It was easy to see he was desperately unhappy in his marriage. With a family to support, he claimed that his wife felt he wasn't in the position to go to medical school. It was a major source of friction between them.

The navy had first brought him to Rhode Island. His wife was a nurse at the Newport Naval Hospital when, in 1973, they married at the Chapel by the Sea.

It was at this time that Hightower, discharged from the navy, returned to school, and enrolled at the University of Rhode Island, where he studied zoology and graduated with a Bachelor of Science degree in 1975.

At the time Susan and Chris met at the Creamery, Chris and his wife were living on Bedlow Place in Newport, Rhode Island, with their two young daughters.

Susan listened with rapt attention to this man who was confiding his innermost thoughts to her. He sounded like a person with an enormous desire to make it. She was flattered that he would take so much time with someone so much younger, never thinking that the fact that he seemed to have an overwhelming need to prove something might stem from frustration that had already tainted much of his adult life. She never wondered from where these needs sprang. All she really knew was that he was kind and attentive and charming, and he seemed to enjoy talking to her, telling her all about himself.

"In high school, I ran track and played baseball and basketball," he told her. "I even earned enough varsity letters to become a member of the Letterman's Club."

She was moved by the apparent wistfulness beneath the proud recitation of accomplishments, as though he missed the more innocent time when he could enjoy athletics without all the family responsibilities.

"I even became a member of the Interact Club," he grinned. "That's a community service organization sponsored by the Rotary. And I was vice president of the Science Club."

"You've done so much. . . ."

"I was always ambitious. Still am."

It never occurred to her that their intimate discussions usually concentrated on him and his background. Even if she had realized it, the seduction of their secret relationship had intensified to the point where it wouldn't have mattered to the girl. Then there were all the romantic dinners; candlelight, bottles of wine, holding hands, intimate corner tables for two. None of the girls at the Creamery knew him the way she did. He wasn't a martinet at all once you got to know him well. He was actually a very romantic man. A charmer.

With the concentration of romance, flattery, and candlelight, it wasn't long before the inexperienced beauty, who had been raised in a tight-knit, loving, religious family, was falling in love, so much so that she rationalized away his failing first marriage and all of the little peculiarities he continued to display at the Creamery, particularly his need for perfection. The other girls still found his obsessive demands annoying and unreasonable, but Susan had come to find his perfectionist insistence on these details endearing. An excusable idiosyncracy. She never associated the behavior with obsessive-compulsive tendencies. She knew management liked him. William Ahearn, personnel manager of the Newport Creamery, would one day state when asked by a local newspaper what Chris was like:

Susan: *He was a crackerjack. Very conscientious. Well groomed. You'd want this guy to be your next-door neighbor.*

There were times when Susan felt profoundly sorry for him. He told her how awful his wife was. Perhaps Sue was only hearing one side of the story, but she had a young, generous heart that had been expertly won over and was full of love. Every instinct of hers was geared to believing the persuasive lamentations about his marital state. The poor man had this horrible wife. It was obvious that he wanted out of his marriage. He wanted to go to medical school and his wife wouldn't let him. She was opposed to his advancement. She absolutely refused to go along with his plans.

Then he found Susan. She was wonderful. She supported him. *She* understood.

What he never told Susan was that he wanted his wife to sell their home to support his studies, that there would be no money coming in, that he had applied to medical schools just about everywhere he could, in and outside of the United States, from

Poland to South America, and had been rejected by each school except for one in the Caribbean. His wife, a registered nurse, had no faith in him or in his ability to complete the demanding studies required. The Caribbean! He didn't have the money for tuition, and on top of everything else, he was too old. She wasn't about to jeopardize their entire future and that of their daughters for a goal she was certain he would never achieve. In her mind, failure was a given.

With all of his dreams spelled out in rosy expectations to the girl seated across a candlelit table in a darkened corner of a little restaurant, "I want to go into medicine. Be an obstetrician. . . . Or research. Maybe find a cure for hypertension . . ." it was not surprising that Sue encouraged him. "If you want to go back to school," she said, "go ahead. Do it." The dream was, after all, a noble one.

That was enough for Chris to decide what he wanted. He wanted a divorce.

But he never applied for one. Despite all his talk, it was his wife who ultimately had to initiate the proceedings. She was fed up with his not having a real job, and with all of his impossible aspirations.

She also found out about Susan.

She filed for divorce.

The romance between Chris and Susan continued.

Throughout the summer, they continued to date. He repeatedly assured her his marriage had been on the skids long before he met her. She should not feel guilty about the breakup of his home; it was inevitable.

Susan was impressed with the fact that he was still very ambitious. In her bighearted style, she encouraged him to talk. Little by little, Sue found out all about her new love.

At least, as much as he wanted her to know.

"I'm the oldest of five kids," he told her. "I always took care of my two brothers and my two sisters."

"What about your mother?"

"Oh, she was a carhop in a drive-in restaurant. She had crazy hours."

"Still, who took care of you?"

"It was okay. I didn't mind."

"And your dad?"

"Him!" Chris snorted. "He took off. Left us cold. When my mother got married again"—not mentioning that his mother and father had never married—"I had my birth record changed to that of my stepfather's."

He became Christopher Jemire Hightower.

That's how much he thought of his natural father, Susan thought. Her heart went out to the young man who had tried to create another identity for himself out of a stepfather until he, too, abandoned the family and left Chris as the head of the household.

"My mother still calls me Jemire."

Christopher Jemire Hightower grew up in the Florida coastal community of Titusville, less than twenty miles from the Cape Canaveral Space Center. Jemire was always thought of as an intelligent young man. He was the family's golden boy. Always working hard. Always trying to improve himself. He was the one who was going to become the great success and help out his younger brothers and sisters. All family aspirations centered on him.

As the eldest, he was often responsible for taking care of his four younger half siblings, his two sisters and his two brothers. His mother never had to worry about him as he assumed the parental role. It was he who worried about her. In his estimation, his mother couldn't handle money and was incapable of making good decisions. He had to do it all. His sense of responsibility was strong and dependable. Even though he claimed to have a good relationship with his mother, she worked all the time and was often an absentee parent. Then there were hints about being beaten with a broom, about how he was a difficult child, always getting into trouble, rebellious, all of which, perhaps, stemmed from having too many responsibilities at too young an age, Susan thought sympathetically. While in high school, he went to work in a Piggly-Wiggly to help support his siblings. Then his mother divorced his stepfather, and Jemire ended up being the one who had to make sure all the kids were dressed, fed, and off to school. Although Jemire was only twelve when he took over these responsibilities full-time, he had basically assumed many of them earlier, even while his mother was still married.

When Jemire graduated Titusville High School in 1967 at the age of seventeen with 395 other "Titusville Terriers," their class motto was, "Each step in life leads to a greater one." His mother liked that. And she knew her Jemire believed it.

Fiercely ambitious, Jemire didn't let much time slip by once he had graduated. By the fall he had enrolled himself in the Indian River Community College in Fort Pierce, Florida. The college was only about one hour south of his hometown. He remained at Indian River a year, taking general academic courses.

Then he suddenly decided to quit and join the navy.

His mother was sorry to see him go, but Jemire was quietly glad to get away from the demands of the family. It was one of the motivating factors in his decision to join the military. The other was that he could get an education and training in the field that interested him most—medicine.

Still, part of that implanted sense of responsibility remained with him. When he went into the navy a portion of his pay went home every month.

A letter came.

Susan's boyfriend from college finally broke his prolonged silence. He wrote to Susan to tell her he was going to visit her in Barrington at the end of the summer. A wave of anxiety rushed over her. She was eager to see him again but she was no longer sure of how she felt about him. Somehow the eagerness was dampened considerably by thoughts of Chris.

When her boyfriend finally came to visit, he broke off their relationship.

Despite the silence brought about by his lack of contact, she hadn't anticipated his move. If it had happened several months earlier, she would have been devastated, but now she was working with Chris every day and she almost couldn't believe how well she took the rejection. Still, it was troubling. Even her lack of despair was troubling.

Now both Chris and Susan needed to talk; he was coming out of a marriage, she was coming out of a relationship. Having Chris in her life seemed to mitigate all prior problems and heartaches. There was even a subtle sense of relief. Perhaps her joy with Chris was the result of an emotional reflex; she had cared a great deal for her inattentive college beau, and his rejection placed her on the quicksand of an emotional rebound. Chris seemed so much more together than her college boyfriend, so much more mature.

She could never pinpoint exactly when she fell in love with Chris, but by the end of the summer when she had to go back to school, all she knew was that she did not want to leave him. For the most part, their time together had been romantic, not physical.

She knew he was falling in love with her, too. But she couldn't help asking about his wife. Feelings of guilt were marring the beauty of their newfound love. She couldn't help it. Every ounce of decency she had cried out in her. She didn't want to be responsible for the breakup of his home. He assured her again that she wasn't.

Now he told her how it had *never* been good with his wife. It had been a mistake from the beginning. She never understood him. The only thing that kept him in the marriage this long was the love he had for his daughters.

But something was wrong. She knew he was still living at home.

"It doesn't matter," he told her. He and his wife no longer shared the same bedroom. The only reason he remained at home while their divorce was pending was so that he could stay with his children as long as possible, and also, so that he could save some money.

For him and Susan.

For their future.

* * *

Susan's younger sister, Kathy, first met Chris during the fall of 1980. She had spent the summer in Finland as an exchange student and when she returned to the states, Sue was getting ready to return to school in Ohio.

"It's my kid sister back from Finland," she told Chris. "She's only fifteen but she's awfully sharp. Could you help her to get a job here?"

"Have her come in to see me."

He hired Kathy in September. It worked out fine. She would not turn sixteen until November and until then, all he had her do was work the cash register.

Kathy got to know some of the other managers at the Creamery. In comparison, Chris seemed a typically basic manager, except that she, too, found him to be more of a perfectionist than the others. The rigid litany of his job requirements struck her also:

. . . The coffee cup had to be in the same direction with the spoon in that direction. . . .

. . . Scoop the ice cream this way. . . .

. . . Make the sundae that way. . . .

Kathy: *He'd make you do it again. He'd look at you in that way he had, and you would know you did it wrong.*

He could be daunting, but Kathy never felt intimidated by him. She knew there were those who didn't like him because he was too severe, but her sister, Sue, liked him, and that was good enough for Kathy.

When Sue went back to school the separation was painful, but Chris knew how to keep her attention. He knew how to use the distance between them, spanning it with romantic letters full of love and yearning and confidences. Unlike the last separation from a man, when Sue had waited daily at the mailbox for letters that never came, this time the letters were there in a steady stream, reassuring and full of love. There were also the flowers—a dozen red roses, and another dozen. Four, five dozen roses delivered to her dorm during the course of the school year.

Susan's popularity rating at school soared. She was being courted by an older man who had the means and the manners to woo her with charm and grace. When a jealous friend gave her a hard time because one bouquet of roses was yellow instead of red, Sue smiled confidently and said, "That's because the florist ran out of red. He bought them all."

She was very happy, breathlessly ecstatic at her good fortune.

Kathy kept working at the Creamery after Sue left. Chris was always nice to her. He even treated her a little bit special.

One day he called her into his office after work, looking pleased and excited.

"Can you keep a secret?" he asked.

"Sure."

"Promise?"

"I've always been good at keeping secrets," Kathy reassured him.

Still, he swore her to secrecy. "Especially that you won't tell Susan."

"I swear, I swear. What is it?"

Slowly, almost ceremoniously, he opened up the little jewelry box he had hidden in his hand. The stone glittered in the reflected light of the room as he slowly tilted the box back and forth. It was seven-tenths of a carat.

"Is that for Susan?" Kathy asked, impressed.

He nodded proudly.

How beautiful. He had bought a diamond engagement ring for her sister.

"A secret," he whispered.

* * *

It was not like Susan to keep secrets from her parents.

Clyde and Mary Lou had always been understanding and supportive. Throughout Susan's life, her relationship with them had been even-keeled and free from conflicts. The entire family unit was accustomed to sitting down and discussing problems to resolve them. Sue could not remember ever hearing her parents argue. They always managed to resolve their differences in a loving, civilized manner.

But this time, Sue did not share. Something kept her from telling them about Chris. Even in their gentle way, she was sure they would disapprove and she could not bear to hear anything negative about Chris. Her own qualms about the twelve-year age difference between them, his marriage, and his responsibilities to his two little girls made her unnaturally secretive with her parents. She did not trust them to understand.

Chris wanted to move in with her while his divorce was pending, and made it clear he wanted to marry her. More than anything else in the world, Sue was certain that marriage to Chris was what she wanted. "I could come to Ohio with you," he said. They could live together until the divorce was final in June.

They could be married soon afterward, perhaps in July. Meanwhile, they could both go to school, and at last, he could study medicine or apply for graduate work in a related field.

What about getting admitted into school? What about transcripts? Susan asked.

No problem. His undergraduate grades were nearly perfect, he lied. He had already figured out a way to solve that problem. He had no intention of getting rejected again, not when so much depended on his being accepted. The important thing, he told her, was that they would be together.

She had to finally let her parents know about him.

There was immediate concern on the part of her parents. Christopher Hightower was certainly not the match they had anticipated for their beautiful daughter. He was much older, married, a father. But down deep, despite Sue's unusual reticence, she knew her parents would accept the relationship even while they held their breaths, hoping that if they didn't make any noise about it, he would just go away.

She was right.

"I love him," she told them.

Because they loved her, they were willing to set aside their immediate concerns and look at the situation objectively. If he made her happy, then they were willing to discuss it and even work at it. They were going to handle this matter in the same way they handled all of life's problems; they would talk about it. With that objective in mind, Chris was invited to their home.

The four of them sat in the comfort of the Slicker living room on Chantilly Drive to talk it out. Chris and Sue sat close together on the couch. Sue was a bit nervous, but Chris radiated confidence.

It was a long evening. They discussed Chris's present separation from his family, the upcoming divorce, his two daughters, their plans for school . . . all so important . . . all so delicate. Their desire to live together in Ohio until the divorce became final was a major issue. "I want to know what the person is going to be like before I marry him," Sue had said when she told her mother their plans. "I have a very good idea of his habits and dreams and the way he feels life should be. I don't want a college boy I've got to figure out."

Mary Lou didn't have a problem with his age and previous marriage. Mary Lou and her husband did not like the idea of their daughter living intimately with Chris, certainly not before his divorce was settled. They disapproved wholeheartedly, but were afraid to object. They sincerely tried to accept the mores of the current generation. Societal behavior had changed considerably in the last twenty years. The upheavals of the sixties had put a new twist on everything.

Clyde and Mary Lou listened carefully. Maybe Sue had spent enough time with Chris to know she wanted to live with him. Maybe she had to spend some more time with him to know what he was really like before anything as serious as marriage could be contemplated. Nowadays, couples tested it out first. Maybe it was better. Despite all of their unstated misgivings, the Slickers tried to understand and asked the necessary questions. Sue and Chris had answers for all of them.

What about Susan's school . . .

Sue had told Chris she wanted to finish school. They had discussed it throughly. It was never a question.

You have to finish your undergraduate degree. . . .

She would do that even if she were married.

He agreed.

How would they support themselves? . . .

They would both get jobs.

What was going to happen with his daughters? . . .

They were his and he loved them. He could never give them up completely. Sue would help him care for them when they visited.

She agreed.

It was a long session in the living room, but it left Clyde and Mary Lou impressed that Sue and Chris had thought over most of the issues they raised. The two of them had answers for almost all the tough questions on money, sex, school, children. There were a few gaps. The most important was money. Chris hadn't put it all together in a package and said, "This is how the next five years should look." Where was money coming from? He had ambitions, but he also had child support to pay. He had bright ideas, but implementation didn't seem to be fully thought-out. Yet the convictions of the two in love were powerful, easily overriding parental hesitations. They would work it out. They were in love and wasn't love supposed to conquer all?

Mary Lou was impressed with Chris's sincerity and with some of the goals he had in life. He appeared confident that with hard work he could become a doctor. He seemed a hard worker, the kind who would decide to do something and work hard at it, even becoming obsessive in his determination. She had no way of knowing how successful his efforts would or would not be, or where the pattern of obsessive traits would lead.

On a more fundamental level, moral issues were involved. The Slickers were profoundly concerned that the man still had a wife.

All promises aside, he was not free, and despite societal mores, it distressed Clyde and Mary Lou that the couple were going to live together. But both knew if they seriously disagreed with the intended plans, Sue would go through with them anyway. With heavy hearts, the Slickers decided not to throw up roadblocks that might drive Sue away from them. Confrontational approach had never been their style. At least Sue wasn't talking marriage. Mary Lou's nephew had already done something quite similar.

"It seems you've thought it through pretty carefully," Clyde said after a long, thoughtful pause.

Yes.

Mary Lou found herself liking Chris. She could find nothing in his demeanor to dislike. This was the man her daughter had chosen.

So it was settled. Mary Lou decided to get to know him better.

While the plans for the move to Ohio were being finalized, Mary Lou often stopped at the Creamery near the end of Chris's shift. He was very happy and more than willing to sit and talk with her. She was as different from his own mother as night and day. Mary Lou was a retired elementary school teacher who did a great deal of volunteer work with the Girl Scouts, both as a leader, training adults, and with the state board, eventually becoming the first vice president of the Girl Scouts of Rhode Island. She also did volunteer work in schools and churches. Several times she ran the entire Barrington Congregational Church Arts & Crafts Fair. She was always involved in charities and community projects. Always interested with an intellectual vibrancy that belied her soft-spoken demeanor.

His mother, on the other hand, had nothing more than a sixth grade education. Chris told Mary Lou that as a child he often had to eat sandwiches made out of two pieces of bread, a little mayonnaise, and lima beans. Sometimes the meager fare was substituted with an even more meager ketchup sandwich. His mother used to eat in the kitchen while the kids ate in the living room so they wouldn't know there were times she didn't have enough food for herself.

Although Mary Lou and Chris got along very well together, and she could feel the charm that had captivated her young daughter, Mary Lou believed that Chris considered his mother ignorant, racist, and stupid. There was little sense of respect, only an intense but burdensome attachment that often revolved around money or the lack of it.

A man who had such ambivalent feelings about his own mother . . .

But there was little time to think about how early impressions and deprivations would impact on Chris's adult life, possibly to affect his relationship with Susan. There was a diametrical difference in their backgrounds, tempered only by his great desire to improve himself and move forward in life. At the Creamery, Mary Lou noticed that he was left-handed, and often transposed numbers . . . perhaps he was dyslexic. Ideas came easily to him. She thought he was bright, not brilliant, ultimately deciding he probably could do what he intended to do if he kept at it and planned well ahead.

Everything moved swiftly, leaving little room for deep contemplation. Susan was forced to dispel her doubts in the growing excitement of planning the move to Ohio. A couple of trips west were going to be necessary. He had some furniture he wanted to take that he had in storage, the Slickers had offered some furniture they weren't using, and there were Susan's own things.

Their new apartment was in Fairborn, about half an hour from Wittenberg, where Sue was going to college. Now that he was moving out to be with her, Susan was going to have her own apartment. It was a terribly exciting prospect:

Susan: *I felt really grown-up. Special. Lucky to have found somebody who cared that much about me and wanted to do so many things for me.*

Susan was glad they were all going to drive out to Ohio together in two cars. Her parents could visit her paternal grandmother, who lived in Ohio, and bring Sue back at the same time. All doubts were obscured by the overwhelming details necessary to coordinate such a trip. Chris drove his car out to Fairborn and left it there so that when they all returned to Rhode Island, Susan and he could drive back to Ohio again in the truck loaded with the furniture.

Should the Slickers have said anything? Objected? Demanded they wait until his divorce? They were moved by Chris's solicitous attention to their daughter and by Susan's breathless happiness.

Good-byes. A new life. Hugs. Kisses. "Good luck." "Call us if you need anything."

Clyde and Mary Lou looked at each other in the silent aftermath of their departure.

Mary Lou: *It was a hard day when they took off in that truck.*

Susan, on the other hand, was ecstatic.

Susan: *When we moved in together that summer in 1981, things were really good. He paid attention to what I thought. He listened to everything I believed was important. It was wonderful.*

They lived together for a year. It was a good year. A perfect year.

They both spent the summer working at Friendly's and going to summer school. On their off-hours, they drove around, exploring different places or simply enjoying each other's company. Sometimes they rode their bikes looking at houses, sharing with each other their preferences, dreaming about what kind of house they would like to have someday. They didn't have much money but that was okay. They were happy to wait for the great future he assured her was beckoning to them. Life was moving forward, bright with anticipation and promise.

Living together was everything she could have hoped for. He was warm, considerate, and a caring, tender lover. He was also vulnerable just often enough to melt her heart. She would never forget the time they were driving down the highway discussing his daughters. He became so emotional about losing them that he began to cry. He pulled over to the side of the road and sobbed, "I can't believe I'm losing them. I love them so much. I miss them terribly already. They're going to grow up and I won't be there to watch."

Susan: *That just turned me to mush. Here was Mr. Tough and he actually had the heart of marshmallow. It also convinced me how much he loved kids and I wanted to be married to a person who felt that way about his family.*

In the fall, they went back to school.

For the first time since she began college, she was off campus and away from most of the people she knew. Chris wanted her home whenever she wasn't in class. Although it was an adjustment for Susan, she thought it was sweet that he couldn't bear to have her apart from him.

There were so many decisions to make. It was exciting to plan, discuss, adjust, and make them together . . . more or less. At first she thought he was going to go to medical school, but he decided, instead, to apply to a graduate program at Wright State. He was accepted into a biomedical science program. He told her, it was better than medical school. He had great ideas. It was almost intoxicating to hear the enthusiasm of his plans. He talked of how he was going to go into research to find a cure for high blood pressure. Or at least, find the cause behind it. He wanted to make an impact on the world. Susan thought his goals were both exciting and commendable. They were willing to hold down the fort and be tight with money until he could finish school and then get a job at a university or research setting where he could move on with his career.

They were wonderful times, happy times, exhilarating times.

By Christmas, when they returned to Rhode Island for the holidays, they knew they wanted to cement their relationship with marriage.

* * *

Chris had really romanced Susan, sent her dozens of flowers, written countless letters, spent what money he had on presents for her, lived with her under the best of courtship circumstances taking care never to upset her, always the considerate partner and lover. He told her he had bought the diamond engagement ring he gave her when he received his half of the profits from the sale of the house he had lived in with his first wife.

Christopher Hightower was finally going to get what he had wanted all along.

The wedding date was set for July 10, 1982.

The first time Susan began to feel some qualms was just before the wedding. For some reason, she was terribly nervous. She had the uneasy feeling her family was still uncertain, that her parents were not that crazy about him, and that most of her friends didn't really like Chris but were too polite to say so. She became protective and defensive. Chris had very few friends and he did not make new ones easily. Among her own friends, she found him to be strangely uncomfortable. He didn't seem to know how to act at a party, or how to talk to people. His behavior was sometimes inappropriate; too loud, too crazy.

"Kathy," she asked her younger sister, "do you like Chris?"

"Sure."

"You don't think anything because . . . well, because he's divorced, for instance?"

When he first started dating Sue, Kathy hadn't known that much about him, but she did know he was getting divorced. It didn't seem that odd to her. It happened all the time.

"Lots of people get divorced," Kathy reassured her.

Some of her friends thought he was too controlling. Susan didn't sense it at the time, but he had a habit of putting her down in front of other people in subtle ways. "You don't look good in that color," he would say. Or, "Well, you know her," he would joke. "She really isn't too bright about those kinds of things."

Some friends couldn't help wondering why she didn't look at the warning signs with an objective eye rather than through rose-colored glasses. Romance can be deceptive, especially in the hands of a manipulator. But how to tell that to a young woman just prior to her wedding day? The plans had been made. The wedding invitations had been sent out. The beautiful white lace wedding gown had been purchased.

Susan finally convinced herself that her doubts were nothing more than prewedding jitters. There was never any thought of canceling the wedding.

They were married in a storybook setting in the White Church, where she had been confirmed. At the reception, she beamed with happiness.

Then they returned to school in Ohio to begin married life together.

Susan did not know the reason why Chris's mother did not attend their wedding.

Chapter 5

Changes

"Late Monday afternoon, police roped off the Brendel property on Middle Highway and Christopher Hightower's business office a few miles away."
        —*The Providence Journal-Bulletin, 9/23/91*

Their marriage began with great promise. Both bright students, Susan was completing her senior year at Wittenberg, while at Wright State University, Chris was working on his master's in physiology. They seemed to have everything going for them, including academic futures full of exciting prospects. Life was pleasantly uneventful.

At first the changes were so subtle as to be almost imperceptible. Susan *had* to be reading him wrong. Everything was still wonderful.

Except . . .

She knew that marriage would be different from the romantic haze that cloaked the wonderful days when they lived together and both of them were always on their best behavior. After all, there were no legal bonds at the time; too much dissatisfaction and either one could walk out of the relationship without any legal scars. Now, as a married couple, there was a settling-in process that had to take place. The passionate molds of courtship had to be recast into the routines of marriage, but Susan had no idea the adjustments from those days would be so great.

It was a gradual buildup. He started to treat her differently. She had the feeling she had become less precious to him. She was more of a thing than a person.

Susan thought, *It's my fault.* She wasn't doing something she should be doing. This pattern of blaming herself began early in the marriage and would continue during the coming years.

Susan: *After we got married was the very birth of noticed insecurity.*

When she moved out of the dorms and into the apartment with Chris she was separated from her friends and from the things she liked to do by twenty miles. Many of her friends did not have cars on campus, and, although she did, after the wedding, it was always: "No. You're a married woman now." Even keeping in touch with friends by phone was difficult since calling them was a toll call. "Long-distance," he said. "We have to be careful with the telephone bill." Her parents were paying for the remainder of her college tuition, but Chris and Susan were still short on money. Maybe he was right.

She remembered he had started his minor interventions into her lifestyle when they were living together. It hadn't really mattered at the time. It used to be that he couldn't bear to be separated from her, that he wanted her with him always. Now, he felt he had the right to demand she subordinate her schoolgirl needs to the greater demands of their union and to what would be good for them as a married couple. Or, to what was good for him alone, she sometimes found herself thinking.

When she complained that she was beginning to feel a bit lonely, he immediately stated with a smile and a hug, "That's not important. You shouldn't need anyone else." She didn't know what to make of it. She smiled back uncertainly, trying to minimize the pang of hurt she felt at his sudden lack of understanding. That he loved her and wanted her all to himself she could understand. But combined with his often-stated desire to have her around all the time, were unexpected restrictions on her movements and a subtle shrugged-off containment of her needs. It often seemed as though he planned to isolate her from friends.

He decided that he would determine where she could go. She wasn't exactly sure when she began to feel manipulated, but she slowly became aware that he was trying to control all of her activities—what she did, whom she saw, with whom she spent time, even with whom she could talk. Susan had always been fairly independent by nature, and she didn't know how to deal with this domination. He certainly wasn't like that before they married. Her role in his life seemed to have changed significantly. Her desires and wants were constantly being subordinated to his. She was the one who had to be adaptable. She was the one who had to have the resilience to withstand all the changes in the rules of life without complaint. Slowly his subtle demands became tinged with annoyance. "Why do you need anybody else? You've got me."

Perhaps she just was being too sensitive.

She was unsure, doubtful of her own abilities. Her grades were good, but she never seemed to have the right response for him. With a haunting sense of *déjà vu,* she realized his way was becoming the only way things could be done, just like all of the spoons and all of the bills in the cash drawer at the Creamery.

* * *

The beginning of Susan's nightmare was tenuous but penetrating. Loyalty forced her to minimize her growing concerns and to look the other way. Chris could be so wonderful, sometimes exacerbating her growing suspicion of a possible Jekyll and Hyde aspect to his personality. Even though he hated cats, he encouraged her to take home a beautiful kitten, making two cats in the house, and he did it just for her, knowing how fond she was of cats. He was very tender and loving with children and animals. He even cleaned and nursed the cats when they came home chewed-up from a fight.

But the uncomfortable little suspicions continued.

She heard rumors from his sister of another ex-wife. Was it possible that she was his third wife rather than his second? There were unanswered questions about a girl from Thailand. Had he kept important secrets from her? He certainly had kept secrets regarding his family background; little by little, she discovered the truth of his dysfunctional family. When his stepfather, like his natural father, abandoned his family to flounder on its own without any financial or emotional support, Chris decided he was going to have to make up for the sense of paternal deprivation left in the wake of yet another abandonment. He had started out as the Golden Boy of his family, the oldest of the five children, who took care of his four younger siblings while his mother worked as a meat cutter in Titusville, but . . .

"I thought you told me she was a carhop," Susan interrupted.

"She's done both," he said with an impatient edge that ended her intrusion.

. . . it was he who was going to make it big and take care of all of them.

But something went wrong.

Despite hard work and almost making it a number of times, he would invariably fail at most of the things he attempted. To her surprise, he was not a good student. He had a difficult time in school and was a slow reader. With all the comprehensive medical books and journals he had to absorb, poor reading skills were bound to impact heavily on his studies. He had never been diagnosed, but she was beginning to suspect he might be dyslexic. He had told her that once he was fitted with prescription reading glasses, he had done "all right" in grade school and high school, but he almost flunked out of junior college and struggled with much of his undergraduate studies.

Once again, she had to be wrong. The combination of a left-handed male and poor vision does not add up to dyslexia. And his transcripts were excellent. Maybe it was something she was doing that was distracting him, something about their marriage. Lord knows he certainly indicated often enough she wasn't measuring up to the expectations he had had of her. It was nothing he actually said, just the gnawing feeling of a constant sense of disapproval over everything, even sex. That was one of the most painful reproaches he hinted at, reaching right to the core of her being. All of a sudden she wasn't good enough in bed. He had never hinted at any dissatisfaction before. His reproaches only made her want to please him all the more.

In the early days of marriage, they had some disagreements, even some fights in which she yelled her frustrations at him. "You have no right to raise your voice to me," he stated categorically. "No right at all." And when, at times, she instinctively rebelled and wanted to expand her activities beyond the limits he had set for her, he got upset and accused her of sleeping around. She was profoundly shocked at his accusation.

"How can you say that?"

He had been the only man in her life. He knew that. She had never slept with anyone before Chris. Early in their marriage, he began accusing her and he never relinquished his lack of trust. It was, he told her, one of the reasons he had to keep a tight rein on her.

She had always enjoyed working in college theater productions. He forbade her to participate. "No," he declared in his growing court-of-no-appeals manner. "You're a married woman now."

The hours were too long. The camaraderie that built up amongst the cast and crew was too dangerous. People who worked in theater were promiscuous and not to be trusted. There were a dozen reasons why she was not permitted to participate, not the least of which was her primary function to be a good wife, to cook dinner and "be home with your husband."

"Chris," she tried to reason. "I really love theater. I've always worked on the school productions, and . . ."

"You're being stupid," he interrupted a bit contemptuously.

No one had ever called her stupid before.

"You're not really attractive enough for theater anyway," he said. "You're okay for me, but not for the stage." It was the kind of criticism that was meant to degrade. Suddenly, all of his other criticisms flashed into her mind, the ones she tried to ignore: he didn't like her to wear jeans . . . they were too tight . . . she talked too loud . . . too fast . . . she didn't make sense . . .

"All right," she finally acquiesced, stunned at the kind of undermining comments he was capable of saying to her. She didn't want to hear any more or have them fuel the present argument. "I won't join the theater group . . ."

"Now you're finally being sensible."

". . . but I'd like to go out with some of the other women."

"What other women?"

"In the neighborhood. They go out once a month."

"To do what?"

"Talk. Socialize."

"No."

"But . . ."

"I don't like it, Sue. You're already out too long by staying at school so much. That's not very fair to me, is it?" he complained. "First it was the theater. Now, you'd rather be with friends instead of me."

"Don't put it that way," she pleaded. "It's just to have some fun."

"What kind?" he demanded.

And then she realized, he thought she was going to "do something else."

He didn't talk to her for a week.

She finally admitted to herself that the idyllic storybook romance had metamorphosed into a tension-filled life. The walls of pretense and secrecy were becoming psychologically draining. She wondered if this was the way he had been with his first wife or if this was why he wanted a younger woman, one less likely to demand equality.

She told the women she couldn't join them because she had too much schoolwork, and she told the drama coach she was too busy now to participate in the productions. She loved the theater and became very depressed when she realized she had to give it up. She couldn't tell anyone the true reason. It was too degrading. "I have too much work to do," she fibbed.

Susan: *I remember feeling sad that I was losing friendships and connections that were just mine. I was letting go of most of the personal interests that I had that were apart from him.*

All of the friendships and activities that helped to define the individuality of Susan's personality were put at risk. Little by little, he was molding her into Christopher Hightower's wife and little else.

She knew that jealousy was playing a large part in his demands. "You're too friendly," he often commented. He was afraid of other men intruding into their relationship. "You dress too sexy," he reproached, accusing her of being a flirt, overtly implying her behavior was generally too promiscuous for him.

Promiscuous. She couldn't believe he was saying that.

The feeling of repression was beginning to suffocate her. She still wanted desperately to be a good wife to him, to be everything that he expected, but he had to give her a chance to learn.

She tried harder.

He sulked.

She did not recognize how manipulating his anger and disapproval were.

* * *

It was all very confusing. What was going wrong? Sometimes he was so sweet and other times so forbidding, so emotionally distant from her.

One night she found him sitting in almost-total darkness. He liked to keep the shades drawn as though keeping light out of the room kept him safe and protected. When she asked him what was the matter, he told her quietly that he had always felt like the square peg in a round hole, and she knew, with a surge of sympathy, that she had to try to be a more-understanding wife. She realized he must have deep-seated pain somewhere in his psyche that he was unable to share with her. He tried, but could not seem to get it out. She deeply believed in marriage, with all of the attending implications of bonding and sacrifice implicit in the sacred vows they had taken before God. She wanted desperately to make her marriage work. To make him happy. Perhaps the strength of her love could make up for the love that had been denied the little boy he used to be. It was up to her.

While still trying to be a good wife, Susan began to admit her growing resentment. She remembered the reservations she had about marrying him during her junior year. She hadn't paid much attention at the time. He's been married before," she had thought, generously excusing his behavior. "He's used to a married state." She fondly reminded herself how they used to go grocery shopping together, but she also remembered how she had experienced some big reservations, and had written them off as nothing more than prewedding nerves.

Had she made a mistake?

More and more, she found herself thinking of her parents and the way they shared their lives. She had always taken a backseat when her father and mother spoke, especially with bigger issues like politics and religion. She had never been in the habit of challenging her elders. Was that part of the problem? An ingrained habit? She thought about how life used to be at home in Rhode Island and tried to recapture the happy aura of those days. Unlike Chris and herself, Mom and Dad shared their household tasks pretty evenly. Susan and Kathy tended to go to Mom for some things and Dad for others, but Clyde and Mary Lou always made their important decisions jointly. Wasn't that the way it was supposed to be? They rarely fought, making sure to keep it in private. The atmosphere they tried to maintain at home had always been pleasant and secure.

Susan: *They didn't let me fail very much. When I was in sixth grade, everybody took a music test. I wanted to play flute in the band badly. I obviously didn't do well enough because I ended up playing clarinet and I really didn't want to play that. So they went out and bought me a flute to circumvent the disappointment.*

Susan was beginning to sense some of the unexpected disadvantages to such a protective environment. Was it possible to be too loving?

Susan: *I was a normal kid with a sloppy room. After a while, my mother got tired nagging me about it so she cleaned it up herself. In some ways, she didn't teach me to live with the consequences of my actions.*

Susan recognized that sort of protection could have both good and bad ramifications. Her parents would always say, "Just do your best," but she would translate that into believing she never did well enough for them. Some of the time she felt they expected more of her, and in many aspects of her life, she felt unworthy. Her parents had recognized and tried to ward off a tendency to low self-esteem.

Susan: *I was a fat kid. I got teased a lot. The college chunk. All the way through the seventh grade. I took it personally. I carried that image of being fat with me till three years ago. Now I'm right where I like it . . . but I carried that image for a long time. I was poor in math. I ended up getting caught up and aced it in college. But certain things stuck as a kid. Like I wasn't attractive.*

Chris knew that. How could he use it against her?

"You're not attractive enough" progressed to, "You're not smart enough," even though her grades were excellent, almost as good as his. It soon became clear her grades didn't count for much to him. They placed her in a competitive role he did not appreciate. Her role as a student was a subordinate one to her role as his wife. He set the rules by which she was to behave, and although she didn't think she needed a supervisor over all of her activities, somehow, as her elder, he always intervened and always had to have the upper hand.

Susan: *Chris was getting to be too heavy. I was supposed to be home after school. Even if I wanted to stop and talk to someone I couldn't. He actually forbade me to, and if I was late, I would have to go through a humiliating third degree when I got home.*

She did not recognize the classic patterns of an emotionally abusive husband. The demands became increasingly oppressive. She was never quite sure when his attitude turned to bullying. She did not realize she was beginning to fit the classic pattern of an emotionally battered woman. Nothing was ever good enough for him. She could sense the erosion of her own self-esteem. It had taken her several years to build herself up to really liking herself, but she was not mature enough nor emotionally equipped to salvage it at the expense of peace within her marriage. There was no balm for her battered ego.

"Why are you late?" he asked. "You could do your work at home. You don't have to stay at school to do it." And then the first of a long line of suspicions, "Who were you with?"

"Nobody."

"You weren't alone."

"Nobody," she insisted.

"Who!"

"I was with a friend."

His eyes narrowed. So she *had* been with someone.

"A girlfriend," she hastened to add.

"You don't need friends, you have me."

"I know, Chris . . . but . . ."

"Aren't I good enough?"

"Yes, of course . . ."

"Why isn't dinner ready yet?"

She was supposed to be there to cook and clean, but she wasn't supposed to have fun or friends, she thought resentfully. She tried not to feel oppressed and neglected while he tunneled in on his own schoolwork, but she couldn't help herself. She was offended by his self-absorption in his own studies, even if, as he always reminded her, he was struggling through them to build a future. After all, who was he doing it for? It was for her. All for her. And she was too young and too stupid to understand or appreciate it.

In his own egocentric manner, Chris loved Susan very much. All he wanted was to show her the way and guide her in the proper direction for a happy marriage. He had already been divorced once. That wasn't going to happen to him again. He could not lose Susan. He had to mold her into a pattern of behavior that would make him feel secure. Why couldn't she understand that everything he did was for her own good and for the good of their future, one in which it was he who was going to be at the top of the world, creating financial security for her as well as for his family out of the strength of his very intellect alone. She must not thwart his goals with petty girlish needs.

The strain of living with his domineering personality manifested itself in an unexpected way. Susan found herself attracted to another man.

Had she been more experienced, she would have realized the attraction was a rebellion against Chris's domineering behavior. Instead of blaming herself for her lack of emotional fidelity, she might have insisted that the two of them had to seriously think about the abusive direction in which their relationship was progressing.

Susan: *This guy was funny. He wasn't so heavy, so serious, so*

controlling. So we flirted some. I went back to his place once. I
kissed him. Other than that, nothing happened and Chris as-
sumed I had slept with him. That's something he threatens me
with even today. He says when he gets out of prison he's going
to tell his story and everybody will know what I'm really like.

She was honest with Chris about the incident. She wanted
the marriage to work and she believed that honesty was a large
factor in the equation of trust. She needed him to help her
understand what was happening to their relationship. Telling
him about kissing the young man was a major miscalculation.
He never forgave her. Instead of opening the doors of communication and understanding between them, he threw a barrage
of invective at her.

"You have broken your vow!" he exploded while his wife
sobbed and begged for forgiveness. "No wife of mine . . ." "How
could you be so cheap? . . ." "I'll never be able to trust you
again." "If this is the way you really are, you'd better get out! I
won't have a flirt for a wife . . . or worse . . ." "I was right . . ."

It was a violent, angry justification of the abusive manipulation and control he had maintained over her. She was completely
out of her element in trying to deal with the complexities of a
personality that had such profound, unexamined psychological
problems.

She couldn't stop crying.

What had happened to the man who had courted her? Was that
all make-believe, or a con? Her own inexperience made her a
party to his domination. Had she been more his equal in age and
seasoning, she might have fought him on his own terms, but he
made it very clear that he was older, more experienced, and,
without question, her superior. She was just a kid.

Pleasing Chris became of paramount importance: if she only
could, it would make criticism of her in his forbidding tone less
likely.

"You have a lot to learn."

She cried a lot.

The romantic candlelight that had softly illuminated their courtship had been permanently snuffed.

The incident about the young college man never really came to an end. Susan was confused. She didn't understand why Chris continued to remain so upset. What more could she do? How could she make it up to him? Despite his attacks on her, she was never angry; she didn't know how to be angry. Mostly, she was hurt. She was always on the defensive end of their disagreements. She covered up her feelings and tried to make explanations. It turned out that it was always something she had done.

Susan couldn't handle her despair in silence any longer. She had to call her mother and tell her all about it. The collect telephone call from Susan frightened Mary Lou and Clyde.

It was September 25, Clyde's birthday. Susan had called to wish her father a happy birthday, but after the good wishes had been extended, Susan broke down.

Mary Lou realized her daughter was deeply upset and didn't know what to do. Susan told her how she had remained at school after some of her classes and gone to a boy's place, how she told Chris about it, and how he held that over her all the time.

"He won't let up," Susan cried. "I'm afraid he's going to throw me out. He threatened he would . . ."

Mary Lou was terribly worried.

They had only been married two and a half months.

What could they do? How could they help? Mary Lou sat and wrote them a long letter. It discussed how a marriage was based upon trust. "We all have our individual lives to lead, but the true essence of a relationship comes down to trusting each other." The letter, written with care and without any prejudicial defer-

ence to either Susan or Chris, was read by both and thought
about. But nothing seemed to calm the emotional storms. The
newlyweds ended up going to a marriage counselor the first year
they were married. Susan was disturbed and concerned that in
her segregated environment, she found other men interesting to
be with and talk to when she was out of her husband's control.
The counseling didn't do much, but she was hoping it would
make Chris at least sit up and pay attention.

He did.

Chris had his own solution to their problems. "You see," he
said with genuine sincerity, "I really miss my children. Wouldn't
it be great if you were pregnant during school and had the baby
right after graduation?"

"Oh, not yet," she protested.

But he didn't want to wait for anything. When he begged her
to have children right away, he was sweet and loving, and she
caught a glimpse of the man he used to be, kind, thoughtful,
persuasive. She wanted children eventually. Just not yet. But he
was convincing. He knew how to make her acquiesce. He was
adept at manipulating her into agreeing to something she was
not certain about.

She could understand how he would want to start another family, but something told her what he really wanted was for her to
be pregnant the moment she graduated from college in order to
keep her tied down.

She didn't want to deal with such a troubling thought and
swept it under the rug.

"I don't want to wait," he said, seeming to sense her unstated
feelings. "I'm getting older. I've practically lost my two children
to their mother."

She knew he was only calling his daughters sporadically, and
usually only when she reminded him.

"But . . ." she began.

"I've lost my two little girls," he cried in distress.

Her sympathies were aroused despite her doubts.

"It will be wonderful," he insisted. "We'll take care of the
baby together. It's our future. We're building a life."

As a form of self-protection, she had subconsciously planned to take the path of least resistance in any decisions they had to make. She would give in to his requests. Her own family's method when confronted with something unpleasant had always been to internalize it. Now, she wished that she had learned how to fight. The more pressing exigencies of life did not always succumb to such a civil approach for solutions.

She did not really want to give in to this request. She did not want to have a baby yet. But he was very persuasive. "You'll see," he said fervently. They would be closer than ever before. "It will be ours . . ." Something to share. Someone to love together. Someone who belonged to both of them. A bond cementing their love for each other with the sacred blessing of a new life. It would solve whatever minor little problems they had been having. The outside world was trying to pull them apart. This would keep them together. He sounded like the old Chris, all his ardor geared to color and control the outcome of their joint decision. He knew how to influence her, leaving her little room to maneuver or offer resistance.

She had to agree.

He knew she would.

"Oh, Sue, just think. Our baby. We'll do it together. All of it. Even labor. We'll do it together. We can go to classes for natural childbirth and do it together . . ."

If this would make him happy, her position as an equal would be possible. Perhaps he would be less demanding of her.

"The minute you graduate," he determined would be a good time.

But natural childbirth . . .

He spoke authoritatively and convincingly. Natural childbirth was a good idea. The only way to go. She worried a little about what natural childbirth would be like. Still, his enthusiasm was contagious. Maybe a baby would change a life that she hated to admit had become almost intolerable. Natural childbirth. She shouldn't worry. It was definitely something they could do together.

He already had two daughters. Maybe if she could give him a son . . .

Chapter 6

Home Sweet Home

"I think about (the case) all the time. It's difficult when a family disappears into thin air."
— Barrington Police Chief Charles Brule
The Providence Journal-Bulletin, 10/17/91

Susan graduated magna cum laude with a 3.78 grade point average that she felt almost obligated to play down. Chris's average was better. A perfect 4.0. Maybe she played down her grades because he never commented on them.

When they had their first anniversary on July 10, 1983, she was apprehensive but pleased when she realized she was pregnant. She knew Chris would be thrilled at the news, and he was. But once the first rush of joy passed, he went back to the old pattern of ignoring her. He was paying more and more attention to the demands of school. How could she complain? He was doing it all for her, wasn't he? But she was young, and she was lonely.

Susan: *I was disappointed that he wasn't more attentive. I rationalized that he already had two kids and number three was less likely to cause excitement.*

She began feeling poorly and wanted some special treatment. This was going to be their last nine months together before there would be someone else in their lives. She was ill for the first three months, so much so that she started to think to herself all she wanted was just to get it over with.

Morning sickness. Unable to eat. Mild depression. She lost weight.

He joked about it. "Well, you were too fat anyway."

Was that supposed to make her feel better? How could he be so insensitive? She was genuinely hurt inside but couldn't get him to understand how much his comment bothered her.

"What's the matter now? Are you angry about something?"

"No," she denied. "I'm upset, not angry."

Despite denials, she *was* angry. It was a mean thing to say, but she still did not know how to deal with her anger. She buried her feelings in silent anguish and the rationalizations that subconsciously helped her to cope.

That fall, Chris began his long-sought-after program in biomedical sciences. It was a difficult combined masters'/doctoral approach to a degree. Only the best students were accepted. Not only were Chris's grades perfect, but he came with high recommendation from former professors.

The Slickers were concerned that their daughter had become pregnant too soon. Sue and Chris had been living on student loans. Mary Lou thought Sue should get a job after graduation to earn some money first before taking on the responsibilities of a family, but she knew Chris had convinced her to do it, even though he, himself, would still be going to school and not earning any money. It was troubling. Chris and Susan had hardly gotten used to each other yet and already they were taking on a major change in their lives, one that would affect every thought and every decision they made from now on. The Slickers had been supporting Susan's college education; whatever money Susan would have needed had she remained in her dormitory was sent to her just as though she had not married. They always had planned to do that and they continued sending the money that had been set aside for her education.

But they knew the money could only help in the short term. Now he wanted to buy a house in Dayton.

"It's much smarter to own than to rent," he told Susan. "We'll be building up equity."

She wasn't even sure she wanted to settle in Ohio.

Once again, though, he was so enthusiastic about buying a house, she had to listen. All of his old charm emerged when he was enthusiastic about something. They were going to have a baby. They had to have a place of their own. They were on their way to the bright future he had promised her.

He didn't have any money of his own. He knew that Susan's grandmother and her great uncle had left small amounts, $5,000 each, to both Susan and Kathy.

He was loving, attentive, charming, wonderful. The moment she agreed to buy a house in Dayton, the personal problems that had plagued them calmed down considerably. She wasn't totally opposed to buying a house, just nervous about being so far away from home, especially in her condition. She remembered how they used to ride around on their bikes dreaming about the houses they would like to own. That had been such fun. She had been so deeply in love.

The old two-story corner house with the barn-shaped roof that he selected for them in Dayton was not really what she had dreamed of. The house on Elsmere Avenue had seven rooms and was only $24,000, but it was run-down both inside and out. The concrete front porch was cracking and in need of considerable cement work.

The house had a living room, a dining room, and an old kitchen on the first floor. The second floor had two bedrooms, a very old bathroom with octagonal black-and-white floor tiles, and a third room that was not considered a bedroom since it had no closet. There was a full basement with another bathroom, a driveway on the side of the house, and a backyard. The house was in what

Susan considered a marginal neighborhood on the city's north side. Around the corner were nice homes, but most of those on Elsmere Avenue were a bit dilapidated.

Chris minimized all of her concerns. He convinced her the racially mixed neighborhood was actually in the process of re-generation. He would be able to fix up the old house and once the remodeling was completed, they would be able to get more than $24,000 for it. It was a good investment. "Trust me."

They put $5,000 down.

Her parents were happy to see they had gotten beyond their difficult first year of adjustment and had moved on to planning their future. Clyde and Mary Lou even gave them some money to help their transition into the new home.

Once the deal had been consummated, Susan became excited about the move. She looked forward to cleaning up the house with paint, wallpaper, curtains, new floor coverings. She couldn't wait to plan the nursery.

Even though Chris selected it, it wasn't good enough for him. Everything had to be perfect. Susan thought when he said they would fix it up, he meant wallpaper, paint, a little plumbing, but the minute they moved in, he began to gut the house. He ripped out practically every interior wall. He removed all the lumpy cracked plaster and horsehair insulation. Then he began the slow process of rewiring and replumbing most of the house. The second floor bathroom with the very old floor tile had to be redone. He ripped out every tile as well as the old pedestal tub because the water pressure was so low the sprinkler wouldn't oscillate. "We'll put in a new bathroom," he reassured her.

The bathroom was unusable during renovations. For months.

He tore down a kitchen wall. The dirty plastic drop cloths that were hung to separate the kitchen from the dust of the unfinished living room remained in the same place. For months.

Trying to keep house in such turmoil and mess was very difficult. By the end of October, the morning sickness was over and Susan was feeling physically better. They were living in one room, heated only by a kerosene space heater. It was dark and dirty with exposed pipes. The only usable toilet was in the basement. From the bedroom on the second floor, needing to use the bathroom meant a two-story trek down to the basement and back up. So they lived in a second floor room with a couch, a television, and a space heater, and they slept in the room next to it, which had nothing. For months.

She couldn't believe she was going to bring a new baby home to such disarray.

Susan: *I couldn't believe I was living in these conditions. I was embarrassed to tell my family. My parents would have been shocked. It was awful. It was filthy. I couldn't tell them.*

She was only three months pregnant and not showing yet. When their next-door neighbors invited them to a Halloween costume party, Susan wanted to attend very badly. Chris didn't want to accept the invitation but he finally gave in to the supplication in his wife's eyes. He was tired of seeing her chronically depressed state. To please her, he agreed to go, telling her it was his love for her that made him relent.

Susan was thrilled. She excitedly put together a country-style costume from bits and pieces she had lying about. Even Chris agreed to wear a costume. Together, they created one for him as a mad scientist, with a lab coat, a stethoscope about this neck, his glasses perched on the tip of his nose, and military-style, grounded, green operating room shoes. It was great fun. Usually, if they were invited somewhere, there would be an edge to the acceptance of the invitation; Chris would start an argument just before they were about to leave and Susan would wind up saying, "Forget it, let's not go." But tonight it was okay. He had agreed. No fight just before leaving. Nothing to mar the evening.

* * *

The neighbors, Glenn and Vicki, lived in a duplex next door, only a driveway apart from their own home.

Gaiety and cheerful silliness were the standing orders of the night. There were about forty guests at the party. Vicki was dressed as a witch with a long pointed nose and a tall pointed hat, and Glenn as a Kabuki-style Mikado, with chalk face makeup, black-painted slanted eyes, and long fingernails. One guest made a hit dressed as Lady Godiva in a long blond wig and a flesh-colored bodysuit that left little to the imagination.

It was the first party they had attended since coming to Ohio and Susan felt excited. Even Chris's denigrating comment about her to one of the guests who had brought up the subject of foreign affairs, "She's ditsy. She wouldn't know the first thing about that," didn't bother her on this night.

After sampling the finger foods placed about the rooms, hors d'oeuvres, chips, dips, and quail eggs skewered on long toothpicks, Susan sat down on the couch in happy relaxation and started a conversation with the man seated next to her. He was young, friendly, in his mid to late twenties, and, with his mask removed, nice-looking. They talked for about twenty minutes about the party and school. It was refreshing, easy, comfortable. It felt like old times. She paid attention to what he said. She offered her opinions. He listened. She smiled and laughed. She felt wonderful.

Chris was standing across the room talking with someone else but watching her through the corner of his eye the entire time she sat on the couch.

When she finished the conversation and was about to get up to look for Chris, she saw him across the room. Her heart jumped a beat; he had "that stare" on his face.

He decided it was time to go home.

"Not yet," Susan tried to protest. "It's early."

"It's time now."

Susan didn't want to leave. She was having a good time for the first time in a long while. The anger he had barely been able to contain only increased at her reluctance to leave. He was certain she was challenging him because of the other man. Susan didn't want to leave because of *him*.

"What do you think you're doing making eyes at another man."

"Chris, no . . ." she began to protest, suddenly realizing he was escalating an innocent incident. He was whispering, but he was so angry, everyone in the room could hear him.

"Do you have any idea how embarrassing it is to me to see my wife coming on to another man," he hissed furiously.

"I wasn't. I was just talking . . ."

"We are going *home.*"

The man she had been speaking with almost got up from the couch to protest. He was disturbed at the false accusation. They had only been casually talking. But he decided to stay out of it. It was a domestic dispute. Susan's husband was very red in the face and acting crazy. Maybe the guy had reason to be so angry with his wife. It was best to stay out of it.

Chris's outburst was discomforting to their hosts. They tried to intervene as gently as they could, but Chris wasn't about to be appeased.

"We're going home," he insisted. "Now!"

Susan, her face ashen, her eyes beginning to blur with tears, turned to Vicki, "I'd better go . . ." She didn't want to cause a scene. The whole thing was awkward enough without giving him cause to intensify the incident into a public third degree.

"I'm sorry you have to go. . . ." Vicki said.

"Thank you . . . a nice party . . ."

Susan rushed home ahead of him, crossing the narrow driveway between their houses quickly to escape what she knew was coming. He started the moment he slammed the door shut.

"You were flirting with that guy!"

"No."

"Right there in front of me! I saw how you looked at him."

"I look into people's eyes when I talk to them," she cried, trying to convince him she had done nothing to warrant his accusation.

"Don't take me for a fool, you bitch. I could see."

"That's just the way I am," she tried to explain, "the way I've always been. I look into people's eyes when I . . ."

"You were flirting with him!" he insisted. It dawned on her he would always look on her natural behavior as flirting. "Every time I turn around, you're flirting with another guy."

"I didn't think that was what I was doing."

"Acting like a whore."

She was shocked. "Chris, I'm sorry. I would never do anything like that."

"It's disgusting!" he shouted violently, pulling off his wedding ring and throwing it at her. It missed her and rolled across the floor.

"I didn't realize I was doing that," she said, bursting into tears.

"If you're going to act like this, that's the end of this marriage. The end!"

Her eyes traced the track of the fallen wedding ring. She bent to pick it up. "Chris."

"You can just get out!"

She was terrified of his rage. His teeth were clicking in agitation. Scared to be alone, she felt helpless. Susan apologized over and over again. She did what she felt she had to do in order to survive. She practically groveled at his feet, thus perpetuating her loss of dignity and self-esteem. It was degrading to apologize for something she felt she had not done.

She hated the kerosene space heater. She hated living in a house in which the rooms were always dusty and dirty, cold and uncomfortable. The staple gun had lain next to her bed for months, as though her dressing table were a toolbox. The downstairs portion of the house had nothing but the exterior walls. They lived in dispiriting deprivation all through the winter.

When she came down with the flu, he refused to fuss over her, walking off instead. How could he do that, she wondered tearfully through a coughing spasm. His only comment before leaving the room was, "Get a grip on yourself."

Yet, he was very good about other things. They were going to natural childbirthing classes together. Despite her initial reluctance to his insistence on natural childbirth, she had begun to believe it was what she wanted too, since they spent close moments together in training. But, except for the time they spent going to the classes together, she saw little of him.

She had to find ways to keep herself occupied without him. She took a job baby-sitting. It served a double purpose.

Susan: *He would never let me have money, I always had to ask for it. I got a baby-sitting job while I was pregnant so at least I had a little money coming in because I couldn't stand not having any money.*

Since being pregnant made her so unattractive, Chris decided baby-sitting was safe. It would keep her from being lazy and from trying to socialize with her school friends.

Susan: *It took me about five years to admit that money was an issue because I didn't want to let money come between us. I'm middle-class. I had more than one change of clothes. He came from a dirt-poor background. Money was very important to him.*

When they ran short of money for remodeling the house, he charged her with mismanagement.

"It's all your fault!" he insisted.

"Why?"

"Because you have problems with money. You don't know how to handle it. You let it slip through your fingers. You can't manage well!"

He pulled open the refrigerator door. "Look," he exclaimed pulling out spoiled leftover spaghetti and broccoli. "Look at that! How could you waste food like that! Your kind doesn't understand what it's like to be poor. Money doesn't grow on trees. You should use up everything instead of letting it go to waste."

* * *

The renovation stopped completely.

He kept saying, "I'll get to it," but he didn't. He was doing schoolwork. She recognized it as one of his behavior patterns. Whenever he got stuck with something, he just stopped.

Even when Susan was pregnant, he still didn't trust her completely.

One day her purse was lying in full view. He picked it up and opened it.

"Wait," she protested.

"Why? Do you have something to hide?"

"It's not that."

"Is there something that shouldn't be there?"

"Chris, that's mine . . ."

Slowly his hand came out of her purse holding some folded-over bills. "Where did you get this?"

"I saved up."

"Who did you get it from?"

"Nobody. I had it. I saved."

"You've been hiding it from me."

It was the old senseless, unwinnable argument. "I need to have some money of my own."

"Why? Exactly what do you propose to spend it on?"

"That's not the point," she cried, trying to justify her needs. "Nothing in particular. To me it's a safety cushion, because if I didn't have something put away . . ."

He slammed her purse on the table at the same time he pocketed the bills. "There can only be one set of controls over the household finances and I'll take care of it. How many times do I have to tell you that!"

"I hate being without a dime of my own."

"I give you enough. I give you plenty."

"I have nothing in case of an emergency."

"I can't understand that."

"I don't think you should go into my purse," she objected.

He advanced on her. "I'm your husband," he said in a forbid-

ding tone as she stepped backward. "I have the right to be in
your purse and look through everything in there."

She felt utterly violated.

Susan: *It gives me the creeps to think about it now.*

At the time, Susan jotted a few feelings in her private journal.
She hadn't written in it in a long time. Now she felt she had to
express her private feelings somewhere.

SUSAN'S JOURNAL—March 19, 1984

I have a hell of an attitude problem.

Question: How do I go about correcting it though? Everything I do is only temporary—the attitude always comes
back. It's like I'm just deluding myself. Maybe plain old
hard work will help. I want my home to be a place Chris
wants to come home to. I don't want to drive him away. I
also want our baby to grow up loving himself and his world.
That requires change on my part so my poor attitudes etc.
don't rub off on him.

Susan's notes in the margin of her journal read: *"Keep busy
and think of your family."* And then a big question: *"Is patience
a virtue?"*

Susan felt panic at the first labor contraction, but she wasn't
really afraid. She remembered everything Chris had said to her
about how they were going to go through this together.

The birth of their baby showed a side of Chris she had never
seen before.

Susan: *I will never forget this day.*

*After being in slowly increasing labor the whole day, Chris
took me to the hospital after dinner—a rather large one of pizza
with all the works. The nurses looked at each other with that
"she's going to lose it all" look on their faces.*

He had been very supportive all day: "Just keep breathing slowly."—"Let's go walk the mall to keep things moving."—"Remember everything they taught you at natural childbirth classes."

Chris had accompanied me to the series of classes and I was comforted by the fact that he had been through this twice already and knew what to do. I also assumed he'd be pretty patient. I was wrong.

The contractions intensified and she began having back pain. It was getting more intolerable by the moment. Chris kept reminding her how to breathe, doing it with her—in—out—in—out. He stood by the side of the bed and held her hand. She didn't know what she would do without him. He kept talking to her, rubbing her stomach. "There you go. That's it. Breathe." Watching her body writhing back and forth as the pains intensified.

Eventually, she couldn't take it anymore. "I can't," she cried.

"Sure you can," he insisted. "Hang in there."

The pain was too much. She couldn't finish without an anesthetic. They had never really discussed the idea, both assuming she would be able to go natural. There was the extra cost to consider, as well. He reminded her it would be astronomical and they had already had to borrow money from her sister to pay the hospital bill.

Hours were passing and it was too much.

Finally she said, "I can't take this anymore. Get me something to make the pain go away."

"You're fighting against it."

"No. I can't." She grabbed onto the bars of the hospital headboard overhead for support. "I can't do it anymore."

His face changed. "You told me you wanted to do this with no anesthesia. You can finish this without any artificial help."

"I don't care what I said."

"Or are you too much of a wimp!"

"I've never been in so much pain in my life. Just get me something to make it go away," she begged. *"Anything."*

The contempt on his face was shocking. He leaned toward her

so no one else could hear. "If you want anesthesia," he declared in a harsh whisper in her ear, "you can have it, but then you don't need me."

"Chris . . . it hurts," she gasped as another surge of pain arched her body.

"I'll just walk out of this room and go home," he threatened through his teeth.

"How . . . can you . . ." She could barely breathe through the spasm. ". . . say that . . . ?"

"You're on your own now."

She couldn't believe what he was saying. She was frightened. She had never felt anything like this before, slicing through her, forcing her to cry out with each contraction. All she wanted was a little something to ease the pain. Could he really be that insensitive to what she was going through?

She watched in panic as he walked out of the room. "No!" Her emotional need to have him with her was much stronger than any physical pain she was going to endure. "Come back," she cried out. "You can't leave me!"

He stopped at the door and looked back at her. "You don't need me."

"I'll make it without the anesthesia," she sobbed. "Stay with me. You promised."

"You promised you'd go natural!" he said bluntly just as another contraction took her breath away.

"I will," she gasped. "I will . . ."

He came back.

They finally moved into the delivery room and Chris left to be outfitted in hospital greens.

Susan: *I thought I was going to have the baby without him being there after all because things were moving along so rapidly now.*

But he made it back in time and insisted on taking pictures of the delivery. . . .

Not my favorite idea.

He started to become more insistent as she began the final stage. "Push harder!" he snapped. "Harder!" It seemed to her that all his concentration seemed to be with the doctor and the baby—she was just there to deliver "his" child.

When the baby was delivered she was so wrapped up in what her body was doing that she didn't hear them. "What is it?" she finally called out.

It was the nurse who replied, "It's a boy!"

She was exhausted but thrilled. He had had two girls. Now she had been able to give him a son.

Susan: *They laid him on my stomach, and I was in awe that such a perfect little person had been created by us. Chris was so proud to have a son! He was all over the delivery room making sure he was being properly cleaned and cared for. I'm sure he gave me a hug and kiss and told me he loved me, but I have no specific recollection of him paying much attention to me—it was all focused on the baby.*

I had always liked the name Mitchell . . .

The next day, Chris sent her flowers at the hospital. She was expressionless as she looked at them neatly arranged in the vase next to her bed. Roses. Just like when he was courting her.

She turned her head away.

She had made it through the delivery without the aid of anesthesia, but down deep, a hate was growing in her for his blackmailing her into unnecessary suffering by threatening to abandon her at a time she needed him most. "Are you too much of a wimp?" he had said. She always caved in.

Lying in the hospital bed, holding her beautiful, brand-new son, with Chris, the proud papa, standing over her beaming, she told herself she forgave him for being so mean to her during her labor.

But she would never forget.

* * *

By the time they brought Mitchell home, her negative attitude
had improved. The baby's room had new walls and paint. When
she had left for the hospital, the old windows still had gaps
around the edges, and there were no doorframes or doors. He
had put the old woodwork back and it looked wonderful.

Susan: *It was mine, my first home. He did let me decorate the
way I wanted. I got to pick colors and the wifey type things.*

"Go ahead," he said. "I don't have time anyway. As long as
you don't have striped wallpaper."
"Why not?"
"My first wife loved striped wallpaper. I don't want to have
it around."

Susan: *I liked it when it was finished. I loved the big wide woodwork. It had solid wood doors. They called it fruitwood. Kind of
a golden, oaky color. I loved that in it. It was older, had character
to it.*
Chris had been right, after all.

The birth of Mitchell had only a temporary positive effect.
The 50/50 partnership he had promised her in taking care of
him disappeared within the first few weeks. Susan became the
constant recipient of criticism over her mothering. "You're not
picking him up as much as you should. Don't you know anything about these things?" "You're picking him up too much.
Let him cry it out." "Your should have changed him." "You
change him too much." They had talked about being partners
in parenting, and she had believed his promises to help. He
was leaving it all to her, the same way he did when his daughters came to visit.

The implication was always that she couldn't do it right and
that she wasn't a good mother. And she believed him. She *wasn't*
an experienced mother. Chris knew what he was talking about.
He had already had two children, so he knew. She didn't know
a thing about it except for what Vicki had taught her.

Susan's bad attitude returned. She had no one with whom to

share her growing daily desperation. It was becoming easier to do as he wanted. Easier not to argue back. Easier to apologize and beg for forgiveness. She hated it. She no longer recognized herself. She hated the arguments even more. It was such alien territory. Protesting was useless.

"You have a lot to learn about motherhood."

The bottom line, now clearly readable, was that she felt she was forced . . .

Susan: . . . *to stay with this man whom I was finding I really didn't like very much. Yet, I had a baby. I felt I had no choice. I was stuck out here in Ohio so I did it. He would get mad and not talk to me at all for days. My family doesn't do that. We discuss things. He taught me how to fight. But when I started to yell back at him . . . "You have no right to raise your voice to me."*

I was always caught in a 'catch-22.' If I had dinner ready when he walked in the door he didn't want it, but if I didn't, "What have you been doing all day? Goofing off? Talking with your friends again?'"

This and that.

Couldn't win.

Walking on eggshells for years and if he came home late and dinner was cold or spoiled, it was always, "You should have thought of that." He made me hypercritical of myself, believing that I was always the cause of what went wrong. He was never wrong.

There were times when it would look real bad. It would get better for a while and I'd shut up but he could read people. He knew how far to push and how to get to you.

I was always afraid . . .

She could not figure out why she was so afraid of being abandoned since her family had always been supportive. What had she not gotten from them that made her so vulnerable in her relationship with Chris? She thought about that a great deal. She was beginning to think that part of the reason she stayed with Chris was because to leave him would have been an admission of failure, and she rarely failed at anything.

Susan: *Maybe they just didn't give me enough of a chance to fall on my face. So when I came face-to-face with big-time failure, it was hard to accept that I had made a big mistake. That's also part of my family's background. You don't give up on something.*

Chapter 7

Fire! Fire!
And Then Another Fire . . .

"Our main concern at this point is to account for the family, and we're optimistic that they are still living."
—Barrington Police Chief Charles Brule
The Providence Journal-Bulletin, 9/24/91

Susan was too inexperienced to see the controlling mechanism behind what her husband was doing with his put-downs and all the little jokes made at her expense. Women should be kept barefoot, pregnant, and in the kitchen, he would laugh. They were supposed to be housekeepers, nannies, and girlfriends. Sometimes she felt like a housekeeper and a nanny, but she was beginning to feel less and less like a girlfriend. Sometimes she thought he didn't really like women.

Susan: *I wanted him to make the world right for me. I was always trying to be good, to get an "A" from him.*
But it was draining.

Her conciliatory efforts only magnified her own sense of failure, a feeling he encouraged since her self-doubts helped to make her more malleable to his demands. "It's a good thing I'm around," he said. "What would you do without me? You're not bright enough to hold down any kind of real job . . ."

It was impossible to look at the reality of their situation plainly; a clear assessment was simply too threatening. She had been brought up to believe in marriage, duty, morality, honor, and all the important controls and restraints placed on behavior by religion and the God she deeply believed in. Her family went to church every Sunday. The Slickers were an intimate part of their congregation. At home, they practiced their beliefs both below the threshold of conscious perception, as well as overtly. Ever since Susan could remember, they had always preambled their meals with bowed heads and hands clasped in intimate familial communion around the dinner table as they said grace. The pattern of relying on family and God and of acquiescing to a higher authority was difficult to break. Susan knew what constituted the duties of life; they had been etched into her personality long before she had ever met Christopher Jemire Hightower.

Still, part of Susan knew no one should be held hostage to these guidelines, particularly if they impinged too seriously on happiness. There was a subconscious part of Susan that had begun to fight back surreptitiously.

Swallowing her pride at his constant attacks at her inability to do anything right, she told Chris she would like to go back to Wright State University to get a graduate degree in counseling.

He looked at her thoughtfully. Even with the GI Bill, student loans, and a graduate fellowship he had received on the merit of his excellent grades, they still could not make ends meet financially. They had even had to borrow $1,700 from Kathy's inherited $5,000 to pay for Susan's hospital bill when Mitchell was born. They had no medical insurance, no earned income, no more undergraduate stipend from Clyde and Mary Lou. "It's either that," Chris had told Kathy when she offered to lend them money if they needed it, "or Sue won't be able to have the baby in the hospital."

Susan: *I'm still embarrassed about that.*

It was money they had not been able to pay back.

When Susan broached the subject of returning to school, she had it all worked out. Not only did she qualify for a work-study program, a graduate assistantship in the Education Department, she had also arranged to get a part-time job. Vicki took children into her home in a private home day-care program she ran to supplement her family's income, and she would mind Mitchell.

"I'm not against it," Chris said.

Susan was almost surprised that Chris supported the idea of her return to academia, especially since that meant she would be around other people again, but he offered no objection. "If you can work out the finances, it's okay with me," he told her. "If things get bad," he joked, "I guess I can always rob a bank."

Mitchell was five months old when Susan returned to school for her master's.

Susan: *Vicki was a godsend. She took Mitchell on my way to school and gave him breakfast. Mitchell loved her. I was thrilled. I knew he was safe there. He was with three or four other little kids, and it only cost me $30 a week.*

Chris deemed Vicki suitable as a caretaker of his son, and was happy to have the baby next door.

Susan: *I no sooner started classes than Chris began making noises about where I was, what I was doing, who I was with.*

In her graduate assistantship, Susan had to work closely with one of her professors. It was her job to do research for his projects. It wasn't long before Chris accused her of sleeping with him. "You must be," he shouted over her objections. "You spend a lot of time with him."

She also spent a good deal of time crying and apologizing for making him angry. It only propelled him to criticize her further for her excessive emotionalism.

Nothing had changed.

In some ways, it was worse. Now, if she rebelled, he made it clear that since he was twelve years her senior and a Ph.D. candidate, he obviously was cut in a superior mold. He felt justified in putting her down. Although he displayed the classic symptoms of the emotionally abusive male, Susan never saw his behavior as abuse, simply because he wasn't physical.

The tooth in the trunk has been identified as belonging to Ernest Brendel.
—The Providence Journal-Bulletin, 9/23/91

Susan was highly stressed-out. Married July 1982. Mitchell born April 1984. Back to school October 1984. Now, a new year, and still things, though certainly different, were no better.

She hadn't touched her journal in a long time. Now, she picked it up.

SUSAN'S JOURNAL—January 9, 1985:

Reading through this book it's fascinating that "the more things change the more they remain the same." Except for a couple of entries, literally years have passed since I wrote in here. A husband, a baby, a new house. The mind reels at the drastic changes that have taken place within the last 3 years. No wonder my stress level is almost off the scale.

Chris doesn't trust me and may never do so—not a happy thought. He's so complicated, keeping emotions in—it's frustrating! I wish school were over and we could have some more *excitement* in our lives (parties, etc.). How much patience do I have (or rather how much am I willing to extend). I really think my love for him is a comfortable love now that the passion's gone.

She had talked herself into believing she still loved him. But when did the passion go? Why? She tried not to think about it.

Chris's bachelor's degree had been in zoology, his master's in physiology. He was still taking courses in physiology since the combined master's/doctoral program into which he had been accepted was in biomedical science. For his master's thesis, he chose a laboratory project on the examination of the water weight of baby rats. He sometimes joked about the project and his little subjects; after dissection, he wrapped the rats in little plastic bags leaving their tails exposed before placing them in the lab freezers to be thawed and examined later. When they froze solid, with their stiff little tails protruding from the plastic bags, he called them his little "ratsicles."

Susan: *He was spending more time with that and less time at home. Granted he was doing research. He had lab rats he was dealing with and all kinds of odd hours, but there was a strict double standard. There always was time for him to go off in study groups, to the library, talking with professors in the research lab. Whenever he needed to go he was out the door.*

The same freedoms did not apply to her. When not in class, Susan was expected to stay home. She had to be where he could find her at all times, either in class, at her job, or at home. There was to be no deviation.

Susan: *He'd call me to check up—to make sure I was where I told him I'd be. Then, later, at my job at the church, there were all those hang-up phone calls.*

Chris began to pull away. He withdrew into an almost-complete secrecy about his work. He was paying less attention to her, positively and negatively. She went to school, tended house, did the shopping, cooked the dinners, took care of the baby at night, and kept up with her studies. He barely noticed. She made excuses for his interest in his own work and lack of support about her own life. She resented his never attempting to help at home, but rationalized away his neglect. "It's just that he's so busy."

Schoolwork did not come as easily to him as it did to her, and she became aware that he was struggling very hard in spite of his 4.0 grade point average.

When he wrote his thesis on his little ratsicles, he would be able to prove to his professors, who had begun to noticeably challenge his intellectual abilities, just how brilliant he was, a very important matter to establish in order to maintain his ego.

Chris's withdrawal into his studies was a welcome breather for Susan. The once-demonstrated regard for her that had long since deteriorated under a barrage of criticism now retreated behind a barricade of self-absorption. Now he was too busy with his ratsicles even to pick on her.

But even as he isolated himself from her and baby Mitchell, she could tell he was terribly worried. Despite the long hours spent in the lab and all of his hard work, he began to show signs of failing in his studies. His grades were not commensurate with the standards needed to remain in the doctoral program.

She couldn't understand why he was doing so poorly.

The transcripts that had placed Chris in his combined master's/doctoral program had had a perfect grade score, 4.0, even better than her own excellent 3.78 average. She was doing very well while he flunked several major written exams in a row.

Why was he suddenly failing now?

* * *

When he finally completed his thesis, his name, "Christopher Jemire Hightower" was boldly stamped in gold onto the glossy black cover:

"Body Water and its Distribution in Neonatal Rats: The effects of Adrenalectomy and Adrenalectomy with Aldosterone and/or Corticosterone and Replacement."

The dedication read:

"To my mother for her support and belief in higher education. Also to my wife, Susan, for encouraging me to return to school and for providing the support and understanding necessary to complete my studies. Finally to my children ... for they have had to do without while I succeed."

He hadn't succeeded yet. Despite his accompanying written declaration that his thesis was the first to show how corticosterone may have biological activity in fluid volume regulation in the twelve-day-old neonatal rat, it was a pedantic, overwritten fifty-page paper that barely squeaked him past the standard written requirements set by his committee. Now he had to face the really tough hurdle of oral exams in order to be permitted to continue to the next level of the doctoral program.

The orals loomed before him. Hidden beneath his patronizing arrogance, he was concerned about being up to the scholastic challenge before him.

Because of his secrecy about his work, Susan never fully realized how badly his grades had been sliding. The only thing he would say was, "This is hard. I'm having to spend a lot of time reading. The reading is slow."

Susan: *He struggled all the time. I probably noticed it the most when he was studying for his exams.*

He studied . . . and studied . . . and studied . . .

"Evidence shows at least one body was in the Toyota."
—*The Providence Journal-Bulletin*, 9/23/91

March 5, 1985

It was about seven-thirty on the morning of March 5. Susan had an early class.

She took eleven-month-old Mitchell to Vicki's as usual, leaving Chris behind with his studying. "Mmmmaamma," was beginning to be clear and he was just starting to toddle, give kisses and hugs. Susan went over last-minute details with Vicki, and then was off on the twenty-minute ride to school.

A little more than five minutes after she arrived, she received a call from Vicki.

Instinctive maternal panic welled up. "What's wrong? Is Mitchell okay?"

"Mitchell is fine," Vicki told her, "but you have to come home."

"What is it?"

"Your house is on fire."

Susan couldn't believe it.

"I wasn't going to call you until I saw the fire trucks come," Vicki said, "but now they're here."

"I'll be right there!" Susan cried.

She telephoned Chris. The telephone in his office rang and rang. He ordinarily left home for his office at school shortly after she left with Mitchell. He was not in the office yet. She grabbed her purse and ran out to the parking lot they both used. She looked around, up and down the lines of parked cars. His car wasn't there. She *had* to find Chris. Susan dashed across the WSU campus parking lot to his office. Arriving out of breath, she banged on his door, but he still had not arrived.

She could wait no longer. She dashed back to her car and headed for home.

Fire. What would she find when she got there?

Fighting back her anxiety, she drove hard and reached home in less than the twenty minutes the drive ordinarily took. Even from a few blocks away, she could see heavy black swirls of smoke clouding up the blue sky. She could barely get into Elsmere Avenue. Fire trucks were parked across the road almost completely blocking the entrance. Hoses were everywhere. The stench of smoke reached her through the car window, now wide-open, as she called out to one of the firefighters, "I live here. That's my house. I have to get through."

She managed to get close enough to see the streets were crowded with neighbors. The smoke was so thick in the backyard she could barely see from house to house. She switched off the ignition and jumped out of her car.

Susan: *I was shocked, looking at my house with the windows bashed out and black smoke pouring out of the top windows.*

"How bad . . . how bad?" she stammered to another fire-fighter working with the long tangled line of hoses crisscrossing the street. "That's my house."

"The fire's out now," he told her.

"Can I go in? Can I see?"

"No, ma'am. Not yet."

"But . . ."

"Sorry."

Vicki put her arms around Susan and held her until she stopped shaking and asked, "Mitchell?"

Vicki went to get him.

Hugging the baby. Holding him close. Safe. Protected in her arms.

She called Chris again from Vicki's. He was finally in his office at school. "Chris, come home," she said.

The tone of her voice put him at complete attention. "What is it, Sue?"

"The house is . . . there's been a fire."

He raced home.

When Susan and Chris were finally permitted to enter their burned-out home, they were ankle deep in dank, smelly puddles of water blackened with soot and ash. The shambled home raised a pungent, sickening stench they would not soon forget.

Susan: *I remember walking through the house. Just walking around looking at what heat can do. Plastic sheeting lying all over the floors because the firemen tried to save the carpeting by doing that, and it stinks. It's a stench I will never forget. It permeated everything.*

We had a family portrait of the five of us, the two girls, Chris, me, and Mitchell. It was a beautiful picture and I took a look at the wall where it had been hanging and the wall was gone. I thought I had lost the picture but the fireman had taken it off the wall and saved it. They were so careful and so good about it.

No matter how careful the firemen had been, all of the windows were broken and the back end of the house was wide-open. Their clothes and all of the baby's things were smoke-damaged. Their refrigerator, now blackened by smoke, was standing forlornly in the middle of the backyard.

They were going to have to move out of the house.

They were in shock. The basement and the kitchen were burned-out. The fire had taken out everything Chris had done to fix up the house, including the plumbing, the wiring, all the new oak and fruitwood doors and windows. All of his work had gone up in smoke. Chris was devastated.

This was one thing he did not blame on Susan.

It was officially confirmed that it had started by spontaneous combustion—fertilizer in the damp basement sitting on top of a case of motor oil.

What were they going to do? Where were they going to go?

"Do we have insurance?"

"Yes," Chris reassured his wife, putting his arms around her, holding her, comforting her. Susan cried and clung to her husband, feeling closer to him in their pain and loss than she had in a long time. He was crying, too. "I've lost everything I've worked for," he whispered. She held him tighter, now comforting him. "Everything I've built. Everything's gone . . ."

The local Red Cross put them up in a hotel for the first night. Their insurance covered the expense of a hotel for another week until they were able to rent a house from a friend.

They didn't tell Clyde and Mary Lou about the fire until after they were settled in the hotel.

Mary Lou had been planning to visit Mitchell for his first birthday next month, but when she learned of the fire and how uprooted they were, she had second thoughts. "Sue," she said over the phone, "maybe I'd better postpone coming out under the circumstances."

"No, come ahead," Susan begged. She was anxious to have her mother visit.

"But where would you put me? I don't want to be in the way."

"Friends of ours are going to let us use their house. We're renting it and they're thrilled to get the rental. It's only a few blocks from our own house, so it's going to work real well. Please, Mom. Don't change your plans. There's plenty of room."

They had to inventory the contents of the entire house for the insurance company since so much was gone, lost to the combined damage of fire, smoke, and water. Pages and pages of details. Six four-ounce jars of peanut butter, half a tube of toothpaste, Chris's darkroom and photography equipment, his scuba equipment, three fish tanks, an old baby carriage, the computers, the television, their furniture, his tools . . . and the cost of the renovation.

When they finished the inventory, they found they had actually salvaged more than originally thought. Chris stacked all of their remaining belongings in the middle of the living room. "It's safer like that," he told Susan. They carefully put the lists together and submitted total estimates worth $100,000. When the insurance company offered to pay only $10,000 for replacement value, Susan was so disappointed she backed away. Chris was furious and combative, repeatedly, getting into arguments with the insurance adjuster. "We only had that couch a year!" he exclaimed. "You can't depreciate it that much!" But they did.

Not making any headway, Chris was livid at the insurance company's position. "The best defense is a good offense," he told Susan through taut, white lips. "That's my motto. Hurt the sucker before he can hurt you, and screw what anybody else says."

His intensity was both understandable and frightening, but he patted her shoulder. "That's all right," he told her quietly. "I don't want you to worry."

They were in their rented house only a week when Susan found him seated in the living room, his rage dissipated, looking completely depressed. With the shades drawn, as he often liked to keep them, the room was almost dark. She knew what he was upset about. With the way the insurance was planning to have the house repaired, it looked as though their home was going to suffer through a slapdash job of carpentry covered with a coat of paint. Neither one was sure how it would look once completed. They had both heard horror stories of lack of money, cheap materials, and poor repairs. They had spoken and worried about it together.

"It's not that," he said.

"What, then?"

"How could I possibly be expected to do well on the exam with all this going on," he exclaimed.

"What do you mean?"

He removed his glasses, wiped his eyes, and replaced his glasses on the bridge of his nose. "I took the orals," he said quietly.

"Oh." He hadn't told her he was going to take them. She was almost afraid to ask, "How did you do?"

He quietly admitted he had failed.

He had dreamed of this all of his life . . . "Dr. Hightower" . . . His dream was slipping through his fingers. And now this.

It wasn't common for him to turn to her with his troubles, but this time he did and she felt bad for him. She tried to comfort him. He blamed his failure on the fire. "How could anyone concentrate with all that going on?" he rationalized.

He was required to take the orals again. She could see that he was almost despondent over the prospect, but there was no getting around the requirement if he wanted to remain in the program. The orals had already been rescheduled.

9/26/91—Hope for the Brendel family was fading.

A dog from the Connecticut State Police searched in Haines Memorial Park in Barrington.
                    —The Providence Journal-Bulletin, 9/26/91

March 19, 1985—2:00 A.M.

Mary Lou's visit was soothing and welcomed. Fortunately, Chris liked her. It was so good to see Mom after all this time. She had always had a calming effect on her surroundings. She was supportive of both Chris and Sue and delighted to take care of her first grandchild while they tended to the pressing needs generated by the fire.

Mary Lou did not usually sleep well in strange places. A bed had been made up for her on the living room couch in the little bungalow they were renting. She tossed and turned, dozing on and off.

In the middle of the night, she heard the fire sirens blaring a distant, melancholy sound. She was sleeping so lightly, the sirens' wail wakened her completely. She opened her eyes in the darkness and stared at the ceiling. "That siren," she intuited with fear, "has something to do with their house again."

The phone rang, shrilly breaking the silence of the sleeping house and she knew she was right. She could hear Chris answering the telephone in the adjacent bedroom, his voice raised to an incredulous, "What . . . ?"

Mary Lou's sixth sense had been right. The house was on fire again.

It was two weeks, to the day, after the first fire.

This time the damage was more substantial. By the time the fire was extinguished, there was little left but a roof and outside walls.

Susan: *It was awful.*
You could go up the stairs but if you tried to go through the upstairs landing you would have fallen through to the first floor. There were places on the first floor, too, where the floor gave way to the basement.

Something was wrong.

They had gone back to the damaged house every day since the first fire. They had taken out the Oriental rug to get it cleaned. They had removed pictures from the walls to have them cleaned and reframed. They had been trying to get their life back in order. Fortunately, records that had been on the floor of one of the closets were still in pretty decent condition.

Susan couldn't understand it. How could another fire have started. She could understand the first one—spontaneous combustion. But this one? Only yesterday Susan noticed it looked as though someone had been rummaging around in her desk, one of the salvaged pieces of furniture that Chris had stacked in the middle of the living room for safekeeping.

"Chris, have you been in the desk looking for stuff," she had asked.

"Why?"

"Things look different."

"Someone might have been in the house," he said.

She had gone to her desk and decided she didn't want to leave all their important papers in the house—his discharge papers, his divorce papers, their marriage certificate, her private journal. She hadn't touched *that* in a long time. She had removed them all.

It's a good thing I did, she thought, looking at the total destruction from the second fire. She had managed to save their most important papers. She had even taken her flute out of the house the day before.

But something *was* wrong. This time arson was suspected. Sifting through the rubble and ashes, investigators determined that, this time, the flames had been deliberately set in at least five separate points.

Later that evening, all that was left was the stench of smoke and charred ruins. An opaque smoked-drenched sky hovered over them as Chris and Susan were taken to the police station for questioning. The police believed Chris was responsible for setting the fire. "I don't know what you're talking about," Chris said when he realized he was under suspicion. "I was asleep when the fire started. Ask my wife. She'll vouch for me."

"Chris was there with me," Susan agreed, but a silent little suspicion began to form itself in the back of her mind.

"Would you agree to taking a lie detector test?" the investigator asked Chris.

"Absolutely not. How can you accuse me of something like that."

He let it be known, in no uncertain terms, that it was beneath him to do anything like that. "Are you going to press charges?" he demanded to know.

"Well, I'll tell you," the investigator said calmly. "Somebody set that fire, all right. We know it wasn't a pro, because if it was a pro, he would probably have set a fire inside the front door so the first guy in falls in and they spend all the time rescuing him and the rest of the house goes."

Chris stared at him.

"This was set in five or six different places," the investigator went on. "Top of the stairs, upstairs, downstairs, over here and there. Too easy to trace for a professional job."

"Do you think I'd set fire to my own home!"

"Happens all the time."

"That's an insult."

Susan: *I'm surprised they didn't question me as much as him. I don't know why they had a sense he was connected with it, but they did.*

The only reason they didn't arrest him was because they didn't have enough proof.

Listening to the questioning, Susan had to believe the second fire had been deliberately set. In the quiet of the night, when left alone with her own thoughts, unintimidated by either his anger or his sense of outrage at the unsubstantiated police accusation, she couldn't help wondering if it was true. It was so odd the way it happened. She could not shake her gnawing suspicions.

Carefully, she broached the possibility with her mother, even though Mary Lou was almost as upset as Chris when they returned from the police station and he told her he was under suspicion.

"No, Sue," she said. "I can't believe Chris had anything to do with the fire. He was here in the house when the alarm was sounded."

"I was asleep," Sue said. "He could have gone out and come back. It's only a few blocks away."

"No," her mother disagreed. "I didn't sleep that well. He couldn't have left the house in the middle of the night without me knowing."

"I suppose . . ."

"I guess," Mary Lou added thoughtfully, "he could have sneaked out, but I don't see how."

"I don't think he did it the first time, even though he had the opportunity."

"The first time? You mean the first fire?"

"Mom," Susan sighed, "I'm not sure about anything anymore."

Mary Lou looked about the house. It was like a big bungalow. Elsmere Avenue was out toward the back. She tried to imagine how he could have done it. He would have had to come out of the bedroom through the living room to get to the kitchen, where there was an outside kitchen door, or out past her to the front door. "Either way he would have had to go past me," she mused. "I was on the couch. I don't see how it would be possible."

"Unless he had some kind of slow fuse to set it off."

"Sue . . ." Her mother was stunned. "You don't really think that."

Susan said, "No . . . of course not, Mom. I don't really think that." But the suspicion that Chris would solve a problem by committing a crime was planted.

"There is a substantial amount of blood in the garage on the property, and a gun was found in the car (Hightower) was driving when he was stopped."
—State prosecutor Patrick Youngs
The Providence Journal-Bulletin, 9/25/91

No one was ever brought up on arson charges. Gasoline cans bearing Chris's fingerprints were found close by. "Those are my gasoline cans. Why shouldn't my fingerprints be on them?" Although that seemed a reasonable answer, nevertheless, the police were sure he was responsible. The case has yet to be closed, according to Lt. Arnold Meyers of the Regional Fire Investigations Unit of Dayton.

Susan: *The insurance company did pay off. It wrote out a bigger check than the first one they had stinted on. But it still wasn't enough. I would say the total bill for contents was about $54,000, and we thought the house was worth about $120,000. They only paid $54,000.*

One thing after another.

As suspected, the contractors did a terrible job after the second fire. The floors were not level. A pencil would roll off the kitchen counters. The refrigerator door wouldn't shut because the angle was so bad. We had to make the contractors come back because they had clogged up something in the main drain for the toilet and it backed up into the sink. They put in cheap, thin woodwork. My solid wood doors were gone, they wouldn't replace those. They did remodel the kitchen, but they didn't pay for that. Chris ended up doing the kitchen himself. He changed it from a breakfast nook to a sliding glass door. That was bright and shiny.

Everything was clean. At least, for the first time since we bought it, the house was finished, because Chris had never finished his remodeling. He was still working on the upstairs when the first fire struck.

Chris reported his problems to his biomedical faculty at Wright State University. He had lost all his books, he argued persuasively. All his notes. He couldn't possibly take the oral exams now. He needed more time. Chris's professors couldn't help wondering about the bad luck that seemed to plague their unfortunate doctoral candidate. A second fire!

"I've already spoken to my professors about it," he told Susan.

"What did they say?"

"What could they say?"

Under the burden of such personal crisis, they had to give him more time to prepare. He had convinced them that his rescheduled oral examination had to be postponed. "Anything else would be unfair," he stated categorically.

Somehow, it was ringing hollow.

But then, he could con people into anything.

Susan: *His sister was having financial trouble and he gave her a couple of thousand dollars. It wasn't money we could afford to give away.*

I had no say in that.

And yet we had to borrow money from my grandmother to cover some of the cost of the fire.

Her grandmother's loan was in addition to the $3,000 he had borrowed from Mary Lou just before she left to return to Rhode Island. Susan wondered how he intended to pay them back.

He could convince people that he would have to have the best of whatever it was he wanted.

"There, you see?" he said, proudly uncarting his new acquisition. "A new stereo system."

He had gone out and bought a very expensive stereo system including a CD player. He seemed to think he was doing a wonderful thing for her, but all she could think of was they were short on essentials, and she was furious with him.

"How much did that cost?"

"Fifteen hundred dollars," he boasted. Everything had to be the best.

"With everything we've lost," she insisted, "how could you spend the little money we have on something so frivolous?"

"Because I know how much you love music," he replied with a tender smile. "You lost your stereo in the fire. I just wanted to give you something positive after all the losses. Something just for you, Sue."

She didn't know what to say as she stared at the stereo.

"Come on," he coaxed. "You're not really mad, are you?"

She couldn't help it; she burst out laughing at his puppy dog look as he insisted on convincing her they actually needed the stereo. A lot of his charm was that she never knew what to expect from him. He could so often easily catch her off guard and just often enough so that she could justify any less-than-positive behavior or attitude on his part. It always kept her trusting that he really was a good person underneath.

Susan: *It's like the rats who only get a pellet periodically although they push the lever all the time. Those sporadic rewards just make the habit stronger!*

Susan realized she had other things to think about. She was pregnant again.

Chapter 8

"You Got Nothing on Me"

"I am innocent!" Hightower declared.

There was little doubt in the minds of the relatives of the Brendel family that Christopher Hightower was intimately involved in their disappearance. The belief was so strong that on September 25, 1991, Susan Pandich, Ernest Brendel's youngest sister, issued, on audiotape, an emotional plea directed to him to assist in the search, especially for little Emily:

> *". . . I am Ernie's youngest sister. I have a daughter eight years old, same age as Emily, and both of them are only children, and they've been brought up like sisters. Emily is like a daughter to me.*
>
> *I would like to propose something that might be of help to both of us.*
>
> *Given the past events, you may not be in a position to provide the advantages that you might want your own children to have, I would like to help you do that, and I'm willing to put in a trust account for your children for college, or whatever their particular needs might be in the future, $20,000 for your youngest son or $10,000 each for both of your sons. In return, I beg you to tell me Emily's location.*

*If she's alive, she needs our comfort and support. If she's
dead, we want a Christian burial, and we want to properly
grieve her.*

*Right now, we are living in a hell of uncertainty and pain;
please have mercy on her sweet soul. I will write a letter of
intent for your lawyer to witness, and I will do that before
you receive this tape, which will assure my delivery of the
money as soon as we recover Emily. But you must tell us
her location in the next six hours.*

Please consider my plea. That's all I ask."

Chris refused to listen to the tape.

Susan was at her office in school working on one of her professor's projects when Chris unexpectedly came in and said, "We
need to talk. Let's go down to the cafeteria and have lunch."

She had not been planning on having lunch but he seemed
troubled. *What now?* she worried. Was it something she had
done?

As they sat over lunch, he dropped his bombshell. "I'm quit-
ting school."

She couldn't believe it.

"I've decided to leave the program and take a leave of absence."

"But . . ."

He had never given any indication he wanted to leave the program. Becoming Dr. Hightower had been all that mattered to
him, even above and beyond his family.

"Because I flunked the exams," he confessed. "I need to take
a break."

"But what would you do? Get a job?"

He dropped his second bombshell.

"I'm going into investments full-time."

Investments? What kind of investments? What was he talking
about?

"I'm sick of school. I want to put all my energies into making money by working my brains." He implied working his brains in school rather than in real life was a waste.

Susan wasn't opposed to his making money. As students, they had not had much spending money since coming to Ohio.

But investments? The stock market? And without completing his doctorate, when he had already invested so much time and effort, and was now so close to completion.

He had it all worked out, even though he had never talked to her about the stock market before this very moment. . . . The economy's booming now. . . . You'll never see better opportunities. . . . She remembered he had spoken to her dad about it once. Clyde had a modest interest in the market and Susan knew he dealt in stocks a little. He had done some dabbling in safe blue-chip stocks. Never making any big money.

"Sue, everyone's doing it these days," Chris was going on. "These are the eighties."

"I know, Chris, but. . . ."

"Everyone's making money in the market. This is the best possible time to get into it."

The probability theory in mathematics determines what can be expected when results depend largely on chance and time. The longer one participates in a venture that requires the investment of time coupled with chance, the more likely one is to obtain the desired result. But the determining factor to overiding success is that one must have enough financial backing to cover all the losses before the venture breaks even or turns a profit.

Susan: *I was worried because we had so little money as it was. I had a toddler. Things were not going well . . . the house fire. We were just beginning to get settled in again.*

"But what do you know about the stock market?"

"Plenty," he interrupted, a bit annoyed at her dampening approach to his decision. "I've always been interested in stocks," he said with the old enthusiasm bursting through her uncertainties. "Especially commodities. I've been studying them. And I intend to learn more. It's an incredible challenge."

Susan knew he had always loved a challenge. He used to tell her about the injured boys who came back from Vietnam when he was in a medical unit in the navy. It was a horrible way for them to end up but he had never indicated that it was a trauma for him. To him, the injuries were a challenge. There was a time when she thought Chris should have gone into forensics. He loved a puzzle, the research, the medical side of it, the crime side of it. It is not surprising that Chris chose the career of commodities investment counselor to serve as his express lane to obtain all the things he felt were rightly his but had somehow evaded his grasp. Status. Power. Wealth. It had the right combination of chance and challenge.

"I've signed up," he informed her.

He was going to attend what, in her estimation, was a "get rich quick course" in the stock market. It was going to cost "only" fifteen hundred dollars, of what was left of their meager savings. He saw it as an investment in himself and the business of trading in commodities futures.

The course was in Chicago where most of the action took place. He didn't ask her; he told her. "I'm going to take a year off from school and work the market when I get back from Chicago."

She resented his not consulting her in making this critical and surprising decision, but she was afraid to protest or question him. Instead, she became so docile she could hardly say anything at all. But her heart was pounding and her mind racing. She wanted to scream, "You can't do this, we need money. We have no resources to live on until you begin *making* money. We've got to finish this stuff. If you're not going to do it schoolwise, get a real job. You'll have two babies to support and a wife. I won't be able to work. Do something . . ."

But she didn't say any of it. She could not get her genuine feelings out. All she could manage to say was, "Are you sure this is what you want to do?" hating herself that she could not stand up for herself.

Susan: *I've never forgiven him for making such an important decision and never letting me be a part of it. I'm pregnant the second time, I have a toddler, and he makes a life decision without talking to me about it, and there is hardly any money. I couldn't believe it. He was enthusiastic. But I thought it was irresponsible.*

Later on, alone, she started to cry. If she could only confront him with her feelings. But she couldn't. She still internalized almost everything.

"It's just a leave of absence," he insisted in the face of what he perceived as her unspoken objections.

Susan: *The sense he projected was that he was going to go back to school and this was temporary. But by the end of that winter, I knew he wasn't going back to his studies.*

She said nothing. He could tell she was disturbed. When he realized he had failed to convince her of his great plan, he returned to personal put-downs and intimidations, ending with, "Well, if you're so unhappy, why don't you move back in with your parents!"

He knew she would not.

Clyde and Mary Lou were distressed when they heard he was giving up on the doctoral program since they believed he was so close to completion. While he was studying, it hadn't bothered the Slickers that Chris and Sue had little money. Chris had gotten some loans and Sue had had a scholarship and a work-study program. Mary Lou thought that was the way Chris was working it, too. Being the new mother-in-law, *You try to work it so you don't offend,* she thought. Up until the fire, Mary Lou had thought he had it together. He had his master's degree.

At least, he had a diploma with his name on it. She knew he worked hard at his studies, and that he was within reach of his doctorate just when the fire hit.

But now? While Sue continued making sacrifices, he was

switching to a totally new and unrealistic venture. Both she and Clyde worried. Chris always had a plausible explanation for everything he did, so they said nothing. They didn't want to offer advice that could be interpreted as interference.

Chris went to Chicago to begin the expensive course in commodities trading. Susan remained in Dayton with Mitchell and continued with her studies at the university. Chris wasn't gone long, but she was surprised at how peaceful and relaxed she became while he was away.

Still, she was lonely.

When he did return to Dayton, he was filled with excitement. Susan was always happy to see him when he was like this; he was the old Chris she still loved and missed so terribly. That Chris had been missing from their lives for a long time, and now, here he was, back again, smiling, full of spirit, and affectionate.

In Chicago, Chris told her, after the course work, he had taken and passed a computerized test to become certified by the CFTC as a commodities trader. He was shocked that he had passed it so quickly, but he was quick to boast to Susan. "You see? It's not an easy test, and I passed it on the first try."

He had also passed the background check needed to become a full-fledged, registered commodities trade advisor. "Our worries are over!" he exclaimed. He was on his way.

He could not do any trading on the market himself. "There are all these rules," he explained, "but there's this guy in Chicago. His name is Russ. He works for one of the big financial companies there and he'll do the actual trading for me. I've got it all worked out with him. All I have to do is call him . . ."

Chris realized he couldn't invest too much time in training, but it didn't matter. He had ideas and there was Russ. He had every confidence in his abilities, and knew that he had to make the big money right from the start. But he neglected to look into his soul. He really didn't know who or what he was or how far he was willing to go. Until tested by a financial crisis, even Chris didn't know how willing he would be to stretch the legal and ethical rules in order to succeed.

"I'm taking you out to dinner!" he said jubilantly. Just like the old Chris.

Susan: *One of Chris's favorite things to do with me was go out to dinner. He would come home and say "Let's just go out. Where do you want to go?" At the beginning they were ritzy places. He'd order from an extensive wine list and tell me the bottle cost $100. Another time he just told me "Get all dolled up. I'm going to take you out on the town." He wouldn't tell me where—I love those kind of surprises.*

Sue was glad he was doing something he was so enthusiastic about. It made him easier to live with, but there was still no income and grocery money was scarce. He couldn't be distracted by such basic considerations. He became obsessed with trading in the commodities market, something she knew he really knew little about, despite the crash course in Chicago. She knew he was having visions of hitting it big.

Susan: *He believed he had come up with this great formula to read the charts, to know exactly what to buy and sell, and, more importantly, when.*

Susan didn't know if it was a dream or not. But he kept telling her this was the way to make the big killing. Quickly. It was the way the big boys did it, and without risking their own money. She realized the entire concept of trading had stimulated his gambling instincts.

He tried to convince her. He talked. She listened.

He used to talk with the same kind of enthusiasm about his interest in biomedical science. A disloyal doubt began to plague her. Something suggested that if he so quickly passed that advisor course he took, it must not have been very difficult, and if it was not very difficult, it could not have been very comprehensive. She wasn't sure when she started doubting his intellectual abilities. Was it because he had failed at school? She felt guilty thinking such thoughts. Anybody could flunk an exam. She should be more supportive. After all, he was doing all this for his growing family.

"The trick is to use other people's money," he kept saying. That was how to make the really big killing, with little or no risk to their own finances.

All she knew was that commodities trading was known to be a treacherous business.

What was he getting himself into?

Dozens of local and state policemen gathered at Primrose Hill Elementary School to search for the child and her parents.
—The Providence Journal-Bulletin, 9/29/91

Susan was deeply worried. She tried to talk to him about her concerns, but he unceremoniously shunted her aside every time she began to voice her feelings. In the grand scheme of the course he had set, her feelings were not important. He knew what he was doing.

He informed her he was going to work out of their house. She didn't know how she felt about that. She didn't think an address in a borderline residential area looked good for business, but it was all they could afford.

Eventually, Lady Luck smiled on Chris when he answered a newspaper ad placed by a local investors group consisting of amateur stock market enthusiasts who were interested in investments. Most of the sixteen men and women in the group were either retired or close to retirement age. Their life savings were now mostly at a finite point of growth, but they were willing to try to improve their bottom lines. They met in the basement of a nearby library once a week. The shared concept was that they would get together, deliberate over different stocks, discuss trends, and calculate where they thought the market was going before individually making investment decisions or pooling some of their resources and trading cooperatively.

Chris decided to join the group to see what he could learn.

It wasn't long before he believed he knew more than all of them put together. Within the group, the con man in Chris became fully operational. He looked mild-mannered and almost professorial with his wire-rimmed glasses and light, Freud-like beard. He was articulate and well educated. He let it be known in his soft-spoken, high tenor voice, that he was a registered commodities trade advisor, certified by the Commodities Futures Trading Commission (CFTC). He spoke glowingly of commodities futures as the only way to make any real money in the market. Some conservative members were concerned about the high-risk factor inherent in trading commodities futures. "True," Chris agreed readily; conservative stocks might be safer in some respects, but the returns were minimal compared to proper trading in the slightly riskier prospects in the market.

Having mastered the language of the commodities world, if not the subtleties and intricacies, Chris began to impress the members of the group with his smooth interjections into their discussions. He was adept at explaining the great potential of the commodities market. Commodities exchanges exist in eight major cities in the world. The credit for creating and developing the markets went to the Japanese. They'd invented contracts that guaranteed both the rice farmer and buyer a set price for a particular quantity delivered on a date set in the future. This stabilized prices and the contracts themselves became valuable and were traded. That was the beginning of commodities trading.

He explained how the data from the various world markets projected onto an orbiting satellite overhead came almost instantaneously to the satellite dish he had had installed on top of his roof and, thus, onto the screen of his computer. Such instantaneous inside knowledge permitted him to trade through his partner in Chicago before most of the rest of the market could react to the changing figures. It was an extraordinarily challenging and profitable operation.

He agreed it was a speculative gamble, but it was deeply exciting, and the place to make quick profits and the really big money. He, himself, was earning huge profits that could soar as much as fifty percent in a single morning of smart trading using his techniques. Futures could be bought in metals, meat, woods, grain, soy beans, pork bellies, even orange juice. The profit was in the paper and trading. It was a fast cutthroat world of sly professionals—and the amateur should approach this world with extreme caution, he warned. Statistically, they have a better chance of winning at a casino rather than tempting the fickle fates of the commodities markets. "You have to know what you're doing."

The more Chris talked about when to buy and sell through the great formula he had devised to read the graphs and charts churned out by the overhead satellite, the more he quoted catch-phrases from Financial News Network telecasts, and threw about imposing predictions from the *Dick Davis Digest,* and the *Wall Street Journal* the more some of the group members were lured by what he was saying. He was highly effective. He talked a good game. Passing himself off as an experienced investment broker, Chris convinced them that the best way to go about investing was in a cooperative manner, pooling their resources and investing together rather than individually. The trick was to do it through his system.

They never knew that part of his credo included, "The trick is to use other people's money."

Since he understood his system better than anyone else in the group, it would probably be wiser if he did the actual investing for them. He never let on that he had little field experience and knew practically nothing about investment management or that his credentials were those of an eager beginner. He convinced them. They trusted him.

Susan: *I think he said something like, "How about I put together a partnership agreement?"*

They all agreed that $3,000 was the minimum investment for

each member of the new corporation, that Christopher Hightower was to make the investments, and that he was to give them a monthly financial report on how the corporation was doing. With the highest individual investment at $24,000, Chris began Investors Guild of Dayton, Ohio and set himself up as president and CEO. His first and only client was the library group of retirees. They pooled their resources and came up with $100,000 for him to invest for them.

Chris was ecstatic with his new clients' $100,000. It was an incredibly good beginning. Now he could test his formula.

Susan: *He told me about it. He was excited about it. He probably withheld information from me. He withheld what he was actually doing with their money. He drew up a partnership agreement. That's all I knew about it. I knew the group was there and they used to come to Investors Guild at the house. I met one or two of them. They seemed nice. Retired gentlemen.*

Working out of the house, he subscribed to Stock Market Cable Network. Financial News Network was on all day, every day.

Susan: *He made me crazy being in the house. I never got away from him. He put in an office upstairs with a computer. Then he started buying equipment for "the company." He couldn't feed his family but he was buying stuff for the company.*

"Oh, well, it's necessary," she rationalized when he kept saying, "It's got to be done right if we're going to do this so that people believe this is a legitimate business. It's going to be great, a little tough in the beginning, that's all."

That's not the way you start out in a business, she thought, trying to put up a front to convince clients of your legitimacy.

Susan: *But he was very positive with continued enthusiasm. He pumped me up. He got me to believe this was going to be a winner.*

She didn't really believe it, but as usual she went along with it. When he was like this, he was like the old Chris once again, and right now, in her uncomfortable early stage of pregnancy, that was all that mattered. He was easier to live with when he was in a good mood.

Susan: *He decided he needed a new computer. 'Put it on the credit card.' he'd say. When he decided he needed stock newsletters,* Dick Davis Digest, Wall Street Journal. *The subscription costs were running between $150 and $250 a year. He had three or four. He was always calling Chicago, where the trade board is. Racking up bills. During this time he got his mother's money to invest. He had been sending her money when we didn't have any. He ended up convincing her to give him her pension to invest. We had a separate checking account for her. I used to spend more time running back and forth to banks trying to get money in the right place before the checks cleared.*

By January of 1986, Susan was about three-quarters of the way through her master's program. She had only two internships left, one major paper to write, and one other class to take. She had taken one fall semester of classes while having to deal with both her pregnancy and Mitch, who was growing into a bright and very active toddler. It proved to be too much for her. Their second child was coming along sooner than they had planned. She had gotten pregnant in October and she was uncertain as to whether Chris was even pleased. He never said anything about it. Susan wanted another child, but she would have preferred having her children three years apart.

She was not feeling very well and decided she could no longer continue in school. Since she was only twenty-four years old, she felt she had plenty of time to go back.

Susan: *I really thought I was going to be able to do that. I didn't feel like I was being forced. I knew I could go back and finish later. With the way things were going in my own life, I was worried about going into an agency setting and counseling people, anyway.*

She was studying to be a counselor, but she wasn't ready to

deal with other people's problems, not while she had so many of her own. With all that was going on with Investors Guild, Chris paid no attention to her at all. Sometimes it was as though she were not even there. Even worse, once the initial excitement of his new venture had become the mundane daily rituals at the computer, Chris had become moody. He never discussed business. The waves of enthusiasm that had sustained him in the beginning had transmuted to a kind of obsessive solitude.

Susan had the distinct feeling he still didn't know what he was doing, no matter how hard he worked. He spent hours at the computer, but nothing seemed to happen. When she read the business profile he had written about himself to attract clients, she found herself thinking it was only hype:

"Hightower utilized his skills as a technical analyst to purchase and sell securities to provide support for his family and parents. His continued efforts as one of two general partners of the Investment Guild of Dayton, Ohio, a stock commodity partnership, have allowed him to develop his own technical trading system for common investment decisions."

Other partner? He must mean Russ in Chicago. Technical trading system? So far, his system had produced little, if any, results. There was still no money coming into the house.

Sometimes, she would suggest, "Wouldn't it be better if you just got a regular kind of job."

"What do you know about it?"

"Well, we need money."

"If you knew how to handle money," he accused, "we wouldn't be in this mess."

"I don't care what you do!" One of the few times she answered back. "Just get a job. Carpenter, whatever . . ."

"You can't talk to me that way!"

He slammed the door as he stormed out of the room.

Any questions from her about his business brought nothing but derision and emotional abuse. He frequently called her stupid and incapable of understanding the complexities of stocks.

All she knew was she was struggling to buy the necessary daily household items. She couldn't imagine how he was paying the other bills. Bill collectors were calling up all the time. He wouldn't even talk to them; that was her job. "If you knew how to handle money . . ."

She was deeply distraught. Literally starting to feel the weight of her second child, she often found herself sitting alone at home sobbing.

Susan: *He never listened to me if I tried to talk. I had a very active toddler. I was tired. I wanted to be near people who cared about me. I wanted to go for two weeks, just a short visit, to my parents, but I didn't have the money to do that. I was isolated and unhappy with him. I had this nice new house after the fire, and although I eventually grew to love the house, it didn't matter.*

I didn't know where to turn. I felt my husband didn't like me. I hated myself because I was pregnant, fat. He wasn't paying attention to me. It was hot. I was miserable. I had no money. I saw no future. My one support system was hundreds of miles away and I was miserable.

My friend, Vicki, could tell I was at my wit's end, depressed, scared, no family, in the middle of nowhere with this man who didn't care a thing that I was pregnant and needed support. He made me doubt myself. I hated that.

Now it makes me angry.

I used to take it.

Vicki, unwilling to watch her friend's pain in silence any longer, finally took it upon herself to make some inquiries. She urged Susan to "call this number and go talk to somebody." She put the scrap of paper with the telephone number in front of Sue. "I'll watch Mitchell for you."

The number Vicki had given her was a family counselor at the Good Samaritan, a Catholic hospital in Dayton.

Susan agreed. She had to do *something*.
She did not tell Chris about it.

Susan: *He would have shot me for talking to anybody about our private affairs.*

Susan tried to make herself look as presentable as possible for her appointment with the counselor. She wore a bright green maternity jumper and a plaid blouse that she had made herself.

In the counselor's private office, she tried to explain her frustrations with her life, holding her tears in check. She carefully expressed her disappointment in her relationship with Chris, choosing her words so she did not condemn her husband. She just needed help in how to deal with him. She was willing to talk, to try anything to get closer. She told the counselor of her unfulfilled basic needs. Her pregnancy left her feeling vulnerable and fragile. Tears began to well up.

The counselor listened attentively, nodding with understanding, but from Susan's point of view, the session was a total disaster.

Susan: *Basically, what she told me was that I had to be more forgiving and try harder. She gave me these pamphlets to read about "forgiveness" and "learning to love someone despite their imperfections," and all this crap, as I see it now. Looking back, that person did a terrible job. It was just a bunch of platitudes about being married and taking care of your husband.*

It was the worst advice she could have received. A form of institutionally condoned martyrdom with no expectations of reciprocity or mutual respect. The counselor actually encouraged her *not* to stand up for herself.

Susan went home more depressed than before, still believing that the emotional estrangement from Chris was all her fault. She sat at the kitchen table sobbing because she felt so alone: her life had become nothing but misery. The tears were running down her cheeks and wetting the front of her bright green jumper when Chris came in. "What is it now?" he asked, annoyed.

"Chris . . ."

"Listen to yourself!" he said. "You're such a baby. A sissy."

She reached for him. "It's just that . . ."

"Grow up and get control," he ordered. "Stop being an emotional female."

Susan: *When I look back, this is the part of my life I have a harder time dealing with than what happened later. I have more mixed feelings about it. I made stupid moves. I was young and afraid. I was completely apart from a support system. If I had been living here in Rhode Island, I might have done something about Chris earlier than I eventually did.*

It turned out that Susan had been wrong all along. She should have had more faith in him. Chris *did* know what he was doing. Investors were very happy with Investors Guild and with Chris's management of their money. They kept receiving glowing reports of how well the investments he made for them were doing—growing—looking good—multiplying—outdoing their wildest expectations.

"I got them to set me up an office," Chris told Susan, grinning broadly.

"Who?"

"One of the guys in the investors group," was all he would share.

Sue couldn't get over it. He could talk people into anything. He had convinced one of them that the Investors Guild was working so well he needed larger office space. They were so happy with him they were willing to help support him in his growing office needs.

Susan: *So he moved to Centerville, and I really started not to see him much.*

At first she resented his long absences from home, but it soon became clear that she was happier when he wasn't around. She began to feel a sense of independence again.

Susan: *He wasn't on my case all the time. I could watch what I wanted on TV, discipline Mitchell the way I wanted to, eat what I wanted to and when. He'd come home at ten o'clock at night, leave the next morning at seven-thirty, Come home for dinner. Go back to the office.*

The negative side was that she was always by herself. Months passed. It was the end of June and she was almost at term. It was almost as though she were going to have this baby by herself. That was okay in some ways. She certainly didn't want Chris in the labor room; not after he'd almost walked out on her the night Mitchell was born. Thank God Mom and Dad were going to come visit when she was due to deliver.

She didn't know about the phone call Chris had made to her father from his office.

Clyde: *I knew Chris was involved with a group of investors and that he was kind of their leader, or guru, trying to help them make money, and I knew they weren't as successful as he wanted them to be, but he never shared any of the details about dollars, or whether they were upset about anything, I remember he called and said he needed some money because he had to replace some stock that had gone downhill too far. About $6,000. So I sent him the money, but I never got it back. I didn't mention it to Sue at the time.*

Mary Lou: *I knew money was tight, but did not know much more than that until we were in Dayton. Clyde had gone early to be with Susan when the second baby was born. I was working and arrived in Dayton just as Susan gave birth to a beautiful, healthy baby boy on the third of July. They named him Paul.*

Mitchell was just a little over two. He was very bright, into everything, adorable. With his full capacity for curiosity and mischief in overdrive, he was a real handful. Susan's parents stayed for a few weeks after Paul's birth, until Susan got on her feet and was able to manage again.

Mary Lou did not question the subtle indications that Sue might not be happy, and Sue covered up her feelings in front of her parents. Mary Lou attributed the edge of moodiness to post-partum blues.

It was Chris who was obviously in some kind of trouble.

Mary Lou: *I knew something was wrong with Chris from the way he acted and looked during the entire time we were visiting. Withdrawn. Quiet. Except when he and Clyde talked about stocks. Then his enthusiasm level swung high. But mostly quiet and apart.*

On the way home, Mary Lou kicked herself hard on the plane that she didn't push Chris to find out what was the matter. She felt they had a good enough relationship for her to have asked him point-blank what was the matter and get an answer. They had always gotten along very well. But for some reason, she couldn't ask.

She had always sensed a schism between him and their family. He had come from a different background but she could tell he wanted to create a similar environment for himself. His financial troubles had widened the schism and he no longer seemed approachable.

The call came soon after they had returned home to Rhode Island. Things continued not to go well . . . financially, businesswise . . . they needed additional money.

Everything had begun to fall apart.

Susan: *He confided to me after Paul was born that the Investors Guild wasn't working. That he had made a bad judgment call and he lost some money and people were on his back. He made it sound like, "Poor me."*

Chris did not tell her the full story. He had been sending the investors periodic reports showing huge profits. When one of the investors wanted to withdraw some money out of his account, Chris had told him it wasn't possible as none of the money was in liquid assets.

On July 7, the Guild members had a picnic during which they planned to discuss with Chris some of the details of his trades. He never showed up at the picnic, even though he was the guest of honor. Rebellion and suspicion began polluting the sunshine that warmed the day. Some of the investors decided to go to Chris's home to confront him with their growing suspicions, learning the reports for the past six months had been doctored. Chris had lost virtually the entire amount they had invested with him. He had never reported the legal fifty percent fail-safe point to them to give them the option of pulling out to salvage part of their investment. He merely ignored it, and like the gambler that he had become, he had attempted to retrieve the monies he had lost by continuing to invest until he had lost it all.

Of the $102,000 that had been pooled, only $231.35 remained in the account. The sheep had been shorn. Realizing that they had been lied to all along, the investors were livid. They threatened physical violence as well as legal action.

"You got nothing on me!" he told them defiantly.

Susan was not at home when they came. She did not know the investment group had come to the house and called her husband out to fight. She had no idea that the losses ran in the six figures. Chris had never told her. He made it sound like he had lost a little of the money and they were being unreasonable about it. After all he had tried to do for them, they were even talking about reporting him to the CFTC. Anyone could make a bad judgment call. That was the nature of the investment business. They had taken their chances. It wasn't like they hadn't known there were risks involved.

"I made one little mistake," he cried, "and now everybody's on my case. They're talking about reporting me to the CFTC."

"For losing some of their money?"

He nodded.

She was devastated when she realized Chris was being accused of fraudulent investment dealings by the Ohio group. She didn't know if the accusation was true or false. Chris did not deny any wrongdoing, only telling her that they were after him.

"How much did you lose?"

"Not much, but they want it back."

"What are you going to do?"

"I don't know, but we have to do something."

Now, all of a sudden, it was "we."

"I need your help."

He had always told her to stay out of the things and she was too stupid to understand, demanding that she trust him. Now he was turning to her for help. "We'll have to take a second mortgage on the house. It's the only way I can raise any money."

He told her he had already inquired. They could get $22,000 on the house.

"Twenty-two thousand? It was that much of a loss?"

"I need you to sign the mortgage," he went on. "It's the only thing I can see to do. Otherwise, I don't know what will happen to us."

He'd only told her about it because he couldn't get a second mortgage without her signature.

When business reason and cold dollars and cents overcame the hot anger, the investment group opted to accept the second mortgage on his home as partial compensation for their losses. They had made inquiries to the Commodities Futures Trading Commission about what action they could take against Hightower. The federal regulatory agency informed them that if they reported him, they would get the legal action they wanted but, most likely, would get no monetary return. They voted to accept partial payment of pennies on the dollar instead of taking the legal revenge that could have cost him his license, the minimum punishment they felt he deserved, and might even have had him jailed.

* * *

Chris never told Susan he had gone beyond the fifty percent point of losses without informing his clients. She did not have the facts to assess what he was doing, and was unable to see that this behavior was a portent of future dealings with other clients. She did not know he had mismanaged everything so badly, or even the true extent of the loss he had incurred with the group. Susan would not learn the full truth of what happened until after the murders in 1991. He never gave her any indication that he had lost almost *all* of the money that had been placed in his trust, a net loss of approximately $78,000.

Chris continued vehemently to deny any wrongdoing. Susan knew only that the accusation ultimately cost them their home.

Two weeks after the Slickers had returned to Rhode Island, Chris completely let his guard down. He sat halfway up the stairs with his head in his hands and said "Sue, I just don't know what to do. I don't have the money to continue on. I don't know how I'm going to take care of you and the boys. I have these people demanding back money. What am I going to do?"

Susan: *There he was sitting on the stairs to the second floor, in misery, this poor puppy who finally admits to me that he doesn't have any money and he doesn't know what to do, and of course like the good wife and sucker that I am, I felt sorry for him. He looked like a lost little boy, and so, I came to his rescue and suggested talking with my parents about moving back with them till we got on our feet. If we could move back with my parents for a while, he could make some money and get his feet back on the ground.*

We did want to move back to New England. I wanted to get out of Dayton before the kids were school age.

Clyde and Mary Lou agreed immediately.

Susan thought it was her idea. Mary Lou thought they were the ones who brought up the subject. Actually, it was Chris who had said, "Maybe your parents . . ."

Susan: *We agreed we had to sell the house. It took three years to sell it at a loss. I took a cash advance on my credit card to pay off the difference so that we could get the house off our backs.*

It was sad to lose the house. Sue had grown to truly like it. But the overwhelming feeling was one of relief that she was going home to where the bill collectors wouldn't be calling her and she wouldn't have to worry about where her children's next meal was coming from.

Susan: *At this point, my surface feelings for Chris were, I felt bad for him. The underlying ones were that I was angry at the position he'd placed us in. I didn't realize that I felt unsafe. And if moving East wasn't going to work, at least I was going home to my support system. I was feeling utterly hopeless at that point, and I saw going home as a chance to escape from Ohio, where things were so lousy, and try to make a better life for me and my kids.*

They moved back to Rhode Island on the Columbus Day weekend of 1986. They piled everything they owned into a U-Haul truck and escaped back to Barrington to move in with Susan's parents on Chantilly Drive. Susan remembered when her parents had driven with them when she and Chris first moved out to Fairborn, Ohio. That had been such a wonderful time, full of so much love, excitement, and anticipation. She had been so in love with Chris and with the future he projected for her. It had been one of the happiest times of her life.

The return trip was far less joyous.

She couldn't help wondering what Chris was going to do in Barrington.

Chapter 9

Home in Barrington

Nearly two weeks after the disappearance of the family, the massive, intensive searches of Barrington from shoreline to woods had turned up nothing.

Within the Bosom of Family—Chantilly Drive—October, 1986

After four years of marriage and two children, Susan and Chris moved back to Barrington, Rhode Island.

With a thirteen- to fourteen-hour car trip stretching before them, the Slickers felt there was no way that, alone, Sue and Chris could bring back car, truck, furniture, and two little children. Clyde offered to take time off from his job at Rhode Island College to go to Dayton to help them make the move.

He helped them load their material lives into the U-Haul truck. Packing up generated ambivalent feelings in Susan. Elsmere Drive had been her first home, and, despite all the problems, she had grown to love it. She felt a wistful sense of loss at having to leave it now, so abruptly, and with a second mortgage attached to it.

However, going back home to Barrington had become something she wanted. She was bringing her children back. Home.

Such anticipation. A huge weight was being lifted off Susan's heart. Things would *have* to get better once they got home.

How discouraging it is to live in a world that is possessed by so much evil. . . . And of the "Evil One."
                              —Pastor Ryden's Sunday sermon 9/29/91
                              St. James Lutheran Church, Barrington

Mary Lou knew Sue was desperate to return to Rhode Island. She didn't have all the pieces put together yet, but she just knew that, as a couple, Sue and Chris didn't want to live in Ohio any longer and preferred to return East. In many ways Mary Lou was excited about having them back; her family was reuniting for the first time in four years. Even Kathy was living at home, having just graduated from college. Mary Lou did not dwell on any potential problems that could arise with all of them together under one roof; the house on Chantilly Drive was not very large, but Mary Lou concentrated on the happy aspects of family solidarity. She and Kathy did a lot of housecleaning in preparation for Sue and Chris's arrival, to make more room for them and the children.

Kathy, too, was happy they were returning. Living together was only going to be a temporary measure until Chris got himself going again. She knew they had had trouble getting back on their feet ever since those awful fires. This would give them the financial respite they needed. Mary Lou knew that Chris was going to go off in business on his own. It took time to get started. They were lucky to be in a position to help. When she and Clyde were young and struggling, they had been fortunate to live with her parents for two years. They moved in with two girls, a dog, a cat, a piano, and a freezer. *What goes around comes around,* she thought with a smile.

"I'll really get to know my grandsons," she said delightedly to Kathy.

* * *

Susan looked about the familiar New England landscape as they reached Barrington. It had been a long, tiring trek, this time with a toddler and an infant in tow. But, now, it was worth it, just to be back.

She had almost forgotten what a beautiful town Barrington was.

Government Center. Town Hall. The library, a pretty redbrick building with a slate roof that had once been the high school. Huge trees and massive stone walls giving a sense of solidity to the town. There was some new construction but most of the houses gave the feeling of timelessness, the appearance of having been there a long time, even a sense of history.

Home.

Could Susan recapture the essence of who she was, who she had been, who she could still become now that she was home?

One thing she felt certain of: she could not let her family know the truth. She had to keep it hidden from them.

Mary Lou: *We knew nothing about the way she was treated at that point. I didn't know any of that until just before the murders. She kept it to herself. And that was one of the biggest shocks for me. She pulled it off. Now I know she had become afraid for herself, her boys, and for us if she did say anything, literally afraid for all our lives.*

Who could have known?

It was crowded and cramped in the house on Chantilly Drive, but it didn't matter too much. The Slickers were warm, loving, and generous people and they went to great lengths to make Chris feel comfortable in their home. Chris responded warmly. He was deeply attracted to the piety and the goodness of the mild-mannered Doctor Slicker and his efficient wife, Mary Lou, who was warm, artistic by nature, and interested in her son-in-law. He still could not get over the fact that the family held hands around the table and said grace before meals, often with personalized messages of gratitude for their good fortune. They attended the Barrington Congregational Church every Sunday morning, sang in the choir, and volunteered on several church committees. As an established and important part of their congregation, the Slickers enjoyed a close personal bond of friendship with most of the pastors, including Rev. Skip Waterbury and Rev. Joseph T. Dye, and their families.

The sense of roots and of belonging was something Chris had never known. Living with the Slickers, he had inherited, overnight, true respectability for the first time in his life.

> *"We have a hard time understanding that evil can come to Barrington . . . but evil has been done."*
> —Rev. Joseph Dye
> Barrington Congregational Church

Susan's parents had deep faith in Chris. He was very charming and seemed deeply devoted to his family, particularly to the boys. Still, they could tell it would be a long time before Chris and Susan would be able to make it on their own. They were willing to be patient.

Chris liked Clyde. Bright, intelligent, soft-spoken, mild-mannered. He relied on him. Talked to him. In a very real, important sense, Clyde became the father figure he had always wanted. How different Clyde was from the father and the stepfather who had abandoned him and his family in Titusville all those years ago.

Chris became like the son Clyde never had and, as such, it was part of his nature to want nothing more than to support him and encourage him in his studies. "When will you go back to complete your doctorate?"

"Soon."

Clyde told him he was sorry Chris had given up his doctoral program. "It's worth getting," he encouraged. "If you plan to return to the medical field or plan to teach at the college level, you need to earn your doctoral degree. My doctorate allowed me to become a full professor in the field of early childhood ed, teaching both undergraduate and graduate courses, supervising practical teaching. These are students interested in positions working with infant/toddlers, preschool up to grade two in schools as well as grad students."

Chris was interested. He asked many questions. Clyde had an infinite amount of patience and answered each as thoughtfully and thoroughly as he could.

Susan watched the family interaction carefully.

It warmed her heart to see how well they got along. Maybe this was the clue to making her relationship with Chris work. Maybe here, at home, with her parents, with Mitchell and Paul blossoming under the glow of the grandparents' love and attention, Chris would see how families really were supposed to be when they lived and worked together in mutual respect and support. Moving back to Barrington could help Chris if only he could learn to take advantage of the Slickers' serene stability. Maybe the solution to her unhappiness with Chris lay in introducing him to a different way of life than the one he had grown up with. It wasn't his fault. It had been a life that had obviously not given him the foundation he needed to become a truly loving and involved person.

Maybe. It was possible.

Probability, however, was a different matter, Susan thought, but she believed she still loved Chris. She pushed the cynicism aside and concentrated on optimistic expectations.

Kathy liked Chris. She had no reason not to like him. He was her sister's husband and she accepted him fully. Still, life on Chantilly Drive raised a few challenges. She wasn't used to the kids. One weekend at a time with crying children was enough for her when she used to visit them in Ohio. There were other living adjustments as well.

Kathy: *I remember he always took long showers and that was a bother.*

About the fact that he never had a job: It seemed like he had done a little bit of everything. Car racing, dog training, medical school, the service. But now I realize he never held down anything. In the way of a job. . . .

One of the first things Chris did in Rhode Island was to notify the National Futures Association of his new address. His fantasy world of brokering investments with the new formula he had personally created had not faded merely because he had had one setback. He was ready to start over—with other people's money. In less than a month, Chris had begun Hightower Investments, Inc.

It was the fall of 1986, and he was back in business.

Chris enthusiastically shared his business dreams and plans with his in-laws, using all of his charm and powers of persuasion.

He spoke to Clyde and Mary Lou glowingly about his prospects. At different times he sat down with them and told them some of his plans—that he only needed this amount to get involved with that aspect of it, then he could pull it all together.

Susan did not have strong negative feelings about Chris's starting Hightower Investments, Inc. even though she knew he had done poorly in Ohio.

Susan: *He told me he lost some money. I had no idea it was $100,000. I only learned the actual amount after he was arrested. For murder.*

Because of this, when he started Hightower Investments, Inc., it didn't bother her. At least, he was working, which meant there was always the possibility of an income.

Her parents were willing to give him some money to get started. She wasn't sure if he had asked or if they had offered it. She just felt that he was quick to capitalize on their faith and generosity. Susan had ambivalent feelings about it. Mary Lou wrote out the first check for Hightower Investments, Inc. to pay a lawyer to incorporate the new business.

Susan: *On top of everything else my mother wrote the check for the lawyer. It was her money!*

Susan was worried.

He advertised Hightower Investments, Inc. as a corporation designed to engage in the business of personal and business financial planning.

It sounded impressive but, once again, he was the sole officer and he had no credible track record. What if clients *did* suddenly materialize, Susan wondered to herself? Was he truly capable of handling their investments?

He rented a little office in Warwick. "It doesn't matter where I work," he told the Slickers enthusiastically, "since I do all of my work via computer and phone to Chicago."

They encouraged him.

He had never before experienced such a solid sense of support. He was excited as well as stunned by their apparent interest. He even tried to explain some of the intricacies of his business to them—how he was going to create an important newsletter, how he was going to introduce a formula for buying, how he was going to set himself up as someone other investors could turn to for advice.

They were thoroughly ingenuous, trusting and unsuspecting of either manipulation or ineptitude on his part.

No one in the family knew the exact details of why he and Susan left Ohio. Susan never offered explanations since she didn't know all of the details herself, and they never asked.

Kathy knew it had something to do with the Investors Guild of Dayton, Ohio. She remembered how she had seen him absorbed in his computer when she visited them, but she, too, never knew how badly his business had performed or that there had been an undercurrent of fraud.

Every time she saw him, he was busily working at the computer, with printouts spread out every which way. He was putting all his effort into it, she thought. Still, Kathy wondered if he knew enough about commodities. She didn't know that much about the futures market herself, but she knew one needed special licenses and special techniques, especially when dealing with commodities. It seemed odd that he didn't work for an investment company first before setting himself up as an advisor to others. Kathy, who had a bachelor's degree in political science and sociology, and was an administrative assistant for a personal trust company, had asked Chris about his business and he willingly explained what he was doing. But, mostly, his explanations went over her head. There were times when she felt he was being deliberately confusing about what he was trying to do.

She didn't want to make waves so she never discussed it with Susan, but she couldn't help wondering to herself if her brother-in-law knew what he was doing.

Kathy: *He kept reading different theories of cycles for the market. Margin accounts, and I could never tell if there was just a whole new set of words that went along with that area of investing or whether he was making it up.*

While Chris worked hard at his new business, Mary Lou and Clyde worked equally hard to make him feel at home. He was polite, helpful, and seemed to have both a plan for their life and a method of obtaining it.

But while he borrowed money from his in-laws and courted their favor, Chris surreptitiously became even more psychologically abusive to their daughter. In private—"The least you could do is take care of the boys properly."—"You're not much of a lover anymore."—"I'm going to turn you in for a new model," while in front of her family, he was careful to put an endearing spin to the persistent put-downs: "She's too ditsy to really understand."—"I have to take care of everything."—"That's what comes of marrying a child."

It was as though he wanted to preempt her position in her own family and become the most important person in the household in the eyes of the Slickers.

He was extremely helpful to his in-laws around the house. He did the dishes once a week. He raked the grounds. He joined their church and attended weekly services with them. He became increasingly active in church functions. He taught Sunday school, headed the Junior Pilgrim Fellowship, and offered to work with young people as a youth group leader to counsel troubled teenagers.

Susan: *I remember him telling me one day, that he couldn't believe the things some of the junior high kids shared with him. Problems that they were having at home. He said, "I can't believe these kids can appear so together and have such problems at school or home." My sense was that he was amazed that other kids faced problems and shame like he had—that he wasn't the only one.*

Why couldn't he be that understanding all the time? Susan thought wistfully. He could be so wonderful when he wanted to be. With his soft-spoken, high-pitched tenor voice, his wire-rimmed glasses, and the conservative manner in which he usually dressed, he looked genuinely mild and sincere. He became so well liked and respected by the congregation that he was even voted chairman of the Board of Christian Education.

One of the activities he enjoyed most was coaching the youth soccer team on which Paul played. He also volunteered to be den leader for Mitchell's Cub Scout group.

The Slickers were pleased with their son-in-law. He smiled at his wife in their presence but continued to keep her psychologically subdued behind their backs. Susan's inability to act verged on emotional paralysis, and she continued to demonstrate the subtle signs of the psychologically battered wife.

When she was bereft of positive spins, all she could think of was:

Susan: *I couldn't find enough legitimate reason to get out of it because there was no physical abuse. I did not understand the powers of psychological abuse.*

He was a master at it.
I was frightened and quiet.

But she could feel herself changing inside, where it really counted.

It was a slow process, since she really did not want to fail at her marriage. The two sides of her personality were at war with one another. How could she make it work? He was self-isolated. Worked for himself. Office always locked. Shades always drawn. An image of darkness shadowed their lives. She always had the sense of living in a dark room with him. He insisted on pulling the shades and keeping the lights dimmed, as if the sunlight would expose all of the lies and ruin his illusion of prosperity and honesty. In each place they had lived, Fairborn, Dayton, and Barrington, he had kept the shades pulled in his office, their bedroom, and any other rooms he could close up.

Susan: *He kept our relationship and our finances that way—never showing the public the reality.*
For me it was like a slow death sentence. I thrive on fresh air and sunlight. It was like putting a living plant in a closet—failure to thrive, until I "died."

Back with her parents, she realized she didn't know how to fight. She had never heard her parents fight, or argue, or even raise their voices to one another. Whenever they had a disagreement, they always sat down and discussed it through to a mutually agreed solution. Beautiful though it was, Susan saw the crippling flaw for the first time. Everyone should learn how to fight, she thought. At some point in life, knowing how to stand up for oneself could become a matter of life and death.

Life with Chris was sometimes a seesaw, sometimes a roller coaster ride, always unpredictable. Suffering through his mercurial nature, from scathing invectives to charm-laden attempts to win her warmth, Susan, nevertheless, finally summoned up enough courage to insist on initiating a family conference to discuss Chris's lack of income. She wanted him to get a job. Chris managed to manipulate the situation by convincing them he was so close to success that bailing out now would negate the foundation he had laid for success. It was a master stroke. Instead of getting a paying job, he convinced the Slickers to back him further. They agreed to loan him $1000 a month toward his expenses until all of his work paid off. The money added up quickly.

Despite long hours, Chris still did not bring home a dime. Thoughts of the Investors Guild of Dayton, Ohio, haunted Susan. She wanted him to have clients, but clients simply didn't walk in from the street. He had little or no track record he could point to in order to attract them.

"What do you think about computers?" he asked Susan one day.

"What about computers?"

"Going into a computer business," he mused. "You know, opening up a computer business."

"What kind?" Susan probed.

He immediately became annoyed at her question and left the room.

One church member to whom Chris spoke about investing was far from impressed. Chris could usually talk his way through a direct approach to a potential client, but this man knew something about the market himself and found Chris to be rather unknowledgeable. The lingo he threw around to impress him, "Upscale." "Progressive." "Can't lose." "New formula." "Everyone can make a lot of money," struck him as more the talk of a fast-talking salesman than a sober, down-to-earth investment advisor dealing in large sums of money that did not belong to him.

Chris's lack of clients forced Susan and her children to live entirely off her parents. She started to feel ashamed and unhappy.

"I think you ought to try something else," she ventured to him.

"Can't you see," he said, this time with genuine supplication in his tone. "This is my only chance. *Our* only chance. It's for us. I know I can make it work."

"But there's no money."

"Yes. Yes there is," he said almost desperately. "Small amounts, maybe, but it's growing. I just have to put it all back into the business, that's all, but I'm getting closer to making it work. Much closer. We just have to hang in there together a little longer. Please, Sue."

When he spoke that way he melted her heart. She *wanted* to believe him.

She tried because she had to, and she did.

But while she tried so hard to be understanding, the other side of his nature prevailed in their everyday interactions; he continued to berate her for the mismanagement of their funds.

What funds? Six months had passed since their move to Barrington. He had not had one client nor earned one penny, and even though there was no income, it was *she* who did not know how to manage money. He made that very clear. She was on the receiving end of those accusations again.

She realized if she didn't get a job herself, there would never be any income for their family and they would be forced to continue to live off Mom and Dad. It was the last thing in the world she wanted. They didn't deserve to be taken advantage of. They were too good. Too generous. All of Chris's basic needs were taken care of: shelter, heat, food, electricity, most of the necessities for the children. The Slickers even paid for health insurance for Chris, Susan, and the children. The only bill he concerned himself with was the telephone bill for Hightower Investments, Inc. He seemed perfectly satisfied to maintain the status quo. Susan was not.

A job. But how? She tried to come to grips with her options.

SUSAN'S JOURNAL—Summer, 1987

"First I must find child care. I want to give the boys happy memories, but without clothes and food there won't be much to be happy about. How will I send them to college? Where will I get the $ to live on when I grow old? First I must deal with the child care area and then worry about other things. One step at a time. Somehow I'll make it—I always have and with little thanks to Chris!

I have this nagging feeling he was one of the biggest mistakes of my life. It's been an awfully tough 5 years being with him. Granted it isn't all his fault, but things could have been a lot different.

Not surprisingly, as the months passed, he was not having much client success.

By April of 1987, when Kathy moved out to her own apartment in East Providence, Chris had decided to move his office from Warwick to Barrington. There were many good reasons to consider such a move besides a lack of clientele. It was cheaper, closer to home, and would save on gas.

Susan: *He didn't like the landlord over there, but I didn't know he didn't pay his rent either.*

In the fall of 1987, Chris moved Hightower Investments, Inc. to a little office on Maple Avenue in Barrington.

The small building with a shake roof was in an older section of town where the houses were less imposing, some in good repair, some not, but the section had a definite turn-of-the-century kind of charm. Chris had a two-room office suite on the second floor, up a narrow wooden staircase to the right of the building. The office, with its pitched roof, looked like attic space, but it was neat and clean, and it was more in keeping with the image of success he wished to project. There were other successful businessmen located in the building, lending additional prestige.

Paul Ryan, a lawyer, shared the other office on the second floor with a few fellow lawyers. There was also the Mortgage

Exchange on the ground floor, owned by Dennis Murphy and Ray DeWall, who were the landlords and owners of the building, and a well-established hairdresser opposite them. There was plenty of parking and a bicycle path in the back leading through the woods.

As far as Murphy and DeWall were concerned, as long as everyone paid the rent, there would be no problems. The local real estate market was in some disrepair and the owners could maintain their own economic head above water with this building only if everyone pulled his weight.

Blood (in the Toyota) could be Ernest Brendel's.
—*The Providence Journal-Bulletin,* 10/2/91

Chris paid $600 in rent for his small, new office.

Actually, the Slickers paid it.

He had managed to move Hightower Investments, Inc. from Warwick to Barrington by borrowing $20,000 from Clyde and Mary Lou. He intended to really set himself up right in order to give the business the necessary financial foundation it needed while it was establishing itself. Underfinanced businesses were always in jeopardy of failing, he pointed out.

Susan was worried about the effect Chris could have on her unsuspecting parents. His oft-repeated phrase, "other people's money," haunted her. In one respect, she wanted to warn them. But warn them about what? That he had made a few bad judgments in Ohio? That he wasn't nice to her? And how would he react if he found out she had thwarted his need for seed money? He had never been physically abusive, but he vehemently warned her to stay out of it! The *look* in his eyes when he said, "You're too stupid to understand, anyway!" truly frightened her. For the first time, here, in the safety of her parents' home, she felt the pangs of genuine terror. A new element had been added: an undercurrent of violence she suddenly believed he was capable of. It was something about the way he looked at her, the intensely implicit warning, not only in the words, but in the look he focused on her as he said, "Stay out of it!"

It was as though he had finally come upon a situation in which his worries were over, and *nothing* was going to stand in his way. He was going to make Hightower Investments Inc. succeed, by trying, by working hard, by intimidation, by fraud, by insinuating himself deeply into the affections of his benefactors any way that he could. *He simply had to be successful.* If he were not, it would not be for lack of trying. If nothing else, Christopher Hightower worked very hard at every endeavor he undertook.

But Susan simply could not stand by and do nothing.

Aiding Chris in his quest for the big killing, were the conflicting motivations, denials, avoidances and pure good-hearted generosity and naïveté of the entire Slicker family. When Susan mentioned her concerns to her parents, they assured her they wanted to help their son-in-law. He had no income. He needed to be successful in order to become financially independent. They had given him two years to pay back the loan. It wasn't such a long time. He deserved a chance. They wanted to give it to him, and to her, to try to ensure the success of their financially troubled young family.

Susan wished she could tell them everything, but she was afraid.

Susan: *If I told my parents about my fears and the state of my marriage and finances, the repercussions from Chris when he found out I'd confided in them would have been physically and emotionally devastating.*

Still unable to deal with him at this point on an equal basis, Susan continued to keep the pain of his maltreatment from her parents. He intimidated her objections into silence. She prayed that, this time, his efforts would work for her parents' sake as well as their own. At least, there was a two-year time limit on the loan. Maybe he'd make it this time.

* * *

But there were other things to consider besides their perennial lack of money. Now, the persistent pattern of emotional abuse slipped behind the closed door their bedroom.

"There's someone else," he began as they lay rigidly in bed in the dark besides one another.

"What?"

"Isn't there?" he insisted.

"No, of course not."

"Don't lie to me, Sue. You just lie there. You're nothing but a cold fish."

"I can't help it if I'm just too tired," she said evasively.

"No. It's more than that," he insisted intensely. "And don't talk to me anymore about infections! You don't have any infections. That's not it. You don't want to do it as often as I do."

She didn't respond. She did get infections. Too many and she didn't know why unless, subconsciously, her body was physically resisting his advances. He was right about one thing. The sex part of their marriage was almost gone. They only made love about once a month. Even at that infrequent an interval, she didn't enjoy it and he knew it. As they spoke, her mind raced backward, like a tape rewinding their married life until she stopped it . . . here . . . then there . . . and she came to the stunning realization that she hadn't regularly enjoyed making love to Chris since the second year they were married.

"You're interested in someone else, aren't you?"

As if the only reason she could be unresponsive to his love-making was because there was another person in the picture.

"Aren't you!"

"No," she murmured.

"You don't want to do it as often as I do," he said again.

"I can't help that."

"You're just not a very good lover anymore."

"I can't help that, either."

"Who's the guy?"

"I'm always home," she flared. "How could there be someone else?"

"You're lying!"

"I'm not . . ."

"Don't expect me to believe you. I've always known what you were like," he whispered aggressively. "You were always such a damn flirt. From the day I met you."

Not that again. First he tried to convince her that if it wasn't for him, nobody would want her because she was so thoroughly unattractive. Then he accused her of having an affair.

"There's another guy!"

He was convinced he was right in his assumption.

There was no one in Susan's life. It was an argument without resolution.

"Well, I'm telling you right now," he warned, "if I ever find out the truth, I'll leave you and I'll take those kids with me!"

An overpowering alarm rose in her. She couldn't control the waves of anxiety. He was capable of doing such a thing. Taking the boys. This had been one of his controlling themes from the day Mitch was born.

"You'll never see them again!"

By the time he turned over and left her staring at the ceiling, she was in a complete panic. All she could think of was the boys. He had always said he would never lose his children again as he lost the girls to his first wife.

She had to make this marriage work. She had to. But how?

Although she continued to remain quiet and uncommunicative with her family regarding her worries about money and her marital problems with Chris, she used her diary as a confidant. Not only did she need to vent her hidden feelings, it was as though something told her it was important to keep a record of everything that was happening. She had finally come to the decision that her only salvation lay in getting out.

SUSAN'S JOURNAL—Spring, 1987

I just want to get myself out of this mess. Granted there are no collectors repossessing our furniture but things could be a lot better. I feel a real distance between Chris and me. Right now he's providing me with nothing. No financial support, no emotional support and very little support with the children. I guess I'm really disappointed in him. I've lost confidence in him and his judgment. Therefore, it's easier to just be distant, once I get myself on my feet. Then I'll do some more deciding about our relationship (business-wise I should just cut my losses— him—and go on). Money is the key to the entire thing. I need to be independent of Chris. Do I go towards a job that simply pays good $ and benefits and forget about advancement and interest, or do I go for something that may pay off better in the long run?

It was a persistent deterioration.

Here in her parents' familiar atmosphere of support and love and yearning to recreate the same atmosphere in her own relationship with her husband, she saw her marriage slipping away. She was terrified that the intense love she had originally felt had almost completely disappeared behind a reaction of bitterness and deep disappointment.

She was unwilling to give up, yet she did not want to live in constant intimidation. She wanted to make it better. Desperate to try anything to mend their relationship, for the sake of their children and for the sake of the vows they had exchanged, she spoke to Chris of counseling.

He refused.

She tried speaking directly to him of their problems.

He chastised her for her stupidity.

She pointed out their obligations to their sons.

He would not listen.

She spoke to him of money and their growing dependency on her parents.

He became furious.

She became quiet.

She grew to know, with increasing frequency, the withering stare that had become his trademark. That was the chord of terror that, once struck, usually put an end to all rebellious conversations.

But resentment was growing, a by-product of the strength she was slowly regaining from her surroundings and the support that had been denied her for the last five years. It was the strength that she had lost under the spell of his dominance. She actually began to answer back. Carefully, at first, but once she began, the crack had been made in the wall of intimidation that had kept her silent for so long.

Now her mother could look the other way no longer. She began to admit the suspicions that all was not well with them. Her first instinct was to preserve the marriage. The thought of the toll her daughter's family breaking up would take on her grandchildren made her believe it was something that had to be avoided at all costs.

Mary Lou: *There were times Sue thought I sided with Chris against her and maybe she was right. There were times that I did, if it dealt with working to save the marriage and a family of four.*

The first year of Paul's life, Sue had stayed home to take care of him. She felt she had to trust that Chris knew what he was doing and would make it. But it was slow in coming.

After five years of marriage Sue came to the decision that if Chris wasn't going to earn a living, she would *have* to get a job. Completing her master's in counseling would have to continue to remain on hold. She would take any job she could get—anything that would give her a beginning sense of financial independence.

Mary Lou was certain that something was seriously wrong with her daughter's marriage. Sue never complained and, consistent with the family pattern of nonintervention, it wasn't in Mary Lou's nature to pry, but in the wake of Chris's long shadow, Susan seemed to have undergone a private sort of emotional metamorphosis. The shimmering brightness of her daughter's personality had darkened considerably in the four years they had been away in Ohio.

Her opinion was always important. She was the holding force in the family. But they weren't asking, so she wouldn't interfere. Still, something had to be done.

Mary Lou decided to give up her job as the secretary of the Barrington Congregational Church in favor of Susan.

"I've been talking to Skip," she told her daughter.

"Skip?"

"Reverend Waterbury."

"Oh."

"Sue, I'm going to leave my job at the church. He said he'd be happy to interview you for the job if you want to work there in my place."

"I can't let you do that," Sue protested.

"I was ready to quit anyway. I'll take care of the children." her mother offered. "You need the job more than I do."

Her mother was giving Susan an important opportunity. It wasn't only that she had no money, and she was feeling guilty about living off her parents. Sue wanted to go to work to try to rid herself of the angst that was building up inside her.

Susan interviewed for the position along with several other candidates and was offered the job. She couldn't have been happier to have been selected.

Now, while she went out every morning to earn their daily bread, Mary Lou remained at home with the children, thoroughly enjoying her two grandsons. Now she even had the time to devote to crafts. She made anything she could think of that looked new and interesting. Wreaths, quilts, afghans. Weaving with wheat and even some metals. She did not consider herself an artist by any means. She had to see a pattern first before she could work with it, but her life had become full again, with a rich blend of the needs of the children interspersed with the joy of her crafts.

* * *

Susan's own life eased up a little, at both her job and at home. Chris could no longer be as overtly manipulative or critical. With her out of the house daily, his core of control was dwindling.

Susan: *The job was a good place for me. I felt like I was worth something again.*

But Chris wasn't about to let go gracefully. He often checked the odometer on her car to see how far she had driven. "There's an extra six miles on here. Where have you been?"

Sometimes she answered. Sometimes she did not.

Then the mysterious phone calls began at her office.

The phone would ring. She would answer the phone. The party on the other end of the line would hang up.

Susan could not be sure, but she believed it was Chris checking up on her to see if she was really at the office when she said she was going to be there. She could not put such behavior past him with the way he was acting. The minute she stepped out of the tight circle of his control, jealousy spread its ugly green shadow again. The image of a leashed dog began to haunt her. He frequently checked her rings to see if she had them on backward—his rationale being that she would have taken them off to sleep with someone else and made an error putting them back on in a hurry. He often checked to make sure they were still on. Susan came to realize that when she had the wedding rings on, he felt he was in charge. They were his symbol of power and control over her to the outside world. She belonged to him—like a dog with a collar and tags.

Susan: *The rings were a very powerful symbol to him and he often threatened to take his off it he thought I had been unfaithful. This was always done with great theatrics.*

There was no trust, and he was getting more and more secretive, as though he suspected everyone around him was a potential enemy. "Never tell anyone anything about our relationship," he warned her. "Never."

"What's that?" he demanded as Susan leafed through the morning mail.

"Nothing. Just . . ."

He took the envelopes out of her hand anxiously.

She realized, as he looked through them with a frown creasing his brow, that he thought any mail that came through the door was either a potential adversary or from a member of his family asking for money again. Chris claimed that no one in his family knew how to manage money and that he was the only one who did.

"They think I have all this money," he often complained.

If only they knew how little he had, Susan thought. She never could accept the insidious demand behind their frequent requests. His family came from a different mentality than one she understood; other people "owe me something," whether it's the government or their son who has this college degree and must be earning money.

Susan knew he had inherited a great many burdens from his family, but that did not excuse his oppressive behavior.

He went through her purse and read her journals. When he read, ". . . I should cut my losses and get on with my life . . ." he was livid.

"What do you mean, 'cut your losses,' " he demanded.

"My journal," Susan cried, horrified. He had invaded the only private place she had left in the world—her mind. "You've been reading my journal!"

"You'll never get away from me!"

She was becoming desperate.

"You'll never see those boys again, I'm warning you!"

It was an old story—one Susan was not willing to accept anymore, but she still could not win any argument with Chris, and his threats about the boys literally terrified her.

SUSAN'S JOURNAL—Late summer, 1987

I need to create a support group outside of my family. I can't ask them to do much more for me. Someday I'll make them proud of what I've done. The boys are my best creation so far.

Try to look forward to a brighter tomorrow.

Try . . .

But no matter what she wrote in her diary to cheer herself and to optimistically hope for changes, down deep, Susan knew she was living a horror story.

Chapter 10

Tradition and the Smell of Money

The search expanded.

"Police and firefighters from Seekonk and Rehboth, Mass., and Bristol and Warren, along with sheriffs from Bristol County, Mass., will assist in today's search."
—*The Providence Journal-Bulletin,* 10/2/91

The journal had to be kept hidden. It reflected, too clearly, the rage that had grown in Susan.

SUSAN'S JOURNAL—March 2, 1988

I have this incredible anger that builds up inside me and I hope that taking my thoughts and feelings to paper will help release the anger and bring some order to my thoughts.

But where to begin . . .

Once again my husband has become a grumpy uncommunicative enigma. He is so paranoid about so many areas of my life—who I talk to, what I do, what I think. It's a good thing he can't hear what I think. That feels like the only private place I've got left.

Last night he said, point-blank, that he didn't care to communicate with me. Now how are we supposed to make this marriage work if not? If he'd only die my life would be much simpler.

Tonight, I will sit down and talk at him again so he has no grounds to say that I haven't told him how I feel and what's going on with me. That's the most *I* can do. But what if it does no good? Deep inside I still love him, although I don't know why. Maybe the memories of what it used to be like.

I guess I want to stay with him. What other choices do I have but to wall him off emotionally. He's hurt me so much. It's depressing and embarrassing to be around him. Look at the choice I made for whom I decided to marry! What a mistake! But I'm willing to live with it and work with him to make things good. I think they can be, but not if he doesn't try.

I feel like our lives are on hold waiting for him to make it big or go bankrupt.

July, 1988—The Move to Jones Circle

They all sat around the living room. Mitchell and Paul were on the floor next to one of the massive, round legs of the grand piano, playing quietly with a Lego set. They were so engrossed in their activity, they paid little attention to the serious family conference that was going on between their parents and grandparents.

"How much longer do you think it will take to make a go of the business?" Clyde asked.

Chris hesitated.

"Do you think it will be a few more years?"

"Probably not that long."

Clyde knew his son-in-law was still hoping to make a lot of money in his investment-counseling business. Clyde based his expectation on his belief that Chris shared the normal male desire to take care of his family himself.

"We don't have the money to move out yet, Dad," Sue added.

"Well, here's the thing." Clyde continued with a nod. "Your mother and I don't have a problem with you living with us, but it's been a couple of years now, the boys are growing, and even with Kathy gone, it is getting crowded. . . ."

"I just need a little more time," Chris said quickly. "It's all beginning to fall into place now, and if . . ."

Clyde: *I never thought he was conning us. I was with him every day and I didn't see anything there that raised a big red flag. He would ask for my advice. I would give it. Sometimes he took it. Usually he distorted it. But I didn't realize that until later.*

"It's okay," Clyde interrupted Chris. "That's not what we're getting at . . ."

Clyde never objected to his son-in-law's overenthusiastic business projections, even though they never saw any funds materialize out of all his efforts. He seemed to be able to talk in a manner that made sense and they wanted to have faith in him even though Clyde was beginning to suspect Chris was more of a dreamer than a business man.

Clyde knew he should have asked more penetrating questions. He dabbled with the stock market himself, but he never invested money that he could not afford to lose. He had little interest in the kinds of investments Chris was talking about.

Susan: *It was all options, the kind of thing where you have to understand bonds sold across the world . . . the exchange of monies. That calls for a lot of dedication to the computer and to a great deal of information. And even then, interpreting the information is tricky and requires a great deal of skill and experience.*

It wasn't for Clyde. He thought it was too risky, but, like the others in the family, he didn't want to probe.

"What we're getting at," Clyde continued, overriding Chris's hasty explanatory excuses, "is, we know it takes a long time to get a business going, and under the circumstances, Mary Lou and I think we should look for a larger house."

Chris stared at them.

"Move?" Sue asked.

"In a larger house," Mary Lou added, "we would be more comfortable. We could all have more privacy."

Chris didn't know what to say. He was certainly aware that the house on Chantilly Drive had a great many precious memories for the Slickers. He was astonished that they offered to sell the home in which they had raised their daughters to buy a larger one to accommodate needs they should no longer have to consider their responsibility.

Susan: *Just like he was always amazed that my family gave gifts because it pleased the receiver—not as a bribe. He always claimed that was what his first wife's family did. Give gifts as bribes.*

There was something very sad and wistful about such a feeling. Now here he was again, astonished at such an incredible display of altruism.

"So," Clyde said, "how about we look for another house . . ."

"The money . . . ?" Chris asked.

The money needed was part of an inheritance. Mary Lou's mom and dad had died in 1986 and left her a considerable sum, but they also had money of their own. Part of their estate came from living through the easier real estate market of the fifties, sixties, and seventies. First they had rented for three years. Then they'd bought a house for $17,000. In five years they'd sold it for a 35% gain. They'd moved to Connecticut and bought another house. A year and a half later, they'd sold it for a 26% gain. Then they'd moved in with Mary Lou's mom and dad for two years while Clyde finished his doctorate before moving to Barrington and buying their house on Chantilly Drive. Through the combined effects of Mary Lou's inheritance and a process of steady upgrading in their property acquisitions, they had reached the comfortable stage of upper-middle-class affluence.

Chris knew there was money and he remembered it as he and Mary Lou, both of whom had free time during the day, went to look at new places to live. He pledged to himself that, someday, he would pay them back.

To Clyde and Mary Lou, the house on Jones Circle, an upscale neighborhood, represented their whole life. It was large, beautiful, quietly elegant, and brand-new. There were no windows or furnace to replace, no remodeling as in some of the older houses Mary Lou and Chris had looked at. It was sandpiper beige in color, with forest green shutters set back on a spacious lawn bordered on one side with a split rail fence. It was perfect for a family of four adults and two children.

The only glitch in the family move from Chantilly Drive to Jones Circle was that Susan had begun to make noises about leaving Chris. It was the only time she had given any overt indications of the problems her parents sensed and strenuously avoided bringing out into the open. Susan wasn't sure she wanted them all to settle in together again, not if she and Chris weren't going to make it. Sue even gave Chris a deadline to make his business work or give it up and get a job. Mary Lou thought it was not a good thing to do at this time, especially with the uprooting aspects of their imminent move.

Sue felt betrayed. Her mother was sticking up for Chris.

It wasn't that, her mother explained. It was just that her parents thought her timing was not good. Not at this time. They hoped the move to the new house would help to resolve whatever problems they had. This time, they spoke up and convinced Sue that the move would be beneficial to all of them, even to Sue and Chris's marriage. They knew how difficult it was for them living in such cramped quarters. Things would change once their living arrangements became more comfortable.

SUSAN'S JOURNAL

I hate being powerless and, without money, you are powerless in today's society.

Chris is paranoid of my parents' generosity and jealous of their ability to buy things. I'm jealous too but if he'd do something about the $, he could have more too. I feel like he's starting to take advantage of Mom and Dad's generosity.

Chris appears to be resentful, jealous, of everything I do. Somehow he's afraid I'm going to run off on him. If he keeps up this non-communication stuff he will force me to talk to my friends and my family. He hates for me to go out anywhere with my friends or inconvenience him in the slightest way.

He has no right to demand everything and give nothing in return. I feel really used—for sex, for parenting, for support, for money. Nothing I say or do seems to get through but I will try one more time (isn't that always the case!!!) Am I being a complete idiot to keep trying? Sometimes I feel that way and that everybody's wondering why I married him and why I put up with and stay with him. I dread talking "at" him but what have I got to lose—at least I know in my heart I'm doing the absolute best I can."

Living with her parents made staying together easier than if they had been on their own and were forced to deal with the realities of their financial needs alone and without help.

Jones Circle

Decorated for ease and comfort, the new house reflected a nostalgic touch of Americana, full of four-poster beds, Early American picture frames with the children, Early American spindle-back chairs and bookcases, *Cosmopolitan* magazines lying casually about, handmade little teddy bears, quilts, and samplers with colorfully embroidered homilies like:

"Love is pulling together against all odds."

The children's room had a one-foot-high dinosaur-decorated tape around the center of the entire room, a bulletin board tacked with learning activities, bookshelves topped with stuffed toys, clowns, seals . . . soft, cuddly, comforting.

Chris was truly overwhelmed, feeling he belonged. He repaid the Slickers' generosity with help around the new house. Shelves had to be built. Mary Lou's assorted crafts and hobbies had to be set up in the basement. Everything he did was completed with the precise, almost-obsessive perfectionism Susan had come to know so well.

The solid family tradition, fortified with a gallery of family photos, was very appealing to Chris. Preserving the ancestral line in a proud display of family photos going up the staircase, reaching to the second level of the house, fascinated him. "Where did they all come from?" he asked Clyde. "Are all these photos of the family?"

"Yes. Families of all ages," Clyde responded proudly. "My side of the family with my grandfather, grandmother, and at the bottom of the steps would be my grandmother and grandfather on my father's side, whom I never met. They died six months before I was born."

"You've had them all this time?"

"The pictures had been in my mother's attic and she decided that they would either throw them away or give them to me. I was there in Ohio at just the right time to save them. The other pieces are Mary Lou's side and they go back pretty far. The idea is for the children to see what is in the family history. Eventually we will have a gallery of people in the upstairs hallway, too. That's Mary Lou's idea. Her mom and dad had it in their hallway on the second floor and it worked out well for them. They could bring up people and show the children whom they were talking about. Tradition."

"Yes," Chris murmured. "Tradition."

Chris became a fanatic about hanging the pictures correctly. Clyde would take a picture and hold it up and say, "Well, that looks okay," but Chris insisted on getting a tape measure and measuring every angle to make certain the frame was hanging properly. Always a little obsessive-compulsive, Susan thought. Just like at the Newport Creamery . . . all the spoons had to be the same way . . . all the knives . . . but, bottom line, she had to admit, it did look terrific when it was finished.

Chris was trying to latch on to the family tradition by becoming a part of it. Someday, maybe his picture would be up on the wall. Maybe family members, generations down the line, would talk about him and point him out to the children.

"I reserve some hope that Emily and Alice may still be alive, but that hope is a candle in the void of space."
　　　　　—Christine Scriabine
　　　　　The Providence Sunday Journal, 10/6/91

The move did not produce the desired effects for Sue and Chris. By the time Kathy visited them, she could see Sue was not happy with Chris. But even if her mother hadn't finally confided her own suspicions, Kathy could tell, herself, that something wasn't quite right. She didn't say anything. She didn't want to pressure her sister.

"Not happy" was hardly an apt description. Too often, under the guise of not intruding, deepest feelings are not revealed. Within a month of the move to Jones Circle, the relationship between Susan and Chris was tearing at the seams, again.

Susan was coming into her own. The job at the church helped considerably. More and more, she was standing up for herself in the face of Chris's demands. Sometimes Clyde and Mary Lou could hear them yelling at each other behind the closed door of their bedroom at the foot of the stairs.

Susan: *He always wanted the car. I didn't mind sharing but he wanted it five days a week. My parents couldn't understand why we were fighting over this. They didn't understand it was a power struggle. It had nothing to do with the car. He was trying to keep control over me. He assumed I was having affairs. That's why he always had to check up on me and take the car. He wanted to leave me stranded at the church.*

She was so miserable, she often talked to Reverend Walter "Skip" Waterbury, who, realizing the severity of the young woman's problem, eventually recommended a marriage counselor.

Summoning up all of her courage, "Either we go to marriage counseling," she finally said to Chris, "or we call it quits."

"Don't be ridiculous."

"I mean it."

"Don't think you can push me into—"

"It's that, or this marriage is over!"

He looked at her quietly. There was something about the way Sue said it this time that was a little different.

"I really mean it, Chris," she continued in the wake of his unusual lack of response. "Here's the name of the counselor Skip Waterbury recommends."

"You've been talking to him!" he accused.

"It doesn't matter."

"About us!"

"It's too late," she said stubbornly as she put the card with the name of the counselor on the table before him. "You go first. You set up the appointment and you go to the first appointment and after that we'll go together. Or it's *over!*"

He stared at her, but her eyes didn't budge from his.

"I love you, Sue," he said softly.

". . . You'd never know it. . . ."

He looked down at the card and slowly picked it up.

They went to marriage counseling together from September 1988 to June 1989. Initially, the sessions were covered by insur-

ance but they weren't happy with the person they were seeing,
so they went to another counselor, who wasn't covered.

Despite the expense, Susan, insisted upon going, even though:

Susan: *It was like ripping my guts out.*

*It was horrible. I understood what counseling was all about and
it made me vulnerable. I was being honest, I was playing the game.
I was doing things the way they were supposed to be done. I was
being honest and I was afraid he was going to use it against me.
He appeared to have no ability to define what he was feeling. He
couldn't comprehend a lot of counseling or communication con-
cepts. He had no comprehension that things he said could hurt me
in ways that they did. So I would come out of there exhausted.*

All to no avail. In the privacy of their bedroom, Chris *did* use
their sessions against her. Everything was her fault. He threatened to use the children against her. He regularly tried to intimidate her emotionally, and continued to treat her like a child. "I'll
disappear," he persisted, "and take the boys if you even so much
as think of divorcing me."

"You can't take the boys," she cried.

"You're replaceable. The boys aren't, but you are. If you try to
interfere with me, you could be eliminated just like that," he threatened, penetrating her diminishing resolve with a deep, cold stare.

"What does that mean?"

He would not amplify.

Susan almost believed the veiled threat. She had come to think
he was capable of violence. But he couldn't mean it. Not really. He
was just being melodramatic, trying to frighten her into obedience.

*Twenty officers and eight specially trained German shep-
herd dogs were used in a search of Aquidneck Island.*

*Barrington Police Sgt. Richard E. McInnis: "I am satisfied no
bodies were buried at any of the places searched yesterday."*

SUSAN'S JOURNAL
Again he's become hypocritical expecting perfect com-

munication from me and giving no indication that what I tell him makes any difference or is of any importance.

He says, "You don't communicate and that's why our marriage has become so poor." But he won't listen or talk to me about his problems. He says it's none of my business.

He wonders why I don't want to make love.

Would you want to with someone you feel you hardly know and who makes you feel trapped and angry?

Part of me wants to give in and be a doormat.

Lock out all my feelings!

Figure out how best to live with Chris and *stay out of his life at the same time*.

That idea is utterly depressing.

Yet, I don't have the energy to fight him and that's what seems to perpetually happen. All we seem to do is bait each other these days. For example he would decide the child was sick enough to need to go to the doctor, but he'd insist that I take him. I'd take him to the doctor to get checked, we'd get home, and he'd say, well, didn't you ask about so and so, and I'd say no, I didn't ask about that, and he'd say, well why not, and I'd say, cause I didn't think of it! Chris would say, You should have thought of that, how couldn't you? Then I'd say, well next time you take him!

He sets me up to bait him.

Very critical.

There were times when I would not tell him things because I was afraid of his reaction. Then he claimed I was uncommunicative, and I'd say, well I thought I told you that! I think subconsciously I was afraid of what he'd say. The time would come for me to go out with friends on Saturday night and I'd say, Well, I told you I was going. But I actually hadn't.

She felt as though their lives were on perpetual hold, waiting for him to either make it big or go bankrupt. He still claimed he could be successful.

"Just hold out a little longer."

* * *

For a while, he actually started listening at the counseling sessions and their lives began to get better. She began to see some traces of the old Chris—the Chris she had fallen in love with.

They ran out of money and had to stop the sessions. Once they stopped, it wasn't long before they skidded back to where they had started.

Susan: *He had a tantrum one time when I went back to work at night. If I go back one night in a year to that church it's unusual. But I was really jammed up. A new minister, and the computer went down. So I had to go back to work that night and he had a fit. He didn't believe me.*

"You can't go back to work tonight," he stormed, "I have better things to do than just take care of the kids. I have my priorities, too! You should have given me more notice!"

Tantrum or no tantrum, she left him raging and walked out the door. She went to work wondering how she had summoned the strength to ignore his anger. Maybe there was more steel inside of her than she realized.

Emily always thought there was.

Emily Carroll was Susan's best friend and had been since they met in a seventh grade science class wincing over the dissection of frogs. They trusted each other with each other's lives and every triumph and defeat was equally shared without judgment. Susan had told Emily more about her unhappy marital state than anyone else because she knew Emily would never tell a soul. Emily never told her what to do unless she directly asked for advice. She simply listened and supported her friend.

Now, Susan felt she needed more than the comfort of a friend's ear. She needed direct intervention.

* * *

The moments of strength she occasionally was able to muster actually made her feel worse and worse about herself. They only proved there was room for positive improvement.

She was desperately tired of enduring life instead of living it. She was beginning to worry that so much daily unhappiness would have a negative effect on her sons. She wanted Mitch and Paul to have the happy memories of childhood they were entitled to.

Chris was a good father. Too strict, maybe, but he loved the boys and they knew it. But their parents' inability to get along had to have an impact on the boys that could set a poor pattern for their own emotional development.

In August she approached Rev. Skip Waterbury for some guidance. He was ready to take a position at a different church and referred her to the local Methodist minister, Rev. Tom Thompson. After a preliminary evaluation, Tom would make a recommendation as to how best to proceed in a professional setting outside of the church, since it was not the policy of the ministry to offer long-term counseling.

After two or three private meetings, Tom asked if Susan had ever considered going to Al Anon.

"Al Anon?" she asked in surprise. "Isn't that for alcoholics?"

"It's for the families of alcoholics."

"But that's not the problem," she protested. "Chris doesn't drink."

The very idea startled her; there were no problems with alcohol in their marriage or within her family—close or extended.

"Perhaps so," the minister commented, "but you exhibit many of the behaviors of someone who lives with an alcoholic."

That was an even more startling concept. She couldn't accept such a jump in attitude.

"I couldn't attend meetings like that."

Just the idea of opening up her innermost anguish, her very heart to a bunch of strangers . . .

"It's okay," Tom assured her.

Now he encouraged her to seek the more traditional course of action, marital counseling, and gave her the name of a woman in Providence whom he strongly recommended.

Reluctantly, Susan went, but worry about counseling increased. In the quiet of her room, she poured her anxieties onto the pages of her private journal:

SUSAN'S JOURNAL

Counseling never really helped for long. Admitting to him what I needed in a relationship only caused him to use that need in a power play. So it's hard to figure out what to work on and how to communicate without making myself so *vulnerable*.

During the first session, the new counselor asked Susan if she would try going to Al Anon.

"Did Pastor Thompson tell you to say that?"

"No."

"Because he suggested it, too."

"Did he."

"Yes, and I told him then I didn't think it was the right choice. Chris is not an alcoholic."

"Al Anon isn't only for alcoholics. It is a support group for the members of families who live with extremely difficult, controlling, even addictive situations, alcoholism being only one. Drugs is another. Abuse is still another of many possible situations that require learning how to behave with those who demonstrate controlling behavior through their addictions."

Learning how to behave . . .

It was the first time her own behavior was being challenged as possibly adding to the marital problem. Sue admitted that, in her own way, she had probably contributed to Chris's persistent abuse by permitting it, giving in to it, caving in, and reacting to it in programmed ways that allowed the abuse to continue. She sensed Chris instinctively knew which buttons to push to control her. What if she could learn to deny him access to those buttons? What if she could learn to stand up for herself to the point where she could ultimately stand *alone?*

Without him!

It would require an entire process of reeducation, even consciously eliminating past parental and religious ideals and manners of acceptance. Learning a *new* way. Was it too late? She was no longer a kid. She didn't believe it could happen.

She asked Emily's advice.

"Go to it!" Emily told her. "What do you have to lose?"

There was a chapter close to her home, almost prophetically convenient. Still reluctant, Susan agreed to give Al Anon a try.

Susan was very nervous and had no idea what the people would be like. The first thing they did was put some pamphets in her hand. Pamphlets again! Like that time in Ohio where they suggested she "forgive" and "accept" everything her husband did!

On the outside, the pamphlet said, "One day at a time." She turned to the inside cover and read the prayer that had sustained so many through their respective ordeals:

THE SERENITY PRAYER

"God grant me the serenity to accept the things I cannot change, courage to change the things I can, and wisdom to know the difference."

It sounded so simple.

Now her life was going to be restructured around one of Al Anon's basic tenets: "One day at a time," and some of the suggested rules in Al Anon's concept of Detachment from another's problems.

- Not to suffer because of the actions or reactions of other people.
- Not to prevent a crisis if it is the natural course of events.
- Not to cover up for another's mistakes or misdeeds.
- Not to allow ourselves to be used or abused in the interest of another's recovery.

At the meetings, she discovered the goodness of people whose lives were far worse than hers, yet they accepted the tremendous struggle she was going through to make a better life for herself and for her sons. It was all such a wonderful surprise that it was almost too much to bear.

Susan: *After I stopped crying each time I was there, I gained enormous strength and courage from these folks to change how I thought, felt and behave with Chris. What a liberating feeling!*

I began to believe in myself—to learn that my thinking was crazy! because it was the only way to survive in a relationship that was unhealthy.

As I learned to stop thinking and acting like a victim, my self-esteem rose. That created a snowball effect and, bit by bit, I had the courage to try new behaviors, to calmly state what I would and would not tolerate Chris saying and doing to me and to "act not react."

Chris was neutral about her going to the meetings, although he thought it was all a lot of hooey, but going there was the beginning of the new Susan.

Eventually the day came when she consciously chose not to react to one of his tantrums. Rather than crying and apologizing for something that wasn't her problem, as had often been her habit in the past, she told him, "Come back when you can behave like a human being and then we'll talk about this situation."

He stared at her. "I don't know what's gotten into you," he responded. "You've changed so much!"

Susan: *He didn't know that was the biggest compliment he had given me in years!*

We had separate checking accounts. I cut him off. I don't know where he got money from.

I learned to not react when he did things, to ignore stuff. This brought on tantrums. For years I've listened to his threats and believed them. The threat of him taking the children, making my life miserable. Threats that I was a bad mother. When I ignore it he only gets madder.

I won't be roped into the head games he tries with me. I won't! It's time for things to change. And so they have.

There is no panic now like there used to be. Because I started to believe in myself.

AL ANON helped with this. I was secure with my job. My family was around.

That was 1988. She still backed down. She still wasn't ready to break up her children's home.

"One day at a time . . ."

When it's time to learn the lesson, the teacher comes along.

It wasn't quite time yet, but it was getting close. Even her closest friend, Emily, one of the few people who insisted she open up and confide to her, could see the growing changes in her attitude. "Welcome back," Emily told her. "You've been gone a long time."

At one point, Chris was behind in his child support to his first wife. The official papers of complaint he received sent him into a rage.

"If you don't get it together," Susan warned him, "she could have you thrown in jail, or they'll find you a job flipping burgers."

"She just won't let up!" he said, reaching for Sue's purse.

"Why should she?" Sue objected, knowing he was looking for her pay. "She thinks you should get a job, too, to help support your daughters. Why should I be the one to pay your child support? You should get a paying job." ·

"Can't you just be a patient a little longer?"

"It's been six years."

He turned his back on her.

"Talk to me, Chris!"

"There's nothing to talk about."

Now, *she* turned her back on *him*.

SUSAN'S JOURNAL

How things have changed from what I wrote in March. Emily is right. My whole attitude has changed since then. So much has happened and there's so much more to come. . . .

I have given things one last chance and have given Chris every opportunity to decide that he wants to make this relationship work, to no avail. Having talked with Skip and now working with Tom, my self-confidence is being restored.

Now I need more guidance but it will have to wait until Tom is back from vacation.

I will no longer be a doormat and martyr. I have given 6 years of everything I had to him. I have taken up all of his responsibilities except his business which has only made me miserable. I've listened to his threats and put-downs and believed them. It's time for things to change and so they have.

Chris now has responsibility for his daughters, child support, student loan, gas and his business. All credit cards are his or mine and checkbooks are now separate. The only things left are the house and a Visa bill.

I think emotionally we're already divorced. I don't want him to touch me, or even be around. He's hurt me too much for too long and I won't allow myself to be abused any longer.

The more independent and self-assured I get the nastier he gets—threatening to take away the children, put-downs, verbal abuse, etc. When I ignore it he only gets madder. I won't be roped into the head games he tries with me. *Not anymore!*

If I really think about what he's saying I can find the lack of logic or bluffing he's doing.

The latest is that I spoke to both my parents and Emily about things and it was just too much for him. He stomped off to sleep somewhere else and told me this morning that in Sept. he's going to file for separation and then probably divorce depending on how the boys were handling things. I think he's upset I didn't fall apart when he said that. For the first time in all the times he's brought up divorce, it didn't send me into a panic.

I have to trust that the Lord will take care of me and the boys and it will all turn out ok. There was a coldness inside me this morning which left once I got busy and there were people in and out—also a sadness that he truly didn't want to make it work.

No panic. To me that's significant. I'm trying to accept that things may not turn out as I hope but *I will survive* and make the best out of what I'm given. All my instincts tell me this is the right thing to do and when I start to let up a bell goes off inside and says "this doesn't feel right, you don't really mean what you're saying/doing."

Do I wait and see if he files (save me some $?) I doubt he will, he needs me too much and can't afford it. See what happens with child support, court, jail, job? Get things going myself?

Most likely to keep things looking normal. If I wait till Sept., Mitchell will be started in school—another reason for Mitchell to stay with me.

I've also started to be more concerned with how the breakup will affect the kids (all 4!) I know their pain will make me feel guilty but in the long run, they'll have a more stable home with competent care.

I'm so tired from fighting him but I can't give in—I'd lose my self-respect. I know things will be much tougher and there will be lots of things I haven't anticipated but this is the right decision with the facts and feelings I have so I have to go forward from here.

No more being stuck!

No more being a victim!

Al Anon had one other effect. Once she began to stand up to him, living with him wasn't as bad as before. She now felt good about herself. It gave her a breather. It put off making the ultimate decision while she enjoyed her newfound position in the relationship.

But whether she decided to divorce him or not didn't matter at this point. What mattered was that she had found her guts at last.

PART III
Ernie

Chapter 11

A Fatal Meeting— Ernest Brendel

Anyone having any information about the Brendel family that they want kept confidential can write to: Barrington Police Dept., P.O. Box 350, Barrington, R.I. 02806

Early 1989

A strong Teutonic heritage gave an aura of strength and firmness to everything he did. Ernest Brendel was only five-six and 160 pounds, but he was broad in stature and gave the appearance of being big. At fifty, he had a full, rich head of curly, chestnut-colored hair with flecks of gray. Excelling in sports during his school years, now in mid-life, he looked as strong as a boxer and appeared almost tough, until a warm smile, sparingly used, belied the hard edge. He was a New York City corporate lawyer who had moved to Rhode Island to start a new business. Alice Bobb Brendel, petite, with short-cropped light brown hair, was his second wife, his first marriage having ended in divorce in 1969 after seven years. Alice had been a librarian at the New York City Public Library when they met at a Brown University alumni gathering.

After marrying in Alice's hometown of Reading, Pennsylvania, the Brendels moved to an upper east side apartment in Manhattan. They enjoyed a yuppie kind of existence, taking full advantage of the city's endless restaurants, museums, theaters, and concert offerings.

Eventually, yearning for their own home in greener pastures, and always with the possibility of starting a family underscoring their decisions, they moved out of New York City, first to Tarrytown, New York, then to Providence, Rhode Island. Alice secured a position as a librarian at Brown, and Ernie set up a patent law practice out of their home, specializing in the protection of copyrights through international licensing.

Attorney Paul Ryan, a former Barrington probate judge, was one of the lawyers who rented offices in the small suburban office building on Maple Avenue where Chris Hightower had set up Hightower Investments, Inc.

Sometimes Ryan was visited by his longtime friend, Ernest Brendel. Ernie and Paul often shared business clients. They had handled the international account of a cosmetics company, and collaborated on the legal representation of a Japanese pinball machine manufacturer.

Since leaving New York, Ernie had attempted to go into partnership with the makers of a wine cooler beverage distributed in the southern part of New England. To his disappointment, the association didn't work out, and he was able to back out before taking any losses.

It has been 13 days since the Brendel family vanished. 100 police and firefighters begin the most massive search yet.
    —The Providence Journal-Bulletin, 10/3/91

It was during one of his visits to Ryan's office that Ernie met Chris. Brendel accurately perceived Hightower as a struggling commodities advisor who was desperately down on his luck and having a hard time attracting clients.

Ryan knew only that Hightower was always glued to his computer screen. He had never had more than brief conversations with him and was surprised when he learned Brendel had befriended the man. He was even more surprised when he told him he had decided to make a couple of small commodities investments with Hightower.

After twenty years of privately dabbling in the stock market, Brendel had signed a management agreement with Hightower.

"Why invest with him?" Ryan asked doubtfully. Commodities. Those were highly volatile markets they were talking about. "I don't think he's up to it."

"It'll help Hightower become a trader," Brendel said generously.

Even though he knew Hightower was registered as a licensed commodities advisor, Brendel was aware that Hightower was not permitted to execute the trades himself without the aid of firms that had access to the Chicago markets. "Actually, he's doing it with Balfour McLaine Futures, Inc. They're based in New York."

How much did he sign for?

"Only $2,000."

Awfully risky.

"Well it might lose, but it will be a voluntary loss. The guy is so desperate and broke. I'd like to help him out."

"But . . ."

"And you never know," Brendel added. "He might be able to do something. He certainly thinks he can."

Brendel had come to think Hightower had some interesting formulaic notions. The surprise in Brendel's sudden interaction with Hightower was that he was usually very cautious where business was concerned, and Hightower was a complete unknown with big, untested ideas.

Ryan realized that Hightower had sparked a latent, but potent, interest in his friend. Leaving corporate law was a welcome relief from the rat race, but Brendel's business in Rhode Island usually left him with little to do after noon. He had been dabbling in business for the last few years trying to latch on to a venture about which he could become excited. He was a minor partner in the Newport Trading Company, and he had his usual clients, but none of them represented the excitement or the potential for fulfillment that he was seeking. He wanted something else. There was the time he almost bought a manufacturing company with a New York corporate lawyer he'd met through their mutual association with the Brown University Alumni Club in Manhattan. They had been looking for some kind of business together since 1980 and had spent four years investigating companies up for sale.

Brendel had told Ryan once that they had actually analyzed a total of sixty different businesses. They were taking no chances. Even so, they could never agree on which business to embrace.

Ryan attributed the lack of agreement to a divergence in where they were in life. Brendel, the younger of the two, was interested in making quick profits, while his partner was not in that much of a rush. He eventually lost interest and moved back to Westchester County in New York.

That left Ernie on his own, still looking, until he met Christopher Hightower.

They had a great deal in common. They both enjoyed athletics, Hightower was involved in the youth soccer program in town, Brendel was a devoted Boston Red Sox fan, as well as a football devotee, never missing a Brown-Yale game. They were both family men and solitary entrepreneurs. They enjoyed discussing business deals and big money. While Hightower never considered getting a normal paying job Brendel was growing tired of an unsteady income and had begun sending résumés out to law firms in New England.

But it was the business deals he was really interested in exploring. The men were a perfect match.

After 28 days of continuous searches, there are still 'no leads' as to their whereabouts.
— *The Providence Journal-Bulletin,* 10/18/91

Chris and Ernie were going to be partners. Susan thought Ernie was a good, solid friend for Chris and she could tell he liked Ernie.

Susan: *I remember the first time they got together, I thought, this is great! Ernie seems to be a loner, Chris is a loner. Maybe he's found one good buddy.*

Ernie had asked him to come over to his house to look at one or two things. He wasn't as handy with household stuff as Chris was, and Chris went to help him out.

My nature is social, outgoing. Friends. Chris had submerged that entire side of me. I thought with Ernie in the picture, it would get him off my back.

Ernie and Alice decided they would have Chris and Susan over to their home. The invitation was for dinner, but the purpose was to discuss their business association. There had been some talk of a partnership and putting out a newsletter together. Susan was not privy to the details of their discussions, only that they seemed to get along and that Chris was excited about it. The invitation to dinner at the Brendel home in a Barrington suburb was the first time they got together socially.

The Brendels' large, white colonial farmhouse was comfortably situated on two acres of land next to St. James Church. Coming slowly up the driveway, they parked in front of the huge, barnlike structure that served as the family garage. To the left of the barn, Sue noticed that the house, clearly in need of a paint job, was a charming old, clapboard house with a huge porch in front.

"How long have you been here?" Susan asked Alice.

"Only a few years. You?"

"I grew up in Barrington."

"Lovely town. We moved to the suburbs because of our daughter, Emily."

It wasn't surprising that, as a librarian, Alice knew the colorful history of the house they had bought. It had originally been constructed as the caretaker's house on a large estate. Its most recent owners were Leo Patrick and Doris McGowan. Mr. McGowan had been considered one of the more flamboyant members of the Rhode Island State Legislature. When he died in 1984, his widow remained in the house for an additional four years until she finally made the decision to sell the house to the Brendels for $225,000.

"There's a very good school system," Alice added, "and living here we're right near the school."

"Primrose Elementary?"

"Yes. In the Alternative Learning Program. It was all because of Emily."

Susan immediately liked Alice and Ernie. Although they struck her as studious and quiet in close conversation, it was easy to see they were intelligent, warm people who appeared close enough to each other to be termed a perfect match by their families and friends. Ernie seemed more sociable by nature. Alice, a bit less gregarious, was sweet, with a quiet, but rich, sense of humor.

Their conversation indicated a tendency to veer away from parties with large groups of people, preferring a modest, intimate social life that, when not involved with their extended families and a few precious old-time friends, revolved almost exclusively around the privileged social comradeship of Brown University.

Susan didn't get to learn much about Ernie during this visit. She didn't know exactly what he did for a living, only that he didn't go off to a job every day and had a legal background.

Eight-year-old Emily was beautiful, with short-cropped dark hair and vivid, sparkling brown eyes. In the short conversation they had, she seemed not only polite and well behaved, but exceptionally bright as well. Watching the close interaction between parents and child, it was obvious that Ernie and Alice adored their perky little daughter. They let her talk enthusiastically about how she and her father met her mother at the bus stop every day without fail, and then they would all go home together, have dinner, read, talk, feed her pet turtle, watch TV—a pleasant routine that gave a solid foundation to the tight family unit. Together, the three of them projected as one.

After politely saying "good night" to the adults, Emily had retreated to her second floor bedroom to read herself to sleep. Surrounded by an army of cuddly, soft, stuffed animals and covered by her favorite "Blankie," she propped herself to reread one of her favorite books, *Just a Dream,* by Chris van Allsburg.

* * *

As Sue and Alice spoke during the last-minute meal preparations, Susan discovered their common religious backgrounds.
The Brendels went to Central Congregational Church, her family
went to Barrington Congregational Church, the two being UCC,
United Church of Christ denomination. They both knew the conference minister.

"We went on a trip to Israel with him last year," Alice told
her.

After dinner, the men adjourned upstairs to see Ernie's tiny
home office situated in the hallway on the second floor close to
where Emily now slept peacefully. While the men discussed
bonds, stocks, futures, commodities, prices, and how to maxi-
mize potential investments with bold new ideas, Sue helped to
put the dinner dishes on the partially rusted rack of the old
KitchenAid dishwasher that had come with the McGowan house.

Alice laughed, saying one day they would replace the old relic.

The kitchen was decorated in a rich, warm colonial style with
bricks circling the cooking area and solid wood beams overhead.
Comfortable, Sue thought.

While the dishes were being done, Sue and Alice discussed
their children.

"You're lucky to have two. I always wanted children," Alice
confided. "There was a while there when I didn't think I would
be able to have any. Then along came Emily."

"How wonderful for you."

"Yes. She's a special part of the family. We try to do as much
together as we possibly can. Emily is always included if it's at
all possible," she explained. "We couldn't take Emily with us
last year to Israel, but"—she smiled—"we're planning a special
trip with her next year to France and England."

Susan: *She would never say anything negative to the rudest person in the world. She was typical of what you think of as a librarian. Good cook. Loved her daughter, and loved her husband
as far as I could tell.*

From the wine served with dinner, it was apparent the Brendels understood wine. It was a pleasant, uneventful evening, the kind shared by people who were on the way to friendship.

Four state troopers, at least two Barrington police officers and four FBI Agents are still working on the case full time.
                    —*The Providence Journal-Bulletin,* 10/18/91

In the annual filing with the Commodities Futures Trading Commission in August of 1989, Chris reported his biggest year since he received his license. His report stated the assets on deposit with him totaled $30,722.21.

Brendel was one of only two clients he listed on his report to the CFTC.

Mary Lou: *It appeared that he had some clientele. But he couldn't understand why people just off the street couldn't come in and invest with him. He didn't seem to have understanding that, unless he had a proven track record, no one would.*

Once or twice, Ernie came to visit Chris at Jones Circle to look at some figures on the computers.

It was all very friendly and pleasant. Chris even borrowed Ernie's bicycle for a while to go riding with Mitchell. The bike remained in the garage at Jones Circle for months.

Not surprisingly, Chris had Mary Lou believing that he had started to make money and that the first quarter of the year was good.

"Is it time for a celebration, Chris?" she asked.

"No," he hedged, "let's wait for one more quarter."

The longer they were all together, however, the less Mary Lou felt that the success he was always talking about was going to happen. He never paid toward the upkeep of the house. It was only Susan who contributed monthly from her church salary.

Mary Lou: *I thought he was contributing to Sue.*

Instead, he was always asking for money. I had trouble saying "no" because we could afford it. The big monies went to him before this last year. I think some of it was the summer right after Paul was born.

At least now Sue had a job and could contribute part of her salary toward their board at home. It was more important to her that she pay their way than to us, although Chris's lack of financial participation to the household was beginning to get to me, too.

And then, partly because of the money, Sue started making noises again about leaving him. Or at least she was thinking about it. I got to know that stare of his. I saw it directed at Sue, mostly when she did something he didn't like. When her friend Emily was here, for instance, and they went out to the Creamery for coffee and a chat, he was absolutely livid.

And when she got home, there was that stare . . .

Shortly after one of Ernie's visits, Susan suggested that they invite the Brendels for dinner. Chris was not receptive to the idea.

"Well, we should reciprocate their invitation."

"No, no," Chris said. "Ernie's going sour on me."

Sue could barely believe it.

He admitted to Sue that he and Ernie weren't really getting along very well and that Ernie was going to pull out.

Susan was surprised as well as disappointed. Everything had seemed to be going so well. She couldn't imagine what could have gone wrong.

Mary Lou was the one who spent the most daytime hours with Chris since they were both often at home during the day. Now she could tell that something was weighing heavily on his mind. She began to notice a very subtle change in Chris around the house. He was always strict with the boys, but now his disciplinary tactics seemed excessive.

Mary Lou: *I think sometimes he went a bit overboard, especially if he was in a mood. If the kids didn't do exactly what he wanted, he'd get upset and they would have to sit in a corner or go to their room, or get deprived of something. If they were working on something, like building with Legos, and they didn't do it in exactly what he thought was the correct way, he would insist they take it apart and start all over again. I did a lot of cross-stitch, and I found it a challenge to take what I may have done wrong and rework the pattern so it looked correct. Not pull the whole thing out and start over again.*

I just assumed that was the way he was, a perfectionist.

But it was more than the demanding temperament of the perfectionist that was at play. Less than six months after Ernie had opened the trading account with Chris, he closed it at a small loss. He later wrote to the CFTC that "Hightower seemed unable to trade client accounts." He further stated that he intended to "keep in touch with Mr. Hightower since we both live in the same small community and I supported his efforts to become a successful commodities trade adviser."

Ernie's letter was kept on file at the commission.

Paul Ryan: *Ernie viewed that investment as a voluntary loss. He gave Chris that money to encourage him to see how it would do . . .*

It didn't, and now Ernie retreated. He took his loss in a gentlemanly manner. It was Chris who became furious that he backed out.

"He's not a believer," Chris raved to Susan behind closed doors. "I'm writing him off!"

It was as though he had been let down by his best friend. Susan could not understand Chris's attachment to Ernie, except that she realized that, somehow, Chris believed Ernie was going to be instrumental in turning the tide of his bad business luck, for that's all that it was: bad luck.

Despite his statement to the CFTC about staying in touch, Ernie virtually disappeared from their lives.

* * *

Today the search will move back north to St. Andrews School in Barrington and along the powerline right-of-way near Gate of Heaven Cemetery on the East Providence-Seekonk border."

—*The Providence Journal-Bulletin,* 11/5/91

1989

Chris pulled out of their daily life. It made living at Jones Circle easier, but that also meant that there would be enough breathing space for Susan not to have to act. Two more years would go by before she would be forced to do something about her marriage.

Chris continued to live in an imaginary world, and Susan continued to go to the Al Anon meetings.

Susan: *It was just what I needed. It got me through so much.*

Chapter 12

High Hopes and a Con

On 11/5/91 searchers dragged a pond in East Providence . . . Nothing . . .

The Spring of 1990

One year later, Ernie was back in the picture again.

* * *

Chris and Susan finally returned the bicycle because Ernie wanted to take Emily out for a bike ride. When they arrived at the white clapboard house on Middle Highway, Alice and Emily weren't around, but Ernie was. In putting the bicycle inside, Sue got to see the interior of the barn.

Christopher Hightower (on the witness stand): *It was in the barn that the Chinese and Hispanic men killed them . . . Right there. In front of me. You just don't kill a child . . .*

It was a worn-out old horse barn. Sue was fascinated by the bizarre things in it, antique bits and pieces of odds and ends, pews from the church next door, a load of toy slot machines, and bags of peat moss lying about.

The police found a jagged, steel point of an arrow imbedded in one of the bags of peat moss.

Chris was excited again. "He's going to give me money to buy computers to start a financial newsletter."

Susan thought it amazing how Chris could talk people into parting with their money. He seemed to want to work with Ernie at all costs, and now Ernie was even talking of converting the old barn into an office where he and Chris could work. Ernie had tried, unsuccessfully, to obtain a variance from the Barrington Town Planning Board to convert the barn into an apartment for his aging mother, when it appeared that she would no longer be able to live by herself. For his own use, as a business rather than an apartment, he might have better luck with the planning board.

Ernie loaned Chris $2000 to buy computer equipment to help him run his trading business more effectively. It wasn't going to be as easy this time, as Ernie had reservations about investing with him again.

Why Chris attached himself to Ernie as though his entire business future depended on him was one of the things Susan never understood.

Susan: *Anybody who wants to deal in commodities is a gambler at heart. They probably both had that streak in them. Chris picked up on that in Ernie.*

Desperate to get back Ernie's business, Chris came up with what he thought was a daring and inventive idea; it didn't matter to him that it was also fraudulent.

He had to do *something!*

Susan was talking about divorce again. Mary Lou was showing signs of impatience that he had not been able to pay back the money he had borrowed, even with all they had! He was getting terribly annoyed with her for pressing him for the money, no matter how infrequently or how gently she went about it. One time when he made the mistake of mentioning he wanted to buy something he needed—*for his business*—*didn't they understand?*—she interrupted with, "Have you given Sue money for shoes for the boys?" Mary Lou was starting to bring these matters up to him on a regular basis. He'd answer, "I know, I know," but it was beginning to bug him.

He was even beginning to see a subtle difference in Clyde, too. Clyde still was always polite and supportive, but less willing now to discuss the possibilities of the success in commodities Chris kept projecting.

"I know it didn't work too well the last time," he told Ernie eagerly, "but I've worked the bugs out of my computer program."

"I'm glad for you, Chris," Ernie answered doubtfully, "but I'm not too anxious to get into commodities again. It's a real gamble."

"Sure! But that's where the real profits are," Chris urged. "And I've got it down now. I've been working on it night and day. "Look," Chris said, showing him the figures on two accounts he had been trading. "This one has netted nearly one hundred percent profit," he boasted.

Ernie looked at Chris's handwritten trade record.

"Here, look at this," Chris urged insistently, knowing that he had taken the bait. "The Spaziano account."

Ernie knew how to read the figures. The record showed $65,567 profit on a $75,000 investment during a four-month period of time. Nearly 100%.

That was impressive indeed.

"You're not buying all that," Ryan asked Ernie a bit incredulously when Ernie told him about it.

"Well, he does seem to have gotten his act together," Ernie responded thoughtfully.

What Ernie did not know was that Chris had falsified the entire account. There was no $65,567 profit on a $75,000 investment. Like the falsified monthly records he had sent to the members of the Dayton, Ohio, Investors Guild, it was all a lie. Chris's plan had been to pretend things were going great in order to get Ernie's interest—and money—again. This time, it was the lie that opened the door to Ernie's gambling instincts.

In looking back, Louis Olt, one of the Ohio investors who lost the most money, regretted that the group did not turn Hightower in when they discovered his treachery.

Louis Olt: *If we had gotten him at that time, he wouldn't have gotten out of the county. If that had happened, perhaps the Brendels would not be dead today.*

Ernie succumbed. He agreed to permit Chris to manage another commodities account for him. On May 24, Ernie reopened his account with Hightower Investments, Inc. At the time he re-invested with Chris, Ernie listed $385,000 in liquid assets. He was willing to set aside $15,000 of his assets for commodities trading. Chris was to receive a twenty percent fee of all earnings. That Ernie could be so thoroughly conned was a testament not only to Chris's powers of persuasion, but to Ernie's own deep-seated wish to strike it rich.

Three people would be brutally murdered over the results of this ill-omened $15,000 account.

In his October 1990 annual filing with the trading commission, Chris listed one client: Ernest Brendel, with assets of $13,947.30. His only other client, unhappy with Hightower's handling of his funds, had taken what was left and had terminated his account with Hightower Investments, Inc.

When Ernie's family heard about the flimflam after the murders, they were surprised that Ernie had been willing to risk the highly volatile commodities market at all.

Nephew Fred Bobb: *He had always been into very, very conservative investments. He always advised me to stay away from commodities. He said, Fred, it's very risky. Stay away. Don't touch one.*

At home, Ernie's name was constantly on Chris's lips again. He couldn't stop talking about him. There was an urgency in his excitement about his friend and all of their business prospects together that bordered close to the edge of fantasy. He had managed to convince Ernie that he had been successful—now he had to produce.
But how?
In the three years since he had received a license Chris had spent only one day actually observing a professional commodities operation. It was held in Braintree, Massachusetts.

Two commodities veterans spent some enlightening time with him—Raymond Dumaine[1] and Scott Weins,[2] both of whom had very strong negative impressions of the man who was ostensibly looking for advice.

Dumaine, a successful veteran broker, had already heard of him; one of Hightower's clients had called him earlier in the year to complain about some of Hightower's investment tactics, even questioning some of his earning records.

Raymond Dumaine: *What Hightower did to this individual was definitely wrong. It's not kosher; it's not right to conduct business in that manner. I think Chris had problems. I think he had them long before this. He lived in an imaginary world . . . trying to set up a one-man operation, which . . . struck me funny.*[3]

Scott Weins: *I thought his ideas were kind of pie-in-the-sky. He didn't have the fundamentals to make money in this business. You need a lot of well-capitalized customers. He didn't have many. Paine-Webber, for example does not allow anyone with a net worth of less than $100,000 to trade commodities.*[4]

Raymond Dumaine: *He had pretty much made up his mind how he was going to operate, and did not seem to want to learn much.*[5]

Chris's imaginary world of high finance, formulas, and brilliant trading was deeply operative despite the fact that those brokers in Braintree, in his opinion, "didn't seem to understand or appreciate" the subtleties of his methods.

---

[1] Currently a commodities broker for R.G. Dickinson in Boston.
[2] Currently a broker for Paine-Webber in Springfield, Massachusetts.
[3] *Providence Journal-Bulletin*, 4/29/92.
[4] Ibid.
[5] Ibid.

With the new Brendel account, it looked as though luck was shining upon him and things might finally go well. All the old persuasive contagious enthusiasm was back. He even borrowed another large sum from his in-laws to pay for his operating expenses.

The next time Chris and Sue went to the Brendels' house for dinner, Sue began to suspect that perhaps Ernie drank a little too much.

Susan: *He drank a lot that night. I think Ernie was basically an honest guy. Chris had a thing for preying on these people. Ernie always seemed like he had something under there that could explode. Alice, on the other hand, wouldn't hurt a fly. She was like one of those ladies of the church.*

The more Sue learned about them, especially about Alice, the more she liked them. She was the daughter of a successful ophthalmologist, and, at one time, had even considered becoming a doctor herself. Her entire life seemed to have abounded with studies, reading, traveling, and music. She was even a fairly accomplished pianist.

This time, at dinner, business took a back burner. Ernie and Alice talked a great deal about their daughter. Ernie always took Emily to her third grade class. They either drove or walked together, depending on the weather. A little overprotective, perhaps, but at so tender an age one couldn't be too careful. She was much too precious, and, fortunately, Ernie's schedule left him plenty of time to start his daughter's day off in the right way.

They also told Chris and Susan about the joyous occasion of Emily's eighth birthday in which they had given a big party for her at the Caratunk Wildlife Refuge in Seekonk, Massachusetts. With a beautiful June day bursting through the trees and lighting the extended nature walks they took with twelve of her school friends, it was a perfect day. They particularly enjoyed the live animal exhibits at the refuge.

*After the family disappeared, the police found no trace of
the painted pet turtle given to Emily by her parents for her
eighth birthday. They did not even find the glass bowl in
which Emily had built a special home for her little pet.*

"Where's Emily now?" Sue asked.

"Upstairs reading in her bedroom," Alice smiled. "Usually
we read together, but tonight, she's on her own."

Then at some point during the dinner they were asked if they
would be emergency contact people for Emily at the YMCA.
They were friendly enough with them to take on the responsibility, Sue thought. That's fine. "Of course," Susan replied. "I'm
in town. So is Chris."

That was 1990. It wasn't renewed for the next school year.

Susan: *Things seemed fine when Alice called me at the church
to find out about buying Christmas trees. She believed in buying
things from youth groups and wanted to know if our church kids
were selling them. That was the only time she ever called me. We
were friendly, not real friends, but I never ran into her anywhere.*

At one point in the summer of 1990, by virtue of the close
friendship between Chris and Ernie, Susan and Chris took Emily
with them on a short vacation trip to her parents' New Hampshire
summer home. Emily got along extremely well with Mitchell
and Paul.

Chapter 13

Decisions—One Last Try

Police came up empty in the continuing search for the Bren-dels.
                                    —The Providence Journal-Bulletin, 11/6/91

Susan was changing and he hated it. Al Anon had warned her about that. By becoming stronger and her own person, she had changed the rules by which they had lived for so long. . . .

"One day at a time . . ."

. . . and that very simple but profound philosophy put into practice was very threatening to a man of Chris's controlling nature.

She had terminated their joint checking account and opened a new one in only her name. She didn't tell him; she was still too frightened to do that. She actually found herself shaking as she made the transfer, but it was her money. She had to keep reminding herself that it was she who had earned it, and he who was spending it. By closing their joint checking account, she forced him to scramble to pay his child support to his first wife. Up to now, Susan had been paying it.

He was furious when he found out what she had done.

Despite all the support and progress, deeply ingrained habits change slowly; she still had to struggle with herself not to let his fury intimidate her into acquiescence to his demands.

Susan: *He's scary when he gets angry. He gets hard. His face freezes up. He becomes very quiet, and his voice gets very calm and level. Measured tones.*

Low but threatening.

I never worried so much when he yelled, but when he gets quiet, that's when he is dangerous. His whole body tenses up. He's had that problem since high school where he clomps his teeth. The more tense he is, the more he does it. He tenses his jaw, his eyes get big. You can almost see him physically restraining himself from doing something violent.

He never hit me though. . . .

Susan was not aware how dangerously close she was to playing with fire by changing the rules, or just how tenuous his self-control had become. The facade he always proffered to her family and to the outside world had thickened to the point of impenetrability even by someone who knew him as well as she did.

But underneath the facade was a desperately struggling man. Everything was falling apart. Only he knew, within the confines of the secrecy he always insisted upon regarding his business, how badly his carefully constructed financial house of cards had begun to collapse around him.

Something had to be done. But what?

He had already overtapped into his in-laws for outrageous sums. If they ever counted the money they had advanced him over the seven years Susan and Chris lived together, the sum would be so high, even he wouldn't have the audacity to ask for more.

Clyde: *Mary Lou and I made the decision together to lend him money. It was at least $46,000. And I certainly would like to have the money back, but we were taken and we can't dwell on it. The money was to help him start the business. We paid monthly rent on the office, electric bills, computer hookups. He rented a sat-*

ellite dish. We paid for that for a year and a half, in addition to the $20,000. I don't want to count, but it's probably up to about $70,000.

While I feel unhappy about it, I can't berate myself. We thought it was right at that time. We had some extra money because of Mary Lou's inheritance, and it was a good time for someone to say, "Hey, let me borrow some of that."

He did on one occasion say to us . . .

"I need some money," Chris said with apparent forthrightness. "Would you like a second mortgage on my mother's house in Florida?"

It was an extraordinary offer.

"Chris, that's not necessary," Clyde answered. "I would feel terrible if I had to foreclose on your mother's house."

"She won't mind a second mortgage," he assured him. "It's only for a little while."

"No," Clyde refused. "If you need the money and you say you're going to pay it back to us, then I'm satisfied."

Clyde: *Many of my friends who are in business find they have to be two different people. They have to act differently. Being in education, I've been able to stay the same person.*

It turned out that Chris was two different people.

Chris knew they trusted him, but he knew he couldn't go to them again for money. Not again. Not yet, anyway. To whom, then, could he turn?

Kathy played in a handbell choir at the White Church. The ten members in the bell choir played once a month during regular services and gave extra performances during the Christmas holidays. Chris knew they met with their director for rehearsals every Tuesday from seven-thirty to nine in a downstairs hall at the church.

Kathy came out of the church building after rehearsal on

January 15, calling a cheerful "Good-night," to her fellow bell ringers, and heading toward the river in the back of the parking lot where she always parked. Kathy huddled into her jacket. A winter breeze was beginning to blow hard off the surface of the river. As she walked toward her car, she saw her brother-in-law coming down the steps from the Education Building where the offices were. It didn't strike her as odd to see him at the church so late in the evening since she knew he was active with Christian Education and his duties sometimes called him in at night.

It never occurred to her that he might have been waiting for her.

When she spotted Chris, she stopped to say hello.

"Do you have a minute?" he asked almost mysteriously after returning her greeting, "because I want to show you something."

"Sure," Kathy responded.

He guided her back inside the Education Building to the office, where he took a seat behind the desk. He nodded for her to take a seat in the chair to his left. He seemed very serious.

"I have something I want you to hear," he said.

"What?"

"And," he went on enigmatically, "would you keep something for me?"

She saw that he was holding a letter he had handwritten on his own stationery.

"I'm going to read you something," he said, "but before I do, I want to know if you've heard about the mob problems I've had this past year."

"The mob? You mean, like the Mafia?"

He nodded solemnly.

"Well, yes, sort of," she said. "My parents told me something about it."

"What did they tell you?"

"Only what you told them."

"Can you remember what?"

She thought for a moment. She hadn't really paid that much attention. They had related to her something about how he told them the mob liked to get involved with small businesses like his just to get them hooked. But she wasn't clear exactly what he was supposed to get hooked on. Kathy had heard about a year or so earlier that everything was going well for Chris, particularly with some new accounts. He was supposed to sign something, but he had gotten tipped off by someone else who was an attorney—she couldn't remember who—that the clients were mob related. Whether they were actual members of the mob or just mob connected was not clear to her. Chris had managed some small accounts for them so they could try him out before letting him manage larger investments for them or something to that effect.

Kathy: *I have a hard time with this now.*

Supposedly, at the last minute I think they had even given him a check. He turned around and said he found out that they were Mafia related and didn't want to have anything to do with them so he gave them back the check.

"Well, the mob people have resurfaced," he said with worry creasing his forehead. "I thought I had gotten rid of them. You want to know how I did that? I got rid of them in the first place by purposely losing their money."

"You lost money for the mob on purpose?" she asked incredulously.

"If they didn't think I could deliver," he explained, "then they'd leave me alone. But now they've resurfaced and are demanding repayment of the money that I lost."

He didn't specify an amount.

"If they don't get their money back," he told her, his eyes now bulging dramatically behind his glasses, "they said they would hurt Sue and the kids."

"Hurt them?"

"Yes," he said miserably.

"Sue . . . ?"

"And the boys."

"Do you believe them?"

"Oh, yes," he assured her. "They're capable of doing anything."

"How much do they want?"

"About $7,000."

"Seven thousand dollars . . ."

"I have the money in my business," he went on, "but I can't get to it because it's all tied up . . . invested . . . and I can't sell it fast enough."

"When do they want it?" she asked slowly.

"They're demanding the money by tomorrow afternoon."

She had no reason to doubt him. Even if his story was bizarre, he was thoroughly convincing. It couldn't be that he just wanted money from her. After all, it wasn't as though he knew about the money she had accumulated in her savings account. And it wasn't that long ago that Mom and Dad had told her that convoluted story about Chris and the Mafia.

But she was deeply worried.

Just the thought of something happening to Sue and the kids was enough to terrify Kathy into complete attention to what he was saying, despite its being a crazy story. The Mafia. This sort of thing didn't happen to people like them. When did the Mafia start hurting wives and children? Didn't they have some kind of unwritten law about that sort of thing? But, she guessed, anything was possible. She had heard that organized crime had made huge inroads into Rhode Island, to the extent that the state had, long ago, been tagged with the nickname, "Rogue's Island." Still, was any of Chris's story possible?

"I'm so nervous about it," Chris continued hurriedly in the face of her worried expression as her mind raced through her limited knowledge of Italians and what she had heard of the Rhode Island Mafia. "I even went out and bought a gun."

"A gun. ."

"Yes, I keep it in my briefcase."

"Oh, Chris . . ."

"Don't worry. The gun is loaded but my briefcase is always locked and never leaves me."

She looked at the attaché poised on the floor leaning against the desk. She knew he never went anywhere without it. Now she found out he was carrying around a loaded 9mm Glock semi-automatic pistol. It was all terribly frightening.

"Are you telling me they'd kill Sue and the kids?"

"I don't know. But I do know they'd come after them. They promised to hurt them. Bad."

He was very specific on that point. He was so completely distraught and beside himself as he related his fears that he thoroughly convinced her.

Now he read her the letter he had written, repeating three or four times, "I'm the only one who has touched this letter. The only one."

In it he had written the events he had just described to her, the names of the Mafia people involved—she had heard of the family—that they had brought money into his business, that when he realized they were Mafia he purposely lost money to discourage their business, and how they now had come back demanding the return of the lost money, or else!

He signed his name to the bottom of the letter in Kathy's presence, turned the letter over to her, and had her witness his signature. Then he placed all ten fingers of his hands on the back of the letter and pressed hard on the stationery so they could prove they were his fingerprints. He sealed the letter in an envelope and addressed it to Ted Gale, a member of the church.

"He works for the state in the organized crime area," he explained.

"I know," Kathy whispered, caught up in the drama.

"Is there some place that you could keep this?" he asked, bringing her further into his plot. "Someplace safe?"

"My safe deposit box."

"Could you keep it there forever?" he urged. "For as long as it needs to be kept secret? Even if it's years?"

"Yes . . . of course . . ." she stammered.

"You are to bring it out only if something happens," he instructed. "Then, and only then, can you reveal what is in this letter."

She nodded. Then she said what he had been maneuvering her to say throughout their entire meeting: "If you need $7,000, I can let you have it. I don't want anything to happen to Sue and the kids."

"Please don't tell Sue or your parents about this," he said.

Kathy: *I volunteered, but now I realize, he set me up.*

Chapter 14

Going Sour

Many Barrington residents, deeply involved in the trau-matic story of the disappearance, refused to give up hope. They were certain the family would be found alive. And while they continued to express optimism, the wide assort-ment of cut flowers and potted chrysanthemums at the Bren-del home gave the appearance of a wake. The assortment grew daily, left at the end of the driveway on the outskirts of the yellow police tape.

Mary Lou wanted her daughter's marriage to stay intact almost at all costs, mostly because of the children, but even she began to lose faith in Chris. There was a growing suspicion of what Chris was all about. A cancer was growing in their relationship.

Mary Lou: *Chris never knew how much money we really had. He was still asking for money right up till the last six months. He juggled credit cards.*

To a degree I resent it. I resent the fact that he cared more for what he was doing than for his family. He wasn't taking care of his family.

I've lost trust in people . . .

In late March 1991, Chris began building a basement room at Jones Circle. It was going to be a gift for Mary Lou, where she could keep all of her crafts paraphernalia. Ever handy with a hammer and nails, he had made an agreement with Mary Lou that they would pay for the wood and any extra tools needed, and he would design and build it. Since he was the one in complete charge, he started off with great enthusiasm, coming home every night at the beginning of the project, changing his clothes, and going to work on it. Then, he ran into a difficulty with angles. Clyde noticed that the times in between Chris's work sessions on the new room became longer and longer.

Eventually, the work would stop altogether.

Clyde: *That's when I began to notice a serious change in Chris around the house.*

In April, the bubble burst.

The banner year Chris had anticipated with Ernie's reinvestment went bust. He had not been able to produce positive results.

On April 1, Brendel terminated his account with Hightower Investments, Inc. It hadn't taken long for the relationship between the two men to deteriorate drastically. The next day, Ernie asked for the bottom line figure on the account he had opened a mere ten months earlier with a $15,000 deposit.

Not only had the commodities account not yielded profits, it had closed with a balance of $3,139. Chris had lost almost eighty percent of his investment. It wasn't a crippling loss, and Ernie managed to control his disappointment, but he was angry at his friend. Ernie refused to accept Chris's excuses for the loss of more than three-quarters of his investment. Not wanting to confront him personally, knowing that they would argue over Chris's illegally going past the fifty percent fail-safe point without client notification, Ernie decided to put the decision he had come to in a letter.

* * *

The first letter he wrote to Chris in April was still fairly amiable under the circumstances. Ernie simply severed the business relationship and said he would take no action as long as Chris made restitution by May 1.

Chris took the reprieve but did not respond to the letter.

Ernie tried to follow up the letter with phone calls, but found he could not get through to Chris.

The longer it took Chris to answer his letter or phone calls, the angrier Ernie became. Ernie was now certain of Chris's chronic ineptitude in the highly competitive field in which he had chosen to operate. He was also beginning to recognize in Chris the growing addiction to the high generated by the gambling aspects of trading in commodities as well as an obsessive desire to make the big killing in the market. That is the kind of gamble one only takes with one's own money, Ernie reasoned to himself, not someone else's funds that have been entrusted to you. Perhaps he, too, had been lured by the prospect of big profits, but Chris hadn't followed the rules. He hadn't told him the money was slipping. He hadn't reported to him when the account had dwindled down to fifty percent of the original investment—the point at which client and investment manager decide *together* in which direction to proceed. He hadn't told him he had continued trading.

Ernie began to doubt the accuracy of the account Chris had shown him earlier in which he claimed he had almost doubled a $75,000 investment in six months.

Ernie personally checked with the people whose handwritten accounts Hightower had shown him. The former clients were quick to tell him the figures Hightower had reported to him were lies. Rather than the huge profits he claimed, Hightower had lost much of their money also, without ever reporting to them, either, that he had reached the fifty percent account loss limit. Ernie realized that the Spaziano account had been falsified specifically for his benefit. He had been conned by a man he had considered a friend.

Ernie was enraged. The entire operation had been a swindle.

May, 1991

Ernie wrote a second letter and this time the tone was considerably less cordial. It was pungent with legalese and serious threats to meet with the U.S. Attorney General to determine whether any criminal violations had occurred. He threatened to take his complaint directly to the Commodities Futures Trading Commission. Ernie's accusations were spelled out in detail. He accused Chris of falsifying the trade record for the Spaziano account in order to convince Brendel to reinvest with him.

". . . I find this information extremely distressing and impossible to comprehend . . . I am unable to discuss this with you since you have apparently disconnected your telephone lines."

He demanded Chris reimburse fifty percent of the initial $15,000 investment, or more specifically, $6,351, plus the $2,000 he had *loaned* him to buy computer equipment. He gave him an additional month, until June 1, to come up with the funds.

Chris could not respond to Ernie's demands. He had no money.

As usual, Chris took his frustrations out on Susan. Behind the closed door of their bedroom, he berated her, yet again, for her inability to understand his business. He was so full of his own angst, he didn't notice that she was eyeing him through calm, narrowed eyes.

Susan: *There's no doubt about it. Ernie felt he had been duped, and he wanted to stick it to Chris.*

Susan was unaware of the fatal drama that was unfolding between the two former friends. All she knew was that Chris was getting worse every day.

Chris was starting to act differently—moody, quiet, withdrawn. Now he spent a great deal of time in the family room sitting in front of the television. He was grouchy all the time. He pressured Susan constantly to get money from her credit card.

He was so manipulative, she thought, but she had learned to change her responses. "Act, not react." It just took a lot of energy. He continued to claim he was on the verge of the big one, the big deal, the big killing. He wouldn't tell her what, but it was always the same thing!

SUSAN'S JOURNAL—June, 1991

Sometimes this relationship is so exhausting and depressing. I've tried hard to take care of my kids, myself and my life and yet still have a decent marriage. Right now it feels like we're doomed to run on parallel tracks, but never meet.

He sits in my office and tries to convince me to give him money. He goes through my purse. My stuff. The sense of violation is just as keen as ever, but now I mask it from him.

I've already told him I can't trust him with money and I guess I don't trust him with my feelings either.

He doesn't trust much of anything I do either.

Its been 10 years we've been together—it seems like forever and none too happily.

By this time, the anonymous phone calls to her office were coming several times a day. She no longer played the game like she used to:

"Hello, is anyone there? . . . Hello? . . . Hello?"

Each time, now, she listened to the silence for only a brief, undisturbed moment, and then hung up.

It was heartbreaking . . .

The Halloween pumpkins left at the Brendel home were beginning to show signs of decay . . . the cut flowers had wilted in the stiffening fall wind . . . some of the simple, little heartfelt notes left by Emily's elementary school classmates as they waited and hoped and prayed, had blown away.

Only the potted chrysanthemums continued to bloom in their brilliant autumnal colors.

July 15, 1991

When Chris continued to ignore him, Ernie's fury exploded. In July, having received absolutely no satisfaction from Chris, Ernie wrote a forty-page arbitration report to the CFTC in Washington. In it, he attempted to arbitrate the case, and by doing so, officially put the complaint on file through his lengthy report.

At one point, Ernie's associate, Paul Ryan, knowing what he was doing, tried to intervene. "Come on, Ernie," he urged. "Is $11,000 worth going to all this trouble? You know what a real hassle these kinds of complaints are."

"It's not the money," Ernie said stubbornly, trying to hide from his longtime friend his humiliation at having been taken. "It's the principle of the thing."

Ryan pointed out that a formal complaint could put Hightower out of business.

"That's the point," Ernie declared. "He is a dishonest man. I'm going to see to it that he never plays anyone else for a sucker again."

The complaint, if upheld, would effectively jeopardize Chris's future in the commodities business. Not having received either restitution or a reply from Chris by June 1, Ernie finally acted and wrote a complaint to the CFTC on July 15.

* * *

On July 29, the CFTC sent a copy of the complaint to Mr. Christopher Jemire Hightower. September 17, 1991 was the deadline set for him to make restitution to Mr. Ernest Brendel. He was officially informed that he could resolve the matter by simply paying the $11,861 sum at issue. Otherwise, he had to answer the charges brought against him by the September 17 deadline or suffer the consequences of losing his license to trade.

The pressure was building.

At home, Chris was enraged by the deadline. "He's trying to ruin me!"

Susan looked at the beet red face, the bulging eyes, the nearly hysterical, terrifying fury as he flailed the letter through the air to punctuate his outburst.

"Who?" Sue asked. "What are you talking about?"

"It's none of your damn business," he threw at her, "and don't ask!"

She pulled back coolly. Always the nasty, condescending attitude regarding her inability to comprehend the complexities of stock trading.

Why even bother anymore, she thought.

". . . the serenity to accept the things I cannot change . . ."

Susan had lost all faith in Chris and had come to admit to herself, "I don't trust him anymore." One thing she had never wanted to admit but could no longer deny to herself was that, far from having fulfilled the too-stupid-to-understand-anything image of herself he had tried to shove down her throat all these years, she had finally come to the conclusion that she actually knew more about most things than he did.

The observable change in Chris started six months before the murders happened. The fruits of his fantasies were closing in on him. His complete financial downfall was imminent. Sliding, slipping, toward the loss of all of his dreams, Ernie could destroy him with his petty formal complaint to the CFTC. Of all who were hounding him, creditors, landlords, in-laws, wife, and ex-wife, Ernie was the biggest threat of all. If he succeeded in putting him in bad with the CFTC, Ernie would cost him his license as a commodities broker. What a rotten thing to do. They were supposed to be friends. He was threatening his very livelihood. It didn't matter that there was, and had never been, any income, only persistent losses, vain attempts to beat the market, and still more losses. Hardly a livelihood.

But in Chris's mind, it was Ernie who was betraying him, rather than the reverse.

That summer Clyde began to sense for the first time the need Chris had to dominate. He needed to be in control all the time. He watched as his son-in-law spent hours and hours working on a computer problem until he got it to do what he wanted.

Clyde: *I didn't really see him as a controlling person in the beginning. I thought that what he did was take a piece of his life, like the business end, and try to become master of that.*

I never saw the abuse. Sue never shared and I never really asked.

Actually, I think I avoided it. I always tried to overlook the unhappiness and look toward things that are going to be better. There was an occasional but not long, outburst in their bedroom when we heard them yelling at each other, but I didn't think that was so unusual even though Mary Lou and I don't yell at each other. In fact Susan was critical of our lives after she had been with Chris for a while, saying, "You didn't teach me to stand up for myself . . . to fight.

I either tried not to know, or I simply didn't know. I was busy with the church.

Chris became odder and odder around the house that summer. The early persistence he demonstrated on the household projects

waned under the burden of the moodiness and depression that
had set in. He never finished either the basement room or the
bookcase and stereo unit he had started to build. He seemed to
have lost interest.

Clyde was not very good at woodworking. Perhaps he could
finish off the last polish-up details, but that was about all. Chris
got started on the projects and then everything just sat . . .

Clyde: *I guess things got in his way, probably from business, but
I really didn't know about that. I wasn't asked for any more
money. He kept things secretive. I always thought it was because
he was tentative about what he was doing and didn't want to
share it until he was successful.*

I was wrong.

But I always wanted to believe the best about him.

Chris sat and brooded for hours for no apparent reason, and
certainly with no explanation either to Susan or to anyone else
in the family.

He did less and less with the boys, less and less in the kitchen,
offered less and less to do yard work. He pulled back from almost
all family interaction. He was so withdrawn by the beginning of the
summer that Paul asked his grandmother, "What's wrong with
Daddy?"

"Why? What do you mean?"

"He won't play with us anymore?" Mitchell corroborated.

The boys noticed Dad was not even going to the office anymore, or if he did leave the house to go to work, he would go to
the office only briefly and then return.

Clyde talked with him a little about that.

"I've gotten the business to a point where I don't have to trade
every day," Chris lied.

Clyde knew one of his goals for his business was to have a formula that he could apply to the stocks and options and the money
market, so that he could trade almost quarterly rather than every
day. But, although he didn't ask, he couldn't help wondering if Chris
was telling him the truth since there was no money coming in. The
money for all of their household expenses still came only from Sue.

* * *

Susan hated Chris's attitude. She felt he was taking advantage of her parents' belief in him and sharing nothing in return. As usual, she concluded ruefully, he always abused those who tried to help him. He was using her mother's car every day since he didn't have the money to buy one of his own. He still paid Mary Lou only for the phone bills that were related to business. Susan never knew where that money came from.

Underneath Chris's withdrawal from the family, he was brooding, unapproachable, deeply angry all the time. Aware that Susan was beginning to pull away from him, his attacks on her become even more piercing and persistent.

He did not notice that she had set her jaw in grim determination.

"Courage to change the things I can . . ."

Once she had started to look at her life and her attitude with the new perceptions instilled in her through her Al Anon meetings, Susan's innate strengths had come forth with a vengeance. She no longer accepted his unjustified tirades against her. While she still found it difficult to fight back openly, hating the confrontational aspects of heated arguments, at least she had learned that she didn't deserve the abuse; she now turned her back on it. She had, at least, progressed to the halfway plateau toward separation by leading a totally separate emotional life from him.

A sense that liberation was close at hand was quietly beginning to excite her solitary moments.

"One day at a time . . ."

At the same time, the CFTC deadline was fast approaching.

Chris's internal desperation regarding the deadline had transmuted to total rage at being treated so poorly and to fury at Ernie for putting him in this position. He accepted no responsibility for Ernie's course of action but blamed Ernie entirely for trying to ruin him. His thoughts were black; they were grossly wrapped around salvaging his business and in planning retribution against the one who threatened it.

Chapter 15

The First Crossbow

Christopher Hightower, in custody at the Adult Correctional Institution since being apprehended driving Ernest Brendel's blood-soaked Toyota, continued to stand mute.

August, 1991

Chris managed to talk Susan into getting away to her parents' summer home in New Hampshire for a one-week family vacation with the children. She didn't want to go but she finally agreed for the sake of the boys.

"We have to figure out how much money we need to have with us," she told him.

"I'll be bringing money," he said. "We'll have enough."

"How much?"

"Enough."

He wouldn't tell her the amount. Knowing his past unreliability where money was concerned, she decided to take some extra cash along without telling him. She had learned how to hide money since the day he began going through her purse.

* * *

She really wasn't looking forward to this time with him, but the boys were anxious to go, and if nothing else, Mitch and Paul needed the vacation.

Susan: *So we went up there but he didn't want to do anything. He just sat there, wouldn't even swim with the kids, so I said, fine, I'll ignore you.*

I got depressed about it. I must have spent three whole days being depressed. This was at the end of things and I was depressed about it and about Mitch and Paul having to live like this.

While in New Hampshire, besides sharing the boys' inability to understand their father's lack of participation with them, Sue and Chris got into fights about money. It was always the same story. They finally decided to take the boys on a local train trip through the beautiful, mountainous landscape of New Hampshire. He told her he would pay for the tickets, but when they got to the train station, he dropped Sue and the boys off at the booth. "I'll go park the car," he said. "You go get the tickets."

"Wait a minute," she protested. "You said you were paying for this."

"Well, I don't have any money," he snapped and drove off leaving her standing, looking after him resentfully.

It was always like that. Such petty things, perhaps—who would pay for this, who would buy that—but a perennial, vicious pattern of his always being along for the ride. She masked her feelings of indignation from the boys, but *That's the end of it,* she pledged to herself. *I'm not spending any more money.* He had lied to her again. He had told her he was bringing some money to pay for the family vacation. Instead, as usual, he was depending solely on her to supply the necessary funds for everything.

Stubbornly, the remainder of their vacation, she only encouraged activities with the boys that didn't cost anything; swimming, hiking, games. It was okay. They had a good time, but she was always seething underneath the cheerful facade she tried to present to the boys these days. She knew only too well how to sweep things under the rug. She had had years of practice.

* * *

Then something happened that Susan could never explain.

It was two o'clock of the Thursday morning of their vacation. Chris was fast asleep. She was lying in bed wide-awake thinking, "I'm miserable . . ." when she heard a voice saying, *"Get out."*

She was instantly alert. She had never had anything like that happen to her before. It was eerie but not frightening. "I could separate from him . . ." she found herself whispering into the darkness of the room. "That would be okay, wouldn't it?"

"No," she clearly heard the voice respond. *"Divorce . . . Get all the way out."*

It was a male voice. She heard it. Clearly. She was sure of it. She had been wide-awake so it was not a dream.

"Get out," it had said. *"Divorce. . . . Get out. Now."*

Now she knew it would happen. She wasn't sure about the timing, but she knew she would get out.

Even so, while wondering whether she had heard the voice of God or whether it was her own subconscious actively prodding her to act through sounds she had created in her own psyche, she was still so trapped by her beliefs in the sanctity of marriage that she had to go through one final assortment of mental exercises before she could bring herself to make the decision she knew she had to make. She even made list upon list to convince herself of the inevitability of her actions:

Reasons to get out:
1. He has given no financial support for over 9 years.
2. He has borrowed large amounts of $ from family—none paid back.
3. He doesn't trust anyone.
4. He will not communicate with me about his business or consult with me about any decisions that should be jointly made.
5. He refuses to make commitments on
   - $ payback
   - income

- when projects will be finished.
6. He will not plan ahead or think to the future.
7. He is harsh with the children.
8. He spends more time with church and youth group than his own family.
9. He is unresponsive to my concerns or needs and is critical of everything I do.
10. He is unsupportive of my job and my educational goals.
11. He makes promises to family he doesn't keep.
12. I am much harder on the children when he is around.

"I'm tired of trying," she thought as she reviewed the list she had made. "I feel angry, disappointed, used, unloved, afraid, trapped, sad, and uncomfortable physically. Other than that, everything is great!"

Still not satisfied, she made out two more handwritten lists.

Negatives effects of a divorce
1. Harmful effect on children if he goes away permanently
2. Outstanding bills @ $9,000 plus legal fees
3. Losing someone to be w/children when I must be out— losing another set of hands
4. Stigma—reaction of others

Positives effects of a divorce
1. Enforced child support
2. Peace of mind
3. Stability for my family
4. Getting back my life
5. A life to *live* not *endure*
6. Less tension around house for the children

And then the last, most important reason of all to a young woman of twenty-nine. "I don't love him anymore."

She decided it was time to listen to the voice.

* * *

> *When it's time to learn the lesson, the teacher comes. It was time. . . .*

Late August

Chris demanded to know the specific grounds she was going to cite for divorce. She would not tell him.

It wasn't only that he was losing Susan or that he was also about to lose his standing as a well-respected citizen, but his financial machinations had finally collapsed in on him.

His first wife was nagging him that he was late again on his child support for their two daughters. She was even threatening to take him to court. Ever since Sue had closed their joint checking account, he had not been able to make regular payments. Chris was also three months behind in his $600 office rent. It wasn't the first time he had been late on the rent. The Slickers had been generously contributing $1,000 per month to Hightower Investments, Inc., but instead of applying it toward the rent, he had applied it toward other business expenses. His last two or three rent checks had bounced. He could no longer ask the Slickers for help.

He sat down and wrote out a check for the rent even though he had no money in his checking account. He had to buy some time. The landlords were beginning to get upset with their tenant. Murphy had pegged him as a real loser.

Trying to dodge Murphy and DeWall was almost impossible; they could see every time he entered or left the building. His office entrance was just to the side of the building where their own office was located. Cajole and con as he might, they didn't want to hear his hard luck stories. They had their own problems trying to keep the building solvent. Everyone had to pull his weight or get out. When the last check he wrote bounced, Murphy threatened to file a bad check complaint and an eviction notice against him. One of their shouting matches over the latest bounced check had become almost physical when Murphy, huge, unmovable, and irate, accidently bumped into him to make a point.

Chris was furious. Murphy's name was going on the mental list that was forming in the back of Chris's mind.

Chris bought a small pistol crossbow from Thompson's Sport Shop on Route 6 across the state line in Seekonk, Massachussets. It wasn't very powerful, but it was perfect for practice sessions.

After the murders, Susan would wonder whether Chris's plans to "eliminate" Ernest Brendel were formulated as early as this since it was documented that he bought the first crossbow long before he had any dealings with the "four strange men" whom he claimed killed the Brendels.

September 1, 1991

Murphy and DeWall were furious over the bounced check. Confrontations with their deadbeat tenant had done nothing in the way of resolving the problem, and now his phone seemed to have been disconnected. In desperation, they called the Barrington police to complain that their tenant had sent them another a bad check.

Sergeant John Lazzaro, from the Barrington police, called Chris at home the next day.

"I didn't know the check was going to bounce," Chris lied. "There has to be a mistake. Of course, I have the funds to cover it."

"Certainly, Mr. Hightower," Lazzaro said sympathetically. "But the check has to be made good within seven days or the complaint will have to stand."

"Seven days?"

"By next Monday."

"Or?"

"Or the charge will have to be filed officially."

"No problem."

September 6, 1991

Ernie and Alice Brendel bought a new double bed mattress at
Apex at the Swansea Mall. The mattress was scheduled to be
delivered to their home on Friday, September 20.

September 9, 1991

Robert Cadley was Ernie's oldest and best friend. On September 9, Ernie told him that he was going to meet Emily's
godfather, Jim Page, for the football game. Jim was arriving
in Barrington from New York City on Saturday, the twenty-first
of September, so that they could attend the annual Yale-Brown
football game together. Ernie and Cadley laughed and chatted
about it. Cadley knew how much sports meant to Ernie. Ernie
had always been one of the better young athletes when they
competed in sports together as teenagers in Madison, New Jersey. He was strong, tough, and a good, fair competitor. If Ernie
had been a little taller, he might have considered going after
sports in a big way, but powerful as he was, at five-six he was
just a little too short for the big time. He remained an avid fan,
however, and he and Jim never missed the Yale-Brown game
if they could help it.

It was a phone call from Jim, left on the Brendel answering
machine on the night of September 20, regarding the game that,
most likely, served to extend Alice's life by one night.

Chris had been spending weeks trying to negotiate with Financial Securities of Florida, the company that leased him his
computer. It cost between $750 and $1500 a month for their stock
market service. Chris was behind in his payments to them. He
had been able to put them off for a while. However, like Murphy
and DeWall, Financial Securities of Florida was no longer responding to his usual charm and glib tongue. They wanted either
their money or their equipment.

Chris's desperation was building.

So was his resolve to take care of everything, permanently.

Susan's best friend, Emily Carroll, came north from Baltimore to visit her. It had been several years since they had seen each other and they had missed one another greatly.

"How's it going?"

Susan shrugged.

"No change?"

"Not much."

Emily wasn't surprised. As one of Susan's closest confidantes over the years, she knew more about Sue's situation than anybody else, and she made no secret of the fact that she had never liked Chris.

She arrived in Barrington on Saturday, September 14, at about 7:00 P.M.

Sue and Emily wanted to talk, privately.

"He'll be home any minute," Sue told her, "and there isn't a safe place to talk in this house with him in it."

"Let's go someplace where we won't be disturbed," Emily suggested.

Emily had a new, shiny, bright red car. At eight-thirty they decided to take a drive around Barrington. They were both dressed very casually, in old sweatpants, so they stopped at the Creamery to talk, and huddled conspiratorially across the table toward each other in one of the booths.

"Do you have the name of a lawyer?" Emily asked.

Susan nodded affirmatively.

"Then do it!"

"I know," Susan murmured. "I have to. It's just so hard."

"Why, for heaven's sake!"

"The kids. My parents. . . . Failure."

"Just remember who failed whom," Emily pointed out angrily. "It wasn't you. I've never known anyone to try as hard as you or make as many excuses for a guy as you did."

Hearing her own thoughts coming back at her out of the mouth of a trusted friend was soothing and terribly important.

She told her about the voice she had heard.

"There you go," Emily said. "Sanction from on high."

They laughed together softly.

When they returned to the house at 11:00 P.M., Chris was seated on a lounge chair waiting. Susan caught his eyes as she and Emily entered the house. She thought he had a look of pure hatred in his eyes. She knew he was livid because they had been out.

She ignored him and he didn't make a move since Emily was with her.

Alone now in the bedroom, she was in bed with the lights off when Chris came storming into the room, whipped back the covers, and said, "What the hell do you think you were doing! You didn't tell me you were going out to talk and stop somewhere!"

He was sure they had gone to a bar to meet someone because of the way they were dressed. "If you're thinking about divorcing me," he said through clenched teeth, "you better think again because you can be eliminated."

"Do you mean you'll kill me?"

He didn't say no.

She jumped out of bed and went into the hallway.

"What are you doing!"

Susan knocked hard on her parents' door. Within moments, both Clyde and Mary Lou were standing at their bedroom door in nightclothes. "You have to hear this," Susan stated flatly. "Chris has just told me that he is going to have me killed."

They couldn't believe it.

Mary Lou took Chris into her bedroom, and closed the door to talk to him privately. Clyde remained in the hall to comfort his distraught daughter. Emily stayed in her room but could hear a fair amount of the frantic discussions taking place.

Not wanting to see Chris again that night, Susan said good-night to her father and spent the remainder of the night in the children's room lying on the floor with her back pressed against their door. She was afraid Chris might try to pick up the boys during the middle of the night and abscond with them.

About forty-five minutes later, Mary Lou was through talking to Chris and the lights went out all over the house.

The door to the boys' room opened as far as it could with Sue lying on the floor in front of it.

"What are you doing!" he demanded.

She didn't answer.

"Let's talk."

"No."

From then on, it was full speed downhill. There was no stopping the slide.

Mary Lou tried to negotiate between them in the living room the next day.

"The only way this could work," Susan announced to Chris, "is if we get divorced and you live close by so you can see the kids."

He turned to Mary Lou, "I think *she* should move out of the house," he said angrily. "Let *her* find out what it's like to live by herself."

Susan: *He actually had the nerve to suggest such a thing. He wanted me to leave and he would stay in my parents' house with the children.*

Emily was around this whole time and I spent the next two

nights in the bedroom with her. She couldn't believe his nerve either.

This was September 1991, about a week and a half before I served him with the papers.

There was a frantic edge to the tension in the house. Crises were surrounding the family on all sides. Clyde's sister in Ohio was terminally ill. Mary Lou had been asked by Clyde's mother to fly out to help take care of her in her last hours.

The unhappy situation between Sue and Chris was very difficult for Mary Lou. Several years earlier, she had tried to save the marriage for the sake for the boys and asked Sue some tough questions about becoming a single parent with two boys to raise. She knew there were problems. There were many times she felt he was nicer to her than to Sue—a better father than husband, but that didn't make the thought of divorce any easier. Now, Mary Lou had to make immediate arrangements to leave for Ohio knowing her daughter's family was breaking up. It was the Saturday of Labor Day weekend as she was preparing to leave for Ohio that Sue told her point-blank, "I am getting a divorce." She had never seen such resolution in her daughter's eyes.

Mary Lou: *Almost in anticipation, Chris had already begun cleaning out. It was like he was throwing all of his past away.*

I was concerned about dealing with the divorce and how he would act.

Sue finally shared with her parents the years of abuse she had endured at her husband's hands. They found what she was telling them almost impossible to believe.

Mary Lou: *Sue and Chris were both good actors around the house. I had no idea the extent of emotional abuse that was going on right here. I could "sense" things were not right. Chris would growl, "Has Sue been talking to you?" and my reply was, "I can sense and see how you both look and react."*

But never could I imagine the extent of what was going on between them.

No one had ever truly believed Susan's complaints. Chris and Sue always presented a near-perfect facade. The day Susan was taken to the police station to speak with the FBI was the first day people actually believed what she told them about him.

Mary Lou could not resist one final plea.

She wrote each a letter from Ohio pleading with them to consider their actions from the eyes of the boys; those boys needed both a mother and a father.

Mary Lou: *I had always felt marriage was sacred and you need to try and save it, especially when children are involved. However, trust in each other was crucial for a marriage and I didn't see it anymore.*

Then, as the years passed and he still wasn't making money, was less and less pleasant around the house, delayed finishing projects, and produced his icy stare more often, I changed my opinion and knew a major change on Chris's part had to happen or a divorce was unavoidable.

I told both of them many times—Sue is my daughter and I will support her whatever her decision.

As their story unfolded while I was in Ohio I had more trouble coming to terms with Chris as a murderer than Clyde, Sue, and Kathy. I never saw the anger and pure iciness of that last week.

September 11, 1991—Divorce

By September 11, the Hightower vs. Hightower divorce papers were in the process of being prepared by Susan's attorney, Mary June Ciresi. They cited:

"irreconcilable differences have caused the irremediable breakdown of the marriage."

Mary Ciresi, knowing that there had been a history of abuse in the relationship, asked point-blank, "Do you want a protective order for yourself and and the children?"

"No," Susan refused. He was still her husband. She couldn't demean him in that way. "Not at this time. Maybe it won't be necessary."

Susan: *The day I decided to file the divorce papers I took off my rings at work and put them in my purse. I felt like I'd been released from prison! The rings never went back on.*

That was the first thing he noticed when I went home that night and he challenged me on it. "Where are your rings? Why aren't you wearing them? What have you been up to? Who have you been with?" He was furious that I wasn't going to buckle under his interrogation.

I just said "I took them off, they're in my purse and they're not going back on. I told you I want a divorce."

Chapter 16

Deadline

The white and orange Coast Guard helicopters roared over-head during the search procedures. The deafening roar was a constant reminder of the potential tragedy that could ultimately lie at the end of the search.

The September 17, 1991 deadline that had been set by the CFTC for Chris to respond to the charges or pay Ernie back the money lost was rapidly approaching. It ominously warned:

"Failure to file a timely answer will result in commence-
ment of a default proceeding and a possible reparation order
against you."

In complete desperation, Chris appealed to his fifty-nine-year-
old mother in Titusville, Florida.

When she received the package from her estranged son, she
realized he was desperate for cash again. Now he was asking her
to sign legal papers that would allow her home to be used as
collateral against any money he might lose in his business. But,
this time, she was wary. She had already lost $12,000 in pension
money when he turned to her for money in one of his projects.
The loss of her pension fund led to a total break in communication between them for the six years that followed—the primary
reason she did not attend his wedding to Susan. This time, she
turned his request over to her lawyer. She was told that she could
lose her house if her son's business deal failed. He was putting
her in the position of potentially losing everything she had. On
the advice of her attorney, she refused to sign.

Chris became enraged at her refusal. Even his own mother
was turning away from him.

Now, drowning and desperately looking for any help he could
get, Chris telephoned the Parker Group Marketing Consultants,
based in Newport. He had seen their advertisement for a seminar
called, "How To Sell In A World That Isn't Buying." Maybe there
was a solution. Maybe there was a quick way to shore up the
deterioration of his finances.

He spoke for twenty minutes with a secretary at the Parker
Group. "I'm down on my business luck," he told her glumly.

The girl seemed sympathetic and willing to help. "The Parker
Group's seminar only costs $100," she informed him. "I'm sure
it can help. What is your business background?" she asked, pencil
poised to take notes.

Chris hung up.

He did not enroll in the Parker Group's seminar to find out how to sell in a world that wasn't buying.

Instead, in the gloomy privacy of his office, trying to keep his presence as unobtrusive as possible to his landlords, he began fantasizing a quick financial coup, composing a note he would hand to a bank teller. The note said the bank building would be blown up if his instructions were not followed. He demanded only small, unidentifiable bills, tens, twenties, fifties. He warned that sounding the alarm would jeopardize the lives of everyone in the bank since all police calls were being monitored by his partners, and that if their scanners picked up a police dispatch, the exploding device already in place would be activated.

He had always laughed to Susan that if things got rough he could always rob a bank. Fantasies aside, it was too dangerous, too out in the open. He had something more practical and more surreptitious in mind.

He never bothered to tear up the hastily written solution to his financial woes.

Monday—September 16

Tension and threats of violence were hanging in the air on Jones Circle like a shroud of dense fog. Chris still did not believe that the growth in Susan's strength and determination had set her mind on an irreversible course. He still believed that if he said the right things and pushed the right buttons, he could make her change her mind. He wasn't aware that she had already set the first steps of the divorce process in motion when he wrote to her in mid-September, promising to seek help and expressing sorrow for all the grief, pain, suffering, and embarrassment he had caused her and her parents.

But it didn't matter anymore. Too little, too late. She had had enough. All Susan had to do was steel herself against her own distress at his obvious pain, and keep her resolve from disintegrating under the pressure of her husband's unfamiliar supplications. Although she was still terrified of him, nothing was going to interfere with her determination to rid herself and her parents of Chris's abusive presence in their lives. Nothing.

He was beginning to realize he might have miscalculated. Susan doubled up the boys in Paul's room and moved Chris's belongings into Mitchell's room. It was the last time she and Chris would share a bedroom together.

Damn! He had never seen Sue so adamant. What had come over her. He had a great many decisions to make, many things to figure out. At least, he had to get the threat of divorce off his back. Where would he go if he had to leave Jones Circle? Where would he live? He knew he could get Sue to change her mind one way or the other. He had always been able to control her in the past. Since she wasn't talking these days, another letter would do. He knew that the best defense was a good offense.

In the second letter to Susan, written just days before the restraining order, he repeatedly characterized her as a "promiscuous flirt" who had turned away from him sexually.

Yes, she had turned away from him sexually. He was right about that much. But it was the same old story. The same old accusations.

Susan did not respond to the letter.

Now, what supplication was left in Chris's attempts to alter his wife's resolve dissolved into the usual exertion of intimidation. His icy stare was a constant when turned in her direction. For the first time, her father saw it in full force, seeing for himself the wordless menace that Sue had spoken of just before Mary Lou left for Ohio, but that Clyde had never actually witnessed before.

But no matter the implied violence in Chris's demeanor, nothing was going to stop Sue this time. Not the sanctity of marriage, not the fear of being alone, not even the fear of physical violence. Nothing. It was all over.

PART IV
Murder

Chapter 17

Violence

Still nothing.

Barrington Police Chief Charles Brule decided to expand the search beyond the town's borders.

Chris was beginning to feel as though he were in an enemy camp even though Clyde, gentleman that he was, continued treating him with respect. Mary Lou, his one potential ally, was gone. Sue ignored him. The children, sensing the family disintegration, were quiet.

On Tuesday, the seventeenth of September, he pleaded one
• more time to, "Think it over, Sue. Think what you're doing to our family." He had been pleading off and on from the time he and Sue had the conversation with her mother about trying to make it work just before she left.

By now, the desperation had peaked to a dangerous level. Chris went from being so angry that he wouldn't speak to Sue to trying to corner her at every turn and crying, "What can I do to make it right?"

"Get a job, get out of debt . . ."

But it was asking the impossible.

She had become so overwrought about their continual lack of funds that she fiercely challenged him for his inability to perform as a provider.

Susan: *I got in his face. He tried to yell and walk away from me but I wouldn't let him leave. I chased him into the dining room and backed him into the French doors.*

"What the fuck do you think you're doing!" he exploded. "Get out of my face!"

"No! I'm staying here until you give me an answer."

"If you don't get away from me, I'll hurt you very badly," he warned.

"Then I'll pick up the phone and call the police," she said, not backing off an inch. "It's that simple."

"You'll never be able to prove a thing! I'll hurt you so bad no one will be able to tell. Nothing will ever show."

What was the point! she thought, surprised at her own daring. It never worked. Once, he had picked up a part-time job at a gas station as an evening attendant. He sat in the booth and collected money for gas. That was the only paying job he had held in ten years, but it hadn't lasted long. He considered it too demeaning for a man with his academic background.

Her parents had just kept quiet about it.

Now he wanted still one more chance.

His plan was a combination of charm, contrition, and supplication.

Tuesday morning, putting the CFTC deadline temporarily on the back burner, he came to her at breakfast time, and initiated a long conversation. No anger. No threats. He was sincerely trying to communicate with her.

"Sue," he said, "I'm really sorry that things are not working well for the marriage." He seemed genuinely remorseful. "I'll do anything you ask me to do to try to reconcile."

The tender, gentle approach was difficult to bear. It was easier to brace herself against his invectives.

"Give me a list of things to do that would make it better."

"Chris . . ." she tried to stop him.

". . . a list of things that would make it work. I'm begging you to reconsider divorcing me."

"There's nothing to list. . . ."

"I know I've been moody," he confessed, "and difficult to live with . . ."

She could hardly believe her ears. These were the understatements of the year.

"But," he said defensively, "it's because of the business."

That again.

"When it doesn't go well, it creates a great deal of stress. Surely you can understand that much."

Yes, she understood. More than he realized.

"Will you think about it today?"

"Yes," she nodded. She would think about it during the day.

"Make out a list," he urged again.

She told him that she wouldn't give him an answer until later that day.

It could be better, he promised. It *would* be better.

But she didn't believe him. In her heart all that was left was the legal paperwork.

Chris was eternally confident where Sue was concerned. He made out a list of his own that afternoon, scribbling quickly in his left-handed, loopy scrawl:

Buy a romantic card.
Buy one rose in a vase.
Go to Sue's office at the church to deliver peace offering.
Write her a poem.
Talk to her.

He *had* to persuade her with his charm and loving sweetness to reconsider.

* * *

The next time she saw him that day, was early afternoon.

He appeared at her office at the White Church all dressed up instead of in his usual jeans. He was carrying a rose in a vase and a card. He placed them in the center of her desk.

"You know I want to try and work this out," he said.

She knew it was a gift to encourage her to think favorably of him. In his need, he could not sense that she was unreceptive to his pleas. She took his peace offering and, the moment he left, threw it into the trash.

3:00 P.M.—Repossession

After leaving Sue's office at the church, Chris returned to his own on Maple Ave. He was supposed to answer the CFTC deadline by today, but he hadn't. With the deadline come and gone, his registration as a commodities trading advisor was now seriously jeopardized.

He was sure he had the way to handle it.

Chris perked a pot of coffee grounds into a pleasantly aromatic brew. He usually kept the outside door open, allowing a breeze to filter through the suite where he kept his three computers and the printer that spewed out the results of his maneuvers.

Chris Karmes from Financial Securities of Florida appeared at the Hightower Investments, Inc., offices to repossess his computer equipment. Although Chris had been trying to negotiate with the leasing company for several months to forestall repossession, it was to no avail. When Karmes appeared at the office, Chris told him, "I'm giving up the equipment because my wife is suing for a divorce and I don't want any additional bills."

Looking at his mild-mannered external appearance, one would never have known the internal turmoil racking him as the computers went out the door. Chris even calmly helped Karmes pack up and carry the equipment from his office to the waiting vehicle outside.

Susan Slicker and Christopher Hightower, summer of 1989.
(courtesy of Susan Hightower)

Susan and Chris on
their wedding day,
July 10, 1982.
...urtesy of Susan Hightower)

The Slicker/Hightower residence.   (*courtesy of Susan Hightower*)

Barrington Congregational Church where Chris taught Sunday School and where Susan worked. The church was organized in 1717 when the town of Barrington was incorporated and this building, with its bright blue front doors, has been standing since 1806. (*courtesy of Susan Hightower*)

BRENDEL, Ernest & Alice
Emily

The Brendel family: Ernest and Alice and their daughter Emily, all victims of Chris Hightower. (*Providence Journal-Bulletin*)

At the scene where the Brendel family bodies were found. From the left: Det. Sgt. John Lazzaro; Attorney General James O'Neil; Rhode Island State Police Captain Brian Andrews; Thomas Connell, Public Information Officer for the Attorney General's Office.
(*Barrington Times*)

Media and observers at the crime scene.
(*both: Providence Journal-Bulletin*)

The Brendel home. (*Providence Journal-Bulletin*)

Side of Brendel House just after the crime. (*Barrington Times*)

Prayers and flowers—especially for eight-year-old Emily—covered the driveway of the Brendel home after their disappearance.
(*Barrington Times*)

Chris Hightower, after his arrest, escorted by
Det. Sgt. John Lazzaro. (*Barrington Times*)

Chris Hightower's lawyer,
Robert George.
(*Barrington Times*)

Det. Sgt. Michael Quinn holds the Devastator crossbow seized from
the trunk of the car Chris Hightower was driving when he was
arrested. (*Kathy Borchers/Providence Journal-Bulletin*)

On the witness stand, Dr. Richard J. Evans, Rhode Island's chief medical examiner, holds one of the bullet-tipped arrows that he said killed Ernest Brendel. *(Frieda Squires/Providence Journal-Bulletin)*

Asst. Atty. Gen. Michael Stone reads a statement given to police by Chris Hightower after he was taken into custody. *(Kathy Borchers/Providence Journal-Bulletin)*

Susan Hightower identifies a piece of blue fabric she and her mother used for sewing. On the stand, she stated: "I felt intimidated by him. He stared at me in the way he often did . . . He wanted to make sure I was put in my place." *(Kathy Borchers/Providence Journal-Bulletin)*

Rhode Island state prosecutors Patrick Youngs (left) and Michael Stone. *(Providence Journal-Bulletin)*

Rhode Island Attorney General James E. O'Neil.
(*Providence Journal-Bulletin*)

Christopher Hightower on the stand.
(*Richard Benjamin/Providence Journal-Bulletin*)

* * *

Chris stared up at the small hole that had been wrenched in the ceiling by pulling out the cable connected to the small roof satellite dish. A thin beam of sunshine glared at him through the hole. What would the big Irishman and his partner think when they saw the hole in the ceiling, he mused.

His link to the outside financial world was officially terminated. The repossessed computer had provided him with quotes and information on stocks, bonds, and commodities. Now, without it, there was no more up-to-the-second data. He thought of the voluminous details that guided the commodities and futures markets around the world—a poor wheat crop in Kansas, a bumper coffee crop in Brazil, a devastating hurricane in the Caribbean. So much electronic technology—information—data—feeding directly to him on his computer screens.

Now the screens were black. Silenced. All the colorful, worldwide reports locked high overhead in geosynchronous orbit and unavailable to Hightower Investments, Inc. Anyone could collect information. It took experience, interpretive skill, and know-how to translate the data into sound investments. Anyone could make a mistake! But he did not analyze that aspect. All he knew was that equipment could be replaced. A license to trade, once revoked, however, was another matter.

He was not going to allow that feeling of failure to close in again. He had the solution all worked out. Sometimes a man has to take drastic action. He was doing it for his family—to protect them against someone who was trying to deprive him of the ability to earn a living for them.

He looked around his emasculated office. All that was left was the cardboard bulletin board tacked with printouts and pages of row upon row of now-useless figures. Prominently displayed in the center of the board were photos of Mitch and Paul. He had a momentary sense of panic that he might lose them, too, to Susan and the Slickers. His jaw ground out his anxieties.

Not this time, he wouldn't! One way or another, he was going to take care of everything. He had found his identity as an upright citizen in Barrington. He wasn't about to let himself lose it. Susan would come around. He had the other thing worked out, too. It was time to take Paul to soccer practice. As the team's coach, he knew he was well liked and respected by child and parent alike.

He went home to get Paul and to get Susan's response.

5:00 P.M.

After dropping off his peace offering, Susan did not see him again on that Tuesday until she came home from work at approximately a quarter to five that evening.

He was eating an early dinner with Paul because of the scheduled soccer practice.

"Will you be home Thursday night?" he asked.

"Yes."

" 'Cause I'll be out late and I'm not sure when I'll be home," he explained.

She nodded.

"I don't want to get into it," he said to her, "but I just want to ask you one question."

She knew what was coming. She tensed up.

"Have you thought about it?"

"Yes."

"And what's your answer?"

"I thought about it," she said carefully, "and no, I don't think it can work anymore."

His face became beet red. He was furious. He did not eat any more of his dinner. He barely spoke to her as she moved silently about the kitchen they had to share. She could feel his eyes burning in her back as she stood at the counter.

The tension between his parents had silenced Paul's chatter about soccer practice. Susan's heart went out to the child. This constant tension was terrible for the child. This was not the atmosphere in which she wanted her children raised. It was not a healthy environment.

When Paul finished his dinner, Chris brusquely gathered him

up and they went off to soccer practice in the Jeep Cherokee in which he kept the extra equipment. It was between five and five-fifteen.

When they had gone, Susan sat down heavily at the kitchen table. She wouldn't be able to eat dinner. She had a knot in her stomach. This was not the way to live. She was doing the right thing. She had her solution.

Chapter 18

Total Collapse

6:30 P.M.

The atmosphere at home had become charged with tension. All of the elements of Chris's business and personal world had crumbled, one by one, like a line of dominoes. Although there was a sense of sadness for his losses, Susan was more worried about the growing invectives and the enlarging sphere of his threats.

He returned after soccer practice.

Once the children had been put to bed, the two of them sat in the easy chairs in the family room, not speaking, with only the sound from the television breaking into the thick, painful silence. She was acutely aware they were alone.

Susan and Chris were not accustomed to being all alone in the big house. Clyde was not home. She knew that after he finished teaching his class he was going to play his usual Tuesday tennis game. Mary Lou was in Ohio with her dying sister-in-law. It had been a long time since they had to face each other alone. She dreaded the prospect of the evening with him and fervently wished that her father would hurry home.

It was obvious that Chris was very agitated. He was clomping his teeth harshly and could hardly sit still on the chair. At about nine-fifteen, he got up and went to the bar. He threw a heavy handful of ice cubes into a glass and filled it with scotch. She watched as he downed the drink almost in a single gulp. In rapid succession, he fixed himself two more scotches with ice and proceeded to drink them just as quickly as the first one.

It was very unusual. He did not ordinarily drink. A glass of wine with dinner, an occasional scotch on a Saturday evening, just to relax, but not like this.

At nine-thirty, he decided it was time to talk to his wife.

Fortified with the three scotches, he had pulled himself together. The icy calm he now projected filled her with more dread than his agitation.

"What do you know about guns?"

"I can tell the difference between a pistol and a shotgun," she said quietly after a long beat, "but that's about it."

He did not offer to explain why he was asking about guns and she did not ask.

"What do you now about handguns?"

"Not much," she answered, humoring him, and deliberately not going beyond the scope of his question. "I don't know the difference between them or what kinds the policemen carry or anything. I just know the difference between a small one and a big one."

She thought about the guns in the house. She knew that he owned two rifles and a shotgun that were in the basement and that he had put the .22 in the top of one of the bedroom closets. The .22. How she hated it! He had recently bought it for Mitchell for Christmas. Chris said he wanted Mitch to know the safety of it. She thought it was an inappropriate gift for a seven-year-old.

Why was he talking about guns!

"Do you have a will?" he asked.

"No," she murmured. That was one of those things they always argued about. "I've been pushing you to get a will and you refused."

"I refused?"

"You haven't been interested in doing it so, no, I don't have one."

"Do you know how much a human life is worth?"

"No."

"Let me tell you," he said. "It's worth $5,000. That's the cost of a—that's the worth of a human life and that's what I have paid to have someone kill you if you try to take my children away."

She didn't move a muscle. She didn't know what a man with three scotches in him could do to her, painfully aware again that except for the two sleeping children upstairs, they were the only ones at home.

"And," he went on piercing her with his icy stare, "I paid an extra thousand dollars so it would look like an accident." He was deadly calm. That was always more terrifying that the yelling. The only outward signs of stress was that he was still clicking his jaw very rapidly. "I would never—I would never touch you myself," he said. "It will be somebody else out there so that no one could ever prove a thing."

She just stared at him.

"It may not be tomorrow or next week or next month, but just remember, each time you step off a curb or go out, it may be your last time."

She didn't dare say a word in response to his threat.

She almost liked it better when he threw the personal and profane invectives at her. . . . "You fucking whore!" he would hiss. "You bitch!" That was less frightening than what he was saying to her now in that surreal, hard-as-ice tone.

"I'm going to take care of my business my way," he said. "I've also paid money to have your parents and your sister killed if I get possession—If I get possession of the children and they try to fight me for it, they're dead."

He then repeated the entire conversation, full of threats, at least three or four times, to make sure it sank in, repeating to the silent woman that he would have her killed and that he had paid to have her parents and her sister killed as well.

At the end of his pronouncement, he took the glass from which he had been drinking and threw it violently across the room. It smashed against the fireplace, sending splintered glass all over.

They heard Clyde's car pull up in the driveway. Thank God!

"Go ahead," he said. "Tell your parents, tell your sister, tell your lawyer, tell anybody you want to what I've said. You could never prove it because you have no tape recorder and you have no evidence that I threatened your life. Who'd believe you! All there is, is me and you in the room and you could never, ever prove that I told you I'll have you killed." He looked her straight in the eye. "But I will."

Then he turned, picked up his shoes, and said, "I don't know about you, but I'm going to sleep very well tonight. You don't ever have to worry about me coming after you. I won't, but I'm gonna sleep well tonight."

With that, he went upstairs before Clyde entered the family room through the garage.

He vomited in the tub upstairs and then dutifully went to his room.

When Clyde came in, he could tell by Sue's face that something was dreadfully wrong. "What is it? What happened?"

Susan relayed to him what Chris had said to her. How Chris was dead calm when he spoke to her. How he looked her straight in the eye, deliberately trying to intimidate her, with absolutely no inflection in his voice, and told her exactly what he would do to her, what he would do to his first wife, what he would have done to Clyde and Mary Lou and Kathy, and how he intended to take care of his business his way, all in that flat, very calm, very controlled voice. Susan took him seriously even though she knew he did not have money to bankroll such threats. She knew only that he had proved to be infinitely resourceful where money was concerned. He was not joking.

Clyde didn't know what to think. He believed his daughter.

There was no reason for her to make up something like that. But it was unthinkable.

"Did you believe him?"

"Yes."

"That he was going to have you killed for a price?"

"Yes."

"Are you afraid of him?"

"I'm in fear for my life, Dad," she said solemnly. "For all of us."

They agreed quietly that Sue would have to go see her attorney again.

"In the morning."

"First thing."

"It can't be avoided any longer."

"No."

They both knew what she had to do. She still had not filed the divorce papers, and that omission was making her anxious. She needed to get those papers officially put on file.

Carefully, together, father and daughter picked up the largest pieces of broken glass by hand. It was almost as though the glittering shards represented what was left of a shattered marriage that had started with so much promise and hope almost ten years earlier. Sue pulled out the vacuum cleaner to gather the smaller pieces, worried that the children might sit on the floor during one of their games together and cut themselves on the tiny pieces still clinging to the rug.

"Go to bed now," her father urged. "You look tired."

There was much to do in the morning.

She nodded and went upstairs. The bathroom reeked of vomit. She cleaned out the tub before going into her bedroom.

Deeply troubled, the professor went up to his own room. He earnestly wished Mary Lou was home. He would have liked to talk to her about all this. He didn't like any of it, but he believed the pending divorce was now inevitable and entirely appropriate and necessary. Chris's outward behavior had shifted into a total aloofness and coldness toward Sue during the last year. He rarely acknowledged her comings, goings, or presence in any positive manner. He never appeared to smile when she came in from work, never got up to hug, kiss, or greet her at the door, never praised her for any activity or job she did well, nor thanked her for something she had done for him.

Over the years, Clyde, too, had become painfully aware that Chris contributed nothing financially to the marriage. Sue was forced to use all her salary for her family's operating expenses. Chris always appeared to want to reinvest his few earned business monies back into his company and would not even take out a few hundred dollars regularly each month as a salary to meet the family's needs. Sue was carrying the entire financial burden while Chris indicated that he was entitled to be along for the ride. Chris talked a fabulous financial story but that was all it was.

Talk . . . and now these terrible threats.

There was a knock on the door. Clyde opened it to find his son-in-law standing in the hallway looking a bit queasy, his hair disheveled. "I have to pick Paul up tomorrow morning from kindergarten," he said.

"Yes, Chris?"

"Well," he said through slightly slurred speech, "I may have had too much to drink. I was wondering. Could you wake me up in case I don't get up in time?"

"Certainly. . . ."

Maybe it had been the alcohol talking.

Wednesday—September 18

Wednesday was a relatively calm day. Susan was supposed to go to court but Mary Ciresi had to postpone until the next day.

Thursday—September 19

Susan: *On the morning of my birthday, the nineteenth, I woke up and went to court to meet Mary. I knew the restraining order and divorce papers would be served the next day.*
   Best birthday present I ever had.
   Freedom.

The next morning, with gray clouds ominously hanging overhead, with Chris's recent threat still vividly in mind, Susan left home at eight-thirty with an unswervable purpose in mind. Turning the Jeep Cherokee onto Nayatt Road and then left on Rumstick at a pretty rapid clip, it looked as though she was heading to work. Instead, she drove past the White Church and went directly to meet Mary Ciresi at the family court building. It was time to file the affidavit. In it, she recounted her husband's threats of the night before.
   "I think I have to put them on record," she told her attorney.
   "Yes, you should."
   "That restraining order you mentioned the last time?"
   "Yes."
   "I think I'd better get it now."
   Mary Ciresi nodded in agreement.

Susan's statement was taken down and recorded:

   "The Defendant informed me that he would be taking my minor children and that he has paid the sum of Five Thousand ($5,000.00) Dollars to have me killed and to make sure that it looks like an accident and that he would be sure to have an alibi.
   Defendant further advised me that if my parents attempt to take my minor children, he would have them killed also as he has a sufficient amount of money hidden away to accomplish this act.

I am in fear for my life and the safety of myself, my children and my family."

It took most of the morning. By the time she returned to the Jeep Cherokee, the family court judge had:

1) Allowed the filing of a complaint for divorce

2) Ordered a constable to serve a domestic abuse complaint against Christopher Hightower

3) Approved a motion for temporary allowances to Mrs. Hightower

4) Given Mrs. Hightower exclusive custody of the children

5) Approved a restraining order to remove Christopher Hightower from the premises on Jones Circle.

Instead of returning directly to work, Susan went to a friend's house for lunch.

Eviction

By one-thirty, the September sun had broken through the threatening morning clouds and was high in the sky, spreading warmth. Back at his office, Chris answered the door. He was surprised to find a deputy sheriff standing on the threshold.

"Are you Christopher Hightower?"

"Yes, I am."

The deputy sheriff handed him some papers.

"What is it?"

It was the notice of eviction for his business office on Maple Avenue for nonpayment of three months rent totaling $1,800. Chris set his jaw and accepted it, politely thanking the sheriff.

"I'll pack my things," he said.

"You have seven days."

"Thank you," he said and closed the door with a smile.

Inside, he was seething.

After lunch, Susan was feeling pretty good, until she arrived at the White Church.

When she parked her car, Chris followed her into the church parking lot and demanded to know where she had been. It wasn't until Kathy arrived to interrupt the bitter domestic dispute with a three-rose birthday gift for her sister that Chris left. Once the Caprice station wagon pulled out of the parking lot, Susan finally broke into tears. The weight of fear had been surging ever since he put a price tag on his threats.

Chris went to Thompson's Sport Shop to price another crossbow.

Thompson's was housed in nearby Seekonk, Massachusetts, in a rusty-colored brick building with an Early American cupola on top. The weathervane at the high center of the cupola was beginning to turn steadily in the heightening fall wind as though a forecast of stormy events.

Thompson's was a huge store, stocking everything a serious hunter could possibly need. In the rear of the store Chris found what he was looking for. Slung on pegs overhead was an assortment of vicious-looking crossbows, recalling the weaponry used in the days prior to the advent of gunpowder.

Bill McGovern, the salesman who had served him the last time, offered a pleasant greeting.

"The crossbow you sold me last time didn't have enough power to bring down the crows I'm after," Chris lied. "And there's one raccoon that keeps getting away. I need something a little more powerful."

Not a rifle or a shotgun. He had those kinds of weapons. It was the silence of the crossbow that appealed to him. He didn't

want to disturb the neighbors. Besides, at the range he was planning to fire, accuracy was a given.

The salesman suggested the Bear Devastator, a weapon powerful enough to bring down a full-grown bear.

Printed across the top of the large carton was the word "DEV-
ASTATOR" in big, bold, black letters. Fully assembled and colored a dull camouflage shade, it appeared to be the awesome
weapon it was.

It took great power just to cock it. To demonstrate, McGovern,
a well-built man of six feet, had to put a foot in the steel stirrup.
It took a full twenty seconds, and a great deal of muscle power
to pull back the twenty-six-strand steel drawstring until it finally
clicked loudly into place. Cold metal, a full yard long, a solid
pistol grip, a folding rear sight with high-power accuracy. Fully
cocked, the tension of the crossbow was 150 pounds of pressure.

This was the sort of power he had in mind, but he couldn't
buy it yet. His over-the-limit credit cards would never have been
approved for such a purchase—over $300—and he didn't have
his latest checkbook with him. But there was no doubt about it.
This was definitely the one. He would be back.

Clyde: *My guess, now, is that he knew what he had to do, to get
rid of Ernie. He was trying to find a way that he could do that
and looking for a place that he might bury, at least one body.*
　　Ernie seemed to be his main focus of attention.

A Burial Spot

By now, the plan was formulated. There was no doubt in his
mind what he had to do.

He didn't have to hide his activities too carefully. Once buried,
once in the ground, no one would ever know. No one would ever
find out. He would be in the clear.

It was after everyone had fallen asleep and the house was
perfectly still that he went out into the night to go looking on
foot.

* * *

The Barrington policeman who spotted him walking along a desolate stretch of the East Bay Bike Path, put in a call to headquarters at exactly 1:10 A.M. to check on the man's driver's license. The ID checked out. It was a valid Rhode Island license. There were no outstanding warrants on Christopher J. Hightower.

A little late to be out.

Couldn't sleep. Just walking. Live nearby.

He seemed innocent enough. There had been a series of break-ins in the general area recently, but this fellow was obviously a local resident who seemed to have the kind of mental preoccupation that a nocturnal stroll might be able to clear up. He looked okay.

Officer Bill Dorney thought nothing more of the incident and drove off, leaving the man walking north on the Bike Path.

The moment his patrol car disappeared toward Maple Avenue, Chris turned west onto Middle Highway.

He was alone again, isolated in darkness surrounded by dense thickets. Once he hit Middle Highway, he turned north. He knew the Brendel house was several miles up the road on the left. Slowly, he kept walking in their direction as though magnetized toward the spot.

On his right, about half a mile before coming to the Brendels', just before he came to Winsor Drive on his right, he stopped and looked down the lonely stretch of road. Winsor Road, a quiet semiresidential street, no more than half a mile long, connected Middle Highway and County Road.

Slowly, he retraced his steps until he was standing adjacent to a wooded section of property between Federal Road and Winsor Drive. It belonged to St. Andrew's School, the kind of exclusive private prep school that he could not afford for his sons. The thought of financial deprivation immediately conjured up feelings of resentment. It would be a touch of irony to do it here. He looked about carefully, as his eyes were well accustomed now to the dark. Cutting sideways into a narrow opening in the brush, he started in. It was dark and densely wooded. Less than a hundred yards into the isolated, heavily brambled stretch, he saw a slight opening in the tangled thickets to this left. He cut into the opening, stumbling through the tall weeds and thick brush. From where he now stood in the isolated area, it was impossible to see back to either Middle Highway or Winsor Drive. Beyond the spot was a huge rolling meadow that was owned, but rarely used, by St. Andrew's.

There was a small opening beyond a patch of briars. He moved into it and stamped his foot carefully around the ground. Perfect.

He marked it so that he would be able to find the exact spot again, and retraced his steps back to Middle Highway. He looked up the long stretch of road ribboning away from him to his right. Ernie Brendel's house was only a half mile up the road.

He had found the right spot.

The divorce papers were completed. All that remained was to file them. Just before Sue was to return from work, remembering her abnormal confrontational attitude that morning, Chris left the house and went to his office. No sooner did he get there than the telephone rang.

"Joe Mazza here."

Damn! The guy from the National Futures Association. Not only was he pestering him about the missed September seventeenth deadline but now he wanted to come to the office in the morning with an associate.

"With who?"

Tim Wigand, an NFA supervisor.

"What for?"

They wanted to audit his books. He made up an excuse and put them off.

They just wouldn't leave him alone! All of them!

The clocks hadn't been turned back yet. There was still some daylight left at 6:00 P.M. But the darkness of rain shrouded the approaching evening. It was still pouring when he headed for the Caprice parked at the rear of his office.

It was between six and six-thirty when Chris marched into the house, dashed past the family seated over dinner at the kitchen table, and ran upstairs. Clyde and Susan looked at each other. They didn't want to say anything in front of the children.

Moments later Chris came down. He had his checkbook in hand. "I have something I have to get," he announced over his shoulder as he dashed out again. They could hear the engine of the Caprice start up. They listened to the car leave.

By now it was raining very heavily. Chris drove directly to Thompson's Sports Shop. There were no funds in his checking account, but that didn't matter. The salesman didn't know and would trust him enough to accept a check. When he'd bought the small crossbow, his check had not bounced. There was no reason to suspect his credit was no longer good.

Chris purchased the Bear Devastator crossbow he had held earlier. He could still feel the cold steel against his cheek when he had looked through the sight and envisioned his victim.

He asked for six bolts (arrows), selected the points he wanted, wrote out a check for a combined total of $314.98, and left with his deadly solution in his hand.

He made no attempt to conceal his identity while making the purchase.

Returning home briefly, he left the box that held the Devastator crossbow in the car. He changed into old jeans and sneakers, threw on a heavy flannel shirt, and grabbed his drab, nearly threadbare, green army fatigue jacket.

As he left the house again, he turned to Susan, who was sitting on the couch reading to Paul, "I might be home late tonight. I'm not sure what time I'll be back. Probably not until morning. So don't count on me coming back."

He had not said why he was going to be out that night and they did not ask. It was Susan's thirtieth birthday.

As he left through the garage again, he stopped long enough

to grab Clyde's shovel. His toolbox with the short steel pry bar, small enough to fit into his back pocket, was at his office.

Susan: *The day the computer equipment was to be repossessed, Chris had asked me to drive his toolbox to his office—it was too heavy to carry. I didn't want to see him—he was waiting for my answer, but I dropped it off on my way to work that morning anyway. I was aware he wanted the tools to remove the satellite dish on the roof and disconnect the cables.*

He took off on foot. He would make his way via the bicycle path. Under the heavy blanket of rain, he was sure no one would spot him.

For Sue, his absence was a relief, but frustrating. He could not be served with the papers if he was not at home. It would have to wait until the morning.

Sue and Clyde worked out a strategy to call the police the minute Chris appeared so that they could serve him.

"Call me at work," Sue said to her father, "the minute he comes in."

"Yes," Clyde said unhappily. He knew it had to be done. "But I don't want to call the police." Serving the papers would not be pleasant. Bad enough he would be present when they came to evict his son-in-law.

"I'll do it," Sue said.

They both knew the police would have to be warned that Chris might become unpredictable at the moment he was handed the order.

Early that evening, heading north on I-95, Ernie Brendel left for a financial seminar in Dedham, Massachussets. It started at 7:00 P.M.

Alice and Emily remained at home. They spent a quiet evening together. A new colored picture was hung on the refrigerator door. Dishes were washed and stacked away. Another story was read. Several telephone calls were made to and from Aunt Christine in Connecticut. An animated discussion first about why Emily couldn't have her ears pierced, then about the Viking ships she would see the next day as she and her third grade class went on a class trip to Newport.

It would be the last quiet evening mother and child would ever spend together.

Throughout the evening, in their own nearby garage, a malevolent presence was waiting for Ernie to come home.

"I met with Ernie that Thursday night. The nineteenth. And I was working with him in the garage all that Thursday night."
Christopher Hightower lied to the Rhode Island State Police when apprehended.

10:30 to 11:00 P.M.

Ernie returned from the seminar.
Chris saw the red Toyota Camry pulling into the driveway. He tensed up, crossbow ready. He would shoot the minute he drove into the garage and got out of the car. Chris pressed back into the shadows and strained every muscle in his shoulders to load the steel-tipped arrow into its lethal firing position in the crossbow.
He had figured Ernie would come into the garage to park the car, but it was raining heavily. Instead, Ernie stopped the car by the front porch and ran directly into the house.
Damn.

He waited until the house had become dark for the night.
Stealthily, black steel pry bar in hand, he made his way to the back door. He failed to note the irony of the little plate attached just above the door that read:

"PEACE BE UNTO ALL WHO ENTER HERE"

Carefully, quietly, sticking the clawed tip under the doorjamb, he pried open the door. His forced entry set off an automatic alarm which dialed an old number at a former security alarm company. It kept dialing all night until it burned itself out. Its audible alarm in the house was muffled. Chris heard the muffled alarm and became frightened of discovery. He retreated back to the garage.

If the alarm contract had not been canceled, the night might have had a different conclusion.

Instead of waiting in the garage, wondering whether someone would respond to the alarm, Chris decided to go to the secluded, thickly brambled area he had found earlier behind St. Andrew's School. He found the markers he had left. It was still pouring, but now the rain was an advantage; the earth was softened, easier to handle. He began to dig.

Susan: *I remember sitting on the couch in the living room with two friends the night of my birthday, thinking he's out there in the pouring rain. He'll be out all night. What the hell is he doing?*
And I swear, I remember thinking, "He's out digging graves."

Chapter 19

Point of No Return

When Chris returned to the Brendels' garage, dirtied, muddied, soaked through and through, there was no sign that the alarm had brought anyone to the rescue. He decided to wait until morning when he would confront Ernie alone.

Earlier, he had broken into the huge, barnlike garage through a poorly secured narrow window. He knew this place. It was here that Ernie had promised to set up an office to go into a business partnership together. Broken promises. They were going to start an investment newsletter. Complaints to the CFTC instead.

As his eyes became accustomed to the darkness in the garage, he saw that he was standing next to the three empty, dank-smelling horse stalls, remnants of another era. He could make out all the slot machines Ernie had stored row upon row after one of his deals fell through. The old church pews were still there. So were the stacked shipment of wine they had bought together from a restaurant in Boston that had gone out of business. The black sporty Audi, shining even in the dark, was parked to the side, leaving room for the Toyota. The bicycles were propped up against the far wall. The bicycle he had borrowed from Ernie last year might come in handy.

He shuddered. He could hear the rain pummeling the roof as he tried to doze in a corner of one of the old horse stalls. Wet and chilled to the bone, warmed only by thoughts of murder, he remained in the Brendel garage overnight to wait for the Brendels to begin their last day.

Friday—September 20

It was the beginning of a normal day in the Brendel home. Alice was the first one up, the start of a comfortable set routine. Unless bad weather prevented, Alice always began the day with her morning jog. The rain had finally stopped. As the sun was just beginning to edge out the night, she sat on the side of her single bed in the upstairs bedroom she shared with Ernie, and laced up her running shoes.

Stepping out into the morning, unaware that she was being watched, she jogged through the hushed neighborhood, enjoying the brisk morning air, the silence, the rusty, damp autumn leaves trumpeting glistening colors everywhere she looked as she jogged by.

Back home again, breathing heavier than when she had started out, Alice picked up the morning *Providence Journal-Bulletin* that had been tossed into a corner of the porch. By the time she showered, Ernie was up and Emily had been nudged out of bed and was already dressing herself for the exciting day ahead.

As they drank their coffee, Alice and Ernie discussed the upcoming day. With a light kiss good-bye, she left for work.

It was about a six-minute walk to the corner of County Road where Alice waited for the express bus to Providence. She didn't mind riding the bus to work. It was a short run into downtown and she could scan the morning newspapers or the latest book.

While Alice waited at the little wooden-structured bus stop, Emily was scrambling into the Toyota with her father. The sporty black Audi, Ernie's pride and joy, was in need of repairs, so he usually used the Toyota. Emily was particularly anxious to get to school on time today. The school was only a short distance from home, but Ernie drove Emily every morning. Without sidewalks, Ernie and Alice felt it was a dangerous road for an eight-year-old to walk.

7:55 A.M.

As the bus to Providence pulled up next to Alice, she realized she had forgotten her money. She did not even have the necessary eighty-five-cent bus fare with her. How could she have done that? With a sigh, she watched the bus pull away, with a spurt of black smoke escaping its exhaust as it sped down County Road toward Willet Avenue.

She would be late to her job unless Ernie had gotten back from the school and could drive her to work.

8:00 A.M.—*Primrose Hill School*

Chatting all the way about Vikings, Ernie and Emily arrived at the school in record time. Primrose Hill was a pleasant redbrick building, built low to the ground, with a flagpole in the center courtyard, a playground on the right, and another one in the back.

A quick kiss good-bye, the last ever to be shared by father and daughter, and Emily scampered off to join her third grade class. It had already assembled, waiting for the bus that would transport them to Newport. Her classmates were sitting in an excited group waiting. Teachers milled about; giggles and whispers predominated. Someone took a commemorative photo. It would make the front page. As Emily and her classmates boarded the bus, Alice was on her way back home.

Ernie pulled the Toyota into his driveway.

His murderer was waiting in the garage. Chris had pulled a black ninja mask over his head. Better to keep himself unknown to the victim. He could not do it face-to-face, or chance a look of pleading or of contempt.

A ninja mask with Christopher Hightower's saliva on the inside was introduced at the trial.

Chris was hoping Ernie would drive into the garage. Better to do it there than in the house. But Ernie decided to leave the car outside again. He bounded up the wide porch steps and entered the house to have his second cup of coffee while he mentally itemized all the details of the day's agenda.

Chris waited in tense frustration. He realized Ernie was not coming out to the garage again. He was just about to make his move toward the house, lethal weapon in hand, when he spotted Alice returning. That wasn't right. What was she doing back home? He pulled back into the darkness of the garage and watched as she entered the front door.

Moments passed. Ernie and Alice exited and got into the Toyota. Ernie drove his wife to Providence to get her to the university on time.

Once there, a quick good-bye kiss, neither realizing the finality of it, as he dropped her off in front of the Rockefeller Library. He headed the Toyota back home.

It was the last time anyone saw Ernest Brendel alive except for his murderer.[1]

---

[1]Only one person knows exactly what happened next. The killer. The murders have been recreated through police reports, trial transcripts, and interviews.

This time when he arrived home, Ernie drove the Toyota into the garage. A man with a black ninja mask concealing his identity was waiting for him.

Let him get out of the car first, Chris thought. *Don't give him a chance to recognize danger and attempt to use the car to crash out of the garage.*

The moment Ernie turned off the ignition and stepped out of the car, his fate was sealed. Standing between the Toyota and the Audi, Ernie looked up to see a man in a black ninja mask holding a loaded crossbow pointed in his direction.

Startled, not fully comprehending the insanity of the moment, there was little time even for a "Who are you!" when the first arrow was released at point-blank range. Ernie shouted in shock and searing pain.

The force of it! It was so powerful, it could devastate a bear.

The arrow went right through the front side of Ernie's huge barrel-shaped chest, tore through flesh, and exited through his back. It crashed into the garage wall behind him with a heavy, dull thud.

There was an arrow lodged in the wall by the window. When the police dislodged it, it had blood on the arrow tip.

Stunned, not comprehending the reason, Ernie nevertheless realized he was going to die. His unknown assailant was loading the crossbow again, pulling back the drawstring and inserting another arrow. Ernie turned and tried to escape the lethal weapon aimed again in his direction.

The trigger was released. This time the arrow hit Ernie in the buttock. He fell face forward, the weight of his own body propelling him to the ground with a crashing thud. When he fell, the car keys still clutched in his hand made a huge scratch on the black paint of the Audi. His jaw hit the ground first, breaking and loosening his teeth. The floor was beginning to be covered with blood.

Seething with pain and panic, feeling his strength diminishing as blood gushed from his wounds, Ernie pulled himself up, grasping the handle of the Audi's door on the passenger side, and tore the door open.

The man with the crossbow had reloaded and was now standing between the two cars facing him. Hanging on to the side of the car, Ernie faced him long enough to take the last arrow in the chest, dead center. It went through his aorta and stuck in his backbone.

The deadly arrowhead remained lodged in Brendel's chest. During the autopsy, the tip of what was the fatal arrow could be felt just below the surface of the skin on his back.

The arrow was sticking out of his chest and he *still* would not go down!

The killer was, not only caught up in the bloodlust of the kill, but he was enraged. Incredibly, Ernie somehow managed to climb into the front seat of the Audi. Chris took out the claw-tipped crowbar he had in his pocket and went after him with the round part. At close range, bleeding profusely, weakening by the second, Ernie nevertheless fought back with every ounce of strength he had left in his body. There was a violent scuffle during which Chris was severely bruised in the shins. Despite his valiant attempts to fight off his assailant, fighting with everything he had left, Ernie was no match for a crowbar. As the crowbar kept crashing into his head, he tried to get away. With one last monumental effort, he wrenched himself forward and climbed between the seats to get to the back of the Audi. The man in the hood went over the seats with him. The rearview mirror got kicked and was left bent at an awkward angle.

In the backseat the arrow broke off in the dying man's ribs. He was finally stilled. There were several brutal wounds and lacerations to Ernie's face and head, further testimony to the rage released by the murderer in the assault.

Chris raised his head to listen. No one in the neighborhood heard anything unusual. Except for a sharp "ping" when released, the crossbow was a silent killer.

* * *

The man who used to be Christopher Jemire Hightower—doctoral candidate, family man, Sunday school teacher, churchgoer, and upstanding citizen—now pulled off the ninja mask. He looked at the dead man, his former friend turned nemesis and tormentor. Ernest Brendel never really knew what hit him or why or by whom. Wearing the ninja mask was not only cowardly, but it kept his victim from knowing why he was being killed, one of the things Chris, in his madness, would have liked him to know. He did not get that satisfaction, but at least Brendel was dead and he would not be able to go through with his complaint to the CFTC.

He could now put a stop to that.

With one dead body already on his hands, in the mind of the murderer, the rest of the murderous scenario was inevitable. The point of no return had been reached and crossed over.

He went into the house to get a blanket to put over the windows of the garage so nobody could look inside to see what he had done. Then he went home to clean up.

10:00 A.M.

A constable went to the Barrington Police Department requesting an escort to help serve the restraining order on Mr. Christopher J. Hightower at the Slickers' Jones Circle home. Mrs. Hightower had warned of her husband's potential volatility at being removed from his home.

10:15 A.M.

Chris got home around 10:15 A.M. looking as though he had spent the night in the woods. He came in through the garage, and dropped the shovel in the right-hand corner of the garage just before entering the family room. It was caked with mud, but Clyde was around. He would have to clean it later.

Chris was bruised, dirty, his glasses askew and bent, with mud in his hair and on his clothing. Clyde thought he looked as though he had been playing rugby in the mud. He saw him at the kitchen counter trying to straighten out his glasses. He seemed uptight, agitated, as though he had been betrayed.

Clyde was astonished when he saw him take off his clothes in the middle of the family room and put them in the washing machine. He had never done that before.

Chris went upstairs to take a shower.

Clyde immediately called his daughter. "Sue, he's back."

"Okay," she said. "I'll take care of it."

The moment she hung up, she dialed the police to inform them her husband was at home and could now be served with the restraining order.

By the time Chris got out of the shower, the constable, with a three-man police escort, was waiting for him.

"Mr. Christopher J. Hightower?"

"Yes."

The papers were placed in his hands. "You are being asked to leave. We are here to escort you off the premises."

Chris looked at Clyde.

Clyde had never before seen such a look of hatred in a man's eyes. He knew that in Chris's mind, he, too, had become another father figure who had let him down. Just like all the rest.

Hightower packed a few articles of clothing in a brown paper bag and left without incident and without looking back at his father-in-law.

He was dead calm. He hadn't finished. There was a body waiting to be buried.

Chris could not take the Slicker car he always used. He walked away from the house. He would never return.

He had to get back to the Brendel house quickly. Emily was coming home and Ernie was still in the garage. He walked to Maple Avenue and dropped off the few meager possessions he had taken with him in his office, then headed again for the Brendels'. He came to the end of Maple Avenue, which dead-ends into Middle Highway.

He stopped at the home of John and Suzanne Hoder, friends from the church. Suzanne had always liked Christopher Hightower. He was a real gentleman.

"Suzanne, I wonder if I could ask a favor," he said. "My car broke down and I need a ride to a client down Middle Highway. I wonder if you could give me a lift."

"Sure."

Chris had her drop him off at the St. James Church, next door to the Brendels' house.

Susan: *The large empty crossbow box was in our car Friday morning when he was kicked out of the house, so he kept the crossbow somewhere else. It was either at his office on Maple or at the Brendels.*

Early that afternoon, an unidentified man telephoned the Commodities Futures Trading Commission to say Ernest Brendel wanted to withdraw the complaint he had filed against Christopher Hightower in connection with an $11,861 investment loss.

"I'm sorry, sir," the woman answering the phone told the caller. "A request like that would have to be made in writing."

"Certainly. No problem."

* * *

But first, Emily. Chris knew that she would be arriving home from school.

1:45 P.M.

A man identifying himself as Ernest Brendel phoned Emily's school saying she should walk home from school after the field trip to Newport. That was a change from her family's earlier written instructions which indicated she was to go to the YMCA's afterschool program every day.

3:05 P.M.—Trying to Kidnap Emily

At a little after three, Emily returned from the field trip with the rest of her class. The principal, Elizabeth Durfee, called the Brendels' home to confirm the telephone request that Emily walk home. She waited a reasonable number of rings. When no one answered the phone at the Brendel home, she decided that Emily should go to the YMCA as originally scheduled.

Chris walked to the Primrose Hill Elementary School and said he had come to take Emily home, but Principal Durfee refused. Although Christopher Hightower had been listed as an alternate person to pick Emily up on last year's forms, he was not listed this year.

"I have to stick by the rules," Mrs. Durfee said.

"Of course, I understand," Mr. Hightower said pleasantly.

"Besides, Emily has already left for the YMCA."

Acknowledging with a smile, Chris left.

He had to get her.

* * *

3:45 P.M.—Minutes Later

Chris went to the YMCA. It was only about two miles from Primrose. He parked the Toyota in the parking lot and headed for the administration office.

Once inside, in his best manner, he told Pam Poirier, the program director, he was there to pick up Emily Brendel. Once again the request was denied. It was against the rules to release a child to someone other than a parent unless prior arrangements had been made. In the year Emily had been with the Y, no such arrangements had ever been approved.

Once again, he said he understood. But he was not to be put off. A few minutes later, a man identifying himself as Ernest Brendel telephoned the YMCA. "Mr. Hightower has my permission to pick up my daughter, Emily," the man said. "Thank you for being so cautious. I'll give Mr. Hightower my driver's license as proof."

4:00 to 4:15 P.M.—Success

Hightower drove back to the YMCA in the Brendels' red Toyota Camry, carrying Brendel's license and keys. This time, Emily was released to his care.

Emily went with Mr. Hightower willingly, chatting brightly about the Viking ships she had seen on the field trip.

It was the last time the perky little eight-year-old was seen alive.

5:00 to 5:30 P.M.—Gone

That evening, when Susan returned home from work, Clyde was waiting for her at the door.

It had been done. He was gone. Chris was finally gone.

Sue knew the restraining order that had been served was only a piece of paper and Chris could just as easily ignore it as not, but at least he was out of the house.

The most important thing she had to do was speak with the children about this turn of events. Mitch and Paul listened quietly as she explained to them, how both mom and dad still loved them, but had decided to live apart.

Susan: *One of the first things I did when he was thrown out of the house was open up all the curtains and windows and air out the rooms—especially the bedrooms.*

Then, I removed the rest of his things from the bedroom, including some of his furniture, and rearranged the room so it was mine, not ours. Also any pictures with him came down from the walls. I didn't throw them away, just put them away.

He was out of the family gallery.

5:00 P.M.—Apex Delivery

At the same time Susan was rearranging her bed, an Apex truck pulled up in front of the Brendel home to deliver the double mattress Ernest and Alice Brendel had purchased on September 6.

"They're not here," the lightly bearded man told him.

"I could just leave it somewhere until they get home."

"No."

A man, later identified as Hightower, answered the door and refused the delivery. That pinpointed him at the house on that day at that hour.

Early That Evening

The phone in the Brendel home rang. Chris did not answer it, letting the answering machine take the call and listening to the message as the male voice came into the room.

It presented a problem. Somehow, the man on the other end of the line had to be discouraged from contacting Ernie further. James Page left a message asking Ernie to pick him up at the New Haven railroad station the next day, before the Yale-Brown football game.

That would have to be taken care of.

6:00 P.M.—Now Alice

Returning home from work, Alice waited patiently at the bus stop, but Ernie and Emily were not there as usual. It was only a six-minute walk home. She decided not to wait; something must have kept Ernie.

A neighbor saw Alice Brendel walking home. It was the last time she was seen alive.

At approximately the same time Alice was walking home, Susan was dialing the telephone at Jones Circle.

She was afraid Chris might decide to show up at the scheduled soccer game the next morning. He was the coach of Paul's team, and she knew him well enough to know he would try to test the restraining order. If he did show up at the little playing field in Haines Park, she was afraid, not only that he might cause a scene in front of all the parents, but that he might approach her as well and threaten her again.

She decided to call two other coaches who usually worked with the team. She hated to air her private problems with people she hardly knew. "You see," she began, "Chris and I are . . . we've separated." Better to warn them and ask for their help than take a chance of running into him. "I have a restraining order and Chris is not supposed to be at the game tomorrow."

They both expressed surprise. "You might want to tell him if he shows up," she suggested, "that he's not supposed to be there."

It was a difficult thing to ask them to do; they were friendly with Chris, but they both seemed willing to cooperate with her if that was what she wanted.

The new taste of freedom was heady, but now that the restraining order was in effect, she realized that she was even more frightened of him than before. She knew that he would be livid and vengeful at the legal action she had taken. She also couldn't help remembering Al Anon's warnings about how danger from an abusive husband often escalated at the very moment of a final breakup, when all control over the abused spouse was in jeopardy of being lost.

Susan: *Chris called our house at 8:00 P.M. on September 20. He asked my father for the extra keys to his office and for the address and phone number of his daughters.*

Chris instructed me where to look. The keys weren't there and the address in my phone book was an old one. I knew where to find their current address, but something told me that giving it to him would put them in jeopardy also. His first wife had filed a complaint for nonpayment of child support.

After Chris hung up, I called the police to report the phone call. I wanted every interaction documented in case I needed it in court someday. Chris was as dangerous as they come and I knew I'd need all the hard evidence I could create to keep him away from me.

That Night

Jim Page was not answering his phone. Alice would have to be kept alive until morning to ward him off.

Ernie was still in the Audi. Since it did not run, when the time came he would have to transport them all in the Toyota. It wasn't far, only a half mile away, but he had to be careful. There was no sense in getting caught now. Chris moved Ernie's heavy deadweight from the backseat of the Audi to the backseat of the Toyota, placing him facedown on the backseat. Loosened teeth from the dead man's broken jaw fell out of his mouth and remained on the backseat.

It was no good. He was too big. Too easy to see.

He moved the body again, this time stuffing it in the trunk. He was soaked with blood and still leaving heavy stains of blood wherever he lay.

He couldn't do much about it now. He had the others to take care of.

Since none of the Brendels was killed in the Toyota, the blood in the car would indicate that they were moved to the location of their shallow graves in the car.

Overnight

Hightower remained overnight at the Brendels' home with Alice and Emily.

During intense interrogation, he insisted to the police that he had been invited to stay at "his friend, Ernie's" house that Friday night because they knew he had been ordered to leave his own and he had no place else to go.

Saturday, September 21—7:30 A.M.

Alice Brendel called James Page in New York at approximately seven-thirty the next morning. She told him Ernie would not be able to attend the Brown-Yale football game in New Haven that day because he had to see to his mother, who had suddenly become seriously ill.

Other than the fact she did not seem to want to chat, Alice seemed perfectly all right to Jim. He did not suspect it was a lie.

We don't know if he kept them tied up in the basement. We can assume he kept Emily and Alice alive, and obviously Alice cooperated with him with the phone call the next morning. But there was no evidence he kept them tied up in the basement. There were some signs later that that might

*have happened, but I believe he kept them somewhere in
the house. There weren't any marks on the bodies.*
                              Anonymous Barrington police officer

Sometime during the morning of Saturday the twenty-first of
September, after Alice had been forced to make the phone call
to Jim Page, the murderer drugged her and Emily. The autopsy
report would show that Emily had a nonlethal amount of sleeping
pills in her, just enough to keep her sound asleep for a long time.
Alice had ingested a lethal dose. To make sure he could leave
the house with no worry of her possibly waking up, Chris took
a piece of cloth, knotted it about the unconscious woman's slen-
der neck, and pulled it tighter and tighter until he had strangled
the breath out of her lungs and she died in his hands.

Then he left to go to his son's soccer game at Haines park.
This time he used Ernie Brendel's bicycle.

10:30 A.M.

Susan's friend Diane agreed to go with her to Paul's soccer
game. Following the plan they had created the night before, they
drove to Haines Park in separate cars.

When Susan and Diane pulled into the parking lot to bring
Paul to the game, they saw Chris standing to the side. He had on
clothes she had never seen before. They looked new. Being at
the soccer game was a violation of the court's restraining order.
Not even twenty-four hours and already, Chris was breaking it.
His presence terrified her. To her, he seemed stiff and dangerously angry as he watched the play. Diane calmed Susan's rising
hysteria.

Paul did not see his father's figure across the park.

"Stay here," Diane whispered to Susan. "I'll go call the police.
Keep the doors locked."

The Jeep was almost smothered by large bushes and trees in the secluded area where Sue had parked. Still, she was scared to death that Chris would see her and come over. But he did not notice the familiar car. He was too busy telling the other parents at the game that he and his wife were getting divorced and that he didn't think he would be able to coach the team much longer. He told a convincing tale of woe and they were sympathetic to him.

When the police received Diane's call that Hightower was at the park in violation of a court restraining order, they responded quickly, showing up no more than fifteen minutes later. Chris remained on the field until the police told him he had to leave because his wife wanted to be there with their son, Paul.

His eyes narrowed and scanned the area. He caught sight of the Jeep parked across the park almost hidden in a corner of the parking lot. Susan watched from her distance as he got on the bicycle that was parked along the fence. With the police standing by, he left without incident. She recognized the bicycle as belonging to Ernest Brendel.

Susan: *Saturday, after the soccer game, I had to go to the police station to drop off proof of the serial number of the missing sawed-off shotgun.*

Going in, I ran into his landlord, Dennis Murphy, who triumphantly informed me that the eviction of Chris was not going to take place. He had paid his rent in full.

I was dumbstruck. Where could he have gotten the money?

Now he had a place to stay in town. Much too close for my peace of mind.

Later That Day

Chris searched the Brendel house for money, credit cards and Brendel's business stationery. He had to compose a very important letter to the CFTC.

Taking Ernie's Toyota again, Chris drove to Sears in the Swansea Mall, where he bought clothes for himself using Ernie's credit card and forging Brendel's signature. He drove to the Somerville

Lumber store off Route 6 in Seekonk, Massachusetts, and purchased a fifty-pound bag of lime, muriatic acid, a scrub brush, and a fifty-foot length of garden hose. This time he paid cash.

Susan knew this evidence was circumstantial, but, to her, the purchases only served to solidify her first instinctive feelings about his involvement in the murders.

The jury would one day also wonder why he bought these items. Since he had been removed from his own home, what need did he have of such things at the Brendels' home—except to clean up after the murders.

The Brendels' garage was splattered with Ernie's blood. Chris spent the remainder of the day cleaning up and insanely making bizarre plans for a large ransom. He had to come up with a good story for those rich people in Guilford, Connecticut.

It is believed he buried them on Saturday night. There is a big gap on Saturday night as to where he was. Some of the key things he said was that he made a phone call about the alleged kidnapping, but he told the Scriabines he got the first phone call on Saturday night and would get another call on Sunday night. And they told him to go to the garage and find the car to find evidence, and that's all we had until trial time.

All his stories had big holes in them.
                                        Anonymous Barrington police officer

He never bothered to check whether Emily was dead or alive when he tossed her into the shallow grave. Some believe that the child was buried alive. Her mother was thrown into the grave on top of the child. Then the hasty cover-up, ripping the lime bag open, spreading half the bag of lime. Then the burial of Ernie, large enough to need a separate grave, spreading the other half of the bag of lime and another hasty cover-up.

It was done. He had prevailed.

* * *

That night, Chris slept at his office. He felt no remorse for what he had done, only resentment at what he felt had been done to him.

Ernie represented something that had plagued him all his life—the sense of betrayal from one whom he had trusted and from whom he had expected unequivocal support. Ernie represented a profound acknowledgment of the failure that kept following Chris everywhere he went.

He looked about the empty office with bitterness. Even the murders had not assuaged his anger. He would make them all pay, and he would walk away from this part of his life with enough money to start all over again. At least $75,000, he thought. He sat down at his desk and worked on the rest of his list and on the next part of his plan.

He wished he could have seen his boys once more. But he was already beginning to feel they were lost to him—that they had become a part of Susan and the Slicker crowd.

He sat back in his chair and looked at the evening sky gleaming brightly down at him through the small hole in his ceiling.

Christopher Jemire Hightower had finally made his big killing.

Chapter 20

The Search

Sunday, September 22—A Patrolman at the Parish Door
10:00 A.M.

As usual, on a Sunday morning, Susan, the boys, and her father attended the services at the Barrington Congregational Church.

Rev. Joseph T. Dye knew the home situation between Chris and Susan. Fearing that Chris might appear at the church during morning worship, he asked that a patrolman be stationed outside the sanctuary. Through conversations with Susan, he had become aware of much of the abuse she had suffered and felt very protective of Susan, her family, and the entire church congregation.

Sitting pensively in the pew, depressed over the turn of events for her sons as well as for herself, Susan prayed quietly for continued guidance. She was not aware that Chris had driven Ernie's car to church that morning and was waiting outside.

When Chris saw the patrol car pull up to the curb, his teeth began to click angrily. His thoughts were full of rancor. After all the years he had been a dedicated parishioner and a Sunday school teacher at the church, now he could not even go inside.

He pulled away with a light screech of wheels, passed the patrol car, and continued on to a nearby gas station. He had to fill up for the trip to Connecticut.

He was seen at the station by Dick Brandon, a fellow parishioner, and Armando, the man who ran the Shell station. After gassing up, Chris went to the Newport Creamery to get something to eat and to wait.

2:40 P.M.—The Letter

He waited until the Sunday morning church services were over. All the parishioners had departed and the administration offices were empty. Chris drove the Brendel Toyota back to the church to use the church's photocopy machine. He still had a key. He needed to forge a letter to the CFTC from Ernest Brendel withdrawing his complaint against Christopher J. Hightower, with a copy to Mr. Hightower at Hightower Investments, Inc.

He had Ernie's stationary. Cut and paste. Copy. Make it look authentic. He was pretty good at this sort of paste-up, retouching job. He had to smile to himself as he remembered the last time he had used this technique. Ten years earlier in Ohio. He hadn't been found out then, and he wouldn't be found out this time either.

Later That Afternoon—Where's Emily?

A neighborhood child, a friend of Emily Brendel, went to the Brendel home at approximately four o'clock to ask if Emily could come out to play. The lightly bearded man with glasses who answered the door said simply, "No," and the youngster left.

5:30 P.M.—Kidnappers

It was at this point that Christopher Hightower, the consummate con artist in his own mind, took over. He arrived at the Guilford, Connecticut, home of Ernie's sister and brother-in-law, Christine and Alexander Scriabine. He told them he had an urgent matter he wanted to discuss with them.

Something in the back of Christine's mind told her it was

strange that he was driving her brother's Toyota Camry. She recognized the license plate number. Still, since she had dinner guests, she ignored it and asked Chris to come back later.

He obligingly left.

When he visited the Scriabines . . . "He had rope and the gun in the briefcase, but we don't know what he intended to do with them.

The police fought hard to get that gun into evidence, but no one was shot with it. But we could get the briefcase in, the Scriabines saw the briefcase, but not the contents inside."
State Police Sgt. Doug Badger[1]

8:00 P.M.

He returned to the Scriabines at 8:00 P.M.

Alone with Ernie's sister and her husband, Chris began to weave for them the carelessly constructed story he thought was so clever. The tale of kidnapping and ransom was so convoluted, it immediately aroused the suspicions of Christine and Alexander. He told them that his own wife, two sons, and the Brendels had all been kidnapped, and that the kidnappers were demanding $300,000 in ransom. If the Scriabines could come up with $75,000, he could pay the rest himself. He made a deliberate point of showing them bloodstains in the backseat of the car to indicate the severity of the situation. It was a serious mistake. This time his scam was not well thought out. Alex and Christine were too sophisticated to be taken in by such an obvious tall story.

---

[1]Author's Note: When I asked the state policeman, "Is there any truth that when Hightower went to the Scriabines he intended to kidnap them and search their house for money?" all he would answer was that that scenario had been one of the unproven speculations.

The usual ease of Chris's con artistry was not working at all. He was so accustomed to the success of his cons, he had become careless in assuring the believability of the details of his story. For years he had been able to put it over on Susan and the Slickers, who loved him, and had always wanted to believe in him and give him every benefit of whatever doubts they might have had.

But the Scriabines had no such inclinations. They simply did not believe him. When Chris left their home, after almost five hours of storytelling, he was as empty-handed as when he had arrived, and the Scriabines were worried, suspicious, and about to blow the whistle.

Monday—September 23—Flimflam
1:45 A.M.

After Hightower departed the long night slipped into the early hours of Monday morning, and Christine and Alexander were still discussing the unbelievable situation.

By approximately 1:50 A.M., convinced that the wild story was a lie, and equally certain that it had been concocted in order to flimflam them out of $75,000, they decided to contact their local authorities, who, in turn, contacted the FBI at approximately 2:30 A.M.

After he left Connecticut, Chris returned to Barrington and spent the rest of the night in his Maple Avenue office. The red Toyota Camry was spotted there early Monday morning.

Monday—September 23

When the murderer awoke, he forgot about the appointment he had made with Kathy's friend, David Carriere, to whom he had grandiosely promised a job. He left the office to run the list of errands he had set for himself earlier. He went to the bank to cash the check he had forged with Ernie's signature, leaving just enough to keep the account open. He then went to the post office to take care of what he considered his most pressing problem. He mailed the letter written on Brendel's legal stationery to the Commodities Futures Trading Commission that withdrew his complaint against Hightower.

By the time David Carriere got to Chris's office to talk about the promised employment, the police had already been there looking for Chris.

Chapter 21

Another Nightmare Begins

Monday—September 23—An Unexpected Turn
9:00 A.M.

While Chris was running errands to accomplish his plan, Susan arrived for work. She learned from Pastor Dye that her husband had been at the church the day before to use the church's copier. He had already defied the court's restraining order by showing up at their son's soccer game. Frightened that he was still so close, she called the police.

Susan did not know the police had received word from the FBI about her husband's activities during the night and about his highly suspicious visit to the Scriabines.

9:30 A.M.—Alice Does Not Arrive at Work

At the Rockefeller Library, Steven Thompson became concerned when Alice Brendel was an hour and a half late for work.

Her unusual tardiness, without so much as a telephone call, prompted him to call her home. There was no answer.

10:20 A.M.

Almost another hour passed with no word before Thompson called Alice Brendel's home again. This time, an answering machine responded. He thought that was strange. He couldn't help wondering who had turned on the machine in the fifty-minute interval since he had last called. It could have been Ernest, but for some reason he now began to feel uneasy.

10:30 A.M.

Ten minutes later, Thompson decided to call Primrose Hill Elementary School to see if Emily had gone to school. She had not. That too, was strange. Alice hadn't come to work and Emily hadn't gone to school.

The school officials began to wonder why a stranger had called to inquire into Emily's attendance.

Susan had arrived at the police station and was questioned for approximately six hours. Without being told, she knew Chris was involved in some illegal scheme. *If this helps them to put him behind bars for whatever reason,* she thought, *I'll do whatever it takes.*

Echoes from the Past: "You Got Nothing on Me."
1:50 P.M.

Christopher Hightower, still driving the Brendels' bloodied Camry, was stopped by police on County Road (Route 114) near the Barrington Shopping Center. The first thing he said to them was, "You got nothing on me!" He still had the Brendels' credit cards in his possession.

Inside the car, they made a grisly discovery. There was a great deal of blood, four human teeth, a crossbow, a kitchen knife, and an empty fifty-pound bag of lime. There were indications that there had been at least one body in the trunk of the car, as well. There were scratch marks in the trunk and what appeared to be a small bloody handprint on the inside hood of the trunk.

Hightower was taken into custody.

The car was impounded at the Department of Public Works. When it was determined that one of the human teeth found in the back of the car belonged to Ernest Brendel, and that the blood was Type O, the same as Brendel's, the police began searching for the Brendel family.

They were nowhere to be found.

While his estranged wife was being questioned about him down the hall, Chris was adamantly denying all complicity in the Brendel disappearance. He even said he was trying to help in their kidnapping.

He told police he had spent the night at the Brendels' because he could not go home due to the restraining order his wife had unfairly imposed upon him. He had a gun because he had been threatened by the Mafia. He offered no explanation as to why he had scrapes and bruises on his shins.

Twelve hours later, he still maintained his story, despite the wide gaps in logic. He insisted the Brendels had been kidnapped and he did not know where they were.

He could offer no reasonable explanation why he had told the Scriabines his own family had been kidnapped along with the Brendels other than he did not want them to feel alone.

* * *

When Susan heard that Chris had been apprehended driving the Brendels' blood-soaked car, she became suspicious of his claim of innocence.

Clyde reluctantly accepted his daughter's suspicions. They knew there had been a simmering rage in Chris that was potentially explosive.

It was only Mary Lou, in Ohio, who still refused to believe the emerging horror stories about her son-in-law.

Late into the evening, investigators were scouring the Brendel property as a silent crowd gathered to watch. A dislodged railing on the porch stairway was attracting a lot of attention. They noticed that the police seemed to be concentrating in the barn/garage area behind the house. They heard the whir of chain saws as huge sections of the garage wall near the window were cut away and carried out to waiting police vans.

At Jones Circle, after continued hours of questioning by state police and FBI, Susan walked out to the den where the 11:00 P.M. news was on television. Catching the end of the lead story, about the mysterious disappearance of the Brendels, she knew in her heart what he had done.

Susan: *The week we were in Ohio, every day there was another piece of evidence. One day the bloodstained car, the teeth, more crossbows. We talked about it, but it was like talking about a soap opera.*
I had a sense of being in an out-of-body experience.
Like I was sitting in a balcony watching my life. . . .

No control.
We couldn't stop talking about it.

"Do you think he really could have done it?" Clyde asked.
Susan said, "Yes."
Mary Lou said, "No."
Kathy had no doubt.

Susan: *Mom missed the last two weeks of what Chris was like around the house. Plus she had been charmed by him.*

There was always the possibility the Brendels would never be found. Then what? Would he be released? Were the extortion charges against him solid enough to keep him locked up and away from the family?

Susan: *When we came back from Ohio, the town was still a madhouse. People were glad I was alive. They thought I was dead.*
People know us here. They knew we, too, were victims of this. I have a basket of cards sent to me, with prayers, messages of support and hope, well wishes. Enough to make you cry and cry with the goodness of people. Whatever we needed, they helped us. Ride to work. Food. They came into the church.
They protected us.

In Titusville, Florida, Chris's mother had no idea her son was in trouble with the law until a reporter called to tell her what had happened and to get her reaction.
She had not spoken to her firstborn in a long time, but she swore he could not possibly be involved in anything as criminal as the disappearance of the Brendels. "He's not that kind of man," she told the reporter emphatically. "I just can't believe it. Jemire wouldn't do anything like that."

Shortly afterward, Reverend Joseph T. Dye got a long-distance call at the church from Chris's sister in Florida. "We just don't know what's going on," she cried. "The first we heard was from this reporter, and we just can't understand."

He quickly contacted Susan.

"I'll call them," Susan told him, "and tell them what's happened."

Susan: *And his mother said to me on the phone, "Well if things weren't good why didn't you tell me!" She also said to me at that point, "If he's done something bad, then he should be in jail."*

Tuesday, September 24

While Hightower was arraigned on charges of possessing a stolen car and trying to extort money from Brendel's sister, the police continued their search on the Brendel property and began to expand it to nearby locations.

Initially, Chris had been held as a witness to the possible kidnapping of the Brendels. Later, he remained in custody with charges of extortion hanging over him. At 12:01 P.M., the police held a press conference to announce he was the sole suspect in the family's disappearance. The shocking announcement ran through Barrington like waves of electricity.

Chris denied the charges vociferously and with great feelings of high insult; it was the perpetration of a gross miscarriage of justice. Friends and neighbors were stunned that someone of Hightower's standing in the community could be arrested. Many were skeptical of his involvement in the case. But despite their belief in him, and all of the persistent denials on Hightower's part, little by little the Hightower story emerged in the press. It chronicled not only a long history of misfired business dealings, but many difficult-to-explain details that related directly to the mystery itself: a sawed-off shotgun, a 9mm Glock semiautomatic handgun, a Bear Devastator crossbow, an almost empty fifty-pound bag of lime, and a bloodlike substance in the car.

His friends were left to struggle with the contradictions of the man they knew versus the stranger unearthed by investigative scrutiny: his persistent academic and business failures, a history of domestic abuse and victimization of Susan, chronic ineptitude in the highly competitive and speculative field of commodities trading, a growing addiction to the gambling aspects of trading, and a growing desire to hit it big and make a killing.

That Afternoon—Chris Remains Mute

The police action accelerated. They removed Hightower from the police station to his arraignment at the Criminal Court Building in Providence. He was charged with two counts of possession of stolen property, one count of extortion, and one count of possession of a sawed-off shotgun. He was charged with three similar federal charges.

He was sent to the Adult Correctional Institution, where he remained silent and unresponsive as the search for Ernie, Alice, and Emily was conducted in full force.

Wednesday—Massive Searches

Police searched Haines and Veterans parks. They searched several areas of town with a highly trained search dog on loan from the Connecticut State Police. They covered every conceivable area—the Lion's Head housing development, Haines Park, weeds near Primrose Hill School, Brickyard Pond, Echo Lake.

Facts about Christopher Hightower's misfired business dealings with Ernest Brendel began to come to light as the town tried to grapple with the situation.

* * *

Now Kathy told her sister about the bizarre story Chris had related to her regarding the Mafia that cold January night when she had left bell choir rehearsal. It was the weekend after the restraining order and there didn't seem to be any reason to keep it a secret any longer.

Kathy: *The FBI wanted to see the letter. So I figured he said bring it out if something bad happens, so I did. So they have it. The FBI escorted me to the bank Monday morning. They didn't come into the safe deposit area with me, I think we were outside the bank and I handed him the letter and he gave me a receipt for it.*

"How much did you give him?"
"Seven thousand dollars."
"Oh, Kathy. . . . Oh no."
"He said they would hurt you and the boys," Kathy said quietly. "I believed him. I couldn't let that happen."
Tears sprang to Susan's eyes. Susan was devastated, but, bad as it was, the extortion of her sister's savings wasn't the worst news she would hear this weekend.

Hightower was being held at the Adult Correctional Institution on $100,000 bail on related state and federal charges, including trying to extort money from the Scriabines.

Thursday—September 26—National Attention

On this day, the letter on Ernest Brendel's legal stationery arrived at the Commodities Futures Trading Commission saying that the complaint against Mr. Hightower was dropped. A photocopy arrived at Hightower's office on Maple Ave. The FBI intercepted the latter.

* * *

Ernest Brendel's sister, Susan Pandich, came from New York City at the request of the Barrington police. She was taken to the Brendel home to see if, somehow, she could aid the investigators.

Cpl. Michael P. Quinn was at the scene when she arrived to assist her as she looked about to see if she could determine whether anything had been disturbed.

Emotions rose in her painfully. She had a child of her own who was close to Emily in age and spirit. To Corporal Quinn, the Brendels were flat characters, just possible victims of another crime until he saw Susan Pandich looking through her brother's deserted house . . . the crayon picture taped to the refrigerator, the empty bedrooms, the dolls lined up on the dresser. . . . "The emotion on her face, the sorrow and the pain . . ." They were no longer flat characters. They had become real.[1]

The Slickers' home on Jones Circle was searched by police, as was their vacation home in New Hampshire. The family co-operated fully but there was a profound feeling of shame knowing that their beautiful homes were being searched for clues to a potential mass murder.

Friday, September 27—Fading Hopes
Day 8

The disappearance entered its second week.

The widespread search was attracting the national news media. When an entire family disappears—that is news. When the missing family is middle-class, sophisticated, and well educated, that is even greater news. When there is the possibility of foul play, that adds a touch of speculative interest. When the missing family includes an innocent child, the story straddles the line between crime and high human interest. When the lone suspect in their

---

[1] *The Providence Journal-Bulletin*—"Investigators seize more evidence at Hightower's office." 10/1/91 by Laura Meade and Karen Maguire.

disappearance is a highly respected Sunday school teacher, investment advisor, and former doctoral candidate, the story makes national headlines. *USA Today* sent a team. So did Cable News Network. The quiet town of Barrington had come under the uncomfortable spotlight glare sensational crimes attract.

Now missing over a week, hopes for the safety of the Brendels dimmed.

Susan Pandich issued her taped plea to Christopher Hightower urging his cooperation, at least in the return of eight-year-old Emily, offering a $20,000 trust fund for his own two sons. It was a far cry from the $75,000 he had asked from the Scriabines.

He never listened to the tape. He remained mute and unresponsive at the ACI until he was transferred to solitary confinement later in the week. His prearraignment conference was set for November 26, 1991.

Saturday—September 28
Day 9
3:00 P.M.

A call was put out to the public by the authorities in charge of the investigation for volunteers to assist in the search. There was no shortage of volunteers. In the forefront, standing side by side with FBI agents and local and state police, was a prominent contingent of local firefighters.

Approximately fifty people, walking no more than arm's length apart, conducted a tight grid search, covering a small section of area at a time. They combed through grounds already scrutinized as well as new territory and found nothing.

Sunday—September 29—Pleas from the Pulpit

The ten o'clock service at the Barrington Congregational Church was anything but routine. Television cameras and photographers waited on the sidewalk directly outside church. In his sermon, Rev. Joseph T. Dye told parishioners to do everything they could to help the police. He also asked them to pray that Mr. Hightower would find the courage to tell the truth.

I want to say three things to you this morning. First, the occurrences we have been reading about and experiencing this week are evil. Many evil deeds have been done. The evil that has affected our whole congregation, its ministers, most powerfully, its children and most directly and painfully one of its most respected and beloved families, the Slickers.

. . . Make no mistake, evil has been done. Why am I so insistent upon that understanding? Because we are having a hard time imagining that *evil,* real, hate-filled, demonic evil can come to, or exist in Barrington. We have moved to this quiet, upscale suburb at least in part to escape the more dangerous, more uncertain life of the city. And now we have been confronted by something more horrible than most of what we know happens "out there."
   —Rev. Joseph Dye's sermon
       Barrington Congregational Church—9/29/91

The plants and pumpkins placed outside the Brendel home by friends and strangers alike attested to the growing concern for the missing family. The all-too-frightening outcome that loomed more likely with each passing day only intensified the vigil.

". . . But perhaps the most evil act of all is the damage done to the ability of our children to trust anyone in an untrustworthy world. . . .

. . . Our reaction, at first, is to deny that it could have touched us. We got a lot of calls here early in the week asserting that it surely could not have been *our* Chris Hightower who was involved, or that there must have been some horrible mistake which would soon be corrected and

all would be well. Unfortunately, it *was our* Chris Hightower and it was no mistake. . . ."
                    —Rev. Joseph Dye's sermon
                        Barrington Congregational Church—9/29/91

Counselors were brought in to talk to Sunday school children.

Adding humiliation to horror, since the disappearance, the
ultraprivate lives of the reserved Brendel family were subjected
to intense scrutiny by state and local police, federal agents, and
the news media, who were quick to emblazon their private habits
across the front page.

At the same time the Brendels were being scrutinized, the
authorities were trying to establish what their connection was to
the mute Christopher Hightower.

The desk sergeant at the Barrington Police Station answered
the early morning call. "Barrington Police Sergeant Wilkins
speaking."

"Is this the Barrington Police?"

"Yes, m'am. Sergeant Wilkins here."

"I am from the Audubon Society."

"I beg your pardon. . . . The what?"

"My name is Alexandra Brighton. I am a member of the
Audubon Society!" The woman, whose voice shook slightly with
age, sounded deeply concerned. "Of Rhode Island! And of
course, I know bird patterns. I've been watching them for years."

"Yes?"

"Well this may sound strange . . ."

"Not at all," he said patiently.

"I haven't said it yet!" she snapped a bit testily.

"Haven't said what, Mrs. Brighton?" He automatically made a note of the name.

"The birds behind Primrose Hill Elementary School have been circling around in very strange patterns."

"Birds . . ."

"Several mornings in a row. Unusual circling patterns."

He began to make the connection.

The woman's voice seemed to raise a full octave as she exclaimed. "I think that's where you should look for that family! I've never seen them circling like that before. They're onto something!"

The police searched behind Primrose Hill Elementary School again. Once again, they found nothing. Two of the policemen turned their gazes to the sky overhead to see if they could spot the birds. The sky was clear blue and unmarred.

"Did someone really call up about birds?"

"So I hear."

"Damn. What the hell next?"

Christopher Hightower, whom police felt held the answers to the mystery, remained in prison refusing to talk.

Monday, September 30—Still Nothing
Day 11

The search expanded into neighboring Warren as police looked through swamps near the Kickemuit. Police Chief Charles Brule told a press conference that it was logical to search in Barrington because Mr. Hightower was comfortable with Barrington.

Chief Brule: *If you were going to kill someone and dispose of the body, wouldn't you do it somewhere you know or would you drive out to a highway and risk getting caught by a state trooper?"*[1]

He was actually closer to the truth than he realized when he made the statement.

In response to a question by a *Barrington Times* reporter, Chief Brule said there was no evidence that the Brendels had any pets on the property that might be missing or dead. That wasn't completely true. They never found Emily's pet turtle or even the bowl in which the child kept it.

Pastor Dye: *There was no sense that it would ever come to a conclusion and put an end to our anxiety and wondering.*

Susan tried to maintain a low profile. She almost felt guilty for having been the one to introduce Chris into the community. She vacillated between feeling totally numb and falling into a state of deep depression and despair over what she was beginning to believe had happened to their neighbors. She heard what he said to the police and felt nothing but contempt.

Susan: *What he did was torture the police by sitting in the Barrington police station holding cell and saying nothing. Then when he overheard officers talking about where they were looking for the bodies, he actually said, "You don't need to search there. That's not where they're buried."*
This is like a little boy playing a game.
Very immature.
Very dangerous.

---

[1]*The Providence Journal-Bulletin*—"Tooth in trunk is Ernest." 9/26/91 reported by Judy Rakowsky, Joseph LaPlante, Bob Mello and Karen Maguire. Written by Judy Rakowsky.

Thursday—October 17—No Clues
Day 25

The season was changing. The fall colors had turned to flame. Leaves drifted off tree limbs in a steady downpour of color, blanketing noisy hues across the lawn and driveway of the Brendel home, clinging to pumpkin and flower alike.

In a review of police progress in the investigation, State Police Capt. Brian Andrews said, "There are no leads whatsoever as to where the Brendels may be." It was a stunning and frustrating admission.

It was the not knowing that hurt the most.

Friday—November 1—Still Nothing
Day 39

Police were informed that Emily and her dad had taken twenty-six books out of the Barrington Public Library. Not finding any of them in their home spurred hopes that the Brendels might still be alive and that the missing books were with them.

Wednesday—November 6—Only Prayers Could Help
Day 44

As the weeks passed and the searches continued to yield nothing, the town became more and more annoyed. It was inconceivable that this family had disappeared off the face of the earth. They had to be somewhere. But where?

Vigils continued. Prayer meetings were held.

On November 6, a clergy association of all the religious leaders in town organized a well-attended interdenominational townwide prayer meeting to ask that the Brendels should be found, dead or alive.

Susan: *That was the only one that I participated in. The town was vibrating. There was no closure. The anxiety level was so high. It was held at the Baptist Church. All the clergy from the town agreed to do this. The Baptist minister said he would be more than happy to lead the prayer meeting. There were rabbis, ministers, and priests, and there must have been seventy-five people there. A lot of the folks were from my church. I must have known about eighty percent of the people there. People that I had not seen in ten years came up to me after that service and just hugged me and said they'd do anything for me. It was very emotional for me. I had been scared to go because of the press, but I was surrounded by my close friends. All my friends from high school were there. I was flooded with an overwhelming sense of support. We all went in a big group with my parents.*

I cried. I couldn't sing very well. If I shut my eyes to pray, I still cried. I cried from the loss, the grief, the loss of the dreams that I had with him, the senseless loss of their lives, the loss of Chris's life. The potential of a human being totally wasted.

And then there was the anxiety that he caused the town. The trust that was ruined by him in the children, especially the ones in the church who knew him. Worry that if they couldn't trust him, did that mean they couldn't trust any adults?

I'm glad I went. I made a statement from myself and to other people that we couldn't just fold up, that you can't bury your head in the sand. You have to face this stuff, and then move past it.

I had to make that same statement to my children, who would have to know . . ."

Then came the breakthrough. The Brendels had been found.

Chapter 22

Found!

Susan would never forget this day.

The search had gone on for forty-five days with absolutely no results. The day after the townwide prayer meeting, on November 7, 1991, as though in answer to the prayers of the night before, a woman walked her family dogs in a wooded area near St. Andrew's School only one-half mile from the Brendel home on Middle Highway.

Katherine B. McCloy of Winsor Drive took her dogs out for their normal early morning walk in a nearby field. This time, although taking the usual route, the dogs strained and pulled through an opening in the brush. Then they stiffened, noticeably alert, as they sniffed at a patch of what appeared to be freshly moved earth. It appeared as though another animal had been digging, disturbing the ground enough to draw Mrs. McCloy's dogs to the site. As her dogs began to paw at the same spot with tense agitation, Mrs. McCloy noticed what appeared to be a dusting of lime spread around the entire area.

She immediately became suspicious. Why had lime, or whatever it was, been spread out here in the woods? Why were the dogs so agitated? This wasn't far from the home of the missing family everyone was looking for. She knew the police had already searched this neighborhood. This was within the wooded area off the dirt road. Mrs. McCloy decided she had better call the police anyway. After all, they might have missed something.

Barrington detectives arrived on the scene within minutes of the call. Reining in her dogs, Mrs. McCloy pointed out the spot to them. Maybe it was nothing, but there was that lime-looking stuff all over the place.

How was it possible to have missed it?

The search teams had previously scoured the area not once, but *twice.* During their searches, the police had kept the specially trained dogs tightly leashed because neighbors, fearing for the safety of their pet animals, complained of the dogs being loose. The only possibility was that the leashed dogs simply had not been able to penetrate to the lime-strewn site because of the restraints imposed upon them.

It wasn't long before dozens of policemen, crime scene specialists, FBI agents, and medical examiners converged upon the area. A long line of police cars and CID vans crowded the edges of Middle Highway. Also present were the media trucks, expectantly waiting for news of a breakthrough, ready to bring word to an anxious public if, indeed, this was the spot that would bring the mystery of the missing family to a conclusion.

By 10:30 A.M., dozens had trampled the dirt road into the St. Andrew's field.

Mary Lou's telephone rang with a shrill intrusion into the silent morning on Jones Circle.

"Mary Lou," the friend said, "There might be something happening."

"Why?"

"The coroner's truck and police cars are all over Middle Highway. They may have found something."

Mary Lou's heart jumped a beat.

"Warn Susan," her friend urged. "Just in case the media show up."

Mary Lou called her daughter the moment she hung up the phone. "Sue," she said carefully, "brace yourself. There may be a break in . . . over by St. Andrew's School. Something's happening."

Susan: *I hung up with my mother telling me to "look out" and I moved myself down to the associate minister's office. I knew the minute anything happened the phones would start going.*

Susan desperately wanted them to be found, to have a decent burial, for the Brendel relatives to have some closure on the mystery.

Susan was certain they were dead.

Susan: *Within minutes I saw the Channel 6 news truck pull up. They were there in less than fifteen minutes. I didn't talk to them. Not yet.*

By the time Mary Lou called her other daughter at work, wives and husbands of Kathy's coworkers were already calling to say they had heard something on the radio about a possible breakthrough.

Everyone with whom Kathy worked knew the breaking story concerned her family and that the only suspect in the disappearance was her ex-brother-in-law, Christopher Hightower. Three of the senior management personnel, members of the church, rallied round Kathy as they waited for news updates.

At the excavation site, just a few people had gathered when the police caravan first showed up. In less than a half hour, there were more than two hundred people there.

Everyone knew what the police were digging for and, stoically, they waited for results. Whispered conversations were held in the crisp morning air. Media personnel looked to Attorney General James E. O'Neil, quick to arrive at the scene, for the report of discovery.

12:00 Noon

Clyde came home to await word with Mary Lou. She still was hoping that, even if the Brendels were found murdered, the murderer would be somebody she didn't know. Not Chris. But both she and Clyde already had prepared themselves for the worst.

At lunchtime, Kathy went downstairs with Wally Weatherbee and Dick Brandon, two of her senior managers, to the lounge, where the television set was blaring with the latest report on the grimly developing story. The twelve o'clock news was delivering a special report, bouncing over a reiteration of the well-known facts of the disappearance since, despite all anxious expectations, the bodies, had not been reported found as yet.

Susan: *I just sat in the associate minister's office staring out the window at the water because a lot of things flashed through my mind.*
I felt grief. Mostly I felt numb.

She waited alone.

Traffic-jamming cars streamed into the area, double-parking wherever possible along Middle Highway and spilling off, bumper to bumper, onto the small residential side street, Winsor Drive.

Overhead, five news helicopters roared back and forth, like attacking insects, darting, hovering, trying to get revealing aerial shots of the site where the excavating activity was centered. It was impossible to tell if an exhumation was taking place. They knew something was going on, and they all were trying to get a jump on each other.

State Police Cpl. Michael P. Quinn was in charge of the excavation. Annoyed with the distracting noise and the danger of helicopters flying so close to one another, he was finally forced to have the police call the Federal Aviation Administration demanding that the helicopters leave the area.

By 1:30 P.M., with the green army tents the police had set up flapping breezily along the perimeters of the excavation site, the area was beginning to resemble the grounds of a carnival, but the police did not chase away the hundreds of onlookers; they understood it was more than morbid curiosity on the faces of those who strained against the yellow-ribboned police barricades that had been hastily set up to hold them back. Genuine concern was deeply etched on the grim, waiting faces. These people had been looking, and praying, and hoping for a happy outcome for well over a month.

Discovery

Members of the Bureau of Criminal Investigation team were doing the actual digging while at least two dozen officers and investigators stood by. Several holes were being carefully unearthed at the same time.

Many onlookers continued their prayers during the long wait. They wanted desperately for the search for the missing family to end, but not like this, in a wooded field heavily littered with deadfall, under clods of dirt. For once, despite the need for closure, here, so close to the end, there was some subconscious hope that the police teams, so earnestly on the job, would come up empty-handed.

Another shovel full of dirt was removed from one of the holes. This one was shallow, no more than two or three feet deep at this

point. All of their worst fears were confirmed as the police uncovered the first crumbled sign of what could be a body. A few
more shovels of yielding dirt. Now there was no doubt. It was
the body of a large man. Facedown. The clothing was wrinkled,
filthy from being subjected to a hasty covering of wet dirt, and
smeared with what, to the trained eye, was obviously dark,
brown, dried blood.

Positive identification was not possible at this time, but at the
second hole being excavated simultaneously a few feet away, a
shovel full of dirt that was removed revealed the soiled cloth of
a woman's dress.

Murmurs rumbled through those who stood by watching. The
holes in the ground were obviously makeshift graves. There was
no doubt in anyone's mind that the bodies of Ernest and Alice
Brendel had finally been found.

Lt. Doug Badger: *Several of us uncovered them. I was standing
there. Both graves were being uncovered at the same time. Ernie
was the first to be seen.*

Corporal Quinn swallowed hard. Even though he had always
felt deep inside that the Brendels would never be found alive,
this grim resolution to the search was difficult to take. Capt.
Brian Andrews, detective commander from the Rhode Island
State Police, had been a little more optimistic, but he, too, had
to resign himself to the unacceptable as he stared down at the
dark, graphic evidence of murder before them.

Now they set their jaws solemnly to the remaining task at hand,
calling upon the rapidly draining resources of their professionalism against grief, as they proceeded.

At least the child was not here. Perhaps there was still some
hope for Emily.

To preserve evidence, the team had to move still more slowly,
and the scene took on the aura of an archaeological site. Corporal
Quinn, gently brushed aside the dirt that had covered the two
bodies, working like an archaeologist with brush and trowel, and
stepped into the woman's grave. He bent to the unhappy task,
focusing his attention on the body of Alice Brendel. The edges

of dirt surrounding her were cleared away slowly, methodically, scraping, brushing, moving no more than mere spoonfuls of dirt at a time.

He brushed away some dirt and swallowed a groan.

"Here . . ." he murmured after the brief pause he permitted himself to collect his flooding emotions.

All activity stopped for a moment. In the silence, all eyes burned into the haphazard grave until they identified the point of a tiny soiled sneaker protruding from underneath the woman's body.

There was an unexpected empathetic flood of heartfelt anguish as all eyes stared hard within the grave that had held both mother and child for forty-five days. The deep silence was awesome. It testified to the fact that even the toughest of the professionals on the job was shaken to the core at the sight of the little soiled sneaker.

The child obviously had been tossed into the raw, shallow grave first, then her mother on top of her.

Despite all efforts at self-control, Quinn cracked. His eyes blurred momentarily as he automatically continued to brush dirt away from the sneaker. There was the other, one sneakered foot crossed over the other. He thought of the shoes his own daughter had worn when she was eight years old and shuddered at the thought of how this child had died. He couldn't help identifying with them. It was as though the woman before him was his wife and the child was his own little girl.

The group of men perspired through their task despite the chill of the approaching dusk about them, but they had to keep going.

Captain Andrews watched quitely, sadly. This was different. It wasn't the same feeling as when they were called to the scene of an organized crime shooting, he thought. Many times, in those situations, they were dealing with victims who had not been the best of people. But this was just a family. An entire family wiped out for no reason at all.

* * *

The decision to release the news of the discovery was made. Finally the long wait was over for those who had been patiently standing at the scene for official explanation of all the activity. There was a tense silence as Attorney General James E. O'Neil stood before the assembled reporters and neighbors. During the long fruitless search, each night as he drove home, he would often look in the direction of the Adult Correctional Institution, where Christopher Hightower was being held on related charges. There was an answer inside there, he thought. Now the answer was staring them in the face and it was his duty to tell these people about it. He made the announcement: Alice and Emily Brendel were found buried together in a shallow grave. Emily had been hidden under the body of her mother. A few feet away, another shallow, makeshift grave had been unearthed, revealing the remains of Ernest Brendel.

It was all over.

Chapter 23

Immediate Aftermath

Susan was overwhelmed by the reaction of the community to the discovery.

Donna Proux (Neighbor on Middle Highway): *I believed the Brendels would be found dead but not across the street from my house.*

To have it happen and be here across the street from where I live and know it happened while you were here is a very, very eerie feeling.

No one expected the intensely emotional response. Even seasoned policemen had difficulty controlling tears. It was when they saw Emily's little foot protruding from under the body of her dead mother that the professional composure usually reserved for these ultra grim occasions cracked.

Many thoughts immediately turned to Christopher Hightower, the man being held in relation to this crime. Journalists were on hand to scan the personal feelings and views of those who were intimately involved with the case, either through their presence at the scene of discovery, or through their personal associations with the incarcerated suspect. Speaking to a reporter from the *Providence Journal*, Rev. Rose Amodeo of the Congregational Church expressed her shock and sorrow, knowing full well that the charges against Hightower had changed once again. Now he would be held on suspicion of mass murder. "Our whole world has been shattered," she said with deep sorrow. "To talk about it is just so painful. To share the details of what was a wonderful life—a life of peace and harmony with this good man, who suddenly turned into some man we don't know is too difficult."

Dorothy Combs equally expressed the shock of discovering a side of her fellow parishioner that had been hidden beneath the veneer of his good works at church. "I just keep thinking of the Mother's Day breakfast," she said with a shake of her head. "He was so organized because he used to manage a restaurant. When I went into the kitchen that morning he was all alone scrubbing the dirty pans. That's what he was like."

While many grieved and tried to come up with answers they could understand, the excavation continued. Attorney General O'Neil remained at the site of the graves throughout the day. He knew the support of his presence was important to the men on the job. Corporal Quinn spent the remainder of the afternoon photographing and measuring the makeshift graves, prior to the removal of the bodies.

* * *

Ernie was removed first.

It had been forty-five days since the disappearance of the Brendel family first hit the headlines. After more than a month in the ground the bodies had decomposed badly. Nevertheless, the investigators were able to determined that Ernest had been fatally shot three times with bolts from a crossbow.

Next to be removed from its burial site was Alice. With the cloth garrote still knotted tightly about her throat, it was clear she had been strangled.

The bodies were placed in black plastic body bags, zipped up, and removed to the medical examiner's waiting vans as the TV cameras recorded the grisly scene for viewers at home.

All that was left at the bottom of the grave was Emily. The silence deepened as they prepared to remove her and place her in the last plastic body bag spread open by the side of the grave. Attorney General O'Neil broke the silence. "Hey, fellas," he said solemnly, "how about a minute?"

Policemen, state troopers, FBI agents, and personnel from the coroner's office all froze at the words. With hats off and bowed heads, they paused for a moment of personal silent thought. Not surprisingly, as the humanizing moment cut through professional barriers, emotions that had been submerged throughout the long day, now rose and threatened to spill over. As everyone's composure ebbed, Captain Andrews stared at the ground and wondered how he was going to tell the surviving Brendel family.

It was not immediately clear how little Emily had died. Even after the autopsy, there was no substantiated cause determined for her death. Many would come to believe the child had been buried alive after being drugged with a non-lethal dose of sleeping pills.

With the bodies removed and composure restored, the site was examined further. Many were concerned about evidence, feeling there could be more in the woods.

Lt. Doug Badger was anxious to see if the bodies had bags over their heads.

Lt. Doug Badger: *We knew Hightower bought trash bags and he told the Scriabines that he talked to Alice and Ernie on the telephone and Ernie had a broken jaw. And that the kidnappers had hurt them and had put bags on their heads. Plastic bags. It wouldn't kill them if they didn't tie up the ends.*

But there were no plastic bags on the heads of the bodies. What was found under Ernie, buried in the shallow grave with him, was a piece torn from a bag that had contained lime. Upon examination, it would be determined that the remnant of the bag perfectly matched the bag that had been discovered in the Toyota Hightower had been driving when he was arrested. It was an important piece of evidence.

Lt. Doug Badger: *I think one of the most crucial pieces of evidence is the clothing of the females. When they were found, they had the same clothing they had been wearing on Friday, the day they disappeared.*
   Hightower said they went upstairs to go to bed but they were found buried wearing the same clothing.
   Gigantic piece of evidence.

Mary Lou called her daughters to tell them they were going to meet at Pastor Joe and Sally Dye's house that evening because there was going to be a special news bulletin. They all went: Susan, Mary Lou, Clyde, Kathy, and the children.

Waiting tensely for the six o'clock news, the adults kept the children out of the room. When it came on, the TV screen showed the bodies being carried out of the wooded area in zippered bags.

Painfully graphic as the images were, there was a great lessening of internal pressure now that they finally had been found. The news did not have specific details, merely confirming that the Brendels had been found in shallow graves near each other.

As they listened, they felt a deep combination of disgust and horror at what it all meant. Murmurs and moans accompanied each image on the screen. Even though an autopsy had not yet been performed, the commentator stated that Emily had not been sexually assaulted.

"They can probably prove he did it," Susan cried in helpless bewilderment. "But why Alice and Emily? The one thing that shocks me the most is that he killed a child. He didn't trust adults, but he trusted children. So, for him to kill the child . . ." She broke off helplessly.

No one in the family defended Chris. Innocent until proven guilty aside, no one had any doubt that Chris was responsible for the murders. Not even Mary Lou.

"We all know what a temper he has," Kathy said, "and how Chris wants everything to be very precise and his way."

"But to kill them." Mary Lou said, shaking her head.

"Ernie put a monkey wrench in his plans," Kathy surmised forcefully, "so he became desperate."

"He had an agenda!" Susan declared. "Ernie was first, then his landlord, and then us. He threatened all of us!" Susan insisted in the face of their unwillingness to accept the possibility of their own danger at the hands of Chris.

"It was just talk . . ."

But three dead bodies being moved to the morgue in plastic bags was more than just talk. They also knew he had asked for the new address of his first wife, who was suing him for back child support. Was it possible he would have headed there next?

"For all I know he could have headed to Florida, too," Susan added.

"Maybe Chris murdered the Brendels . . ." Mary Lou said quietly after a long pause as they stared at the television screen. Mary Lou was relieved that they found the bodies. If they hadn't, how long were the police going to be able to hold Chris. Down deep she was keenly aware of the fact that she could have come home from Ohio to an empty house. "I think the potential has always been there," Mary Lou added solemnly. "As long as everything was going well, he was able to keep it under control, but when things didn't . . . the horror exploded."

Kathy looked at the pain on Susan's face. "I have no doubt that Chris killed them," Kathy said firmly. "Sue and Dad put another block in his way with the restraining order. Who knows what else his plans were."

"I believe he did it," Mary Lou said a little louder. It was quite an admission. She had been resistant to the idea for so long, she had to repeat it in order to let the terrible concession to the truth sink in.

"Are you sure?" Clyde asked, knowing how difficult it was for his wife.

"There's too much evidence," she said, "and I know Chris's whole life crumbled in on him. He was desperate and he was going to solve things in the only way he knew how! What a waste of a talented person!"

Clyde nodded. "I think Chris went over the edge," he agreed unhappily. "Something inside him twisted or moved in a direction that forced him to do this. I feel sorry for him, for any human being who feels he has to confront things in this way."

Susan listened to her parents still trying to explain Chris's madness. The tears wouldn't stop. Although there was intense relief that the three missing people had finally been found and that it was finally over, Susan knew the truth in her heart. She still had difficulty believing that the mass murder of their neighbors was the culmination of the love that had begun ten years earlier. The trauma of the brutality inherent in the details of the discovery was almost too much to bear; Susan could barely stop crying.

Somehow, she had to tell her sons why their father had been arrested.

When the police told Susan and her parents they had discovered that Chris had a family Hit List on which they all, including the children, were listed for elimination, as well as others who had offended Chris, such as his business landlord who had evicted him for nonpayment of rent, they finally realized how close they had come to sharing the fate of the Brendels. Susan's suspicions of his agenda had been confirmed.

Now the family had to rally around Susan with even greater

support. Should Susan tell the boys that their father had targeted them, too?

The Brendels' funeral had press coverage. TV trucks lined the streets. It was held in Providence at the Central Congregational Church.

A great many people attended the service: the entire Brendel family, congregants from their church, a lineup of police, all of whom, by now, Susan knew personally. The police were there, not only in honor of the family, but on guard to control the press corps, and to keep them out of the church. They were permitted inside to hear the service, but the police were instructed to keep the cameras out.

When Susan and her family arrived, they found that a parking space had been reserved for them in front of the church in a No Parking zone. The police opened the doors for them. They went into the church and sat. It was a huge cathedral-type church that, for Susan, evoked an awesome feeling with its grandeur. Mom, Dad, Kathy, Rose, the associate minister, Joe, and Sally were there, too, but they had come in another car after they had taken Mitch and Paul to a neighbor's.

Susan knew the minister who performed the service.

Ernie's friend, Jim Page, did most of the eulogy for all three. For Susan, listening to it and feeling the intensely emotional atmosphere that surrounded them, she felt as close to mourning her own death as she was ever going to get. It could have been her. It was God's grace, she thought, that kept her from being in the firing line of her husband's rage.

No one had ever seen the underside of the man. The question remained on everyone's mind why a man of Christopher Hightower's background would brutally slaughter an entire family with such cold-blooded premeditation.

Still, for the grieving family and friends of the murdered Brendels, the why was almost unimportant. Ernie, Alice, and Emily were dead. The whys might become known, justice might be served, but the bottom line for the families of the victims was that they were gone.

Chapter 24

Chris's Family Reacts

He was supposed to be the golden child. The one who was going to earn the big money and make it for all of them. What could have happened!

Deeply upset, Chris's mother, and a sister, wrote to Susan from Florida wanting to know more. The sister was upset, not only because of what happened, but because of the manner in which her mother found out about the murders—through newspaper reporters who knocked on her door to get her reaction to her son's arrest for mass murder. Chris's sister was worried about their mother. They needed to know more.

Susan told them that most of what she herself knew came from newspaper reports.

They didn't want to believe any of the stories.

Susan said, "This is not going to go away."

Susan: *Then I told his family he wasn't a pleasant person, but, not surprisingly, they didn't want to hear that . . .*

It was inevitable that Susan eventually suffered finger-pointing and fault-finding at the hands of the Hightowers. Casting the blame for what happened outside of their familial sphere was necessary to absolve Chris of responsibility. If it was all Susan's fault, not only could it make sense to them, but it could let his own background—and, by association, them—off the hook of responsibility. The tone of the mother's letters went from asking for money, which Susan did not send, to, "Why didn't you tell me something was wrong?" to, "What have you done to my son!"

Susan: *I had a relationship with the sisters but when they started getting on my case like I was at fault, well . . . I was afraid to talk to his family anymore because they were in contact with him.*
   Finally after the letter about "what did you do to my son," I wrote back and said, it is too uncomfortable for me to contact you about this now. When the trial is over, I'll write again.

Susan couldn't help reacting to the bitter irony of the situation; after everything that happened between her and Chris, as far as her in-laws were concerned, it was "all her fault."

When Chris was arrested, the mysterious phone calls to Susan's office stopped.

PART V
The Trial

Chapter 25

Indictment

The Hightower divorce was granted January 21, 1992.

Three and a half months later, on May 6, Christopher Jemire Hightower, age forty-two, was indicted in Rhode Island Superior Court on eleven charges:

Three charges of murder in the first degree
(which included murder of a kidnapped child.)
One charge of kidnapping a minor
One count of breaking and entering (The Brendel garage)
One count of entering (the Brendel) house with intent to
commit a felony
Two counts of check forgery
Three counts of illegally disposing of a body

Since Rhode Island has no death penalty, Rhode Island Attorney General James E. O'Neil intended to seek a sentence of life without parole. If convicted, the maximum penalty the defendant could receive under the law was four life terms plus thirty-three years.

Not surprisingly, Hightower pleaded not guilty. No plea of insanity was raised at this time.

Having little or no money for his defense, except what his sister and brother could raise, Hightower was to be defended by fellow townsmen John Hardiman and Michael DiLauro of the

Rhode Island Public Defender's Office. They kept telling him to remain silent while he sat in the Adult Correctional Institute waiting for the start of the trial that would determine the course of the remainder of his life. They insisted he wait patiently. Since the state had no eyewitness to the murders, it would have to prove what was a strong, but nonetheless, substantially circumstantial case against him.

Hightower believed he knew better than Hardiman and Di-Lauro. Instead of taking their advice, he made intricate plans for his own defense during his stay in jail. In retrospect, once his plans were aired in court, it would appear as though Chris had gone over the edge. However, he was very sure of what he wanted to do, and equally certain that the defense he planned would not only fully exonerate him, but gain him the sympathy and understanding from the court that he believed he deserved.

Not only did it annoy Hightower that his attorneys insisted he leave the structuring of his defense to them, but he also believed he deserved high-profile lawyers rather than public defenders.

As the trial date crept closer, he exercised his constitutional rights and fired Hardiman and DiLauro in the closing months of 1992. Although he had developed his story to the nth degree, he knew he needed someone of great stature to present it to the court for him. With that in mind, he contacted a man in Boston whom he was told through the prison grapevine was a tough trial lawyer—a man who reveled in high-profile cases.

Robert A. George of Boston, Massachusetts, was, indeed such a man. He was the lawyer who had previously represented William Bennett, the prime suspect in the Boston Carol Stuart murder case. Hightower eagerly read the true crime book that had been published about it. Only thirty-eight years old, Robert George was considered a brilliant criminal lawyer and a tough opponent to face in court. Street-tough, court-wise, rhetorically simple but brilliant, there was no doubt in Hightower's mind that Robert A. George was the lawyer for him.

Hightower worked long and hard on the letter he sent to

George. When George received it, he surmised the letter was from an intelligent, literate, highly educated man. George had heard of the Brendel case, and he was intrigued by the apparent intelligence of the accused. The manipulative quality between the lines was not readily apparent. George decided to look into the case.

When the Boston attorney first met Hightower at the Adult Correctional Institute he was even more intrigued. Even in prison garb, forced to shuffle into the room in ankle-restraining shackles, the slightly balding, bespectacled, accused murderer with the finely trimmed light beard, looked gentle, mild-mannered, and distinctly professorial.

George listened carefully as Hightower stated his innocence and begged for his professional assistance. During the telling, the intensity of the accused man's appeal grew. Not only would it be an interesting case to try, George thought, but it was guaranteed to be front-page news throughout the trial.

But Robert A. George came with a high price attached to his services. He, himself, often proclaimed, "I don't come cheap."

That was no problem, Hightower assured him. There was plenty of money for his defense. Not only did he have money of his own, he lied, but his family was taking care of all immediate expenses.

Robert A. George made the mistake of believing him. There was little money for an attorney, and incredibly, Hightower had succeeded in yet another con.

Robert A. George agreed to appear for Christopher at the arraignment and at the trial in Providence Superior Court.

Exactly one day after the indictment, on May 7, two months and two days shy of their tenth wedding anniversary, the Hightower divorce became final. Susan was free at last. It was not over yet. There was still the trial. She would have to appear to testify.

Amongst the authorities who were preparing the case, there was little surprise that the former Barrington Sunday school teacher maintained his innocence throughout the long months preceding the trial. He continued to claim he was caught in the middle of a Mafia plot in which Ernie Brendel was deeply involved, and he, Hightower, had merely been trying to rescue the family members from kidnappers by obtaining the demanded ransom money from Ernest Brendel's sister in Connecticut.

Another reason for Susan's not believing his story were photocopies of newspaper articles about the local mob she had found while looking through belongings Chris left behind at home when he was forced to leave. All of the names in the articles had been highlighted in yellow magic marker, as though he were doing some kind of academic research.

While preparations for trying one of Rhode Island's most sensational cases were under way, Hightower was very busy thinking about his defense. Maybe he could blame a split personality.

In January of 1993, Hightower told his attorney that he believed he suffered from a multiple personality. Perhaps he could plead not guilty by reason of such a disorder. George was willing to try any legitimate tactic to save his client. In a brief presented in a superior court hearing, Bob George decided to mount a two-part defense for him: first, that Hightower was innocent of the charges—he did not torture and kill Ernie Brendel and his family; and second, even if he did commit the murders, Hightower could not be held responsible for his actions due to split personality syndrome, which made it impossible for him to control his actions.

Judge John Sheehan, cherubic-cheeked, looking a little like a white-haired Mickey Rooney, was not pleased with a possible insanity defense. Usually congenial and always with an active sense of humor, now the gruff side of the judge's nature emerged. He was annoyed that Bob George had failed to fill out a formal notification of an insanity defense to the court and to file it within the deadline Sheehan had set to do so. Still, he was always fair.

"I have the discretion not to allow you to put on this defense," he told George sternly "but in the interest of justice, I'm going to allow you to go forward." He assured the lawyer that if the government requested, "I would bar the use of the insanity defense."

The insanity defense came as a surprise to the prosecution, but District Attorneys Michael Stone and Patrick Youngs were ready to proceed no matter what defense was offered.

"The Lynx"

Hightower's mind never rested. He didn't do it. "Lynx" committed the murders.

Always trying to exert power and control over his destiny, he began writing letters in which he asserted:

Hightower is not guilty. This is an FBI coverup.

The Lynx letters, as they came to be known because of the signature "Lynx" at the bottom, also claimed the Brendel family was killed as reprisal for stealing from the mob, an accusation that infuriated the surviving relatives of the Brendels. It was rumored one of the letters had a hit list of names for potential elimination, listing as the targets at least fifteen local residents, including Susan, her children, her parents, Hightower's landlords, and others who had offended him. In one letter, presumably written to a hit man who was serving time at the Adult Correctional Institute, a business question was raised as to whether the sum of $55,000 was enough to cover such murders.

Four Lynx letters in all were retrieved by Atty. Gen. James E.

O'Neil. Kidnap and ransom were prominent themes interwoven in all of them. In a convoluted attempt to place the origin of the letters outside the ACI, they were sent to relatives of a fellow inmate, Michael Giroux, who, in turn, mailed them from different postal zones. The letters seemed to have a dual purpose: one was to deflect suspicion from Hightower as the murderer, the other to try to force Susan to return to him with threats of bodily harm and murder to her entire family if she did not. The letters, called a smoke screen by Barrington Police Chief Charles Brule, were easily traced back to Hightower by Atty. Gen. James E. O'Neil when Michael Giroux decided to talk. Not willing to speculate in public on what impact the letters could have on the trial, the one thing the authorities were certain about was that the Lynx could be traced directly back to Christopher Hightower. When caught red-handed by Giroux's confession, Hightower eventually admitted he was the author.

Robert George offered no comment on the Lynx.

Chapter 26

The Trial

The trial began on Monday, March 8, 1993. It was held in the Frank Licht Judicial Complex in Courtroom #5, a small but imposing room with brown wainscoted paneling. There was an overstuffed leather chair for the judge flanked by the American flag on the right and the Rhode Island state flag on the left. Four dusty old chandeliers hung low from the high ceiling, casting shadowed glows across the breadth of the room. Three dozen spectators squeezed into the visitors' section. Others, who could not gain entrance because of the limitation of space, remained in the hallway waiting for a possible opening at recess.

It was being referred to as a celebrity trial because of all the surrounding hoopla. There was a thick air of expectancy as it was about to begin. Not surprisingly, there was an avalanche of reporters, television cameramen, newscasters. Between fifteen and twenty members of the Brendel and Bobb (Alice's) families would always be on hand, lending the weight of their grieving presence to the proceedings. It was Mary Lou, sometimes joined by Kathy, who represented Susan and the Slickers at the daily event. No one from Christopher's family ever came to the trial.

From the first day Hightower entered the courtroom in a dark suit and a gray turtleneck sweater, he stood against the court alone, with only his attorney, Bob George, and George's two young associate counsels standing for him.

The principal players in the unfolding courtroom drama were: Judge John F. Sheehan, the presiding judge; James E. O'Neil, attorney general; Michael Stone, assistant attorney general; Patrick Youngs, assistant attorney general; Robert George, defense attorney, and Christopher Jemire Hightower, defendant.

10:05 A.M.

Joann Groff, the court stenographer, sat in front of her data-writer prepared to record the proceedings, as Deputy Sheriff Joyce Mota began with an opening declaration dating back to the early days of Rhode Island's history: "Here ye, here ye. All persons having business before this superior court of the State of Rhode Island and Providence Plantations holden at Providence for the counties of Providence and Bristol may now draw near, give their attendance and they shall be heard. God save the State of Rhode Island and Providence Plantation."

Precisely two minutes later, the jury was led into the courtroom and into the jury box by Sheriff Joseph Spivey. The jury consisted of ten men, two women, and four women alternates.

Hundreds of pieces of physical evidence that were to be scrutinized in court by the prosecutorial team at the appropriate time, were housed neatly in a huge stack of cartons. The heavy cartons were handled by state police sergeants Doug Badger and Jim Lynch and by Barrington detective sergeants Kenny Schauble and Gary Palumbo. This was the moment for which they had waited such a long time. Carton after carton. One and a half years of solid investigative work documented, labeled, ready to be presented, a good deal of it aided by the defendant's own compulsive habit of seeming to have saved and neatly filed away every letter, photo, or receipt that had ever crossed his life. Many would relate directly to the murders.

Hightower, walking briskly, entered the court by the door at the far end of the room, escorted by marshals Steve Dagliere, Alan Verdeccia, and Jerry St. James in their deep forest green uniforms. Except for the fact that he was flanked by the three marshals, who would be his constant escort throughout the proceedings, his demeanor gave the impression he was hurrying to a board meeting at which he was to preside.

He sat at a long, lightly scarred, but highly polished, lawyer's table. A yellow legal pad was positioned by his left hand next to a water pitcher, sharpened pencils, and a box of tissues. He was in complete control. In his own mind, he had planned his defense carefully and well. Although the attorney he had gone to such lengths to have represent him strongly advised against his testifying and opening himself up to cross-examination, he knew better. He fully intended to tell his side of the story in his own words. When the time came for him to take the witness stand, he knew he would be fully exonerated. He was ready.

So was the prosecution.

The state, under the precise guidance of Michael Stone, who would handle most of the prosecution's examinations of professional witnesses, and Patrick Youngs, who would deal with the nonprofessional witnesses, was well prepared. Youngs was scheduled to deliver the all-important opening statement to the jury. Many trial attorneys believed cases could be won or lost at this precise moment in the proceedings; the team was primed to introduce in the opening statement what it believed was a powerful case against the defendant.

Hightower leaned forward as Pat Youngs stepped away from the prosecution table to begin.

Youngs's dark jacket was unbuttoned as he stood up. His dark, curly hair fell lightly over his forehead. His tie was pushed loosely up to an unbuttoned collar. This was the moment he had been waiting for. Even the flu he had been fighting for the past week seemed to retreat behind the thrust of adrenaline. He knew the case so well, inside and out, backward and forward, he did not even have to refer to notes during his presentation. Practically every item that had been secured in the Hightower file was presented in the preliminary recounting of the triple murder.

"It's going to be a long road," he proclaimed to the jury, but, he added, one that he was sure could be systematically substantiated by the evidence the state intended to present and prove. His voice was clear and strong as he began to delineate the case against Hightower moment by moment, item by item:

The trip to Guilford, Connecticut, when it first became apparent that a crime had been committed.

The first story the defendant told the Scriabines in Connecticut—a wild tale of ransom and kidnapping, replete with unidentified mobsters in vans communicating via walkie-talkies.

The substantiation of the commission of a crime of violence to the horrified Scriabines by a bloodstained Toyota Camry that belonged to the missing Ernie Brendel.

The demand for $75,000 in ransom money.

The Scriabines' alert to the FBI.

The arrest of the suspect driving the missing man's car.

The discrepancies in the suspect's meandering statements under the intense glare of questioning.

The obvious attempt to remove with muriatic acid the spilled human blood from the uneven concrete floor of the oversize Brendel garage.

Receipts in the defendant's possession for the purchase of muriatic acid.

A photocopy of $1,500 in hundred-dollar bills that Hightower had in his possession when he was arrested, withdrawn from

Ernie Brendel's bank account. A handwriting expert would swear the check was forged by the accused.

Youngs discussed the physical evidence that had been found with the suspect when arrested: the four human teeth that had belonged to Ernest Brendel; the blood-soaked car, the Devastator crossbow that had been determined to be the instrument of Brendel's death.

He continued with a heartfelt account of the frustrating forty-five-day search for the missing family after Hightower's arrest. Finally, the discovery of the bodies, only proving what had long been suspected—that the Brendels had, indeed, been victims of a terrible crime.

Youngs gave a whispered description of the site deep on the brambled grounds of St. Andrew's School, along with a promise to take the jury to the grave sites. They were to see them firsthand so that they could feel the horror of the clandestine burials that took place in the dead of night under the wooded cover of darkness.

Youngs never took his eyes off the jury. He went from one to another as he continued his mesmerizing performance, outlining the murders to an intense, hushed courtroom behind him.

"You'll get to see the crossbow," he said adjusting his glasses on his nose as his gaze penetrated the jurors. It was a torturous instrument of horror. "You'll get to hold it."

Having directly placed the murder weapon in Hightower's possession, Youngs ended with a discussion of the motive that the state claimed had precipitated the triple murder: Ernest Brendel's complaint of financial misconduct to the Commodities Futures Trading Commission with a specific deadline that, if not answered adequately and thoroughly, would have put Hightower out of business.

The state, Youngs told them, could even document that on the morning of Saturday, September 21, 1991, the killer had Alice Brendel rise early. At precisely 6:46 A.M., Alice turned on her home computer and wrote a letter to the CFTC withdrawing Ernie's complaint against Hightower. The fingerprint on the Print key belonged to Christopher Hightower. It was also discovered by Kenneth Schauble and an FBI computer expert that the doomed Alice had tried to leave a clue behind when, unbeknownst to her killer, she had filed the dictated letter on a computer disk she had labeled with the initials, CJH, easily interpreted as belonging to Christopher Jemire Hightower.

The importance of that letter, Youngs said, tapping the table for emphasis, was the heart of the motive for murder. The prosecution claimed that Hightower was so desperate and frantic to have Brendel withdraw the complaint that he made little effort to cover his tracks as he concocted his elaborate scheme of deception, blackmail, and kidnapping. The police were able to reconstruct virtually every move he made from the moment he first went to Thompson's Sport Shop to purchase a crossbow to the moment he was arrested driving the murdered man's car. Thus establishing a motive for the murders, Youngs then stated categorically, "The relationship between Ernest and him wasn't of friends." He almost whispered as he stamped the motive with, "They were adversaries!"

Youngs's opening statement was precise and graphically detailed. Not only was he thorough, but he became quietly and powerfully emotional as he described in a deliberately softened tone how little eight-year-old Emily had been kidnapped from the YMCA's afterschool program by a man later identified as Hightower, only to be discovered murdered forty-five days later, possibly having been buried alive in a shallow grave beneath the body of her strangled mother. From the moment the defendant picked up the child, it was the last time little Emily was seen alive.

Finally, the direct ringing accusation: "One man is responsible," Pat Youngs declared firmly. He turned his sharp attention to the man seated at the defense table with his hands crossed before him on the edge of the table as though in prayer. "That man is right here," he said. "Christopher Hightower."

The opening statement, substantiated by heaps of evidence already piled high across the desk of Court Clerk Linda B. Parsons, was a skillful, carefully constructed set of directions that would later be faithfully followed by the prosecution. It took precisely one hour and ten minutes. To date, it was the most extensive account of the triple murder ever detailed in public.

Robert George did not even present an opening statement to rebut Youngs's ringing accusations. He had no intention, as yet, to disclose the direction he intended to pursue. At the beginning of the trial, his strategy seemed to be: There were no eyewitnesses. It was a purely circumstantial case. Let the state prove it.

Susan was at work in a new job in another town. She had been at the job only three months when the trial began. No one in her new place of employment knew who she was or how intimately connected she was to the murder case that was dominating the news. Since she would eventually be called to the witness stand, she knew it was only a matter of time before the protective mantle of anonymity would dissolve. She was nervous about how her coworkers would react once they found out who she was and to whom she had been married.

Many emotions ran through her, all vying for dominance. She was fearful that, despite the overwhelming evidence against Chris, he would be able to con the jury as he had conned so many in the past. She feared he might be found not guilty by reason of insanity. Sue was convinced that he had been meticulously planning to murder Ernie from the day he bought the first, smaller, trial crossbow, and, once he had reached the end of his rope and everything began to collapse in on him, he had made a conscious decision to proceed with his murderous plan.

The witnesses, beginning with the Scriabines, were powerfully eloquent.

Christine Scriabine walked to the witness stand deliberately casting a withering look at Hightower as she took the oath.

Christine testified in a firm, unwavering voice, retelling Hightower's story of the kidnapping of her brother, his family and Hightower's family, of the blood-soaked Toyota, how she took samples of the blood after discovering the nauseating smell emanating from the interior of the car, and Hightower's request for $75,000. She related to a deeply attentive courtroom how the defendant dictated his incredible tale to her while she captured it on her computer in his own words. She thought the story Hightower told her and her husband was so crazy, she even took his photograph to validate that he had been there. Finally, she related how she and her husband concluded they could not believe him and decided to notify the police once he had gone.

When asked by the prosecution if the man who had come to her home that Sunday night in September of 1991 was present in the courtroom, Christine Scriabine, bearing a distinct familial resemblance to her murdered brother, pointed from the witness stand identifying the defendant as the man. It was as though Ernie, himself, were pointing the accusing finger at him.

Bob George, with his thick black hair perfectly trimmed at the sides, had been sitting next to his client doodling on his notepad. He rose to cross-examine.

As he challenged Christine's interpretation of the weird visit from Hightower that fateful night so long ago, Bob George, dressed in a dark, neatly tailored suit was not above taking a dramatic stance in front of her. With his hands placed on his hips and his feet wide apart, George strongly suggested to the jury that Hightower's visit to the Scriabines was that of a madman who was trying to get them to accept a wild tale of kidnapping, ransom, and men in armored vehicles with walkie-talkies. George finally got Ernie's sister to admit, despite a tense semantic struggle between them, that the man's story was, at the very least, farfetched. That was sufficient ammunition from the mouth of the victim's own sister to help the insanity strategy for which George was beginning to maneuver even at this early stage of the trial. There was no way, he was strongly suggesting, that a normal person could come up with such a stupid, illogical scheme or such a weird story, and, full as it was of holes, tenaciously cling to it!

It had been an emotionally wrenching first day. Both the prosecution and the defense had thrown themselves into the core of their game plans. At 4:16 P.M., when the first day of the trial ended, there was no doubt in the minds of the jurors as to the direction each team intended to go. The prosecution was presenting Hightower to them as a vicious, evil, heartless killer who would even smother an innocent little girl to save what was essentially a failed business, and the defense was highlighting every piece of testimony that could show the craziness and lack of reason on the part of the accused.

During the two-month-long trial, while Hightower sat at the lawyer's table busily scratching notes on the yellow legal pad, Bob George kept his back turned, paying little attention to him. He seized every opportunity he could to damn his own client's lack of logic. Chris continued to maintain his innocence, but his attorney wasn't taking any chances. He knew the case against his client was too strong. It seemed that with the preponderance of physical evidence against him, the only tack to take was to discredit Hightower mentally. The only defense there could possibly be was that the man was not responsible for his actions. The plea for a two-part trial had been a good move on the part of the defense after all.

The prosecuting team was thorough. Witness after witness took the stand to testify to the strength of its case. Alexander Scriabine, Ernie's brother-in-law; Ralph A. DiFonzo, FBI special agent from New Haven; Barrington patrolmen John C. Alfred and John D. Medici; Jack W. McGraw, FBI special agent from Providence, Sgt. John T. Lazzaro, acting police-fire administrator; State Police Lieutenant Hurst; Barrington Cpl. Michael P. Quinn; Ernie's friend James Page; Principal Elizabeth Durfee of Primrose School, and on and on.

By the time the long list of witnesses was finished with its testimony, almost 250 pieces of evidence had been introduced into the record. The evidence continued to pile up against Hightower with an almost-tedious similarity: the billy club and steak knives that belonged to Ernie's mother, Jolene, had been found in a Lord &

Taylor bag discovered under a table in Hightower's office. Christine Scriabine testified that she and Ernie had removed them from their mother's condominium when they closed it up. The entry in Chris's checkbook for $355.34 made out to Thompson's Sport Shop and a receipt in the same amount for the Bear Devastator crossbow. Could there be any doubt as to who had purchased the murder weapon? There was the long damning paper trail that led directly to the defendant: bank slips, and dated receipts—some with detailed descriptions of purchases. Ernest Brendel's stationery had been found in the defendant's possession. The Brendel electronic garage door opener was also found in his possession. A small, white plastic bottle, accompanied by a dated sales slip from a CVS drugstore that contained diphenhydramine pills, an antihistamine, not lethal in themselves but strong enough to induce sleep, with twenty of the newly bought sixty-pill bottle missing. It was enough to have drugged Alice and Emily into sleep. A poem Hightower had written about robbing a bank which demonstrated a dramatic bent of mind that could be construed as a bizarre method of problem-solving. A recent sales slip for a coiled roll of garden hose believed to have been used to wash down the garage floor after it had been scrubbed with muriatic acid. A receipt for the purchase of the muriatic acid. A receipt for a recently purchased bag of Lee Lime. The ragged bag had been found in his car and perfectly matched a piece of the bag that had been found in Ernie's grave beneath his body. Clothes bought by Chris at Sears with Ernie's credit card and a forged signature. The Glock semiautomatic pistol and the length of rope Hightower had taken with him to Guilford on his visit to the Scriabines. A steel pry bar similar to one used to break through the back door of Brendel's house was found in Hightower's American Tourister briefcase next to the pistol, knife, and rope. All the personal items found in his possession when he was apprehended that belonged to the Brendels: Alice's rings, Ernie's checkbook, wallet, and credit cards. There was a legal notepad with the name Ernest R. Brendel targeted in boldly printed letters along the top. A pair of gloves, a piece of blue cloth and wirecutters—all carefully receipted. Photographs, computer printouts, hundreds of letters, all discovered neatly filed away in his office on Maple Avenue. Nothing was ever discarded or thrown away. Everything stored and filed in quickly retrievable alphabetical order. The compulsiveness that had created a minor nightmare for the waitresses at the Newport Creamery so long ago was coming back to haunt and point daggerlike fingers directly at the defendant.

While Hightower sat at the defense table scribbling copious notes, Robert George seemed barely to pay attention. He raised no objection.

By Wednesday, the chill in the courtroom generated by the seemingly endless and damning volume of evidence against the defendant, was matched by the chill outside when the jury, bundled against the weather, was taken by bus to the various scenes of the crime. Hightower could have gone along, but he was so offended when told he would have to be handcuffed and shackled in leg irons in order to be permitted outside prison that he refused.

Not being present, he did not see the solemn reaction of the jury members when they were taken to the Brendel home to view the broken porch steps, the back door with the pry marks of forced entry still visible to the eye, the interior of the garage where Ernie met his death, and the section where the garage wall had held one of the deadly bolts. Nor did he see the grimly silent reaction of the jury members when they were escorted down the cart path in the wooded section behind St. Andrew's School, where the bodies had been discovered. They looked hard and deep at the grave sites now graced with three small pine trees that had been planted in memory of the Brendel family by their neighbors.

By the time the jurors boarded the bus again and were returned, the near-freezing rain, which had been pounding Providence for several days turned into a thin, frigid blanket of snow.

Every morning, before going to work, Susan read the newspaper accounts, but it was her mother's accounts on which she really depended. Mary Lou attended the trial every day, sometimes alone, sometimes with Kathy, always sitting in the back of the courtroom in the visitors' section with a small circle of ladies from the church. Calmly needlepointing a piano seat cover for the baby grand piano that stood in their living room, Mary Lou's hands never stopped their precise, methodical movements no matter what was said during the course of the trial. They did not falter even during the most dramatic moment of the trial, when the prosecution introduced the voice of little Emily to a hushed courtroom. Recorded on the Brendel answering machine was Ernie's voice, ". . . We're out right now . . ." It was painful enough to hear the dead man's voice, but even more wrenching was the voice of the child. One of the messages on the machine was from Emily after her class trip.

"Hi dad, it's me," she said, her light, cheerfully innocent voice entering the courtroom like a burst of thunder.

While the jury leaned forward and the Brendel family could barely hide their emotions upon hearing the now-silenced young voice, Mary Lou's hands continued the needlepoint, even though the stitches blurred together before her wet vision.

"I'm at the Y . . ." Emily said. "What?" she obviously asked someone at her side. Then back into the telephone. "It's three-thirty-five and you called the school for me to walk home, but I came here, 'cause I didn't know."

After dinner at home, the family sat around the dining room table with coffee to hear Mary Lou recount the day's events. Susan was always anxious to hear the news, holding her breath in the hope that it would all be positive for the prosecution. The toughest days of the trial were those when it almost ended in the dreaded mistrial, such as the day one of the jurors had to be excused. In order to keep Clyde and Susan going until after they testified, Mary Lou always tried to be positive. She described Chris's reactions to the various witnesses, or mostly, his lack of reaction. He usually sat quietly in his chair, demonstrating little or no emotional response to what was being said, either about the murders, or about him directly. She described the judge's reactions to the proceedings, and how his sense of humor sometimes dominated the morbid aspects of the accounts, how Robert George laughed aloud, and how the prosecutors did not appear to be amused. Stone had already succumbed to the need for new eyeglasses, his eyes wearied from the overwhelming amount of reading incurred by the mountain of evidence. Youngs had lost at least ten pounds since the beginning of the case, due to a combination of overwork, the flu, and tension. They had spent long, tedious months carefully constructing a case against the man they believed slaughtered an entire family. Now they were dismayed, as well as shocked, at some of the levity being displayed at the proceedings.

The family could not help agreeing with the prosecution as Mary Lou related how Stone and Youngs did not appear to appreciate the judge's humor. They, too, feared it might denigrate the seriousness of the trial.

Mary Lou evaluated for the family each of the witnesses who appeared and how, in her estimation, each of the jurors and each of the lawyers reacted to their testimony. Her accounts left them cautiously optimistic as to the outcome of the trial, especially when a witness had put another nail in Chris's coffin. Both Kathy and her mother would tell about meeting the reporters in the halls outside the courtroom, how they reacted to the proceedings, and how they tried to get sound bites out of them. Mary Lou described how the bailiffs ruled with an iron fist. She kept a running tab of the visitors in the courtroom for the family, including the sad procession of the Brendel family: Ernie's two sisters, Christine Scriabine and Susan Pandich, and Alice's two brother's Arthur and Donald Bobb. The Scriabines made the drive from Connecticut almost every day. Susan Pandich made frequent visits to the court from her home in Tarrytown. Arthur Bobb and his son Fred came all the way from Florida to lend the support of their physical presence to the proceedings, and Donald Bobb and his wife Peggy came north from Pennsylvania to sit in silent heartbreak in the center of the courtroom. Mary Lou also helped to fill in some of the blanks about evidence that the police never shared with Susan at the time she had been brought in for questioning shortly after the Brendels disappeared.

Feeling closer than ever before with emotions unshackled by the tragedy, sharing feelings and thoughts never before spoken of openly, the family sometimes joked about how each of the players in the drama was portrayed by the press and was amazed at how often the television and newspaper reports were in error.

* * *

As the trial progressed, the weather outside became more bitter, as though spring would delay itself until a satisfactory conclusion to the proceedings had been reached.

Seven days into the trial, it was Susan's turn to testify. The police had to escort Susan in and out of the court building. The media was constantly after her and her family, for statements, for feelings, for any word they could use in their coverage of the sensational trial.

It was Wednesday, March 17, the second week of the trial. She had been pulled out of work the Friday before in the event things went quickly. She had spent Monday waiting all day at the courthouse. Even then, people were telling her they did not believe Chris's story, but all that mattered to her at this point was what she was going to say on the stand. How she would say it? Would she be nervous? Would she remember to tell it all? How would she handle Robert George's cross-examination? He would certainly try to break down her story of abuse and threats of violence. How would she feel when Chris gave her that look of his?

The room was crowded. Although there was always a waiting line to get in, there were many church members in the room, seated close to Mary Lou, specifically present this day to give Susan support.

Susan checked out Chris's position in the courtroom before she entered, took a deep breath, and went in. There was a bit of a buzz as she entered. All eyes were upon her.

She looked so perfectly composed that no one would have been able to guess how nervous she was. She was wearing a teal-colored linen suit with a white jewel-necked blouse, simply adorned with a string of pearls and earrings. Her hose were clear-colored, her flats black and fortunately comfortable since all witnesses were required to stand during the entire time testimony was given. None of the jurors had ever seen Susan until she made her appearance. Considered to be mysterious, aloof, and remote, many were surprised when they saw her. Young, lovely, and vulnerable, many had assumed, considering Chris's age, she was much older. Many had also assumed she was blond, which surprised her.

When she got on the stand, Chris tried to stare her down in his usual intimidating manner, but, to her own surprise he did not faze her. She was out of his reach. She had become strong in her self. She made a conscious decision not to look at him until her testimony was done.

At first she was nervous and she knew she was answering too quickly, but she couldn't help it. Once she finally got the rhythm of the proceedings, she settled down to do what she considered to be her part. Question . . . answer . . . question . . . answer. . . . What was it like living with him? Was he ever violent? Did he ever threaten you? Did you see the crossbow? The box it came in? When was the last time you saw him before the murders? Her direct testimony related mostly to the week leading up to the murders. She told where he had been, what he had said to her, how he said he would be out very late the Thursday before the murders and not to expect him home. She related how he threatened to have her killed for $5,000 and how, for an additional $1,000, he would make sure her murder would appear to be an accident. She told the court how she immediately called the police when he broke the restraining order the first day. She gave a brief history of their marriage and how it fell apart. It was painful to relive the lack of trust, the emotional abuse, and the ten years of marriage during which he had never held down a paying job. She also told some of the good things about Chris, particularly how well he related to their sons as a father.

After a while, her feet began to hurt and her mouth became dry from nerves. She got a bit lost in the back-and-forth, "Objection!"—"Overruled!"—"Sustained!" that permeated her testimony. Several times she had to ask that a question be repeated.

The prosecution team always treated her with great respect. They led her through the questions and she followed. They told her afterward she had done a good job on the stand. But, on cross-examination, the part she dreaded the most, no matter how hard George pushed her and tried to trip her up as exaggerating the abused wife syndrome, she refused to be rushed into making an error on the stand. She was quietly thrilled that she was finally able to tell the world just how terrible a provider he had been to his family. She knew with dead certainty that she wanted Chris to be locked up forever. He had to be, she could feel herself thinking as she answered the probing questions, or her life would be worse than the hell she had already gone through with him.

The cross-examination seemed to go on and on. She could feel herself emotionally shutting down. . . . *Just tell it straight,* she thought, *like it happened. Don't feel it all over again in the telling.* She became disquieted at Bob George's persistence. She felt the defense counsel badgered her on numerous occasions until he was stopped by the judge. She finally got annoyed and snapped at George after he had asked her the same question again and again—on what date did she and Chris leave Ohio and move back to Rhode Island. Her eyes never wavered from George's dark, intimidating face as she shot the answer to him again.

After her testimony had been completed and she was excused, she felt relieved and triumphant. She had finally told the world what it had been like to be married to Christopher Jemire Hightower and how he had treated her. She felt that she was believed by the jury and the others present in the court. She was also very proud of the fact that she did not let Bob George trip her up.

George commented later that she was singularly unhelpful.

Just before leaving the stand, Susan finally looked at Chris directly, expecting to find his stare piercing in her direction. She swallowed hard, anticipating that she would be frightened. Instead she found herself disgusted that he would try the sympathy approach, for instead of the familiar glare, he gave her an "Oh honey, you-really-still-love-me-down-deep, don't you?" look. Thoughts flashed through her mind. Emotionally frozen for a long time, she hadn't really permitted herself to think about all the ramifications of her ten-year relationship with him. Now, looking at him across the coldness of a courtroom, all of the long-submerged emotions were pricking at her conscience for attention. She knew it hadn't happened suddenly. It had actually been a slow dawning over the last five years of their marriage that he wasn't who she thought he was, that he was, in fact, capable of physical violence. What had it been like to wake up and find herself married to a mass murderer? She still had not been able to deal with it. When the police had first questioned her, her subconscious jokingly entertained the possibility of violence. "What did he do, kill someone?" she had asked. The reality of his murderous actions only sank in when she heard the newscast about the missing family. She knew immediately what had happened and, in her heart, she knew that he had done it. She was married to a mass murderer. There was never any denial of it on her part, not even when she first heard of it.

Susan did not realize at the moment she made eye contact with Chris, that it would be the last time they would ever look upon each other again.

She turned and left the stand. He followed her departure with his eyes.

After her testimony, Susan met the Brendel family to pay her respects. Unsure of what their reaction to her might be, she was deeply gratified and relieved that they were, and always would be, very cordial and sympathetic to her. Don Bobb, insisted that the public treat Susan and her family as Chris Hightower's victims. Victimized by the intensity of media scrutiny, the police had to escort her in and out of the court building.

Clyde Slicker did not want to testify against his ex son-in-law. Knowing he was duty bound to do so, he became anxious to appear. He believed he had detailed information that could be very important to the case and wanted to share it with the jury. Even so, it was a very pained man who stood in the witness stand, dressed neatly in a dark suit, ready to answer whatever question was put to him. He had always liked Chris. He tried to help him, not only financially, but also spiritually. Clyde had always believed in Chris as an intelligent, decent man. Now, he had the painful task of corroborating the truth of his daughter's testimony about the slow breakup of their marriage and his personal knowledge of the last day before the murders. He spoke of the deterioration of Chris's business despite all the financial assistance he and Mary Lou had given over the years. He told how he watched his son-in-law go from a man who had been helpful around the house, attentive to his business, and active in church affairs, to a man who spent days seated upon the couch in the family room watching television. Speaking in a clear, steady voice, he told about the morning of September 20. After being out all night, Chris had come home with dirty clothes and damaged eyeglasses just before he was served with the court's restraining order. And how it was the first time he had ever seen Chris put his own clothes into the washing machine.

It was the only time Clyde appeared in court. He did not want to sit and listen to the condemning evidence piling up against the father of his grandsons. When he got home, it was a saddened man who told his family that, when he left the witness stand after giving his testimony, he saw Chris looking at him from the defense table with a cold stare that went right through him.

Extensive physical evidence was introduced to the jury to corroborate the prosecution's re-creation of the crime. It suggested intent, opportunity, and motive on the part of the defendant. Youngs, Stone, and their team had done a thorough job, so thorough Judge Sheehan joked they had even managed to throw in "the kitchen sink" when they showed the jury a photo of the Brendel kitchen.

Chris was angry at the direction of the prosecution's case against him. He was even angrier at the tenor of the defense being presented on his behalf. Bob George had managed to defuse some of the state's case by leaping at every opportunity to suggest his client was hardly responsible for his actions. Although it had been partially Chris's idea, the possibility that he might be thought of as mentally incompetent did not sit well with his ego. But he knew he would get his turn. There was no doubt in his mind that he could convince the jury of his innocence once they heard his story in his own words. Contrary to the continuing strong advice of his counsel to remain quiet, Chris was still determined to take the stand.

There was no deterring him.

George shrugged and emphasized to the court that, even with four hundred exhibits and seventy-seven witnesses for the state, what actually happened at Middle Highway was still unknown. The crimes were re-created according to practical evidence, and although the case appeared circumstantially strong against the defendant, there was only one person who knew the exact truth of what happened on the day the Brendel family met with death. All that remained for the jury now was to hear the story of what happened from the man who, although claiming innocence of the crimes, by his own admission was present when the murders occurred—Christopher Hightower.

On the morning of Wednesday, March 31, he finally got his chance. The temperature had dropped a few more degrees. It was still bitter and raw outside, but at least the rain had abated to a thin mist.

Hightower stood alone when the jury entered. Some jurors acknowledged him. Some even gave him a little smile and said, "Good morning, Mr. Hightower."

It was very encouraging. No doubt things were going to go his way.

Robert George asked the judge to dismiss the charges against his client, but Judge Sheehan dismissed the defense's motion, stating that the evidence against Hightower was overwhelming.

According to Mary Lou's description to the family later that evening, Chris became a bit unraveled when he heard the judge make such a damning statement in open court, despite the fact that the jury, itself, had heard the strong circumstantial case that had been presented against him.

* * *

Judge Sheehan cautioned the jury again that opening statements were not evidence. The only evidence they could consider were those statements that came from the witness stand under oath.

Robert George stood up to address the jury. George had finally realized he had been conned by his client. The big fee he had been promised had never materialized. Hightower did not have a dime, his mother and siblings would come up with nothing, Susan and her parents were not about to spend another penny on the man they now hoped would remain in jail for the remainder of his life.

But he had to go on.

"After four hundred exhibits and almost eighty witnesses" George began, "we still don't know what happened. There are only a handful of people who knew what happened on Middle Highway. Despite the fact that the defendant has no burden, that Mr. Hightower has the right to remain silent, he's going to take the witness stand and tell what happened, what he believes happened on Middle Highway. We're here to seek the truth," he said firmly. "We're not here to cast blame or seek revenge . . ."

There were family members of the murdered victims in the courtroom who silently disagreed wholeheartedly. Blame and revenge were very much on their minds.

"Mr. Hightower is going to take that witness stand," George continued, "and tell you what was going through his mind at the time these crimes occurred. He doesn't have to do that," he repeated, strongly suggesting that Chris's willingness to cooperate and put himself through cross-examination should weigh in his favor. "Because the issue here, I suggest, is *why* things happened as they did on Middle Highway. His testimony, I suggest, will show you that. Please keep an open mind for just a few more hours in this case, 'cause, I suggest, what we have to find out is the truth as to why things happened as they did."

* * *

George turned to the judge. "Your honor, Mr. Hightower."

Christopher Jemire Hightower got up. With a sheen to his lightly balding head, he made his way quickly to the witness stand escorted by two of the marshals. Wearing a navy blue turtleneck sweater under the jacket of a grey suit, he appeared, as usual, professorial, gentle, and mild-mannered with his well-trimmed beard and steel-rimmed glasses.

Now it was his turn. He was going to tell his story. What really happened. The air of expectancy that had carnivalized the trial hung heavier than ever.

He raised his right hand.

"Do you solemnly swear that the testimony you shall give to the court and jury shall be the truth, the whole truth, and nothing but the truth, so help you God?"

"I do," he replied solemnly.

What followed was an astonishing display of audacious imagination. Under oath, he was going to attempt the greatest con job of his life from the witness stand.

Chapter 27

Out of the Mouth of a Murderer

Defense attorney Robert George began by bringing "Lynx" back into the courtroom.

R. GEORGE: Have you ever used any other name before?
HIGHTOWER: No sir.

R. GEORGE: Have you ever heard the name "Lynx" before?

HIGHTOWER: Yes sir.

R. GEORGE: Can you tell us how you know of that name?

HIGHTOWER: That was a pseudonym that was used in the preparation of letters that were mailed out of the ACI.

R. GEORGE: Then you used the pseudonym in regard to those letters?

HIGHTOWER: I used some of those.

It was almost as though George wanted to establish immediately with the jury what would be the pattern of holes in his client's logic. Hightower claimed never to have used another name. Then admitted he had used the name of "Lynx" to write threatening letters that were mailed out of the Adult Correctional Institute.

George took him through the usual procedures to personalize him and his background to the court—where he was born, where he went to school, his parents, stepfather, siblings. He led him through a humanizing account of his schooling and sports involvement at Indian River Junior College in Fort Pierce, Florida—why Chris did not finish at Indian River—a poor background, only a partial scholarship that merely paid for his books—how, while attending the university, working two jobs to help support his mother and playing on the basketball team, life became so difficult that he was put on academic probation and decided to leave school.

He joined the navy in October of 1968.

George took him through his sixteen-week basic training program, his hospital school program at Bethesda, Maryland, National Naval Medical Center, his August, 1973 marriage to a nurse, and, finally, how he went back to school at the University of Rhode Island in February, 1973, graduating in December of 1975 with a B.S. in Zoology.

Chris spent the next two years employed as a field representative with Riker, a pharmaceutical company. He claimed he left the job because he was dissatisfied with it. "It involved sales and I did not like sales," he said. "I did not like having to communicate with the doctors." He blamed an average job performance rating on "a bad, very difficult territory."

His testimony, given in a flat monotone, was turning out to be a slow, tedious recounting of his life, from early childhood on. But despite the possibility of raising nothing but ennui in the jurors, George was patiently bringing Hightower through the entire litany of his marriages and career. He wanted the jury to see the man as a devoted son, successful military man, unhappy husband, devoted father, hard worker, and a scholar with great ambition to succeed and great potential due to his superior intellect.

Hightower recounted to the jury, in the same depressed monotone, how he went to work at the Newport Creamery in a management training program because they offered their management personnel the opportunity to go back to school and receive an MBA degree, which they would pay for. He wanted desperately to improve himself and earn a good living for his family. But things were extremely difficult at home at this point. Long hours. "Working too much, couldn't get back into school yet." His wife and he were not getting along. "We were unhappy," he said.

He told how he finally ended up at Newport Creamery in Swansea Mall, where he met Susan and found solace and comfort in her companionship. They had many opportunities to sit and talk. "I was her boss," he said. "In the fall of 1980 she went back to school in Ohio and I was to get a divorce. I applied to several schools in Ohio to be with Susan."

R. GEORGE: Tell us what happened then.
HIGHTOWER: Living in Dayton, Ohio. Started master's program in the fall of 1981. Master's in physiology. Ph.D. in biomedical sciences with sub special in physiology. Marriage had been strained. We got married on July 10, 1982, and shortly after we got married, marriage became strained because my stepfather was ill with cancer and I had gone to Florida to see him. When I returned . . . this was early in 1982, not married yet . . . When we returned back to school I was involved in a research project with a lot of hours,

using rats. Every three or four hours, I had to dose rats . . . spending a lot of time away from home. . . . I returned home one evening from working on the project at the university and had expected my wife to be home and as I walked past the car I felt the heat rolling off the hood and it was obvious she had been out someplace. So I questioned her about it and I believed that Susan was being unfaithful. I have proof. She admitted it to me and I also met the individual that she was with. This was the fall of 1982. I had a difficult time trusting my wife. I wanted to keep a tight rein on her. She was outgoing, she had most of the friends. My wife was my only friend in Dayton.

At no time in their marriage did Susan ever admit to being unfaithful to Chris as he was claiming on the witness stand. This was something that only he had in his head and was thoroughly convinced of.

He told how he requested an extension for his Ph.D. exams. After the written exam, which he had passed only marginally, he had a problem with his upcoming oral exams. He claimed he needed a time extension because of the two unexpected fires at home that destroyed all of his school notes. In deference to the severity of his stated problem, the exams were postponed. Even though he was close to failing, and he admitted he would have to score very high on the orals, he claimed he would have passed them had he taken them at the time.

HIGHTOWER: Mitchell was born in 1984 and Paul in 1986. September 19, 1991, was the last time I saw them. The day before the restraining order. We had dinner together and I had business that needed to be taken care of that evening so after dinner I left the house and my wife put the children to bed.

Having presented to the jury Hightower's sad life through the pain of academic and two marital failures, George began to lead him through the early stages of his career as a commodities investment broker.

HIGHTOWER: My stepfather always had trouble supporting the family and I was determined to provide the support
for my family that I wanted them to have. I got specialized
training in 1985 in commodities through seminars. To become certified you had to take an exam which I had not
done until late in 1985. We moved back to Barrington in
1986 summertime. My concerns were trying to get my business running. The Slickers provided us with support for the
first year. They provided $1000 per month for the business.
I thought I had friends, but not really. . . . Throughout my
business I never had more than five or six customers. The
financial support eventually ceased from the Slickers, but
I don't remember when. It had been sometime before September 1991.

This was quite an admission for Chris to make since he had
been in business for almost six years. He was averaging no more
than one customer per year.

HIGHTOWER: I started working at the church right after
we moved into Jones Circle. Late 1988. Maybe early 1989.
The Barrington Congregational Church. My wife is secretary at the church. I was involved with the Board of Christian Education. Primarily responsible for establishing what
we wanted the teachings of our Sunday school and adult
education classes to receive. Eventually, I became chairman
of that board, so automatically a member of the executive
committee at the church, so I had monthly meetings, sometimes weekly meetings, and ran youth groups. Started with
senior high group and moved down to junior high group.
My oldest son in 1990 was in scouts and soccer. I became
involved with the scouts program. I was leader of his Tiger
Cub den.

He went on to relate how his business was still slow, but that
he had developed a valuable business system. This system would
play an important part in his strained relationship with Ernest
Brendel.

HIGHTOWER: I had been doing research for the development of this system to afford the opportunity to enter into the marketplace with a low potential of risk exposure and seek substantial returns. Worked by computer. I developed it myself. I had not developed it completely by the time I met Mr. Brendel. It was fairly complete but there was a minor problem with market direction. In 1989, I think March, when Mr. Brendel opened his first account with me, I informed him of this situation. I traded the account for six months and we then had a discussion and I told him I was still having problems with the market direction and rather than lose money I would rather close the account and continue to do the research and reopen it at a future date.

The picture presented by the prosecution had changed. According to Hightower's testimony, it was he, and not Ernie, who had closed the account in order to minimize Ernie's losses. This was in direct contradiction to Ryan's statement that Ernie was dissatisfied with the manner in which Chris was handling his investment and had decided to terminate the business relationship.

HIGHTOWER: I was working with commodities, which are highly dangerous instruments because of the leverage. It's easy to make or lose a lot of money very rapidly. My expectations in the development of the system, once I had the market direction problem worked out, was to make vast sums of money to finally be able to support my family.
R. GEORGE: Where is the system today?
HIGHTOWER: There are some people that have the data work and the rest of it is in my head. The data work is missing. I can't find it. I've been incarcerated.
R. GEORGE: When did you meet Mr. Brendel?
HIGHTOWER: Sometime in 1988 or 1989. When I met him I think I had one lady who was working in the office with me at that time.

There was a palpable aura of deep sadness in the telling. The defense was trying to humanize Chris. There was no evil glint in his eye. George was subtly painting the picture of a complex, melancholy loner besieged by inordinate pressures. Strained marriages. Economic stress. Unexplained fires. Academic tensions. Failing Ph.D. exams. An unsuccessful, though visionary, business broker. A man of the church. Had he cracked under the intensity of pressure?

Family members of the victims were untouched by the testimony. They thought he was faking it. They felt no compassion for his travails at all, most of which they felt he brought upon himself though of his own manipulation.

R. GEORGE: Did you have any other clients when you met Mr. Brendel?

HIGHTOWER: No. I met Mr. Brendel through Mr. Ryan. I'm not sure of the time frame. I recall Mr. Ryan's testimony was in 1987 but I can't place the date exactly when I met him. Mr. Ryan had an office next to the office I was moving into on Maple Avenue and I had, in the interim of moving, placed some of the data that I had been working with on the walls of the office space, and Mr. Ryan had walked in and introduced himself and asked what I was doing, and eventually I showed him what I was doing. The research that I was working with. And he said that he had a friend that was a retired attorney and entrepreneur who was interested in finding a small business to work with. So Mr. Ryan told me that he would have Mr. Brendel give me a call at some point, and that's how we were introduced, via a phone call. Sometime in 1987-88. I eventually met Mr. Brendel sometime after the phone call. He would spend a lot of time at the office. He came over on a daily basis, watching what I was doing and showing a lot of interest in it. More than just in the investment aspect. He asked me if I would be interested in expanding the business and going further. Producing a newsletter. He decided to invest the first accounts in March of 1989.

R. GEORGE: Prior to March of 1989, had you met any other members of the Brendel family?

HIGHTOWER: Yes, I had met Alice and Emily. Because of

the meetings we were having with each other we had become friends. Mr. Brendel was not a handy man, had trouble with repairs around the house, and was always asking advice, and I would give him my recommendations on what to do and eventually he would ask me to come over and help him do the repair work. This went on throughout our relationship. Not too much communication between families. We went to dinner together. They came up to the property in New Hampshire and spent a weekend with us. I believe summer of 1990.

I considered Mr. Brendel a friend. No other friends.

In March of 1989 he opened his first account and in May of 1989 he had given me $2,000 and at the time he gave the money to me, we discussed it would be for the purchase of computer equipment. He had given me $15,000 to open the account in March. When he gave me the $2,000 he said, "Consider this my first equity investment in the company." We had progressed to the point in March of 1989, he made it known that he wanted to have part of the operation I was running. With no customers. My primary concern and drive at the time was to continue the development of my system. I had already spent three years working on it and it was my primary goal. Mr. Brendel wanted me to start a newsletter. I didn't want the newsletter, it would take me away from what I was doing with the development of my trading system.

It was never explained adequately why Ernie would want a piece of a business that had no income and no customers, especially since, according to family and friends, Ernie had always demonstrated conservative caution in the past regarding his business investments.

R. GEORGE: Did he introduce you to anybody else in terms of customers?
HIGHTOWER: Yes. Eventually. In November of 1989. Mr. Spaziano and Mr. Bucci, and Mr. Samard and one other, Mr. Perazza. The first account opened in December of 1989

was with Mr. Perazza and Samard. The second account was
Mr. Bucci and Mr. Spaziano. I opened the first joint account
and one weekend I was away in New Hampshire and found
that the second account had been opened. They had access
to my office. Mr. Brendel and Mr. Samard had keys to my
office. They were not partners. The only equity investment
I had was the $2,000 from Mr. Brendel. I had closed Mr.
Brendel's account in September of 1989 because I was having trouble with direction. Not because I lost money on the
account. He had given me $15,000 to open the account and
I gave him back almost $15,000.

This was never substantiated.

HIGHTOWER: The Samard/Perazza account opened for
$30,000. The Spaziano/Bucci account opened for $20,000.
During this time my relationship with Mr. Brendel was extremely good. In September when I closed the account it
was because of difficulty in identifying market direction.

This was in direct opposition to the charge in Brendel's complaint to the CFTC which claimed Brendel had terminated the
account himself because Hightower had lost $11,000 without
ever notifying him that he had passed the fifty percent fail-safe
point.

HIGHTOWER: I continued the development of the system
and he stayed in touch with me on a daily basis and in
November I had solved the problem with market direction.
November of 1989. We had, at that time, started spending
more time together and he became excited and then introduced me to these other four gentlemen to trade their funds.
I ran into problems with trading their funds, but it had nothing to do with the system. When the first account was
opened with Perazza and Samard, Mr. Samard came into
the office with me at that time. He was in the office constantly and Mr. Samard did more than observe. He was involved in everything I was doing. He opened his own

account. He wanted to open up a brokerage account where you solicit the customers and you receive a commission for trading. My operation didn't operate that way. The concern I had was that he was attentive to the numbers that I used to generate my trading signals and I thought he was trying to take what I had, to steal my idea. As a result of this I traded the $30,000 account for a short period of time and slowly lost money on the account down to $24,000 at which time I stopped trading the account and Mr. Samard took over trading. The $20,000 account had not been opened with my permission or knowledge and the account was assigned to me as the trading advisor. I lost $7,000 on that account. Just prior to closing the Perazza account, an article appeared in the newspaper regarding Mr. Perazza and that article concerned me. I contacted Ernie and spoke with him about the article and told him I thought there was a possibility that there were people involved here that we would end up in a lot of trouble with because of the regulations that are involved with the CFTC and the NFA. I believe this was around February of 1991. I eventually severed relations with these gentlemen. Mr. Brendel suggested I close their accounts any way I possibly could, but I had also talked with Mr. Gale, a member of our church and a member of the U.S. Attorney's office, with the department of organized crime. I eventually wrote him a letter. I put the last account in a losing position and ignored it and allowed it to draw itself down to the $13,000 level, at which time they became extremely angry with me and I just closed the account.

This was his hard-to-believe explanation of how and why he deliberately lost money for the men he believed were Mafia connected.

R. GEORGE: How are things at home now?
HIGHTOWER: They're not very good. Not making money. Wife didn't tell me she was going to leave yet. I believe this was February 1991. No, February 1990. When I initially closed the accounts I did not believe I was being followed

yet. I thought I was being followed in March of 1990, I started receiving phone calls and thought I was being followed. No one identified themselves when they called. The calls were referring to the monies that had been lost and the two trading accounts that I had. Never any names. I made the assumption that the people who had opened the accounts were the people making the phone calls. I started noticing I was being followed May or June of 1990. There were times when I would go out in the car and there were cars following me. I specifically made detours, went different places to be sure what I was seeing was accurate. At some point I received a call that was more than asking for money. The call was a threat and at that time I contacted the Barrington Police Department.

There was no record of his ever making such a call to the Barrington police. Several critical questions remained, all unanswered: Was he really being followed? Was he suffering from paranoia? Or was he creating a scenario of danger similar to the one he would soon relate about being followed after the murders?

R. GEORGE: Was there any point when they stopped following you?
HIGHTOWER: I don't believe so. Right up to September 23, 1991. The cars varied. There was a Jeep at one time. There was a white Toyota Camry that followed me. I had seen a Camaro, a white Camaro. Usually men were driving but the white Camaro had a woman driver. I would enter into a semicircle and instead of going off to the side, I would go all the way around and right back the way I had come and the car would follow me. The phone calls were mostly, "We want our money back." Up until the threat. Something like, "He's there, go get him now," and they just hung up. The calls were always a male voice. They were at any time during the day. They were sporadic, not every day, sometimes a week or a month between. Calls always at the office, not at home.

It was at this time that he told his sister-in-law, Kathy, he desperately needed money to pay off the Mafia. He told her the mob had threatened Sue and the children with physical violence if he did not pay them the money they demanded. The $7,000 he asked of Kathy was needed to protect them. Despite the seriousness of the scenario he painted for Kathy, these alleged Mafia threats were never brought up in his testimony.

HIGHTOWER: In March, I had no customers. In May of 1990, I opened Mr. Brendel's account the second time. This was my only account.

R. GEORGE: What about Mr. Werner?

HIGHTOWER: Mr. Werner asked me to open an account for him. He was in bankruptcy, his account was turned down as a result of that. He was trying to get a foothold, get reestablished, and had asked me to take some funds of his and try to do something with it because he was in dire financial straits. My primary point of focus is trying to find a customer that could continue to support my operation. I needed someone I could trust and work with.

I had become somewhat oblivious with things at the house. Things between my wife and I had deteriorated. We had started marriage counseling in 1988. We were trying to resolve problems we had with each other. No psychological counseling.

R. GEORGE: Did you hear Mr. Slicker testify here?

HIGHTOWER: Yes I did.

R. GEORGE: Did you hear him say you started to lose interest in the business and spend a lot of time at home?

HIGHTOWER: That wasn't until 1991. March of 1991.

R. GEORGE: When was Mr. Brendel's second account closed?

HIGHTOWER: April of 1991.

R. GEORGE: Were you being followed then?

HIGHTOWER: Yes I was. And receiving phone calls.

R. GEORGE: Did anything else extraordinary happen?

HIGHTOWER: Mr. Brendel was trying to push me into opening up the newsletter. That was his primary goal and when he opened the second account with me his concern was not with the $15,000 he had invested. It was the newsletter. He was happy with the information I had shown him and when he opened the second account his primary statement was he wanted to trade the account for a while and if he runs it down by February, "I'll put money back in and bring it back up so that there is no problem with the CFTC." As a result of that I allowed Mr. Brendel to make his recommendations for trading and I traded that account relative to his recommendations. He was the only customer that I had but Mr. Brendel kept insisting that once we started the newsletter it really didn't matter, we would have as much money as we wanted.

The implication was obvious; it was Ernie who ran down his own $15,000 account, not he.

R. GEORGE: What was your relationship with Mr. Brendel outside of the office?
HIGHTOWER: Very good when the account was first opened. We were still doings things together. Vacation together. I was constantly over at his house. He came over and had dinner with us . . . ongoing and growing business relationship. At some point, it was around February/March of 1991 the account had dropped down below the recommended trading levels and Mr. Brendel had told me he would replace the funds when that happened and he didn't do it.

There was little evidence to substantiate the constancy of the relationship he claimed they enjoyed, nor did he say why it had soured. In claiming that Ernie knew all about the loss that fell beyond the fifty percent fail-safe point, the loss became the fault of Brendel's own poor trading. The reason for the strain between them became tenuous, if not implausible.

HIGHTOWER: As a result I told him I would have to close the account because now I was legally in trouble. And I closed the account. I did not control that account. I gave the recommendations off the advice of Mr. Brendel. I closed the account in March or April of 1991. I was spending more time at home this time. I was having more problems with my wife and my family. The business relationship had extremely soured with Mr. Brendel. I had been looking forward to him keeping his agreement, not only with replacing the funds in the account but also the fact that he knew a lot of investors who would come invest with us and the generation of the newsletter, eventually.

R. GEORGE: Tell us about your troubles at home.

HIGHTOWER: My relationship at this time had also changed at the church. When I used to go into the office I was always greeted enthusiastically and conversation went on, "What's going on? What are we doing?" And so forth. A lot of happiness, and in March of 1991 this relationship had changed and taken a 180-degree turn. I would walk in the office, no handshake, the minister's head would hang. My wife would turn away from me. He would leave the room and we would talk.

R. GEORGE: Did you start to believe that your wife was being unfaithful again?

HIGHTOWER: Yes I did. This is around March of 1991. I did not at this time accuse of her being unfaithful, (with Pastor Dye.) I just asked her about it and she said, no. She was always going out to lunch with him.

R. GEORGE: Did she deny it?"

HIGHTOWER: Yes she did. The relationship I had with the minister had changed too dramatically for something not to be wrong. I believed it was so.

Once again, Chris made an unsubstantiated allegation that Susan was being unfaithful to him.

R. GEORGE: Did you start to spend even more time at home?

HIGHTOWER: Yes I did. My concentrations now were on my children.

R. GEORGE: What would you do with your days during March of 1991?

HIGHTOWER: I would go to the office and spend most of the day there until it was time for my children to come home.

R. GEORGE: When you came home, what time did you arrive home?

HIGHTOWER: Anywhere from noontime until four in the afternoon. My mother-in-law was also at home. My wife was working.

R. GEORGE: What did you do with your days from noontime until your wife got home from work?

HIGHTOWER: I don't know. Not much. Mowed the lawn. Watched TV.

R. GEORGE: Were you still involved with community affairs at this point?

HIGHTOWER: Yes. I became more active with the youth group at the church. Spending more time with the kids.

R. GEORGE: How long did this continue?

HIGHTOWER: Up until September of 1991.

R. GEORGE: Were you still being followed?

HIGHTOWER: Yes I was.

R. GEORGE: Still receiving phone calls?

HIGHTOWER: At the office.

R. GEORGE: When did you close Mr. Brendel's account?

HIGHTOWER: I believe it was April of 1991.

R. GEORGE: In regard to your relationship specifically with him and his family, did it change after April 1991?

HIGHTOWER: Yes it did. When I closed the account, Mr. Brendel said that he was going to file a formal complaint with the CFTC. However, he would drop that complaint if I would agree to start the newsletter with him.

This allegation was also unsubstantiated. He never explained Ernie's great interest in starting a newsletter with him. At no time did Brendel mention to anyone that he was interested in starting the newsletter to which Hightower kept referring. It had appeared to friends that Ernie was deeply disturbed with Hightower's business practices.

HIGHTOWER: It was a newsletter that would make trading recommendations in stocks and commodities. We were going to establish two different newsletters, one dealing strictly with commodities and one dealing strictly with stocks. The newsletter that we were discussing was to be $1000 for the newsletter. You figure other than the man-hours that you put into producing the letter, the paper, stamps, and data service, over a monthly basis comes out to approximately, you can produce a yearly newsletter for less than $25, the point being if you sold a newsletter for $1000, you've got $975 worth of profit.

R. GEORGE: Does it also solicit business?

HIGHTOWER: Yes it does. And encourages investment.

R. GEORGE: What happened after Mr. Brendel said he was going to file a complaint against you?

HIGHTOWER: I was angry with him because of what he had said, that he would keep the funds in his account, and I was not responsible for the trading of that account. And when it dropped to the level that it did, I thought he had set me up for something. The approach that he was using was not interested in getting his funds back. He was interested in part of my business and the newsletter. I perceived what he was doing was blackmailing me. He definitely wanted a piece of my idea. Like Mr. Samard.

Again, he disclaimed responsibility for the loss in the Brendel account. Not only was it not his fault, but at this point he alleged that Brendel was deliberately setting him up. For the first time, he also claimed Ernie was blackmailing him. The reason for such accusations was not evident.

R. GEORGE: Did he become your enemy?

HIGHTOWER: Yes.

R. GEORGE: Did your wife become your enemy yet?

HIGHTOWER: Yes.

R. GEORGE: Your in-laws?

HIGHTOWER: Yes.

R. GEORGE: What about your children? Were they your enemies yet?

HIGHTOWER: No.

R. GEORGE: Why not your children and everyone else?

HIGHTOWER: The children were young. They didn't know what was going on. We kept our problems away from them. From August until September I spent all of my time with my kids.

R. GEORGE: Does this have anything to do with the fact that you thought your wife was going to take them away from you?

Chris's tearful version of the threat on her life Susan had reported to the police and had testified to under oath earlier:

HIGHTOWER: Yes it did. In September . . . September 7, 1991, my wife had a visitor. One of her friends from Maryland and they had gone out one night, I think on a Sunday. This person's name was Emily. (Emily Carroll) My wife told me they were going out to test-drive her friend's new car and they would be back in a few minutes and they returned several hours later and I was extremely annoyed with her because she lied to me by saying she was going to be gone a few minutes. So that night when we went to bed, I wanted to talk with her. And at this point I asked her if she would talk and she said, "No." I said, "For five years, every time you wanted to talk I'd talk with you, but now you can't talk with me!

Chris began to sob openly.

HIGHTOWER: And I became furious with her and I said, "You're killing us, you and your lover, you're killing us." She jumped out of bed and said, "You're threatening to kill me?" And I said, "No, you know what I'm referring to." And at that point her parents came into the bedroom and Sue left and went to the bedroom with the children and that was the beginning of the end of our marriage. This was September 7, 1991.

R. GEORGE: Mr. Brendel filed the complaint against you in July, 1991?

HIGHTOWER: Yes. Mr. Brendel was still trying to force me to give him part of the business and start the newsletter at that time. I never should have let him have any access to his account whatsoever. It was traded by power of attorney. I was wrong and in trouble and I knew it. I had just previously been audited. That was just before the breakdown of the problems I had with Mr. Brendel. So my records were accurate. They reflected everything that had transpired with very minor discrepancies.

R. GEORGE: September 1991, was your marriage in a shambles?

HIGHTOWER: Yes.

R. GEORGE: How are you paying your rent on the office?

HIGHTOWER: I wasn't paying it.

R. GEORGE: How did you pay for your computer equipment?

HIGHTOWER: I wasn't. I was spending time with my children.

R. GEORGE: Is it fair to say that in September, 1991, the only people you were spending time with were your children?

HIGHTOWER: Yes. They're seven and five now.

R. GEORGE: After September 7, 1991, leading up to the sixteenth of September, did anything happen?

HIGHTOWER: After the confrontation with my wife on the seventh, I went back and started talking with Mr. Brendel. I told him I would be willing to do the newsletter with him.

Now, Chris proceeded testifying to, what many believed was, a total fabrication.

R. GEORGE: But Mr. Brendel is your enemy at this point, isn't he?

HIGHTOWER: Yes he is. But my children were more important to me. He assured me there was a substantial amount of money to be made with the newsletter. And it would provide me with the funds I needed to pay off my bills and should my wife and I end up in a divorce, hopefully allow me to gain control, custody of my children.

R. GEORGE: So between the seventh and the sixteenth you were involved in discussion with Mr. Brendel about this newsletter?

HIGHTOWER: Yes I was.

R. GEORGE: Is there a copy of this newsletter anywhere to be found?

HIGHTOWER: Of the newsletter, no. We had mock-ups of what we were going to do. They were in the office. I was meeting with Mr. Brendel in person. Still being followed.

The mock-ups, or dummies, he spoke of were never found.

R. GEORGE: The week of September sixteenth, do you recall that week?

HIGHTOWER: Some parts. I think the sixteenth was a Monday.

R. GEORGE: Did you meet with Mr. Brendel on September 16, 1991?

HIGHTOWER: Yes I did. About the newsletter.

R. GEORGE: Did anything happen on the sixteenth that we should know about?

HIGHTOWER: No, other than we were making plans to start the production of the newsletter.

R. GEORGE: What was your state of mind?

HIGHTOWER: I just wanted to make money so I could get my children.

R. GEORGE: Did your wife tell you she was going to divorce you on the seventh?

HIGHTOWER: The next morning. The eighth.

Chris told another version of the fight he had had with Susan the night she claimed he threatened to kill her and her family, and of the late-night prowl in the woods when it was believed he was looking for a conveniently located burial spot.

There was no mention of his threats on her life.

R. GEORGE: You heard your wife testify about the seventeenth of September?
HIGHTOWER: Yes.
R. GEORGE: You heard her say that was the day you knocked her in front of a fireplace?
HIGHTOWER: That was Tuesday, yes.
R. GEORGE: Direct your attention to that morning. Did you have any discussion with your wife that morning?
HIGHTOWER: I believe I went to the church Tuesday morning around eleven in the morning. I was trying to reconcile with my wife. I had stopped and bought her a rose. I went in and I talked with her. I asked her if she would reconsider filing for the divorce. She said she would think about it. I left in somewhat uplifted spirits.

I saw her for dinner that night. She told me at dinner. I noticed when she came home that she had taken her rings off at that time. Her wedding rings. I noticed it at dinner and I got up and excused myself, went into the bathroom, and got sick.

I'm a little confused about the things that happened Tuesday or Wednesday night. I recall going out on the bike path Tuesday night. I'm having trouble remembering the night I was drinking. I think that was Wednesday night. I was drunk. There was no way I could have walked on the bike path the night I was drinking, on Wednesday, so I was on the bike path on Tuesday night.

His testimony, proceeded with a none-too-subtle implication that Ernie was trying to sweet-talk him into illegal trading. He was being pushed into it because of blackmail and he was acquiescing solely because of his desperate need to provide for his family and to obtain custody of his children.

HIGHTOWER: I was having trouble with the fact that I had agreed to work with Mr. Brendel and the fact that I was uneasy with what we were going to be doing. I remember

Tuesday night being able to think about what was going on and I don't recall anything about Wednesday. I recall the night I was on the bike path as not being the night I was drinking. I was on the bike path around midnight. Everybody was sleeping. I couldn't sleep so I went for a walk.

R. GEORGE: Was that night on the bike path before or after your wife had told you it was over?

HIGHTOWER: Afterward. The same night.

R. GEORGE: Why where you on the bike path and what were you doing?

HIGHTOWER: I was really confused. I loved her very much. I wanted our children, I wanted us to be together. I was having trouble dealing with my agreement with Mr. Brendel. But I felt that if I could get another five or six years out of my marriage before we were caught, then it would be worth it. I needed time to think.

R. GEORGE: How long were you on the bike path?

HIGHTOWER: Not long. It's probably two miles around the bike path. Walking from the house on Jones Circle up the bike path, I walked around it one time.

R. GEORGE: Did you make any decisions at that time?

HIGHTOWER: Yes. I decided at that time that I was going to work with Mr. Brendel. We would do whatever it was that he requested be done. My wife wanted a divorce. I wasn't happy with it but I would give it to her. But I wanted custody of my children.

R. GEORGE: So the incident with your wife in front of the fireplace was the next night?

HIGHTOWER: Yes.

R. GEORGE: Do you recall that incident?

HIGHTOWER: No sir. I was drinking. I usually don't drink. I had an awful lot of scotch very rapidly and I don't remember much about it. I remember waking up the next morning and I was in the guest bedroom without any clothes on.

R. GEORGE: The morning that you woke up in the guest bedroom, do you recall that day?

HIGHTOWER: I thought it was Thursday morning.

R. GEORGE: Where did you go on Thursday morning?

HIGHTOWER: That would be the nineteenth. Thursday morning when I woke up I went down to the church to see my wife. She wasn't there so I left and started looking for her. I think it was close to lunchtime. I went looking for her at some of the restaurants. I drove back to the church and pulled into the parking lot and she pulled up. I wanted to talk with her but she didn't want to be anywhere near me. She went into the office and locked the door and wouldn't let me in. She came out and we stood in front of the church and talked for a few minutes. She wouldn't listen to me, she wouldn't hear me. Then I went back to the house at Jones Circle.

R. GEORGE: Was anyone there when you got there?

HIGHTOWER: I had to go pick up my youngest from kindergarten. It's only a block away so I walked to get him. This was around eleven or twelve o'clock and I went back to the house with him. Then my oldest son had just started second grade. He came home and I spent the afternoon with my children.

When a recess was called, no one in the courtroom appeared to be pulling for Hightower.

No evidence was ever found of the newsletter to which he kept referring. Members of Alice Brendel's family, who had come from Florida specifically to hear Hightower's testimony, were deeply resentful at some of his allegations.

According to his testimony, he was a pawn. He was being blackmailed, threatened, followed, and victimized by everyone except his children. Not once did he accept responsibility for anything that happened. He made it seem as though he was trying everything he could to reconcile with his wife. He made it clear that most of the problems he had with Brendel's account were Brendel's fault.

After the recess, his increasingly bizarre story continued.

HIGHTOWER: The newsletter being suggested to me by Ernie was illegal. That and the moral aspect of that, I was really confused. I had trouble thinking about what to do.

R. GEORGE: Bringing you back to Thursday at dinnertime.

Did anything change between Tuesday and suppertime on Thursday the nineteenth?

HIGHTOWER: No, not how I was feeling. I still had trouble resolving that what I would probably be doing would be illegal.

Chris told his version of why he bought the instrument of Ernie's murder—the Bear Devastator crossbow.

R. GEORGE: Why did you buy the crossbow?

HIGHTOWER: Ernie had some problems with raccoons getting into the garage that had chewed a hole in one of the upper eaves and was going in, and there was a groundhog that was undermining the carriage house. The carriage house was the other building in the back. Ernie had asked me at one point if I had a .22 so we could kill the "pests" and I said, "No." So I was concerned with firing a weapon in city limits anyway. I said it would have to be done more quietly. We talked about bow and arrow and crossbow and I said I didn't think I could hit anything with a bow and arrow so, "Let's try the crossbow. It's almost like shooting a rifle."

R. GEORGE: Did you tell the Barrington police you used it to shoot crows?

HIGHTOWER: Yes I did. Because by that time my rights had been violated numerous time by the Barrington Police Department and I wasn't about to tell them anything about what happened!

R. GEORGE: Did you need a crossbow that big to shoot raccoons?

HIGHTOWER: You're talking a distance of about 120 to 130 feet from the back of the house to the garage. It needed enough power to strike the target and kill it.

R. GEORGE: Do you have any experience with that type of weapon prior to the nineteenth of September.

HIGHTOWER: Crossbow no, rifles, yes. I had purchased a small hand crossbow, about twelve inches, I think a pull of forty-five pounds. A small version. The smallest they offered. A diversionary action to waste a little time. We had some crows in the backyard. They used to come down in the early morning and create a squawk. So it was for those crows, but the power was too weak and it wouldn't perform its function.

R. GEORGE: What time did you leave your house? (for Thompson's)

HIGHTOWER: I left after dinner, five-thirty or six.

R. GEORGE: Did you have any discussion about your marriage before you left the house?

HIGHTOWER: I don't recall.

R. GEORGE: When you went down to Thompson's, do you know what happened there?

HIGHTOWER: We had some discussion about the crossbow, but I was in a hurry because Mr. Brendel had an appointment that evening and I had to get there before he left. I paid for it with my personal check. Ernie and I had discussed this and the agreement was that when I went down to buy the crossbow, the funds would be reimbursed and I would take care of the raccoons and groundhog for him.

R. GEORGE: After you bought the crossbow what did you do?

HIGHTOWER: I went back to the Brendel residence. I pulled up somewhere around six-thirty. I was in my mother-in-law's station wagon. I pulled up into the driveway, took the crossbow out of the car, and started walking back toward the garage. The garage door was open. There was movement on the inside. There was a white van parked in front of the garage doors.

This was the first mention of the white van that was to play a major part in Chris's version of the murders.

HIGHTOWER: I think it was a New York license plate. It had the Statue of Liberty on it. There was a rack on the upper aspect of it. I walked in the garage and said something like, "Ernie, I got the crossbow. I'll need a check to pay for it now." He came hurrying out very quickly, put the crossbow on the side of the garage, and he and I walked away from the area. I went back to the car. Mr. Brendel asked me to return later on that evening.

It had been established earlier that Ernie had not been home that evening. He had gone to a seminar in Dedham, Massachusetts. He could not have been at home when Chris claimed they had this conversation.

HIGHTOWER: I was only there three or four minutes. I went back to my in-laws' house. I went in and had a small conversation with my wife. It was her birthday, and I wanted to spend some time with her but she informed me that she had invited some of her friends over. I became upset with her even though on Tuesday she told me the marriage was over. I went upstairs. I think I had my jeans on, so I may have changed clothes. I came downstairs and got my army jacket (dirty work jacket). I went back to the Brendel residence. I left around seven or seven-thirty. My wife was expecting her friends around seven-thirty and I left before then.
R. GEORGE: Was that the last time you saw your children?
HIGHTOWER: Yes. So I walked over to the Brendel residence. I was upset. I needed to clear my head. Ernie was gone. He'd be gone for a while. I had plenty of time to eliminate the raccoon. I walked down Rumstick Road through the bicycle path to Middle Highway and walked Middle Highway to the Brendel residence. It took about forty-five minutes.
R. GEORGE: Did you see anybody on the way?
HIGHTOWER: Yes. Some of the children in the youth group passed me and waved to me.

No one in the youth group ever came forward to substantiate this statement.

R. GEORGE: What was your state of mind when you went back to the Brendels' Thursday night?
HIGHTOWER: Distressed, angry, upset. A lot of external pressures on me that I was having trouble dealing with.

Chris began to lay the groundwork for the dirty condition of the clothes that Clyde Slicker saw him throw into the washing machine the next morning.

R. GEORGE: What time did you get there?

HIGHTOWER: Around eight-thirty. I went in and talked with Alice for a couple of minutes because I had expected to be outside most of the evening, lying and waiting for the raccoon to show itself. That's why I had my field jacket with me. It was raining that evening. I went outside and found a place behind the house so I could see the top of the garage adequately.

R. GEORGE: Did you eventually kill the raccoon?

HIGHTOWER: Yes around ten or ten-thirty.

R. GEORGE: You sat in the rain until ten or ten-thirty waiting to kill a raccoon?

HIGHTOWER: Yes I did.

R. GEORGE: At any point were you in the barn?

HIGHTOWER: Yes. I had to reenter the barn to get the crossbow out and the arrows. Alice had a key to the garage. She had given me the key. I didn't see Emily that night.

R. GEORGE: Did Mr. Brendel return home that night?

HIGHTOWER: Yes, very shortly after I killed the raccoon. Probably around ten-thirty-five.

R. GEORGE: Did you have conversation with Mr. Brendel at that time?

HIGHTOWER: Yes. I showed him the raccoon. We left it lying outside in front of the garage and we went back into the house and started a conversation.

The dead raccoon was never found.

HIGHTOWER: We talked about what happened earlier in the evening with my wife and Mr. Brendel tried to get my mind off it and started talking about the business. I wasn't supposed to see him again until that following Wednesday, the twenty-fifth. We had scheduled a trip to New York at that time.

R. GEORGE: When you left the house at Jones Circle, did you tell them how long you would be out?
HIGHTOWER: I told them I didn't know when because I didn't know how long I would be out with the raccoon. I told them I could possibly be out all night.

In Chris's version, Ernie was supportive of him in his upcoming divorce. So much so, that he was willing to withdraw the outstanding complaint he had submitted to the CFTC. Chris still did not explain why the relationship had soured enough for a written complaint. He testified their relationship was not only intact, but on a very solid basis.

He did explain why computer dates showed a discrepancy in his story.

HIGHTOWER: That night I spent the entire night with the Brendels. I slept on the couch in the living room. During the course of the evening, we had gone upstairs and Ernie typed the original letter that was written to the CFTC to withdraw the complaint. He had signed that letter. It was addressed and placed in an envelope for mailing the next day.
R. GEORGE: Mr. Hightower, that letter didn't come off the computer until nine-forty-six on Sunday.
HIGHTOWER: No, the letter that Mr. Brendel typed was typed on Thursday night, to be mailed Friday morning. It was dated September 19.
R. GEORGE: Do you know what disk that was created on?
HIGHTOWER: No. There were two boxes on diskettes there. He opened one of the boxes, took out a diskette, and created the letter on it.

It had never occurred to Chris to check the date programmed into the computer.

R. GEORGE: What time did you awake on Friday?
HIGHTOWER: I was semiconscious when the Brendels got up that morning. Ernie came in and told me he had to take

Alice to work and would be back shortly. I got up and took a shower. I don't recall seeing Alice or Emily Friday morning. I took a shower, went downstairs and poured myself a cup of coffee, sat at the table and waited for Ernie to return. He returned around eight-thirty or nine. I was still bothered by the problems I was having with the fact of what he wanted me to do. (which was illegal)

HIGHTOWER: At that time we went over the plans for the conversion of the carriage house. He was going to move from my office space to the carriage house on his property. So we had to convert it to an office space. I had to run the wiring and enclose the walls to make it dust-free not to damage the computer equipment. The barn is the garage. The carriage house was the small building over to the left of the garage as you face it. (The root cellar.)

HIGHTOWER: We drew a schematic of the root cellar and I outlined where the electricity ought to be run.

The schematic was never found.

HIGHTOWER: When we returned from New York on Wednesday we were going to purchase the supplies needed at that time to convert the root cellar into a habitable building.

R. GEORGE: Did you leave at some point?

HIGHTOWER: Yes I did. Around ten-thirty I went out to the garage, took the bicycle, and rode Mr. Brendel's bicycle to my in-laws' house.

R. GEORGE: Why didn't you walk.

HIGHTOWER: I was running late. I needed to get my youngest son from kindergarten. Mr. Brendel needed his car. I really wasn't planning on returning at that time.

HIGHTOWER: Before I got home as I was coming out of the driveway, because I was in a hurry, I wasn't paying attention and, as I came out, a car came and almost hit me, very close to me, splashed water on me. I fell off the bike, bent my glasses, scratched up my legs. I went back to Jones Circle. Covered in mud. I took my clothes off. I like my

jeans, I worked in my jeans. I had jeans on when I left the
Brendels', and a dark plaid shirt. I wanted the same clothes
put back on, so I took them and put them in the wash. I had
a shower at the Brendel residence but because of the mud,
I needed another shower. After the shower I saw my father-
in-law when I came back downstairs. He put together something for me to eat and I asked about Paul. He said Paul had
gone to a friend's house, so I got my clothes to dry and I
remembered that I had a meeting with a member of the
church re: youth group at noontime. So I had to wait for
that before I could do anything else. I did not see Paul that
morning.

R. GEORGE: What happened next?

HIGHTOWER: My father-in-law told me about a message
I had received from someone, I think Joe Mazza. So I went
upstairs and made the call; it was concerning the complaint
that Mr. Brendel had filed. I told him that the complaint
was being withdrawn.

Joe Mazza was questioning him about his lack of response to
Ernest Brendel's complaint to the CFTC and his failure to meet
the deadline imposed on him. This raised a question in the minds
of many who listened as to why Ernie did not call off Joe Mazza,
since, according to Chris, he and Ernie were now working and
cooperating together, not only in business, but in a personally
supportive manner as well.

Much of the monotone of Chris's recitation was replaced now
with deep emotion as he recounted his version of the day he was
asked to leave his home by the constables, and once again, he
cried unabashedly on the stand:

R. GEORGE: What did Mr. Mazza tell you?

HIGHTOWER: I don't remember. It's before noontime now.
I started eating and someone had come to the door. My
father-in-law answered the door and these people walked
in. One said he was a constable. Showed me a letter he had
in his hands and said this was a restraining order, you have
fifteen minutes to pack and leave. I was not expecting that

to come. I was shocked. I went upstairs, tried to put together some clothes. The constable was walking behind me saying, "Don't you think you should take this or that . . ." The constable basically packed the bag for me. I didn't know what was going on. I was losing it.

R. GEORGE: Did you leave the house?

HIGHTOWER: Yes, within the time frame the constable had stated I left the house.

R. GEORGE: Before noon, before you left the house, had you done Mr. Brendel any harm at this point?

HIGHTOWER: No. No harm to any of the Brendel family. I didn't know where to go so I went back toward the Brendel house.

R. GEORGE: Why didn't you take the bike?

HIGHTOWER: My arms were full. My briefcase in one arm and a bag of clothes in the other. On the way I stopped at the Hoder residence. It was located on Middle Highway. By the time I walked from Jones Circle and had approached her house, I was exhausted. I had reached a stage of burnout and I asked her if she would give me a lift to the Brendel residence and she did. We had very little conversation.

R. GEORGE: Do you recall what time she dropped you off?

HIGHTOWER: Between twelve-thirty and one, I think. I'm not sure. What's time? Everything's gone. She dropped me off in the parking lot of the church next to the Brendel residence. I went inside the Brendel residence at that time. Knocked on the door. Mr. Brendel opened the door and he was surprised to see me. I explained what had happened and I was saying, "If she's going to do this, I'm not going to let her have the children." Ernie said, "Don't worry, we have friends and money. You'll get your children." It was only a twenty-day restraining order and I knew I would see them after that time. Mr. Brendel excused himself. He had to make some calls. I sat at the kitchen table while he made the phone calls. While he was on the phone some people arrived at the house. I went to the foyer area and motioned Ernie. He said, "Let them in." So I did. I don't know who they are. Two were Chinese and the other two appeared to be Latin American.

It was a stunning revelation. There had been no previous mention of these four men.

HIGHTOWER: I let them in through the back door. I went back and sat down, they went into the living room where Ernie was. Shortly after that, Ernie finished his phone calls and they had a short conversation. Mr. Brendel and the others came into the kitchen and said there were things that had to be done. Ernie said, "Don't worry about it. Just do what they ask and everything will be fine." They left and went out to the garage.

Attention in the courtroom was riveted on the witness stand as Chris presented his version of Emily's kidnapping. He never offered an explanation as to why Ernie would not want his daughter to follow her normal routine or why he would want her home early from school while these potentially dangerous men were present.

R. GEORGE: Can you describe the heights and weights of these people?
HIGHTOWER: I thought the two Chinese were tall for being Chinese. They were taller than me. I'm five-eleven so they were six-one or six-two. They were thin and had dark hair. The two Latin Americans were shorter and stockier. One was bald completely, the other had light brown hair. I waited in the house like Ernie asked me to. I guess in about forty-five minutes to an hour one of the individuals came in and told me that Mr. Brendel had made arrangements for Emily to walk home and I was to go down to the crossing and make sure she made it safely home at approximately three o'clock.
R. GEORGE: You took those instructions from a stranger?
HIGHTOWER: Yes I did. I had authorization to pick her up at school. Earlier when Mr. Brendel and I first started working

together, he considered me a friend and asked me if I would be willing to pick up and care for Emily if anything happened to him or Alice. This was for Primrose School and I'm not sure about the YMCA. So I left around three to go pick up Emily. I went down to the school and she had not come across, so I walked over and I saw this lady standing there. So I walked over and asked about Emily and they told me she had already left for the Y. I went to the office area and saw another member of our church, waved to her said, "Hi," and found out Emily went to the Y for certain. I went back to inform Ernie that Emily was at the Y and he became upset that I had gone out into the garage area. Gave me car keys (to the Toyota Camry) and told me to go pick her up.

R. GEORGE: Why did he get upset when you went into the garage area?

HIGHTOWER: There was business taking place between him and these people and I was not a part of it.

R. GEORGE: They're having a business meeting in the barn?

HIGHTOWER: Yes. I was told it was a business meeting. I took the car and left and went to the Y to try and pick up Emily as I had been requested to. They would not let me have her. They said I was not authorized. They said I needed confirmation from one of her parents, so I went back to the house. This time I pulled up and waited in the car. Ernie came out, I told him the situation and he called the Y, came back out and gave me his driver's license, and I went back to the Y and picked her up. I picked her up around four or four-thirty. I drove home, drove the car up to the garage, and we went in the house. Emily went upstairs to her room and I stayed downstairs.

R. GEORGE: What happened next?

HIGHTOWER: I was getting concerned about the fact that I had not made it to the bank yet to take care of the finances that needed to be taken care of. I had irritated Mr. Brendel by going into the garage. He told me to stay in the house and to do what the others said to do, so I was concerned about going back into the garage to discuss this issue with him. Shortly after, around four-forty-five one of the people came into the house and told me that Alice would be coming home soon and wanted to know where Emily was. I said, "Probably upstairs." And then there was a knock at the front door. The fellow said, "Oh that's the bedding that's coming. Mr. Brendel wants that canceled and rescheduled for delivery on Monday." So I answered the door and told him, and he said, "Fine, no problem." This is around five. Mr. Brendel told me to follow the instructions of the others.

R. GEORGE: Was the man that told you to cancel the delivery the same man that told you to pick up Emily?

HIGHTOWER: Yes it was. He was probably about five-eleven. Latin American, I think, and he was bald. Never saw him before that day.

The little details injected into the recitation lent an air of authenticity to the fabrication.

R. GEORGE: What finances were you talking about?

HIGHTOWER: The rent with Mr. Murphy on my office because of some bounced checks. The agreement was that Ernie would cover the checks for me and I was to pay for an extra month's rent so we would have time to complete the root cellar and move my equipment.

R. GEORGE: What about the check that was cashed that evening?

HIGHTOWER: I believe it was $2,700. I signed the check in Ernie's name. This gentlemen said that was not a problem. I went out to the garage with this gentlemen at this time to . . . no . . . I went ahead and wrote out the check. He told me to write it for $2,700.

Chris never explained why the man told him it was all right to forge Ernie's name to a twenty-seven hundred-dollar check which would clean out the Brendel account. Why didn't they have Ernie sign it himself rather than take the risk of detection with a forged signature?

HIGHTOWER: This took place downstairs at a little round table in the living room. We were waiting for Alice to come home because no plans were made for dinner that evening. So I was sitting on the couch waiting for Alice and this other individual was in the dining room. Alice came in. This is around five-thirty. She saw the gentlemen standing there and she knew him. She greeted him by name and went up and gave him a hello hug. This alleviated my concerns about having written out the check. I put Mr. Brendel's signature on the check because the gentlemen that came into the house said it was all right. When Alice came home Emily came down to see her and very quickly after the greeting, the three of them went back upstairs. Mr. Brendel was still out in the garage.

I went to Hospital Trust to cash the check. Prior to that I had to go out and get the car. The car was in the garage. When the people first arrived at the house there was a car in the driveway and it had to be moved. One of them moved the car and I got the Brendel's car to drive. When I went out to get the car I told Ernie what I was doing and he said, "Fine, don't spend the extra cash because we'll need it to buy supplies for the conversion of the root cellar." So I said I was going to Sears to buy some clothes and he said, "Your bills are stretched far enough. Take my Sears card and use that." So I did.

This was a magnanimous act for a man who thought he had been cheated and had lodged a formal complaint against Chris. It seemed incredible Ernie would think about Chris's back rent and his need for new clothes while involved with the four men.

HIGHTOWER: When Alice came home we discussed what to do for dinner and because Ernie was tied up outside, we decided I would pick up food for the four of us. From Hospital Trust I went to Citizens Bank where I got a money order to take care of the rents for Mr. Murphy and I deposited a sum in my account to cover the purchase of the crossbow and another bill that I had written out and kept $100 cash.

R. GEORGE: What was your state of mind when you left the Citizens Bank?

HIGHTOWER: I was doing what I was told to do. Mr. Brendel had become my benefactor at this point. I felt that he had probably effectively ruined my opportunity to make my business succeed, yet he was coming back around and said he would supply the funds to see the business was successful and we would together put together an effective business.

R. GEORGE: At 6:00 P.M. when you left the Brendel house, did you consider Mr. Brendel a friend?

HIGHTOWER: I don't know. He was my benefactor. I hadn't thought about friend or enemy.

R. GEORGE: What time did you get to Rhode Island Hospital Trust?

HIGHTOWER: Around six. I'm not sure. From there I went to my bank. Citizens. These banks are within three to five minutes of each other. Hospital Trust that evening was busy, so I waited in line before I got up to the teller's window.

R. GEORGE: Why were you looking toward the door?

HIGHTOWER: I was concerned about the people at the Brendels' house. I thought they were following me. After I left the two banks I went to Sears out at Swansea, where I purchased some clothing. Socks, jeans. Not much. I signed Mr. Brendel's name, used his charge card. My cards were overextended and Mr. Brendel said to. After Sears I went to a small restaurant on Route 6 called EATS and ordered dinner for the four of us. It was a carryout fish and chips order and a bowl of clam chowder. From there I went back to the house. It was around seven-thirty or eight. Alice and Emily went inside the house. Mr. Brendel was still in the garage with the other four people.

If the four men were still at the Brendel residence, the logical question raised in the minds of those who listened was, who, then, had followed him to the bank?

HIGHTOWER: I think at this time there were three in the garage and one inside the house. When I arrived, I put the car in the garage, interfered with what was going on. There was paperwork all over the floor. I drove the car in and first they started moving it, then they said, "Just drive over it." I got out and took the food and bag of clothes and everyone went back into the house at that time.

R. GEORGE: Was there any conversation at this point?

HIGHTOWER: Very little. I wasn't paying attention. I had problems of my own. I was thinking about what I was getting myself into with Mr. Brendel. My family. So the four of us ate. The people that came into the house with us went downstairs. Mr. Brendel had a lot of files downstairs and they were going through his files down there. Once we finished eating, Ernie and the other people went into the garage. One of them stayed downstairs. One of the other people stayed in the house. So only two went in the garage with Ernie. The one that stayed upstairs with Emily, Alice, and myself was the same gentlemen that stayed in the house earlier. The bald one.

R. GEORGE: Who went into the garage with Mr. Brendel?

HIGHTOWER: One of the Chinese and one of the Latin Americans. They spoke English with deep accents.

R. GEORGE: Did they go by name?

HIGHTOWER: There was only one name that I heard at this time. Names were not mentioned. Except for when Mrs. Brendel arrived home from work and gave him a greeting and called him Raoul, she said, "Raoul, how good it is to see you." So we were in the house. This is Friday evening. Mr. Brendel went back out into the garage and I stayed downstairs in the living room for the rest of the evening. Occasionally went into the kitchen for coffee.

R. GEORGE: Did you attempt to contact your family at any point?

HIGHTOWER: Yes. Before I went to the bank. I attempted to call to get the keys I needed for my office because I left them there and to find out the address of my ex-wife.

R. GEORGE: What time did you go to bed that Friday evening?

HIGHTOWER: Early. I had a busy day on Saturday. Around ten-thirty or eleven. The next day I had to do things . . . when I went to bed Alice and Emily were upstairs and Ernie was still in the garage. They were going through a lot of paperwork. I woke up on Saturday around six. I went upstairs to take a shower. When I went upstairs this individual was with Mrs. Brendel at the computer desk. I went in and took my shower and told them, at that time, things I needed to do for the day. Went back downstairs, put on the coffee, drank a cup, and started to leave the house. I did not see Ernie in the house. When I left, I went back out into the garage and they were still there.

R. GEORGE: Is it your testimony that a letter was printed at 6:46 A.M. on Saturday?

HIGHTOWER: I'm aware of that from the testimony. That was the letter allegedly written by Mr. Brendel.

R. GEORGE: Did you print that letter?

HIGHTOWER: No.

Earlier testimony had shown Chris's fingerprint was on the Print key of the printer establishing that he was the last person to print a document.

HIGHTOWER: I went into the garage to get the bicycle. I knew Mr. Brendel had plans for the weekend and knew he'd be using the car.

The fear of irritating Ernie by going into the garage unannounced no longer seemed to be a factor in Chris's thinking.

HIGHTOWER: When I got into the garage I realized the bicycle was not there, that I had left it at Jones Circle. The bike was located at the edge of the property and I didn't feel it would be a problem. I had no intentions of going into the house. So I left the Brendel house around 7: A.M. I went back to Jones Circle, I walked there. I walked down Middle

Highway to the bike path and cut across to Rumstick Road and walked down Rumstick. I was thinking that I wanted to see my son at soccer. I was one of the coaches. So I got the bike and left. I don't know if anyone saw me. From there I took the bicycle and I either went to the police station or to Newport Creamery. I wanted to make restitution on the check for Mr. Murphy for my rent. I knew I had to be at the soccer field at ten o'clock. I know I went to the police station before I went to the soccer field.

R. GEORGE: Why didn't you tell the police what was going on at the Brendels' when you went to the police station?

HIGHTOWER: I didn't think there was anything wrong. I thought it was business. There was no hostility or aggression or foul language.

R. GEORGE: Do you remember the police officer you dealt with that morning?

HIGHTOWER: No. Officer McGuiness maybe. So I paid what I owed on the check. Had conversation with the officer. I never finished the conversation I started with him. I was in a hurry. I felt uncomfortable. I wanted to get out. I ate breakfast at the Creamery. I got to the soccer game early, around nine-thirty. As the children started arriving at the soccer field, I organized them and started a warm-up session. I was anxious to see my children. I wasn't sure if they would arrive or not because of the conversation I had the previous evening with my father-in-law. He said the restraining order prohibited me from being around the children. But there were other children dependent upon me as their coach. So I thought it best to be there. Before I went to the soccer game I stopped at my office to speak with Mr. Murphy. But he wasn't in. I ran into his associate, Ray Duvall, in the parking lot. I told him that I had lost my keys and asked him if he would make another set off of their master set.

When he related the incident of how he had been asked to leave the soccer field where he had hoped to see his boys, he broke down again.

It had been a long day. Nerves were strained and on edge. A halt was called to the proceedings until the next morning.

Chapter 28

A Helpless Witness to Murder

The Second Day of Hightower's Testimony—April 1, 1993

The second day of Hightower's testimony started late because the judge had to go to a funeral.

Robert George resumed the direct examination where he had left off the day before. His client had regained most of the composure he had lost during his four hours of direct testimony the day before.

R. GEORGE: After the incident at the soccer field, where did you go and how did you get there?

HIGHTOWER: I took the Brendels' bicycle and returned to Middle Highway.

R. GEORGE: What time did you get back there?

HIGHTOWER: I don't know. The soccer game was scheduled to begin at ten, the game had just begun so I assume it was ten when I left the field. It was a ten- to fifteen-minute ride on the bicycle to the Brendels', so I was probably back by ten-fifteen.

R. GEORGE: When you got there, did you see Alice Brendel?

HIGHTOWER: Yes I did. She was inside the house with Emily. I put the bicycle in the garage. Mr. Brendel and the individuals who were with him were there. I went inside the house. Alice was there. I did not see Emily at that time. Alice was preparing some lunch. Very shortly after I had returned, the people with Mr. Brendel had entered the premises and everyone had lunch.

R. GEORGE: In the kitchen?

HIGHTOWER: Yes.

R. GEORGE: Where were people sitting in the kitchen?

HIGHTOWER: There is sort of a breakfast nook area. The Brendel family and myself sat down before we ate, the others stood around the counter. There was not enough room for eight people sitting in the kitchen area.

R. GEORGE: Where were people seated?

HIGHTOWER: Mr. Brendel and Alice on one side, Emily and I on the other side. The others were standing. There's an area behind the table. One was leaning up against that. Two were leaning over against the sink. Maybe one next to the refrigerator.

R. GEORGE: Were they eating?

HIGHTOWER: Yes.

R. GEORGE: Were they speaking?

HIGHTOWER: No. Very little was being said. A hushed atmosphere.

R. GEORGE: How long did this meal take?

HIGHTOWER: About twenty minutes.

R. GEORGE: Around noontime that Saturday, were you still being followed as a result of your activities earlier that week?

HIGHTOWER: I felt that anytime I went out, somebody was following me around. Someone from this group of four people.

Chris had testified the day before that he had gone to the police station to make restitution on his bounced rental check to Mr. Murphy. Why hadn't the man following him questioned him about what he may or may not have told the police while he was there?

R. GEORGE: On that Saturday when you were having lunch at the Brendels' did you have a place to live?

HIGHTOWER: I was staying with the Brendels at that time. No sir.

R. GEORGE: As you were eating lunch that day, what was your state of mind?

HIGHTOWER: Mr. Brendel was, we had entered into a partnership . . . I wasn't thinking about much of anything. It was an association with Mr. Brendel at that time and I did what he told me to do.

R. GEORGE: Did you believe Mr. Brendel was your enemy at this time?

HIGHTOWER: I remember discussing yesterday about enemies and friendship, but this day I believed that he was my friend because of the relationship that had been reestablished.

R. GEORGE: Are you certain that Mr. Brendel was sitting with you at that table at lunch that day?

HIGHTOWER: Yes.

R. GEORGE: How was he dressed?

HIGHTOWER: He was wearing jeans, a shirt, shoes, a shirt. I don't remember the specifics.

R. GEORGE: How was Emily dressed?

HIGHTOWER: Jeans and a shirt, but again, I don't remember.

R. GEORGE: Do you recall what Mrs. Brendel was wearing?

HIGHTOWER: She was wearing a green skirt and the blouse that has been exhibited here, I believe.

R. GEORGE: What was she wearing when she arrived at the house the day before?

HIGHTOWER: I believe those were the same clothes she was wearing at that time.

R. GEORGE: What did you have to eat?

HIGHTOWER: There were primarily sandwiches. Soup had been fixed for Emily.

R. GEORGE: What did you do after lunch?

HIGHTOWER: Again, I was taken into the living room. Mrs. Brendel and one of the people went back upstairs along with Emily. Mr. Brendel at this particular time went down into the basement. I'm not sure how long they were down there before they returned to the garage.

R. GEORGE: Would you say you were taken? Were you a prisoner of some sort?

HIGHTOWER: No. It was suggested that I wait in the living room.

R. GEORGE: Who suggested that?

HIGHTOWER: One of the individuals that was with Mr. Brendel.

R. GEORGE: Can you describe the person that suggested you go into the living room?

HIGHTOWER: I'm not sure I remember.

R. GEORGE: Where did Emily go?

HIGHTOWER: She went upstairs with her mother and the other gentlemen that went upstairs with them.

According to Hightower's testimony, the four men were looking for something and this was the motive for the triple murder. It was not mentioned at this time what the something was.

R. GEORGE: Did you feel anything was wrong at this time?

HIGHTOWER: I'm not sure whether anything was wrong or not. It was obvious that there was something that was being looked for and it was taking an awful long time to find it.

R. GEORGE: After you went into the other room, what happened next?

HIGHTOWER: I was there for a period of time, I don't recall how long I was there.

R. GEORGE: Did you see anyone or hear anyone while you were in that room?

HIGHTOWER: Periodically someone would come down from upstairs, but basically I was there by myself.

R. GEORGE: Do you recall seeing a videotape of the interior of the Brendels' home sometime during this trial?

HIGHTOWER: Yes sir, I did.

R. GEORGE: How did that appear to you compared to when you were there that Saturday afternoon?

HIGHTOWER: It appeared to be about the same. I think the desk area was a little more messy than what it had been than when I was on the premises. But everything else looked to be about normal.

R. GEORGE: What happened next?

HIGHTOWER: At some point Mr. Brendel and one of the other individuals came into the house and stated that they were trying to locate some funds, some money, and they asked if they could go through my records at the office. I said yes and we went to the office . . . One of the individuals went with me. I took him upstairs to the office and showed him where the records were located so that he could go through them. And I left him there.

Why he would agree to allow strangers to search his office for money was never addressed.

R. GEORGE: Describe the individual who went with you back to your office.

HIGHTOWER: He was the other Latin American individual. He had brown, tannish hair.

R. GEORGE: What was his name?

HIGHTOWER: I don't know.

R. GEORGE: How did you get to the office?

HIGHTOWER: We took Mr. Brendel's car.

R. GEORGE: Did you speak with this individual on the way to the office?

HIGHTOWER: No.

R. GEORGE: Did you think anything was wrong?

HIGHTOWER: I was lost in my own thoughts. I wasn't thinking about what was going on that much. I had my own problems I was dealing with.

R. GEORGE: Do you know what time you left Middle Highway with this individual?

HIGHTOWER: I've had trouble reconstructing the time, events as things occurred. I've put together a time line relative to the events that have been stated here in court.

R. GEORGE: Do you know what time you left your office?

HIGHTOWER: Approximately three o'clock.

R. GEORGE: So when you left Middle Highway at that time, was Mr. Brendel alive?

HIGHTOWER: Yes. And Emily and Alice.

R. GEORGE: When you got to the office, what occurred?

HIGHTOWER: I showed him the records and I left.

He never established which records, in particular, he showed the man.

HIGHTOWER: Before we left Middle Highway, Mr. Brendel had stated that she (Alice) had trouble sleeping the previous night and asked me to try to get some sleeping pills for her, which I did. But I don't remember when I went to get them. Either when I left the office or at some point later that afternoon.

It was never determined whether he had a prescription for sleeping pills. It was unlikely that any pharmacist would have given him sleeping pills without a doctor's prescription. However, he could get diphenhydramine, a strong antihistamine, without a prescription.

R. GEORGE: How many people did you leave at your office?

HIGHTOWER: One person.

R. GEORGE: Why did this person want to see your records rather than Mr. Brendel's?

HIGHTOWER: They had been going through Mr. Brendel's records for the last day and a half. And when one of the individuals came in they said they were looking for some funds that had been misplaced and they wanted to go through my records.

R. GEORGE: After you left the office did you see anyone?

HIGHTOWER: No.

R. GEORGE: How did you leave the office?

HIGHTOWER: I walked down the stairs, out to the front, got in the car, and left.

R. GEORGE: Where did you go?

HIGHTOWER: At this time I went to Sears. I don't know if I stopped at CVS prior to going there or later that afternoon. Sometime before I returned to Middle Highway I had stopped at CVS.

R. GEORGE: What did you buy at Sears?

HIGHTOWER: Two gas cans.

R. GEORGE: Why?

HIGHTOWER: There was concern that muriatic acid had not been removed. All of the residuals were still left in the barn.

R. GEORGE: What residual?

HIGHTOWER: Heroin.

There was a light gasp in the courtroom. The story had taken another bizarre twist with the mention of heroin. Robert George seemed nonplussed at the reaction in the court.

HIGHTOWER: So they, at one point, had mentioned whether gasoline should be placed on the floor.

R. GEORGE: Did you ever see heroin there?

HIGHTOWER: Thursday evening when the people left the garage with the van they were carrying cases of what appeared to be wine and loaded it into the van. I did not specifically see heroin. Mr. Brendel told me that's what it was.

R. GEORGE: When did Mr. Brendel tell you that it was heroin and not wine?

HIGHTOWER: That was part of our discussion on Thursday evening. Up until that time I had been kept pretty much out of what was going on and he told me a little bit about what was going on. His comment was something to the effect that the less you know about it, the better off you'll be.

R. GEORGE: Where did that conversation take place?

HIGHTOWER: Inside the garage. Thursday evening. After Mr. Brendel returned home we were spreading muriatic acid over the floor.

R. GEORGE: When did these four men arrive?

HIGHTOWER: They were there Thursday afternoon when I arrived at the Brendel residence with the crossbow.

Judge Sheehan was quick to catch the discrepancy. In the testimony the day before, Hightower had said he was in the house and Ernie told him to let the four men in. Now he was testifying they were already present inside the house when he arrived.

JUDGE SHEEHAN: Excuse me. Correct me if I'm wrong, but you said you let them in . . .
HIGHTOWER: No sir, I don't recall saying that.

Judge Sheehan made a note and the testimony continued.

R. GEORGE: What time did you arrive on Thursday?
HIGHTOWER: Approximately six-fifteen or six-thirty with the crossbow. As I pulled into the driveway, a white van was parked up against the garage. The door was open. The van had backed up toward the garage. The people were inside as I approached. I was very quickly hurried out. I was there no longer than two or three minutes. The crossbow was placed inside the garage at that time. Ernie had asked that I return.
R. GEORGE: When did you have time to spread the muriatic acid at that time?
HIGHTOWER: We didn't. It was done in the evening, after Mr. Brendel had returned from his meeting someplace in Massachusetts.
R. GEORGE: It's your testimony that Mr. Brendel told you at that time, on Thursday night, that you were using the muriatic acid to wash away heroin stains?
HIGHTOWER: Should there have been any residual dust that had fallen off with the moving of the boxes, yes sir.
R. GEORGE: Do you know Mr. Brendel was a patent attorney?
HIGHTOWER: Yes, I did.
R. GEORGE: Did you ever see any heroin in that barn?
HIGHTOWER: No, only what I was told.

R. GEORGE: Was anyone else present when Mr. Brendel said this to you?

HIGHTOWER: No. Mr. Brendel told me that he was receiving shipments of heroin. It was being brought into the country via wine casings, bottles. They thought they had an extremely good method of bringing it in and that the bottles were filled, dipped in the acid, and then in liquid paraffin to remove any residuals to eliminate the ability of dogs to pick up the scent.

A hush fell across the court. Family members of the murdered Brendels were sitting in clenched outrage at the runaway testimony being delivered against a man who could not defend himself against such a serious accusation: running heroin.

R. GEORGE: You had this discussion with Mr. Brendel prior to the discussion you had in the house?

HIGHTOWER: That particular aspect of it, yes.

R. GEORGE: This conversation took place. . . .

Suddenly, Judge Sheehan interrupted.

JUDGE SHEEHAN: Excuse me a moment.

Hightower turned to look at the judge politely.

JUDGE SHEEHAN: There's something there in front of you. Read it to yourself. There's something I really want to . . .

HIGHTOWER: Yes sir. I read it yesterday.

JUDGE SHEEHAN: All right. You understand it then?

HIGHTOWER: Yes, I really do.

JUDGE SHEEHAN: (Doubtfully) Okay.

The judge was referring to the perjury card all witnesses had before them on the witness stand as a reminder against committing perjury.

George continued on to the next allegation against the dead man.

R. GEORGE: It's your testimony that Mr. Brendel was going to turn against you with the CFTC?

HIGHTOWER: The intent was to get control of my business and I do not believe that there was ever an intent to file the lawsuit. The intent was not to carry through with the lawsuit. He wanted control of my business.

R. GEORGE: Did he tell you that?

HIGHTOWER: Yes.

It was the first time Hightower charged Ernie with wanting to take control of his business. He was now accusing Ernie of trying to rob him of his system.

R. GEORGE: After leaving Sears, where did you go?

HIGHTOWER: I believe I went to McDonald's.

R. GEORGE: Where did you go from there?

HIGHTOWER: I could have returned to Barrington and went to the CVS at that time, or from there I went to Somerville Lumber.

R. GEORGE: Is that where you bought the muriatic acid?

HIGHTOWER: Yes. I picked up additional muriatic acid; if we didn't use the gasoline on the floor, then there was more acid to put down.

R. GEORGE: What was your state of mind when you went into the Somerville Lumber to buy the acid?

HIGHTOWER: I was doing what I was told to do by the people that were with Mr. Brendel. Some suggestions that came from Mr. Brendel.

R. GEORGE: Do you have any memory of what you did next?

HIGHTOWER: I either returned to the Brendel residence or stopped at CVS.

R. GEORGE: When you returned to the Brendels', did you see Ernest Brendel at that point?

HIGHTOWER: Yes, and his wife and Emily.

R. GEORGE: Was anyone else there?

HIGHTOWER: The three individuals. When I returned to

Barrington, I stopped back by my office and picked up the individual that I had left there.

R. GEORGE: Can you describe the physical appearance of that person you picked up?

HIGHTOWER: He was Latin American and had blond, brown hair, about my size, maybe a little stockier. He's not the one that I recall that well.

R. GEORGE: Were you still being followed?

HIGHTOWER: Yes.

Chris's testimony was raising more questions than it cleared up. Doubts as to the truthfulness of his account continued to pile up. He had yet to establish who could have been following him. Three of the men were in the Brendel house when he returned and he had one of the mysterious individuals in the car with him.

R. GEORGE: Do you recall the time you got back to Middle Highway?

HIGHTOWER: No.

R. GEORGE: Where did you see the Brendels at that point?

HIGHTOWER: I pulled into the garage with the vehicle and the other gentleman that was with me. It looked like they were starting to put together a lot of the paperwork that had been scattered about the garage. It was being stacked into piles. Mr. Brendel was with them at that time, and we went back into the house. Mr. Brendel went straight into the basement with these other individuals. The things that I had purchased had been left in the car, and I went back into the living room.

R. GEORGE: Where was Emily at this point?

HIGHTOWER: I don't know. I assume upstairs.

R. GEORGE: Did you see Mrs. Brendel at this point?

HIGHTOWER: No.

R. GEORGE: Where else did you go?

HIGHTOWER: Shortly before nine o'clock, I went to the local grocery store. I purchased a box of garbage bags. . . . I don't recall if I was told or if I was just concluding that the trash needed to be collected.

R. GEORGE: So you say when you went to the grocery store you were doing what you were told?

HIGHTOWER: Yes, I believe so. After I purchased the bags I went back to the Brendels'.

R. GEORGE: When you left the house to go to the grocery store, were the Brendels alive?

HIGHTOWER: Yes.

R. GEORGE: What time did you return?

HIGHTOWER: It only takes about ten or fifteen minutes. I took the Brendel vehicle.

R. GEORGE: Were you being followed at that time?

HIGHTOWER: I believe so.

R. GEORGE: Was anyone with you when you went to Almacs (the grocery store)?

HIGHTOWER: No.

R. GEORGE: When you got back to the Brendel home, do you recall what time it was?

HIGHTOWER: Nine-fifteen. I'm not sure?

R. GEORGE: When you got there, what did you do?

HIGHTOWER: I gave the bags to Mr. Brendel and the people in the garage and returned to the house.

R. GEORGE: What happened next?

HIGHTOWER: Two of the individuals came into the house. I don't know what they looked like. I think I was on the couch. They grabbed my hands, and I was handcuffed.

R. GEORGE: What was your state of mind when you were handcuffed?

HIGHTOWER: I didn't know what was happening? Nothing had gone wrong all weekend and we were doing what we were told. There were no threats of danger or anything and I just didn't know what was happening.

R. GEORGE: Did you feel there was danger now?

HIGHTOWER: Yes. I was handcuffed and taken out to the garage.

R. GEORGE: When you got out to the garage, how did you enter it?

HIGHTOWER: Through the garage door. I was taken through the door and as you face going through the door off to the left toward the door which entered into the small room which was isolated from the rest.

R. GEORGE: What happened?

HIGHTOWER: The place was covered with blood. It was obvious that Mr. Brendel had been in a bad fight with these individuals.

R. GEORGE: Do you know what time it was when you went into the garage?

HIGHTOWER: I had been in the house for about forty-five minutes to an hour. Emily and Mrs. Brendel were not in the garage when I went in. They wanted to know where the money was. They kept talking, "We want our money." At that time, I was handcuffed, and they took a shortened piece of stick and ran it through my arms so that I was in a position that I couldn't fight. . . .

Mr. Brendel wouldn't tell them where the money was located. So they brought Emily out. They brought Alice out to the garage. There was one man with Mr. Brendel, there was one that was holding me, and two of them went into the house and got Alice and brought her out to the garage. They were threatening to kill everyone if the Brendels didn't tell them where the money was. I don't know if Ernie didn't believe them or what, but they brought Alice out into the garage. There was some cloth. She came in through the door, she saw the mess that was there, and she called out, "Raoul, what's going on?" And they just wrapped the cloth around her neck and they strangled her.

As he spoke, Hightower was staring somnambulistically into the space in front of the witness stand as though he were re-creating the murder scene in his mind exactly as it happened, and reliving the horror of it.

R. GEORGE: Who strangled Mrs. Brendel?

HIGHTOWER: The two people who went in and got her. I don't know what they looked like or how they were dressed. I don't believe that anyone could kill someone like that. This wasn't happening. It was incredulous (sic). Mr. Brendel was still being held inside the garage. When I first went into the garage, the blood was from Mr. Brendel. He had been beaten up very badly. The cars at this point were in the garage.

R. GEORGE: How was Mrs. Brendel dressed when you saw her come into the garage?

HIGHTOWER: I don't remember.

R. GEORGE: What happened next?

It was never mentioned what Ernie was doing while Alice was murdered, or why, in the face of Alice's brutal murder, Ernie would not tell them what they wanted to know in order to save his daughter.

During the testimony in which he claimed he witnessed the murder, Hightower's eyes behind his steel-rimmed glasses, were wide, almost bug-eyed. He cried and looked as though he was unable to control his anguish.

HIGHTOWER: Ernie still hadn't told where the money was. They went in the house and got Emily and brought her out into the garage. They said they would kill her if Ernie didn't tell them where the money was. I couldn't believe it. Kill a child! It was so crazy! I pushed the guy up against the wall and broke away from him. The guy that had Emily was choking her. I hit him with my shoulder. Tried to push him away. One of the guys that was standing next to him grabbed me and hit me in the groin area. I fell down to my knees. Someone was behind me. They took the cloth they had used to kill Alice and wrapped it around my neck, to hold my head up . . .

When Alice's body was removed from her makeshift grave, the cloth that had been used to strangle her was still wrapped so tightly around her neck that it almost cut into her skin. It did not appear to have been removed and reapplied.

HIGHTOWER: . . . and they stood there and they strangled her (Emily) and he said, "This is what's going to happen to your kids if you don't do exactly as we tell you." He killed her right there.

The medical examiner had testified that Emily's body showed no physical evidence of strangulation. What the autopsy revealed was a nonlethal dose of sleeping pills in her system.

HIGHTOWER: Then they proceeded to kill Ernie. They shot him with the crossbow. They shot him in the chest, twice. No . . . they shot him in the chest once, then he fell down, and they shot him in the head once. And his body was going through spasms and they said, do you think your wife will do this when we kill her . . . and then they shot him again in the chest.
R. GEORGE: How long did this all take?
HIGHTOWER: I don't know. I had no concept of time. I had lost it. I'm gone. I couldn't believe anyone could kill anyone because they wanted money, or kill a child. I don't recall for sure what happened next. I was taken back into the house for a while. . . .

Recess

A recess was called. The families showed no emotion. Although the jury had occasionally looked annoyed during the long testimony, the jurors had been riveted to the defendant's electrifying recounting of the murders. Robert George, who had been dreading Hightower's version of the murders, was beginning to appear pleased with the progress of the trial. He was trying to show inconsistencies in his client's testimony and much of what Chris was saying simply was not believable.

Back from Recess

Hightower began to testify about burying the murder victims.

R. GEORGE: After you were taken back into the house that Saturday evening, what happened next?

HIGHTOWER: I'm not sure how long I was there. There was someone that was always with me. At some time during the evening, a pillowcase or something was put over my head, and I was taken out to one of the cars but I don't know which car it was. They started driving. They drove around, for five minutes or thirty minutes or an hour, I don't know how long.

R. GEORGE: Who was with you during this drive?

HIGHTOWER: I don't know. There was a driver and somebody else in the car with me.

R. GEORGE: Did you have any conversation?

HIGHTOWER: I wasn't talking.

R. GEORGE: What was your state of mind at this point?

HIGHTOWER: I flipped out. I couldn't believe what I had seen.

R. GEORGE: Where did you go?

HIGHTOWER: I don't know. They took me someplace into the woods.

R. GEORGE: Where were the Brendels?

HIGHTOWER: They were dead.

R. GEORGE: Were they in the car?

HIGHTOWER: No. Not in the car that I was in.

R. GEORGE: Did you see them again?

HIGHTOWER: Yes.

R. GEORGE: At some point did you return to the house? Did you go somewhere?

HIGHTOWER: At some point we eventually returned to the house. Prior to that, they had taken me out into the woods, a wooded area. I didn't know where it was. And they wanted me to dig the grave site and I wouldn't do it. I refused to do it. One of the guys said to one of the others that, "We don't want to hurt his family right now. He's too valuable to us. So why don't we kill his sister-in-law. We know where she lives." He got in the car and drove off. I'm going crazy at this point. I didn't want my family hurt.

Unanswered questions:
Why did the four men have him dig the two graves instead of

digging them themselves. Why was Hightower so "valuable" to them?

R. GEORGE: Did you feel that these people were going to hurt your family?

HIGHTOWER: When the guy left, he said, "Kill Kathy." He knew her by name. I picked up the shovel and I started digging and said, "Please, I'll do whatever you want. Just leave them alone."

R. GEORGE: At this point, you were put out of the Slicker home. Were you angry at them for this?

HIGHTOWER: I was upset, yes. But it didn't mean that I didn't still love them. They were the ones that put me out. . . .

R. GEORGE: Did these persons say anything about any other members of your family other than your sister-in-law?

HIGHTOWER: At that time, as I recall, they said, "We don't want to hurt his family now. We can get to them at any time. We know where the boys play soccer. We know where your houses are in New Hampshire. We can get to you at any time we want to."

R. GEORGE: Did they say anything about your other family in Long Island?

HIGHTOWER: Yes. They knew the address, they knew my ex-wife's name. They knew my two children.

R. GEORGE: At this point did you feel they were all in danger?

HIGHTOWER: Yes I did.

R. GEORGE: In danger of what?

HIGHTOWER: Of being killed if I didn't do what I was told to do.

R. GEORGE: Being killed by whom?

HIGHTOWER: By the people who had just killed the Brendels. So I dug the graves. Three of the individuals were there when I did that. The other two had arrived with a second car.

R. GEORGE: After you finished the job, what happened next?

HIGHTOWER: They insisted the graves be small and shallow so the bodies could be found readily.

HIGHTOWER: And when it was over with, the pillowcase, or whatever it was, was placed over my head and I was taken back to the house.

R. GEORGE: Do you know what time you were back at the house?

HIGHTOWER: No. No idea.

R. GEORGE: Next?

HIGHTOWER: I don't remember much from Saturday night, Sunday morning, whatever time it was.

R. GEORGE: What's the next thing you recall?

HIGHTOWER: At some point I fell asleep. I'm not sure how long I slept. But I woke up sometime, or they woke me up, I don't know, Sunday morning. And I wanted to see my family. I wanted to make sure they were still alive and all right.

R. GEORGE: Did you still have handcuffs on?

HIGHTOWER: I don't remember.

R. GEORGE: What happened next?

HIGHTOWER: They said that I could see my family. That if I said or did anything, they would kill them. I drove to Newport.

Chris apparently saw no contradiction in four men who slaughtered an entire family in front of an eyewitness letting the eyewitness leave with only threats of violence against his family if he spoke about it.

HIGHTOWER: Church was scheduled for ten o'clock in the morning. I drove down to the Creamery and I sat in the parking lot facing the road. No. I'm sorry, that's not right. I drove by the house. Went past Rumstick Road onto another road that's right next to the house and I sat waiting to see the family leave the house for church. A fellow that was in the house came out, waved to me, and I acknowledged him.

R. GEORGE: A fellow came out of the house at Jones Circle?

HIGHTOWER: No, across Rumstick Road, the roads are offset. They don't butt each other.

R. GEORGE: Did you see your family at that point?

HIGHTOWER: Yes. I was in the Brendel car. The Toyota.

R. GEORGE: What was the condition of that automobile when you drove over to Rumstick Road?

HIGHTOWER: It was covered with blood.

R. GEORGE: What did you see?

HIGHTOWER: My father-in-law, my wife, my two children. They left the house in the Jeep. They came onto Rumstick and headed down toward the church. I followed behind and drove to Newport Creamery and I sat in the parking lot until church was over.

R. GEORGE: Were they in danger at that point?

HIGHTOWER: I was told if I didn't do exactly as I was told, they would kill them.

R. GEORGE: What happened next?

HIGHTOWER: I took the car to the Shell station and gassed it up. I paid with a credit card. It was my credit card. I didn't see anyone at the gas station. I was just there.

R. GEORGE: Did you see your family again after church?

HIGHTOWER: No. After getting gas, I returned to the residence.

George didn't ask Chris why he went back to the site of the triple murders rather than straight to the police. Hightower maintained all of the actions he had taken throughout this weekend, which had been substantiated by checks, sales receipts, and witnesses, had been threateningly ordered by the four murderers, two tall Chinese men and two short Latin Americans.

HIGHTOWER: The people were still there. I went into the house and they told me that there were things that they wanted done, and I did them. In the house there were files on the floor in the basement. Those files were put into the garbage bags and after that was completed, I was told to go to Summerville Lumber and purchase some items. Lime.

No one was in the car with me, but they were right there in the store with me.

R. GEORGE: What happened after you went to Summerville Lumber?

HIGHTOWER: I returned back to the Brendel residence with the items.

R. GEORGE: What was your state of mind on that Sunday afternoon?

HIGHTOWER: Scared, frightened. Frightened of these people and what they had done. For the safety of my family. At some point that afternoon I was taken back out to the garage and there was more acid put down on the floor. The garage door was washed. I had cleaned the windows on the car and put the baking soda in the backseat. Then I went back into the house and they had the letter that Mr. Brendel had written to the CFTC. But this was a different letter because it wasn't signed and they told me to put a signature on it and mail it.

Chris offered no explanation why four murderers would care about retracting Ernie's letter to the CFTC regarding Hightower's illegal brokering.

R. GEORGE: Did you see anyone at the house during this time?

HIGHTOWER: Yes. These people were still there.

R. GEORGE: Did anyone come to the door?

HIGHTOWER: Yes, a little girl looking for Emily. I answered the door and she asked if Emily could come out and play. All I could say was, "She's not home."

R. GEORGE: At some point did you leave the premises?

HIGHTOWER: Yes. I went to the White Church to put Mr. Brendel's signature on the documents that I had.

R. GEORGE: Why didn't you just sign his signature like you did on the check?

HIGHTOWER: None of this was supposed to have happened. All he wanted was control of the business. I didn't feel it was wrong at the time because it was an appropriate signature because he intended to withdraw the complaint. I was concerned about the legitimacy of the signature. I wanted it to be as legitimate as possible.

R. GEORGE: When had he told you he was going to withdraw the complaint?

HIGHTOWER: Thursday night.

R. GEORGE: When you went to the church who was there?

HIGHTOWER: Initially, when I got into the office I was by myself. But eventually the associate pastor, Rose Amodeo, came in.

R. GEORGE: Did you hear her testify here?

HIGHTOWER: Yes. My conversation with her was I talked about my children and wanting to have my children. I didn't say too much. I was scared and wanted to get out. I didn't know anyone would be at the church when I got there. I didn't realize there was a wedding going on. Usually on Sunday afternoons, the office was empty.

R. GEORGE: Did you tell the pastor where you were going?

HIGHTOWER: I told her I was going to New York.

R. GEORGE: After you were done at the church where did you go?

HIGHTOWER: I went back to my office and I had taken most of the things that had been at the Brendel residence and put them in my office . . . whatever was put in the bag by the individuals that were there. That included the gas cans, bag of items that had been picked up by the Brendels from their mother's house, and so forth. I took it upstairs to the office and left it there.

He never explained why the four murderers would give him so much evidence of murder—gas cans, lime bag, crossbow in the car, bloodied vehicle, etc.—and allow him to travel to Connecticut with the incriminating items that could convict them all. He did say he cooperated in order to protect his family; at no time, apparently, was he worried about his own safety.

R. GEORGE: When did you make the decision to go to Connecticut?

HIGHTOWER: I'm not sure when they started talking about it. It was sometime after the bodies were buried.

R. GEORGE: How did the trip to Connecticut come up?

HIGHTOWER: At some point they said they wanted to get more money and they told me what to do and what to say and that, if I didn't do it and if the police or the FBI showed up at the Scriabines' house, that they would kill my family. I left for Connecticut after I left my office. I drove in the Brendels' Toyota. I don't remember what time I left.

R. GEORGE: Did you stop anywhere on your way to Connecticut?

HIGHTOWER: Yes. I didn't know where I was going. There was a gas station. The only information I had was that they lived in Guilford, Connecticut, and I had the address. I stopped at a gas station and asked for directions.

Christine Scriabine had testified he showed her and her husband a Rolodex card with their address that had been taken out of Ernie's personal Rolodex file at home.

R. GEORGE: What was the condition of the car?

HIGHTOWER: I had washed the windows so that I could see out and I had put the baking soda in the backseat. Other than that, it was in the exact same condition as when the police took the car.

R. GEORGE: Was the bag of lime in the car?

HIGHTOWER: No. The crossbow was in the trunk. Before approaching the Scriabines' house, I stopped at a crossroads just before going on to the road where they live and I took the crossbow out of the car and placed it in a wooded area. I didn't want them to see that. It was bad enough what they were going to be seeing. I didn't want them to call the police. I didn't want my family jeopardized.

R. GEORGE: Was anyone following you?

HIGHTOWER: Yes, there was a car behind me. They were there. It was sometime before dinner that I arrived at the Scriabines'. I was asked to leave and come back at a later time so I left and went to a variety store/gas station and purchased some juices. I felt tired and dehydrated. I drove to McDonald's about two hundred feet away and parked in the parking lot and sat there. Then I returned around eight or eight-thirty. I stayed until about one in the morning. I discussed the story that has been relayed here about the kidnapping of the Brendel family and my own family, but my family had not been kidnapped. I talked to them about money. I told them the kidnappers wanted $300,000. And that I could raise the majority of the money and I asked them to provide, I think it was, $75,000. I told them there were people watching the house, that we were being watched. There was discussion on how to get the funds necessary. But I never asked the Scriabines to give me any money.

This was a direct contradiction to what the Scriabines had testified.

HIGHTOWER: I said that I had been told to raise the money. The damage had already been done. I was just doing what I was told to do. I told them I received a call from the Brendels at my office, but it wasn't true. I was given a story that was fabricated and I relayed it as best I could to the Scriabines. I left the things that had been placed in the car. I showed them the Toyota. I was supposed to have left everything with them that was in the car but somehow the handbags were covered up—Alice's handbags—either with my briefcase or with coats. I had two coats with me. I left my credit card and I allowed her to take my picture. I left a computer statement. I told them that I would keep them informed of everything that happened. Mrs. Scriabine told me that sometime Monday or Tuesday before the deadline on the ransom note they would call the FBI. I really lost it as Mrs. Scriabine said that because then my children would be killed.
R. GEORGE: How were you to get back to Barrington?
HIGHTOWER: The Scriabines wanted me to keep the Toyota there for evidence. I did everything they wanted ex-

cept to call the police. I left in the Brendels' Toyota. I stopped at this area where I had put the crossbow, I picked it up and put it in the car. I don't know why my fingerprints weren't on it because I handled it. I drove back to my office. Around three o'clock I arrived there (A.M.). When I got out of the car I collected my coat and briefcase and realized that Alice's handbags were still in the car so I put them in the trunk. I didn't want anyone seeing them and break into the car. Enough had already been destroyed and damaged. I lay down and tried to sleep. I couldn't sleep. I called the Scriabines and told them that there was no need for them to raise the money. I told them at that time that I could raise the funds. They were already dealing with enough grief. I talked with Mr. Scriabine. It was early Monday morning.

R. GEORGE: Where were these other people at this point?

HIGHTOWER: They were still there. They were not in my office. They were scattered around town. When I was returning from the Scriabines' house, I was unable to maintain control of the car. I was weaving all over the road and they made me pull over and one of the people got in the car and drove me back to my office. On the way I told him that they were going to call the FBI, that I didn't feel I had convinced them not to. He said, "That's all right. You've done what we wanted you to do."

This raised eyebrows in the courtroom. The murderers had followed him, and one had gotten into his car to drive it for him when he was too distraught to drive safely.

HIGHTOWER: That person got out of the car the same time when I arrived at the office.

R. GEORGE: What did he look like?

HIGHTOWER: He was one of the Orientals.

R. GEORGE: After you spoke to Mr. Scriabine, what did you do next?

HIGHTOWER: I believe I went to the post office next.

R. GEORGE: Why?

HIGHTOWER: I had the final instructions to carry through

for the day which were to mail the letter, to cash the final
check, and then I could start running.
R. GEORGE: Did you pay your American Express at that
time?
HIGHTOWER: I don't remember.

Recess

None of Chris's charm showed. His unsubstantiated tale of
heroin smuggling, blackmail, attempts to wrest control of his
business away from him by trying to steal his system and defa-
mation of Ernest Brendel's character deeply enraged everyone.

After the recess, as Hightower reentered the courtroom, he
tried to make eye contact with the jury. Some jury members held
their heads in their hands. Others looked away.

Hightower took the witness stand again, and Robert George
continued leading his client toward the insanity defense.

R. GEORGE: You had told me you went to the post office.
What did you do?
HIGHTOWER: I mailed some letters. The primary letter
was the letter to the trading commission and National Fu-
tures Association, the letters that had been originally written
by Mr. Brendel. Not the original letter but the copy of the
letter you have here. I put the American Express bill in the
mail but I don't remember when I wrote it out.
R. GEORGE: Where did you go next?
HIGHTOWER: I'm confused as to the events that morning.
I'm confused as to the time frames.
R. GEORGE: Do you recall going to the YMCA where you
picked up Emily on Friday?
HIGHTOWER: Yes I do. I had a picture ID taken.
R. GEORGE: Did you speak to anyone at the YMCA when
you went there that Monday morning?
HIGHTOWER: I would assume so. I asked to have an ID
taken.

R. GEORGE: Why did you want an ID taken?

HIGHTOWER: I don't know.

R. GEORGE: Where did you go next?

HIGHTOWER: At some point I went to the bank and I went to Dunkin' Donuts. I was at my office twice during that time frame.

R. GEORGE: Were you alone?

HIGHTOWER: No. I was being followed. The check I cashed was for $1,500. I had been told to go and cash the check. Originally when it was written out the money was to be used to buy supplies to convert the carriage house. I wrote it out when I wrote out the other check on Friday.

R. GEORGE: Then where did you go?

HIGHTOWER: I returned to my office. I was nervous knowing I was being followed. Looking out the windows.

R. GEORGE: Did you think the police were coming?

HIGHTOWER: At some point, yes, I knew they would be coming. But I was also being followed. I was told once I completed cashing the check and mailing the letters I would be free to do what I wanted to. At some point I left my office and went back out to the Brendel car and I waited in my office for a period of time because I wanted to make sure I'd be left alone. As I exited my office and went down the stairs one of the individuals was standing beside the tool-shed next to the office and he told me that I was free at that time. But if I spoke about what had happened within a time frame of four months that they would come and kill my family. I got in the car and this individual got in the car with me. I drove down Maple Avenue down to the gas station on the right-hand side, stopped, he got out and I continued driving to Newport. I was watching to make sure I wasn't being followed. I thought there was a station wagon following me but I had driven up to Castle Hill in Newport and waited for a while. I sat down and tried to organize my thoughts. I was confused. I had been at a scene of a crime, fingerprints, caught in a situation with Mr. Brendel, and it would appear to anyone that he was angry with me, the safety of my family. I was confused. I thought that if I could get to the FBI quietly they could provide safety for my family. So I left Newport and I was on my way to Providence when I was stopped in downtown Barrington.

The first police car that I saw was across the road from me. The officer turned on his lights and motioned for me to move over to the side of the road. At that time another car pulled up behind me so I pulled into the parking lot of the church. I waited for the police officers to approach the car and they asked me to get out and asked me who I was. Explained why I was being stopped and I told them I understood and I'd talk to them. They asked me to empty my pockets and I did. I had my wallet, keys, change, and I had the cash from the check that had been cashed. Credit cards, and I put them on top of the car. My initial reaction was great relief. I could finally provide protection for my family.

Detective Lazzaro and Inspector McGraw were standing behind me. After I emptied my pockets I was told to stand up against the car and spread my legs, which I did. Apparently I had not spread my legs wide enough because someone was banging on the heels of my feet. An officer had gotten down on his hands and knees and was hitting me on the back of the heels. Detective Lazzaro told him to knock it off. "Leave him alone."

R. GEORGE: When you were arrested, describe the motor vehicle.

HIGHTOWER: It was still covered with blood except the windows. The crossbow, the handbags were still in the trunk, the bag of lime was in the car. I think a hammer was in the trunk.

R. GEORGE: Did you talk about the condition of the car with the officers when you were stopped at St. John's Church?

HIGHTOWER: Yes, they asked me what was in the car and I explained to them what happened. I was read my rights and placed under arrest. I was put in the back of the police vehicle on my way to Barrington Police Department. I asked if there could be protection for my family. I was taken upstairs to the second floor of the Barrington Police Department. I went into one of the rooms where they conducted the interrogation. I was, again, read my rights, asked to fill out the rights form, which I did. I began speaking with the officers. I spoke to the police that day until about three in the morning.

R. GEORGE: Did you tell the police at that time everything you told us here today?

HIGHTOWER: No. I was asked some questions by Detective Lazzaro, whose process was very short, like ten minutes, and Inspector McGraw stood up and leaned over right in front of me and said, "Hightower, you did it and I'm going to prove you did it." And he walked out of the room and I flipped out.

At the time, no one knew the Brendel family had been killed. There had been some talk of kidnapping, but up until the time they were found forty-five days after Hightower's arrest, there was always a very active hope that the missing family would be found alive and well.

HIGHTOWER: I told them several times that my family had been threatened. I told them I was going to the FBI to provide protection for my family. And when the FBI inspector said he thought I did it, I didn't trust anybody. I spoke with Detective Lazzaro and Inspector Eaton until about eight that evening. Then I spoke with the state police from eight until approximately three the next morning. I asked for an attorney to be present sometime during my statement I was making to Detective Lazzaro and Inspector Eaton. That wish was not granted. It didn't matter what I said to them anymore. They thought I was the perpetrator and they were going to prove it so all I was going to tell them was what I was told to tell them and that was it. I wasn't going to give all the information. I corrected the written statement before I signed it and handed it to Detective Lazzaro. I told him this is not all the information, just the general idea, so I'll sign the papers, and I did.

Then I was taken in to talk with State Police Sergeant Hurst. They asked me to repeat the story and by this time it didn't matter. About halfway through again I asked for an attorney to be present and again I was denied access to an attorney.

Then they continued their interrogation until about two that morning. At two I was asked to remove all my clothing, my glasses, my watch, and I was taken downstairs. So for the next forty-five minutes I was interrogated, naked, by the state police. I was transferred downstairs to a holding cell with nothing but my jockey shorts to wear. I remember talking about an attorney being present, again.

Eventually, I was freezing. I kept asking for something to put on and they refused to give me anything. I was given a hospital gown to put on.

Victimized and intimidated by the police, Hightower claimed he was tortured by being kept cold, and was denied all of his civil rights by being refused an attorney, even though he was apparently being accused of kidnapping and extortion. He did not tell police the whole story and request his family be put under police protection, nor did he mention the four strange men, or the murder of the Brendels. He was offended at being unjustly accused by Inspector McGraw, so claimed nothing mattered to him any longer.

R. GEORGE: Did you write any letters from the ACI regarding this case?
HIGHTOWER: Yes. In the first week of my incarceration at the ACI, Deputy Warden Gardner came forward with a letter that had been written stating that if I didn't talk about what happened, if I didn't tell people where things were that they knew where my children played soccer and they would kill my children. That letter came from the outside. It was mailed into the ACI. Also during that time, within that first week, I met an inmate named Michael Giroux who became friendly with me. Mr. Giroux approached me and told me about the media and because of the excessive coverage that

this case was receiving that he thought he would write some ransom letters to the Scriabines to take the heat off of me.

When he did this I went crazy. He didn't know what he was dealing with. I did not ask him to write those first letters. He told me that he had mailed these letters to some friends of his, who had then mailed them out to the Scriabines.

R. GEORGE: Did you write any letters after that?

HIGHTOWER: Yes. Since he had done what he did, I asked him if he would help me. No one believed what I was saying. I said something to the effect, "You don't know what you're doing, Mike. You don't know the people that you're dealing with here. You're going to get my family killed. It's the TONG . . ." (The Chinese Mafia) "and you're going to get my family killed." I asked him if he would mail out a specific letter that I wrote saying that the Brendels were dead and that it was too late, "It's over with, they're dead, and leave the situation alone." Mike had told me that the first three letters that had been mailed out were signed by LYNX and I followed suit. We continued to talk and Mike apologized for his involvement. He saw how scared and concerned I was for the safety of my family, and he volunteered to assist, help get protection since the police didn't believe what had been told to them. He said he had friends on the outside that could help watch out for my family. And I wrote a note giving information about my father-in-law and sister-in-law, where they spent their time so they could be watched. These two individuals were the most vulnerable, they were alone a lot. And relative to the night when the Brendels were buried, they had said they would kill Kathy first. I was very worried about her.

There was some question as to how he could be so self-convincing, unless there was some mental illness.

Hightower was crying openly again, so much so that recess had to be called a little early. By the time court was back in session, the defendant was in control again.

HIGHTOWER: What I had done was write a letter detailing events that my sister (-in-law) and father-in-law did in the evening because Mr. Giroux had told me that he had friends on the outside who could follow them and see that there was nothing done to them. However, shortly after that letter was written, he approached me and said that it was impossible to do because it required too many man-hours. There was too much time involved, and it couldn't be done. And that perhaps an easier solution would be to send threatening letters to the family. I didn't care what I did as long as I got protection for my family. I wanted to talk to my wife. She needed to know what was going on.

R. GEORGE: How long has it been since you have spoken to your wife?

HIGHTOWER: Thursday, the nineteenth. (of September 1991)

R. GEORGE: How long has it been since you spoke to your in-laws?

HIGHTOWER: My father-in-law was Friday and that was unbelievable. Brief.

R. GEORGE: How long since you saw or spoke to your two sons?

HIGHTOWER: Thursday.

R. GEORGE: What happened next re: letters?

HIGHTOWER: We decided that threatening letters would be sent to the family. I tried calling the church to relay messages about threats I had been receiving in relationship to them. A block was put on the church phone so I was unable to communicate that way. I was completely shut off from any opportunity to communicate with my family whatsoever. Restraining order or not. So I agreed that we would send threatening letters to my family. Approximately two weeks after this agreement was made, another inmate, a friend of Mr. Giroux's, approached me and told me that everything I was saying and doing with Mr. Giroux was going to the state police. And at that point, it didn't matter anymore. At that point, I didn't care. If they thought I was trying to kill them, fine, but at least I could get protection for them. Then I became more aggressive with the letters.

R. GEORGE: After you were told that everything you were doing was going to the state police you still went through with everything?

HIGHTOWER: Yes I did. This continued getting more and more aggressive until a particular point in February where I had become extremely scared again because one of the correctional officers had come in and made a comment to me, "I see you want to get your family killed." When he made that comment it was after a particular set of LYNX letters which spoke about the deaths of the Brendels had been taken from me at the ACI. They were intercepted from the mail. They were not allowed to go into the mail.

R. GEORGE: You were mailing these letters from the ACI?

HIGHTOWER: There were two letters that I had sent through the mail at the ACI. They were signed LYNX and were in my handwriting. I was sending one of them to a first cousin and I had asked her to send it to John Hardiman, my attorney at the time, and the other letter was mailed out via another individual to go to John Hardiman. I did not send out any other letters.

R. GEORGE: How do you mail these letters from the ACI?

HIGHTOWER: You write letters and on your way to the chow hall, there is a mail box in front of the chow hall. You are supposed to deposit the letters inside the mailbox. Lieutenant Piccarelli was standing there at the mailbox on this particular day that I went to mail this letter and he confiscated it at that time. My understanding, after reading the rules and regulations concerning the deposit of mail, states that no outgoing mail will be intercepted or opened and read unless there is a direct situation where safety is involved at the ACI and these letters had nothing to do with the ACI. The letter had an incorrect address on it, but this was prior to its being mailed. They were confiscated and looked at prior to going in the mail. This should not have been done.

R. GEORGE: At this point, what month are we in?

HIGHTOWER: The letters were confiscated, I believe, November-December. I'm not sure. Prior to mentioning these two letters, I had been referring to a time frame of January-February. January being the time the correctional officer came into my cell and made those statements. When he made those statements I became extremely concerned about Kathy's safety and I started putting out to Mike a lot of information concerning Kathy and relative to the threatening letters that she be killed, knowing that this information was going to the state police. I had no problems with that. I had been given a time frame of four months in which not to talk about this whatsoever. February ended that four-month time frame and as soon as that time frame ended, I ceased all covert activities, if you will. I stopped everything. There was no need to go on. I prayed that my family would be safe from that time forward.

R. GEORGE: Do you believe your family is still in danger today?

HIGHTOWER: I believe that, after my testimony here today, that there is concern for their safety.

R. GEORGE: Do you feel if you were free that you could protect them?

HIGHTOWER: No. I don't believe I could protect them if these people decided they wanted to kill them.

R. GEORGE: Do you feel your in-laws are in danger today?

HIGHTOWER: Yes, a possibility . . . I haven't killed anybody. One of them was named Raoul. I was present as a hostage to the murders.

Although Hightower's entire testimony was telecast live into the living rooms of the regional community, and there were nightly summaries on the evening news, Susan could never bear to watch it. She could not watch Chris's vacant, bug-eyed appearance in what she felt was his inept attempt to con the jury into believing him. When her mother and Kathy passed on to her the incredible gist of his testimony, she was appalled at his audacity. Not only was it cruel and vicious; he was incredibly condescending in thinking he had the strength of personality to pull it off. *Stupid!!* His story had everything but the kitchen sink: the Italian Mafia, the Chinese Mafia (the Tong,) four mysterious and exotic strangers, heroin smuggling in wax-covered wine bottles, a mysterious white van, blackmail, a secret cache of an undetermined amount of money, a brutal triple murder, heroics, threatening letters with secret code names, murder for hire, assassins, being surreptitiously followed day and night, and even police brutality and a denial of his civil rights. As his testimony progressed, it would become even more bizarre with tapped telephone lines, dismembered bodies, and the suggestion that Emily was to be sold into white slavery in South America. It was a melting pot of every good and bad crime movie he had ever seen.

The direct examination was over. Now it was the prosecution's turn.

Chapter 29

Cross-Examination

April 2, 1993

Michael Stone had been waiting a long time to cross-examine Christopher Hightower. Not only had the prosecution built up a strong case, but the defendant had given him a great deal to work with through his own contradictory testimony. The trial had taken its toll on the prosecution team in terms of stress and anxiety, but at this late stage in the game, *nothing* was going to stand in the way of getting this guy. There would be no mistakes. No reason for an acquittal. No reason for a mistrial. However there was cause for concern on the third day of Hightower's testimony. At $4,000 a day, the jury had not been sequestered during the trial, nor would they be during deliberations. Judge Sheehan had each juror brought into court separately to ask each if he had seen the previous night's television newscasts regarding the trial. It had been widely reported that the judge had asked Chris Hightower if "he had read the card in front of him," referring to the perjury card. Some thought the judge's question implied he thought the witness was lying. No juror acknowledged seeing anything regarding the trial on the news.

Joking that he was not conducting a poll for any channel, the judge let the trial proceed.

Smiling thinly and looking self-assured, Hightower was wearing the same beige suit he had worn the day before, but with a black turtleneck instead of the white one he had been wearing.

Stone stood to begin his cross-examination.

M. STONE: Do you recall when you were stopped by the police?

HIGHTOWER: Yes I do.

M. STONE: When they approached you, did they have their guns drawn?

HIGHTOWER: No. The sergeant asked me to get out of the car and informed me they were investigating the disappearance of the Brendel family.

M. STONE: Did you think you were still being followed at this time?

HIGHTOWER: No. I didn't believe so. I was going to downtown Providence so I could get lost in a crowd and contact the FBI. The four men told me I was free to go after I dropped them at the Mobil station on Maple Avenue, about two blocks down from my office.

M. STONE: Did they (the police) handcuff you?

HIGHTOWER: Yes. Then we went to the Barrington Police Station, to the interrogation room. It was a fair-sized room, three or four desks in it. Telephones.

M. STONE: Did they take the cuffs off?

HIGHTOWER: Yes.

M. STONE: You indicated that it was Agent McGraw and Sergeant Lazzaro there?

HIGHTOWER: Yes. That's what I recall. Eventually a third individual came in to put together the photo montage.

M. STONE: Did you understand your rights?

HIGHTOWER: Yes, I understood that I could stop and ask for an attorney anytime I wanted to, but I don't recall being told I was a suspect while I signed the rights form.

M. STONE: But they told you when they stopped you at the red church you were a suspect?

HIGHTOWER: Yes. I knew why I was there.

This line of questioning went on for close to an hour. Hightower was forced to admit that he was offered a phone call and an attorney, and although he said this occurred well into the interrogation, the prosecutor was successful in discrediting Hightower's claim that his rights had been violated. Hightower even said several times that Detective Lazzaro had been very polite to him. In the next breath, he claimed Lazzaro had said to him, "With that bloody car and Alice's purse and everything else, do you think it was so unusual for Agent McGraw to think you were guilty? And you wouldn't tell them the story you told us yesterday because one detective said, 'You're guilty, and I'm going to prove it?' "

Recess was called. The trial then continued.

M. STONE: Did you really think you didn't look guilty?

HIGHTOWER: No. I admit it looked bad.

M. STONE: According to the testimony, the first thing you started talking about with the sergeant was the problems you were having with Ernie Brendel?

HIGHTOWER: I don't remember.

M. STONE: But you do remember that he never asked you to use the phone or for a lawyer?

HIGHTOWER: Not at the beginning. At the end he asked me if I wanted to use the telephone.

Judge Sheehan wanted a precise clarification of the issue.

JUDGE SHEEHAN: You said that at some point they did ask you to use the telephone to phone a lawyer. Did you exercise that right?

HIGHTOWER: No. It didn't matter anymore. My rights had already been violated. I couldn't trust the police anymore, so I just told the story I was told to tell. I asked if my family was being looked after and Sergeant Lazzaro said someone was with them right now. They sent a car right over to the White Church. I knew they took some steps to protect my family.

M. STONE: So they did what you wanted them to do. That was your primary concern?

HIGHTOWER: Yes.

M. STONE: When you were asked about why you had the Toyota, is that when you started talking about what happened that weekend?

HIGHTOWER: Yes.

M. STONE: But what you didn't do was start off by telling them the Brendels were murdered?

HIGHTOWER: I was not given the narrative. I was being asked the questions by Sergeant Lazzaro. It was his discussion and I was responding.

M. STONE: So you were not going to interrupt?

HIGHTOWER: He asked me to cooperate and I was.

M. STONE: Let's talk about Agent McGraw. You said about ten minutes into the conversation he stood up in front of you and told you he didn't believe you, right?

HIGHTOWER: Yes. He said, "Hightower, you did it and I'm going to prove you did it," and walked out of the room.

M. STONE: Did he threaten you or hit you?

HIGHTOWER: I believed it was a threat, yes. I never saw him again. He was replaced by Agent Eaton. Agent Eaton was polite. Sergeant Lazzaro asked me if I wanted something to eat or to use the bathroom.

M. STONE: Is it during this time you recall him asking you if you wanted to call a lawyer?

HIGHTOWER: No. It was toward the end of the statement. Halfway through the statement I asked Sergeant Lazzaro to have an attorney present.

M. STONE: As a matter of fact, you not only read your rights form, you made corrections on almost every page, and at the end, you added a paragraph of your own. If nothing mattered to you anymore, why would you bother to correct this?

HIGHTOWER: I was just functioning, doing what I was told. I was asked to read it and sign it and I did. But nobody forced me. Under duress, I did what I was told to do.

M. STONE: But you were in a blood-soaked Camry, a Devastator crossbow in the car, Alice Brendel's purse, the acid in the trunk, and you think somebody would have a hard time believing you?

HIGHTOWER: I was concerned about it, but I still don't think he had a right to say he didn't believe my story. Sergeant Lazzaro of the Barrington police, called me the week before to tell me I had to cover a check with Mr. Murphy within a week or they would arrest me.

Recess

Another recess was called. The high interest factor had made the morning speed by.

Michael Stone continued with his cross-examination of the defendant, once again standing comfortably on the stand. Hightower still smiled and appeared confident, but Stone was not about to let him relax. He reapplied the pressure.

M. STONE: Did you read your rights and initial each one?

HIGHTOWER: Yes I did. And I signed the rights form. But I was so frustrated at that point.

M. STONE: Why didn't you tell the state police what really happened?

HIGHTOWER: I thought the FBI was a higher authority

and after what Inspector McGraw said to me, I didn't want to tell them anything. I didn't trust them.

M. STONE: Would it be fair to say the story you told them was a lie with a few truths?

HIGHTOWER: Yes.

M. STONE: You stick to the same story, fact to fact, about your activities during the prior week don't you?

HIGHTOWER: Yes I did.

M. STONE: And some of it was factual. You told them you went to Thompson's, some other things that were true, that Sunday you had a hose at the Brendels'. . . . Did the state police mistreat you in any way?

HIGHTOWER: Yes. I asked for an attorney and I didn't get one. And at two o'clock I was asked to take my clothes off. They started to interrogate me again. And I said, "This is the third time I'm asking for an attorney." And Sergeant Hurst threw his arms in the air and looked at the other detectives that were there and said, "Did anybody hear him ask for an attorney the second time?" And for forty-five minutes I was interrogated in the nude.

M. STONE: But you understood your rights and knew you didn't have to say anything, and you tell us that the police officers' testimony here are lies, because they violated your rights?

HIGHTOWER: Yes, they violated my rights.

M. STONE: This story that you told to Lazzaro and Hurst, where did that come from?

HIGHTOWER: That was the story I was told to do when I went to the Scriabines' and I basically told the same story.

M. STONE: You gave day-by-day, hour-by-hour accounts of what you were doing, and you say you were told to say that? When did you rehearse this? When did they tell you, "This is the story you're to tell?

HIGHTOWER: Sometime on Sunday.

M. STONE: For twelve hours you deceived these officers and prevented them from finding out the truth, didn't you?

HIGHTOWER: A deception, yes. Preventing them from finding out the truth, yes.

M. STONE: And all because one agent got in your face?

HIGHTOWER: Yes.

M. STONE: Were you $40,000 to $60,000 in debt?

HIGHTOWER: Yes.

M. STONE: Where was that debt?

HIGHTOWER: It's scattered. Credit cards, the business, banks, people who leased me equipment, back rent, people. Mr. Werner, I owed $15,000, the Slickers I owed about $45 or $50,000, maybe more.

M. STONE: So we're up over $60,000 in debt?

HIGHTOWER: Yes. Probably as high as $100,000.

Laying the foundation for Hightower's desperate need for money—a motive for an attempt to extort $75,000 from the Scriabines—Stone pounded the extent of Hightower's outstanding debts repeatedly before going on to the next point of Hightower's chronic deceptions. During the interrogation, Stone submitted into evidence several substantiating documents to support his allegations. Hightower answered Stone's questions with little emotion, even while admitting again and again, how he had lied to achieve his personal ends.

M. STONE: You were able to get into a master's program at Wright State University with a 2.5 average that you had from the University of Rhode Island?

HIGHTOWER: No. I had contacted an individual at URI and obtained a forged transcript.

M. STONE: Exhibits 409 and 410, what do you recognize those to be?

HIGHTOWER: The transcripts I had the individual at URI send out.

M. STONE: Lastly, I'll show you #408.

HIGHTOWER: It's some of the same paperwork for the transcripts.

M. STONE: Did you graduate with a 2.44 average from URI?

HIGHTOWER: Yes, if that's what it says.

M. STONE: When you applied to Wright State it indicated your average was vastly different from that?

HIGHTOWER: Yes. A 3.97 average.

M. STONE: You said you graduated with the "highest distinction" didn't you?

HIGHTOWER: Yes.

M. STONE: You gave yourself perfect grades in almost every subject you took, didn't you?

HIGHTOWER: Yes.

M. STONE: When you were with . . . [Hightower's first wife], you applied to several medical schools, didn't you, like Poland, Northern Ireland, the Caribbean?

HIGHTOWER: Yes. I was accepted to one of them, the American University of the Caribbean, and yes, I was accepted there from the same phony transcripts.

M. STONE: At Riker Labs, weren't you a terrible salesman and didn't sales drop way back just before you left?

HIGHTOWER: I don't believe so. I left the job because I was unhappy with it. And I stopped performing the duties I was responsible for.

Hightower had testified he filed for the divorce from his first wife because she did not support his desire to sell their house and move to the Caribbean in order to allow him to attend medical school. However, the divorce decree entered into evidence showed that it was she who was the plaintiff in the divorce action, not he.

Michael Stone introduced two of Hightower's résumés into evidence. There was a side-bar conference with both attorneys and the judge before Stone could proceed to explore their significance.

Judge Sheehan ruled to permit the résumés into evidence. It was close to the end of the day, so he decided to end the session, and resume Monday morning.

April 5, 1993

While spring seemingly refused to break through the grey of a morning that still grasped at strong elements of winter's chill, the atmosphere within the courtroom was heating up.

Mike Stone's cross examination of Hightower continued with little preamble.

M. STONE: On Friday we were talking about the two résumés. Do you recognize these?

HIGHTOWER: Yes.

M. STONE: First, the one written when you were living in Newport. Do you recognize that one?

HIGHTOWER: Yes. I wrote it.

M. STONE: Under "Education" from URI, it says you had a cumulative average of 3.97 to 4.0. "Employment" it says 1976-1978 that you worked for Riker Labs. It says pharmaceutical salesman. It says that you increased sales to ninth overall nationwide and increased total sales over thirty-five percent in only two years of employment. That's not true. Now, the other résumé, written when you were in Barrington on Chantilly Drive. The portion where it says 1976 to 1979, would you read that?

HIGHTOWER: (Holding the document presented to him and reading in a clear voice.) "Redeveloped failing pharmaceutical territory. Established working rapport with doctors, hospitals, and pharmacists, increasing sales 25 percent. Third ranking in nationwide sales of several company products."

M. STONE: Read under "Education."

HIGHTOWER: Wright State University, Dayton, Ohio, 1983 to 1987, completed four-year Ph.D. program with GPA of 3.6

M. STONE: This is not true, is it?

HIGHTOWER: No.

M. STONE: Read about University of Rhode Island.

HIGHTOWER: "1973-1975 University of Rhode Island, BS Degree with GPA of 3.97, graduated Magna Cum Laude."

M. STONE: This is not true, is it?
HIGHTOWER: No.

Stone entered three additional items into evidence that had been removed from Hightower's office on Maple Avenue, including falsified letters of recommendations. The defense attorney objected to the introduction of these letters on the grounds of what he insisted was lack of relevance. The judge permitted Stone to continue.

Stone handed Hightower one of the letters he had written when applying to graduate school.

M. STONE: Do you recognize this letter?
HIGHTOERE: Dated March 1981. Probably the letter I wrote for school. "Having worked in hospitals in military and undergraduate school, I've developed a special interest in people having need for a medical professional. I would like to help alleviate the pain and fear these patients face, as well as new approaches to medicinally treating their problems. Because of this desire to find new answers to help resolve the pain and misery of the many ill people, I believe research would be a more appropriate approach in which to achieve my goals. After graduating from college I went to work for a pharmaceutical firm learning as much as I could in the treatment of disease and relief of pain through the use of drug therapy. The more I understand about this phenomenon, I begin to realize the less is known about the principles involved in drug therapy and tissue interaction. I would like to, not only understand, but predict why body functions respond the way they do. I believe my experience in the paramedical field would bring a new and unique understanding to research and the problems these unfortunate people must face daily. Thank you for your consideration."
M. STONE: Now this is basically true Mr. Hightower. You do have a great background with drugs and drug therapy. And the way those drugs interact with people.
HIGHTOWER: Yes sir.

This was an important point for the prosecution to establish since both Alice and Emily had been drugged prior to being murdered.

M. STONE: Does the name Highland sound familiar to you?
HIGHTOWER: Yes sir.
M. STONE: Who is Mr. Highland?
HIGHTOWER: Dr. Highland was a professor at the University of Rhode Island who taught parapsychology. I had him as a professor, but he did not have a supervisory capacity over me there.

Stone got him to admit that he had signed the professor's name to one of the letters of recommendation Hightower had written himself.

M. STONE: Is the name Mr. [deleted] familiar to you?
HIGHTOWER: Yes. He was my district manager with Riker Laboratories.
M. STONE: Do you recognize this letter?
HIGHTOWER: Yes. It's a letter of recommendation.
M. STONE: Something you wrote?
HIGHTOWER: Yes sir.

By now, Robert George was strenuously objecting to the introduction of this "irrelevant" material, which resulted in another side-bar conference. Despite the defense's objections, the judge ruled to permit into evidence yet another letter.

HIGHTOWER: This letter was part of my application to Wright State University for a master's degree.
M. STONE: Please read it aloud.

Hightower cleared his throat and began to read aloud in the courtroom. There was a touch of pride in his voice as he read the words he had written about himself.

HIGHTOWER: "Having the opportunity to instruct Mr. Hightower in undergraduate as well as graduate courses taken at the University of Rhode Island was a pleasure indeed. His drive to consistently obtain knowledge was consistently exhibited in Mr. Hightower. Mr. Hightower always attended classes and was prepared to participate in the discussions. He seemed to have a systematic approach to his inquisitiveness and never hesitated to interject his own knowledge in the subject. His lab projects were clear, concise and on time. He exhibited the forms in which his projects were compared to that of a graduate student. At times he seemed to need a guiding hand with analytical thinking. However, once pointed in the right direction, his drive seemed almost unquenchable. Mr. Hightower will make an excellent student for graduate studies in any field he may choose. I've had few students who want to learn for the sake of learning. Mr. Hightower was one of those students. Feel free to contact me if there are any questions concerning Mr. Hightower's ability to succeed as a graduate student. . . . Sincerely, Dr. Highland."

M. STONE: Now this is a rather stellar recommendation. He wasn't even your supervisor, was he?

HIGHTOWER: No. He was my professor for several courses at Rhode Island.

M. STONE: So you sent this out with your application without his authority?

HIGHTOWER: That's right.

M. STONE: Now read this, exhibit 421.

HIGHTOWER: "Mr. Hightower, while working as a pharmaceutical salesman at Riker Laboratories has demonstrated a capacity for learning, the ability to communicate and the enjoyment of a challenge. Every salesperson employed with this firm must continue their education by completing home study courses. Christopher has consistently scored high on these requirements as well as being on time, while demonstrating an eagerness to learn. While Christopher's line of approach may be questioned at times, his ability to communicate seems to always come through for him.

This was brought out by the increase in sales in Christopher's territory and his ability to keep seeing, on a routine basis, the physicians he calls on. Christopher seems to thrive on challenge. When he doesn't have an answer to a question, he will use his available resources, which includes a hotline to our training department in California, to answer whatever the question might have been. Because Christopher is willing to say, "I don't know. I'll be happy to find out for you," he has earned the respect of the professionals he must deal with. Christopher will make an excellent graduate student and will be missed by us here at Riker Laboratories. If you have any questions concerning Christopher, please feel free to contact us. Sincerely, [deleted] . . . District Manager, Riker Laboratories."

M. STONE: Again you sent this out without his authority?

HIGHTOWER: Yes sir.

The relevance to the prosecution of the letters of recommendation was clear. Stone had effectively succeeded in branding Chris a liar, a braggart, and a man who wasn't above forging documents in order to achieve his desired ends.

When this part of the testimony was detailed to Susan, she could feel her blood rising, even though this line of questioning aroused no surprise in her.

At the time of his arrest, she had frantically gone through Chris's belongings looking for clues to understand, hoping to find some acceptable answer to the question of how the sum of their lives could have come to this.

She had not known he had falsified his transcripts until after he had been arrested and she had dug in the mounds of paper left over from their life together. She had been looking for any kind of evidence to support her suspicion that he truly might have done this horrible thing.

She found the cut-and-paste job he had done on the letters he had sent to Ohio. With all the investigation done by the FBI and the police, and her own private digging, Susan finally learned that he had been accepted into the biomedical science program at Wright State through fake transcripts. There was proof that the transcripts he had used to try to get into medical school were phony as well.

The patterns of his deception were already in operation that far back, even before they had married. She had been in love and had no reason not to trust him. Even after being unhappily married to him all these years, she had never realized the stories he told her about himself were just that, stories. That was one of the things that made her most angry; the foundation to their marriage, the "truths" about his history, his background, and who he was, were not real. They were all lies. It wrenched the entire foundation out from under what she had believed about him.

His academic records were closer to a below average 2.0 grade point rather than the perfect 4.0 he needed the world to believe. No wonder he could never measure up to the academic expectations of his doctoral program. No wonder he flunked his exams!

She sat in shock trying to figure out how he managed to falsify the records and have the seal of the school on it so they looked authentic. It was like being a detective. She found the piece of cardboard on which he had glued all the new records with the old parts, as well as the old one that he had cut apart. She was shocked that he kept such incriminating evidence. A psychologist might suggest it was kept as a trophy to his cleverness at having gotten away with it, but she couldn't believe it. All she could think was that *it was all so incredibly stupid!*

He had used the address of someone with whom he had worked at the pharmaceutical company as the place to write to in order to request his transcripts. When the request from the registrar in Ohio came, he and his friend had sent out fake transcripts. She guessed his usual slick con job had convinced this person to do such an illegal thing for him. This was proof that he had falsified the letter from Ernie to the CFTC. He had spent that Sunday morning at the church cutting and pasting the letter on Ernie's stationery. Again, he hadn't even had the good sense to destroy the evidence of what he had done. He had discarded the trial runs in the wastepaper basket adjacent to the photocopy machine at church. When the police began their search for evidence against Chris, they were still there, as though waiting to be found.

Susan was thrilled about her discovery of evidence that proved Chris's fraudulent past. "I found a piece of evidence to seal that bastard's fate," she had told herself. Then she thought of her sons and wondered how she would be able to explain it all to them. Paul was still under the childish misconception that daddy would be coming home again once the trial was over.

The cross-examination continued relentlessly.

Michael Stone carefully reconstructed Hightower's past, outlining one deception after another. It appeared as though the entire fabric of both Hightower's academic and professional lives was a lie. The Ohio fires were brought up, this time with the strong edge of suspicion that Hightower had set the second fire himself. It had afforded him a legitimate opportunity to have his doctoral exams postponed. Having lied his way into the doctoral program, he, more than likely, would not have been able to pass the orals and he knew it. There was no proof, despite suspicions at the time by the investigating fire department in Ohio. No charges were ever brought against him because of lack of concrete evidence. However, the circumstantial suspicion of guilt weighed like an anvil around his neck in the wake of the long pattern of deception and illegal behavior Stone was showing him to have consistently demonstrated.

Robert George offered little objection to the introduction of unsubstantiated suspicions regarding the long-ago fires.

Originally Hightower had said he just "dabbled" in investments while in Ohio, but he had set himself up as a commodities broker, and founded the Investors Guild of Dayton. It had consisted of a pool of investors who, with a minimum investment of $3,000 each, had invested a total of $102,000. Hardly a "dabbling" amount. Hightower's trading endeavors were markedly unsuccessful; within less than four months, the Investors Guild had lost practically the entire amount that had been entrusted to Hightower, although he had provided evaluation statements to his unsuspecting clients which showed their investments to be highly profitable.

M. STONE: In July of 1986, the Investors Guild had a picnic for you. You didn't show up.
HIGHTOWER: The picnic was by the staff club, members of the Investors Guild, but I didn't show up.
M. STONE: But they came to confront you about the loss of their money and you basically told them, "There's nothing you could do about it. I lost your money."

One by one, in a slow, methodical voice, Stone read the names of fifteen investors who had been members of the Investors Guild of Dayton, all of whom had lost their money as a result of Hightower's trading past the fail-safe point. Hightower blithely informed the court that these people were originally members of a stock group. He acknowledged knowing all but one of the fifteen.

HIGHTOWER: Basically I told them, I invested all your money and then lost it.

The irate group had threatened to take legal action against Hightower and file complaints and charges with the CFTC.

M. STONE: Did those charges materialize?
HIGHTOWER: No. Because we agreed if they didn't file charges I would put up my house as collateral, to reimburse them at the point where we should have stopped trading the account. Fifty percent is the limit to stop trading.
M. STONE: Are you sure it wasn't ten percent?
HIGHTOWER: I think it was fifty percent, the trading limit. I let it go down about ninety percent.

He had invested $100,000, lost it all, and then deceived the investors when he lost it.

M. STONE: Did you invest any money in this?

HIGHTOWER: No.

M. STONE: You told them you did. Your name is on here as one of the investors. . . . January 13, 1986, you are listed as an investor. "Invested $12,000." But you never invested $12,000, did you?

HIGHTOWER: That was for my mother. If it says $12,000, then I would say it was $12,000 I invested for my mother.

He had led another investor, Mr. Werner, into thinking he had a $7,000 investment when he didn't. The check had been returned from the brokerage firm and Hightower deposited it in his account.

M. STONE: You stopped payment on checks returned to Mr. Werner to close his account. Mr. Werner filed complaint with the NFA and the NFA sent two individuals to your office on April 10, 1991 to conduct an audit. And they asked you about the situation with Mr. Werner and you said he wasn't an investor with Hightower Investments, didn't you?

HIGHTOWER: I said that he did not have an open account, that he was an investor in the company.

Recess was called.

It had been a devastating interrogation. Under the magnifying glass of Stone's examination, all of Hightower's usual charm disappeared. He was shown to be a con man, a liar, and an habitual cheat who consistently led people on and falsified documents.

Michael Stone had to establish the motive for murder.

He read in open court, two letters written to Hightower by Ernest Brendel, which clearly delineated the rapidly souring relations between them.

M. STONE: April 10, 1991 letter on stationery of Ernest Brendel to be mailed to you. "Dear Chris, This is to inform you our discussion and agreement of April 1. At that time we terminated the management account agreement between myself and your company. We agreed as follows: You will return the $2,000 which was given to you as a loan/equity. You will return to me the $4,361 which was the difference between the financial account balance of $3,139 and the $7,500, which is 50% of the original account. I would appreciate the return of the above amounts as soon as possible. . . . We did agree that, because of various trading commitments on your part, you have to wait until June 1 to return the $6,361. I believe this accurately reflects honesty and understanding. . . . Please advise if you have any questions. . . . Chris, I'm truly sorry that matters had not developed as we had hoped. I wish you all the future success. . . . Sincerely, Ernie."

And on May 1:

"Dear Chris, I refer to my letter of April 10, 1991. Another far more serious problem has now emerged. You will recall that when I reopened my account with you on May 29, 1990, it was to be done on the basis of totally profitable trading results achieved by you while trading for Mr. Samard and Spaziano. You were then associated with Jonathan Allen. You provided me with an updated record on the Spaziano account which could achieve a gross profit of $65,567.65 between Dec 13, 1990 and April 3, 1991 on a $75,000 principal. I have met with Jerry Samard and he has provided information indicating a far different result. He indicated that this account lost approximately $15,000 and that the Spaziano account lost about $7,500. The trading of both accounts occurred between January and March of 1990."

Those letters showed Chris had been up to his old tricks and Ernie had found him out. In order to entice Ernie into reinvesting with him, Chris had presented false figures of another account, claiming to have solved the little glitches in his "system."

Hightower threw Stone a curve.

HIGHTOWER: When I read that letter dated May from Ernie, that's when I realized I was being blackmailed. Ernie wanted me to start up the newsletter and he wanted a part of my company.

Blackmail, again!

M. STONE: Is it your testimony that Ernie Brendel introduced you to these people to invest?
HIGHTOWER: Yes, it was Mr. Brendel.
M. STONE: Are you familiar with John Sicilini, an attorney.
HIGHTOWER: Yes.
M. STONE: You walked into his office one day, unannounced, to try to find investors for your company. It was Mr. Sicilini who brought these people, to you, (Simard, Spaziano, Bucci, etc.) wasn't it?
HIGHTOWER: No. I asked Mr. Sicilini if he would be interested in investing with me and he said that he had no interest in it.
M. STONE: So you're saying these four investors were not contacts you made through Mr. Sicilini?
HIGHTOWER: Yes. That is correct. I never saw or met those individuals in Mr. Sicilini's office.
M. STONE: If that's so, then why is it that in May of 1990, when Mr. Brendel decided to reinvest in your company, that if he was friendly with Mr. Spaziano at the time, then he would have known the actual trading results that you performed rather than the proposed figures you showed him?
HIGHTOWER: Mr. Brendel was aware of the trading facts. This was all part of the blackmailing scheme.

The end of this day's testimony was left hanging on the intriguing nail of blackmail.

April 7, 1993

After a one-day recess, the trial resumed.
Hightower's impassive demeanor on the stand never wavered.

Always soft-spoken, mild-mannered, and polite, he gave no indication he was bothered that his lifetime pattern of habitual lies
had been disclosed in open court. It was almost as though he
thought being proven a liar, was a far cry from being a murderer,
so there was no problem.

Michael Stone, his jacket open, his eyeglasses hanging loosely
around his neck from a dark string, his tie just slightly askew at
the collar, was ready to refocus his attention on Hightower's earlier direct testimony about the murders.

M. STONE: That morning when you got gas at the Shell
station you went right back to Middle Highway and the
Brendel home?

HIGHTOWER: No, I stopped at the Newport Creamery
first.

M. STONE: But in your direct testimony, you said after you
got gas that morning you went right back to Middle Highway.

HIGHTOWER: Well, I think that's what I said. And if I said
something else then this is what I meant to say. My mind
is confused about all this detail.

M. STONE: Well, were you in the Newport Creamery parking lot at eleven-thirty?

HIGHTOWER: Yes. Now I'm sure of that.

M. STONE: When you got back to the house, were the
people still there?

HIGHTOWER: Yes.

M. STONE: Where?

HIGHTOWER: In the house and garage, but I don't know
how many were in the garage or in the house.

M. STONE: You stated in your direct testimony that "they"
were following you all morning, but when you get back to
the house they are there either in the garage or in the house.

HIGHTOWER: I don't know who it was that was following
me.

M. STONE: So you didn't see anybody following you. So
how do you know someone was?

HIGHTOWER: I guess I don't know for sure. It's just what they said they were going to do.

It was the first time he testified they had told him they were going to follow him. Up to this point, being followed had been something he had noticed on his own.

M. STONE: In your direct testimony, you said you took the Camry and went to Somerville Lumber at some point?
HIGHTOWER: Yes.
M. STONE: You told the police that after having breakfast at Newport Creamery, which consisted of Belgian waffles, that you went to Maple Avenue. But that's not true, is it.
HIGHTOWER: No.
M. STONE: Then you told the police that while you were at the office between twelve and one you got a call from a male caller who stated, we have kidnapped Ernie and his family and we want $200,000 cash for the safe return and if you talk to the authorities, your family will be next.
HIGHTOWER: Yes I said that, and it was a lie.
M. STONE: And you told police that you were allowed to speak to Ernie, and you said Ernie couldn't speak too well, you had a hard time understanding him. So they let you speak to Alice and she thought Ernie's jaw was broken.
HIGHTOWER: I don't know if that's what I told police.
M. STONE: And that was a lie?
HIGHTOWER: Yes sir.
M. STONE: Then you told police he said, go to my sister's in Connecticut for the money. Her address is in the Rolodex at the house.
HIGHTOWER: Another lie.
M. STONE: Yes. Then you told police you spoke to Alice again and she told you that she and Ernie had been hooded. Another lie?
HIGHTOWER: Yes sir.
M. STONE: Then you told the police the kidnappers came on the phone and told you not to tell the authorities. They

would get back in touch with you later and then hung up. Lie?

HIGHTOWER: Yes sir.

M. STONE: So when all this was supposedly happening, you were at Somerville Lumber buying a hose and wire brush?

HIGHTOWER: Yes.

M. STONE: You said it was the killers who ordered you to go to Somerville Lumber in your direct testimony?

HIGHTOWER: Yes.

M. STONE: You said you were followed and you said you did see him follow you this time.

HIGHTOWER: No, I didn't. I was told I would be followed. I can't be absolutely sure.

M. STONE: But on your direct testimony you said, not only did they follow you, but they came into the store with you.

HIGHTOWER: I did not see them specifically, but I believe they were in the store with me.

M. STONE: Did you purchase a fifty-pound bag of lime, a wire brush, and a one-half-inch fifty-foot hose?

HIGHTOWER: Yes I did.

M. STONE: Did the killer tell you to buy all this?

HIGHTOWER: Yes they did.

M. STONE: Still driving the Toyota?

HIGHTOWER: Yes, no one else in vehicle.

M. STONE: Still being followed?

HIGHTOWER: I think so.

M. STONE: When you got back to the house were they all there?

HIGHTOWER: Some in the garage, some in the house. I don't know who was there. When I got back I believe I parked the car inside the garage and went back inside the house.

M. STONE: Well if you went into the garage, wouldn't you have seen what was in the garage?

HIGHTOWER: Not necessarily. I did see people. How many I don't know. I think there was more than one person, and at least one person in the house.

M. STONE: Which one was in the house?

HIGHTOWER: Raoul. I don't know which ones were in the garage.

M. STONE: You told police that the Toyota was covered with blood and that you went into the house, checked all the rooms, and determined the family was not there. Then you said you removed your clothing and you changed into jeans and a T-shirt, got a box of baking soda, Windex, and a rag and went back to the garage and started cleaning the Toyota.

HIGHTOWER: Yes.

M. STONE: You told them you put baking soda on the bloody area of the backseat, washed the windows, inside and out with Windex but you never cleaned any part of the exterior of the car except for the window.

HIGHTOWER: Yes I told the police that.

M. STONE: When the police asked you what you did with the rags and Windex and baking soda, you said you couldn't remember. Then you said you took the hose and washed down the driveway where you had spread the acid previously. Then you scrubbed the floor where the blood was and washed it with a hose. Then you folded the hose up, put it back in the same position where you found it on the grassy area before the garage.

HIGHTOWER: Yes.

M. STONE: Then you told them you came back in the house and changed clothes.

HIGHTOWER: Yes I told them that.

M. STONE: But in your testimony here, you said that you cleaned the windows after cleaning the floor. And what did happen to the bloody rags?

HIGHTOWER: I don't remember.

Stone patiently took him through a few more examples of his doing things that he wasn't told to do. Such as taking items that belonged to the Brendels—the gas can, bag of clothes, steak knives, a billy club—up to his office while leaving other possessions of theirs—Alice's purse and rings—in the car.

Hightower even said it was "they" who told him to take these things.

M. STONE: Hightower, you told the police that the killers told you to go to Scriabines to get more money and told you exactly what to do, and if the police showed up, they would kill your family. So you did. On direct testimony you said you stopped at a gas station and again to ask for directions and then you told the police on Monday afternoon that you left at 4:00 P.M. that you took Routes 114 and 195 then Route 95 south.

HIGHTOWER: Yes, I guess so.

M. STONE: You even stated that you pulled off at the Route 138 exit on 95 south, where you went to the drive-in at McDonald's to have something to eat. You also told them that you stopped at a gas station directly across from a Mobil station for directions, and then you stopped at a fire station and spoke to a fireman who was approximately six feet tall and chewing tobacco.

HIGHTOWER: Yes, I said that.

M. STONE: That's pretty detailed for somebody who says he doesn't care anymore. You said that ten minutes into the interview with the police that you didn't care what you told them anymore, didn't you. Yet you gave them this detailed account of where you stopped along the way to Connecticut?

HIGHTOWER: Yes.

M. STONE: You said that when you left, the crossbow was in the trunk of the car?

HIGHTOWER: Yes.

M. STONE: But before you arrived at the Scriabines' house you took it out and put it in the woods.

HIGHTOWER: Yes.

M. STONE: Did the killers tell you to stop and put the crossbow in the woods?

HIGHTOWER: No they didn't. I stopped and did it myself.

M. STONE: But you said they followed you all the way down there. They were right behind you!

HIGHTOWER: Yes. I saw them following me this time.

M. STONE: How many cars?

HIGHTOWER: One. I recognized the vehicle. A white Toyota Camry.

M. STONE: How many people were in it?

HIGHTOWER: I don't know.

M. STONE: But it's four in the afternoon. It's not dark out!

HIGHTOWER: No. But I don't know how many people were in it.

M. STONE: But you didn't tell the police about putting the crossbow in the woods, did you?

HIGHTOWER: No.

M. STONE: You said that when you arrived at the Scriabines' they had guests so you went and got some juice and then to McDonald's.

HIGHTOWER: Yes.

M. STONE: Were you followed then?

HIGHTOWER: Yes.

M. STONE: When you left the Scriabines', did you have any conversation with the men?

HIGHTOWER: No. I stopped and picked up the crossbow. One of the people was there when I picked up the crossbow in the woods. But no conversation. I picked up the crossbow. I started to leave. I tripped and fell. There was a large rock there when I fell, I hit the walkie-talkie that he had and I broke it and he got furious. I picked up the crossbow and went into the car.

M. STONE: Oh, so now we have walkie-talkies . . .

HIGHTOWER: There were many details that I left out, unintentionally.

M. STONE: How much money did the killers want from the Scriabines?

HIGHTOWER: They said they wanted $300,000.

M. STONE: Is that what you told the Scriabines, that the kidnappers wanted $300,000 for the safe return of the Brendels?

HIGHTOWER: No. I asked them for $75,000 because I could raise the rest on my own. But I knew there was no need to make up the difference because the Brendels were already dead.

M. STONE: But your family wasn't kidnapped?

HIGHTOWER: No. All I was doing was relaying the story I had been told to relay. I asked the Scriabines to keep their concerns with my family as well as with their family.

M. STONE: But the information you were supposed to relay was to ask for $300,000!

HIGHTOWER: That's correct.

M. STONE: But what about your concern for your family, that if you did not do exactly as you were told, something was going to happen to them! You told police that after cleaning up the garage you were told to go to Connecticut. You went to the Rolodex and removed the card with Christine's name and address. Did the kidnappers give you the card?

HIGHTOWER: Yes.

M. STONE: You told police that by accident you took two cards from the Rolodex, Christine's and one with the name of Don Stafford. Now you're telling us that the kidnappers gave you two cards?

HIGHTOWER: I believe they gave me three cards.

M. STONE: But when you got to the police station, you had two cards, and you said you pulled the name out of the Rolodex, and pulled out two instead. Now you're saying the kidnappers did that.

HIGHTOWER: Yes.

M. STONE: But when you were questioned by the police about the ransom from the Scriabines, you told the police you asked for $200,000, but the kidnappers only wanted $100,000 and that you wanted to keep $100,000!

HIGHTOWER: At this point it didn't matter what I told them anymore.

M. STONE: On your direct testimony you said you posed for a photo at the Scriabines'.

HIGHTOWER: Yes.

M. STONE: That's not true, is it?

HIGHTOWER: Yes.

M. STONE: You heard Christine Scriabine testify that she never asked you to pose for a photo, she never told you she was going to take it.

HIGHTOWER: She asked if she could take it, and she asked for identification.

M. STONE: In the statement you made to the Scriabines, you said you got a phone call around five-thirty on Saturday at Jones Circle from the kidnappers, but that was a lie, wasn't it?

HIGHTOWER: Yes.

M. STONE: You told the police something different too?

HIGHTOWER: Yes.

M. STONE: You told us that you met the investors, Mr. Samard, etc., through Ernie Brendel, but this says that you first met Mr. Samard through Jonathan Allen Brokerage firm. He was a broker there!

HIGHTOWER: No, that's a lie. I'm telling you the truth that Ernie introduced me to the investors.

M. STONE: Was there ever a ransom note for the Scriabines?

HIGHTOWER: No.

M. STONE: And you're telling us that the kidnappers told you to take the blood-soaked car and not some other vehicle?

HIGHTOWER: Yes.

M. STONE: Weren't you supposed to carry out the instructions to the detail?

HIGHTOWER: Yes.

M. STONE: Weren't you afraid for your wife and family if you didn't do exactly what they told you?

HIGHTOWER: Yes.

M. STONE: You said that one of the men got out of the car that was following you and got in the car with you at some point on the way back to Rhode Island?

HIGHTOWER: Yes.

M. STONE: I believe you said it was the Oriental one.

HIGHTOWER: I don't know. I'm not positive.

M. STONE: You said that after he got in the car you told

him that you thought you didn't convince the Scriabines not to call the FBI and he said, "That's all right. You've done what we told you to do."

HIGHTOWER: Yes.

M. STONE: So you tell the killer this while driving this blood-soaked car and he didn't care?

HIGHTOWER: I guess not.

M. STONE: At 6:53 A.M. you called the Scriabines and told them there was no need for them to raise the money, that you would raise it yourself.

HIGHTOWER: Yes. I was informed at that time that I was almost done and about to be released and I didn't want them to be out any more. They were going to have enough pain.

M. STONE: Didn't you call them back and tell them this because you were trying to stall them from calling the police?

HIGHTOWER: No.

M. STONE: But now you're telling us that you were more concerned about the Scriabines' financial condition than your family's safety because you were not told by the kidnappers to call the Scriabines?

HIGHTOWER: No. I thought I would be freed in a couple of hours. No one knew I made that telephone call.

M. STONE: But you told the Scriabines before you left Connecticut that their phones were tapped!

HIGHTOWER: Yes. I told them that.

M. STONE: You said under direct testimony that you didn't recall why you went to the YMCA to have a photo ID taken (Monday morning) which, by the way, was not part of the "instructions."

HIGHTOWER: Yes. I don't remember.

M. STONE: You had a family membership to the Y, didn't you.

HIGHTOWER: Yes.

M. STONE: When you left your house, when you were tossed out, you didn't have your YMCA card with you, did you.

HIGHTOWER: That's correct.

M. STONE: Isn't it true that you needed the card so that you would have a place to get washed up because you had been thrown out of the house?

HIGHTOWER: That was part of it.

M. STONE: Well then, you do know why you went there?

HIGHTOWER: I also wanted to see if I was still being followed.

M. STONE: What was your state of mind when you went to the Y?

HIGHTOWER: I wanted to be released. Looking forward to not having to deal with this situation anymore.

M. STONE: Then you went to the post office to mail the letters.

HIGHTOWER: Yes.

M. STONE: You are saying the killers instructed you to mail the letters and cash that check?

HIGHTOWER: Yes.

M. STONE: What was important to them about that stuff?

HIGHTOWER: The exoneration of me through the letter, continuing to set me up, continuing with the scheme.

M. STONE: You said that on Monday morning you were at your office twice. Did you see anyone following you?

HIGHTOWER: Yes. When I went to the post office a car pulled directly behind me. When I returned, that individual followed me to the other places I went.

M. STONE: What did he look like?

HIGHTOWER: He was an American. Tall. Six-two to six-four and elderly.

Now there was a tall, elderly American following him. Stone did not even bother to ask where he came from or what happened to the two Orientals and the two Latin Americans.

M. STONE: Where did you go from the post office?

HIGHTOWER: I don't remember but I know he was following me. I went to Dunkin' Donuts.

M. STONE: You said you saw someone standing next to the

toolshed next to your office and he told that you were free at that time.

HIGHTOWER: Yes.

M. STONE: And then he said don't speak about anything that happened for four months or he would come after your family.

HIGHTOWER: Yes sir.

M. STONE: Which one was this?

HIGHTOWER: I don't remember.

M. STONE: But you said you dropped him off at the Mobil Station. You still don't know which one he was?

HIGHTOWER: No.

M. STONE: Was he the same one that drove home with you from Connecticut?

HIGHTOWER: I don't know.

M. STONE:But you are sure you dropped him off before you drove to Newport.

HIGHTOWER: Yes.

M. STONE: Then you said you went to Castle Hill to decide what to do and that's when you decided to go to the FBI and tell them everything, right?

HIGHTOWER: Yes.

M. STONE: But you were so concerned about being followed and quickly getting to the FBI, why did you pass through Barrington?

HIGHTOWER: It's the shortest way.

M. STONE: Well maybe, but it's taking you right back where you just left these people and there are other routes you can take to get to Providence?

HIGHTOWER: Yes. Maybe easier ways but not shorter. I wanted to go to Providence to get lost in a crowd.

M. STONE: What makes you sure that these people didn't see you when the police stopped you in downtown Barrington, about one and a half miles away from where you dropped this guy off at the Mobil station?

HIGHTOWER: I wasn't sure. But it was my belief that they had left after releasing me.

M. STONE: You talked a great deal about a newsletter.

HIGHTOWER: Yes. It was Mr. Brendel's idea to start the newsletter.

The prosecutor entered into evidence a document entitled "Business Plans for Christopher J. Hightower." In it was a statement that it was Hightower's original plan to start up a newsletter. Stone further suggested that it was, and always had been, Hightower's idea and that it was he who presented the idea to Ernie Brendel, trying to get him interested in investing in it. The document was written by Hightower while he was still in Dayton, long before he met Ernie. There was also the mention of starting a newsletter in the fall of 1986, still well before the two men had met. The fourth page of the document under "Products and Services," stated:

"My company will provide investment information and knowledge from a technical perspective in stocks and commodities. However, my main emphasis will be on the commodity market. I will manage accounts on an individual basis ($50,000+) and through a pool of small investors ($10,000+). Once a steady track record has been established, using my trading system, I will then produce and promote an advisory newsletter to the public."

HIGHTOWER: I meant this to be a newsletter, once my trading track record was established.

Stone gave the defendant a penetrating look and simply nodded as the judge called for a recess.

Hightower's expression never changed throughout the intense questioning. He was in complete control. Occasionally, he stared in front of himself with vacant eyes, but he no longer broke down, not even when shown a graphic photo of the murdered child, Emily. Back from recess, Stone took another turn in the case.

M. STONE: Did any of these people in the garage ever display any weapons to you?

HIGHTOWER: Yes. Semiautomatics.

M. STONE: You actually saw semiautomatic weapons?

HIGHTOWER: When I actually saw them was Saturday in the garage. When they had come into the house and taken me into the garage. But I believe there were weapons prior to that. One of the things that Mr. Brendel and I discussed on Thursday evening when he explained to me what was going on with the movement of the heroin via the wine cases. Knowing that, the next day, I made the assumption that they were carrying weapons.

M. STONE: Assumption aside, you're saying that when they handcuffed you and took you out to the garage, you saw weapons?

HIGHTOWER: Not until I got into the garage.

M. STONE: Who had the weapons?

HIGHTOWER: Everyone was carrying a weapon.

M. STONE: So all four men had semiautomatic weapons?

HIGHTOWER: Yes. Handguns. They were not physically waved in front of me. I saw them in their belts.

Stone was quick to bring up the point that Hightower had his briefcase with him all weekend. Besides the pry bar and rope, his briefcase had a gun in it—a powerful, quick-firing, semiautomatic 9mm Glock pistol with thirty-eight rounds of live ammunition.

M. STONE: Your briefcase remained with you?

HIGHTOWER: Yes.

M. STONE: Did you ever remove any valuables from the briefcase?

HIGHTOWER: No, I never looked inside the briefcase. I don't recall opening it from the time I left Jones Circle.

M. STONE: What kind of a gun was in it?

HIGHTOWER: It's a semiautomatic pistol, 9-mm. I own that gun. I think I owned it since September of 1990.

M. STONE: When you left Jones Circle, you took your

briefcase and the gun was in it. You also said that when you left for Connecticut you took that briefcase with you.
HIGHTOWER: Yes, but I never opened it.

Stone presented the gun and ammunition into evidence. He showed it to the jury, as well as to Hightower, who identified it and the ammunition as belonging to him.

M. STONE: Why didn't you use it to protect yourself, your wife, and your kids if you had it with you all this time?
HIGHTOWER: To protect myself against four individuals would have been pointless. By the time I had seen the Brendels murdered I had never even thought about it after that. My mind wasn't thinking in those terms.
M. STONE: But you have full access to a fully loaded handgun, and you took no action to protect yourself?
HIGHTOWER: No.

Stone turned to his associate Pat Youngs for a brief conference at the prosecution table. He picked up a folder, and began fingering the papers within. It was as though a critical point had been reached in the interrogation. Now came the incriminating paper trail of letters Hightower had written while at the ACI, all of which were cleverly meant to exonerate him, to focus suspicion elsewhere, to clear up details of the murders, to blame the dead man for causing the three murders, and ultimately, to plan additional murders from jail through a hired hit man on the outside.

M. STONE: Shortly after arriving at the ACI one of the correctional officers showed you a letter that was written to you while you were there?
HIGHTOWER: Yes.
M. STONE: And in that letter it was revealed that if you didn't tell everything you knew about the disappearance of the Brendels, harm would come to your children.
HIGHTOWER: Yes.
M. STONE: So. You thought this letter came from the four individuals?

HIGHTOWER: Yes, that's what I perceived it to be.

M. STONE: But the content says they did want you to tell everything that happened!

HIGHTOWER: I perceived it as a reversal of the situation, that if I did talk, harm would come to my children because they knew where they played soccer.

M. STONE: So you are assuming that the letter that tells you to tell everything was written by the same people that said if you said anything within four months they would harm your family?

HIGHTOWER: Yes.

M. STONE: Isn't it true that letter could have come from anywhere?

HIGHTOWER: Yes. But I thought it was a subliminal message telling me not to talk to the police.

M. STONE: So you met Michael Giroux (an ACI inmate.) You said that within the first couple of weeks Mr. Giroux approached you and told you that he thought he would write some ransom letters to the Scriabines to take some heat off you?

HIGHTOWER: Yes. I said that.

M. STONE: You said that this angered you.

HIGHTOWER: Yes.

M. STONE: You said Mr. Giroux apologized to you.

HIGHTOWER: Yes.

M. STONE: So you say you had nothing to do with ransom notes?

HIGHTOWER: I had nothing to do with ransom notes, or the first three letters. But a fourth one was written by me.

M. STONE: But if you were so upset about Mr. Giroux writing ransom notes, why did you write one?

HIGHTOWER: It was a letter stating that the Brendels were dead. I don't recall writing any ransom letters.

The "Lynx" letters were finally presented into evidence. Stone turned to the defendant and holding up a letter in front of him, demanded:

M. STONE: Did you write this?

HIGHTOWER: Yes.

M. STONE: (Reading) "December 12, 1992. . . . We have taken (kidnapped) the Brendel family. You are to raise a ransom of $200,000 for their safe return." Now you just told us you had nothing to do with any ransom notes.

HIGHTOWER: Read the rest. It was just notes I was writing down.

M. STONE: (Reading) "If you go to the authorities we will kill them and then kill the family and kids. (I can't raise that kind of money). You have until midnight Wednesday. Ernie, go to my sister." This is instructions for somebody else, isn't it?

HIGHTOWER: No.

M. STONE: Then, why are you saying "Ernie, go to my sister." Ernie's already dead.

HIGHTOWER: That letter was confiscated from me the day the bodies were found. It was written when my attorney was Mr. Hardiman.

M. STONE: This was not taken from your belongings, Mr. Hightower.

HIGHTOWER: Yes it was.

M. STONE: No it wasn't.

HIGHTOWER: Yes it was.

Stone gave a light, unacquiescent bow of his head.

M. STONE: So, to continue with the letter. "Ernie, go to my sister! The one in New York: No, in Connecticut. Alice, I think Ernie has a broken jaw but we are fine. Kidnappers, go to the house and look in the garage. In the car you will find wallet, ring, and purse. Use this as evidence for the Brendel sister. Go to the store. Buy a bag of lime. Dip it in water and put the bag in the back of the car. We will be in touch." Now you say that one of the Lynx letters was sent to one of your relatives to be mailed out?

HIGHTOWER: Yes.

M. STONE: Would that be [deleted]?

HIGHTOWER: That is correct.

M. STONE: Do you recognize this?
HIGHTOWER: Yes, it's the outer envelope addressed to my cousin. It was taken from me at the ACI.
M. STONE: "[deleted] [address given]." Written by you?
HIGHTOWER: Yes.
M. STONE: The return address on the envelope, "Bobby Moran, [address given]." Written by you?
HIGHTOWER: Yes.

It was strongly suggested that the letters to be presented contained information only the killer would know.

M. STONE: (Reading) "Anyway, I had my bail hearing, and am being held without bail until my trial. Also, please find enclosed a letter a prison inmate asked me to mail out for him. I would really appreciate it if you would mail it in a town other than your own and as soon as possible. He assured me its [sic] nothing bad, so I hope you will do this for me. I've written to my mother and [name of one brother and one sister] but they never get my mail. This is the second piece of mail to you. Can you write me back and let me know if you received everything I mailed to you. [name of brother] is sending me some books so I can start writing children's books. And I'm learning computer programming. Yes, I am optimistic about being found innocent and I refuse to let them confiscate my mail. I am going to learn two new professions while I'm here and when I get out I hope to be making some money. One never knows what one can accomplish until you try. The most difficult part about being here is the loss of my family, but I know God will see that we're all together again, Love Jemire."
HIGHTOWER: That's what my family calls me.
M. STONE: Then on the inside is the letter addressed to John Hardiman, [address given]." Then inside you put another two-page letter. This letter reads: God forgave me, but I cannot forgive myself for being involved in the murder of an innocent child. Hightower did not kill the Brendels. They

were killed because of Ernie's stupidity. Over time he stole over $2 million from me."

It was the first time a specific amount had been put on the money the four men had been searching for throughout that long bloody weekend.

M. STONE: (Continuing to read) "They found out and killed him. Hightower was an unexpected surprise that showed up. It's too bad. He had finally convinced Hightower to work for him. A week before Brendel was executed there was a $50,000 loan that had been granted to Hightower to bail him out and put him under their control. On Friday September 20, Brendel met with four people in his garage. To keep Hightower away, he sent him to pick up Emily. There was much fury when he interrupted us without the child. Brendel had to make a call to secure the girl's release. They found out Hightower's predicament and Brendel's weekend scheduled plans. They told him to make a call Friday night. When the call was not made and the Brendels did not answer his phone, the decision was made to force Brendel to talk before he could run. Around 1:00 A.M. Saturday morning the garage was broken into. The files in the garage were poured [sic] over for the next several hours. We were in the garage when Hightower came in and got the bicycle around 6:35. Had he looked in the horse stall he would have been killed. When Hightower left, three entered the house. We knew the weekend agenda. Ernie had stayed in the garage while Alice was forced to make the phone call. In the garage, Brendel still refused to tell about the money. He was put in the car and beaten with a black crowbar. He still would not talk so was shot in the right rear ass or leg. I couldn't tell for sure. Then he was shot in the left shoulder. He still would not talk so his wife was brought out and was strangled to death right before his eyes. Only when he was told that his daughter was next did he give up the money location. Unfortunately it was too late. Once one was killed they all had to die. Brendel was shot in the chest to be sure he didn't lie. When the little girl was brought out he gave the last piece of information. The little girl was then strangled. Brendel was shot again in the chest. When he fell down he was shot in the top of the head. Five arrows, five shots. The bodies were put in the car that night and buried where they were meant to be found. Ernie had not shoes or socks. Alice had pantyhose, no shoes and Emily had on socks and shoes. A belt was dropped into Ernie's grave. Everyone involved wore skin tight [sic] hoods and gloves. They won't find any prints or hair."

Keenly aware that the writer was not missing a trick, the attention of the entire courtroom was riveted to the sound of Stone's voice reading the long letter written by "Lynx." Knowing that forensics would certainly be able to find evidence of four people inside a house and garage for such a prolonged period of time, Lynx had even invented a feeble excuse for not finding any.

M. STONE: (Still reading) "While searching the house and files we found the letter Brendel had written for Hightower in the checkbook so we laid it on the computer where Hightower could find it. After Hightower's trip to Connecticut, the car was emptied around 4:00 A.M. at his office. We found the piece of lime bag buried in the grave site. Once the entire family was killed, somebody had to take the fall. Hightower slept there. His prints must have been everywhere. Hightower did everything he was told to do. The ransom note, we followed him. There are two things I don't understand, why did Hightower state he received a phone call when he said he had written a ransom note, and why did he say the ransom was only $200,000. We had stated $300,000. By the way, the kidnapping was only a cover. There is a lot more to this story. I'm not sure they plan on telling it all. They never should have killed Emily. It's been eating away at me ever since it happened. And I can no longer take it. I'm not one of them. . . . Lynx."

The letter had been seized by a correctional officer and never mailed.

The more Stone read, the more fancifully warped the writer's imagination appeared to the attentive audience in court. While in jail, Hightower's imagination had soared to new heights. Not satisfied with the first letter, he wrote another several days later, this one addressed to Ray Monese in East Providence with a return address to Frank Monese. Perhaps the first Lynx letter hadn't accomplished the cover and alibi he wanted. A rewrite by "Lynx," with a few more pungent details, was necessary.

Michael Stone pressed his advantage.

M. STONE: (Reading) "December, 14, 1992. . . . God forgave me but I cannot forgive myself for being involved in the murder of a little girl. Brendel was killed because he stole money and he wouldn't give it up. His family was killed because of his stupidity. Brendel had previously been confronted about the missing $2 million. Finally on Friday, four people questioned Brendel. We were also updated on Hightower and the weekend events. It's too bad Brendel screwed up because 18 months of work with Hightower had to be abandoned along with the $50,000 loan."

Unexplained.

M. STONE: (Reading) "That loan would have been put in our pockets for good. We met with Brendel on Friday afternoon. To keep Hightower away we sent him to pick up the little girl. When he returned without her and interrupted the meeting, the people were pissed. Brendel had to leave and call so Hightower could pick up the child. Brendel was told he had till 10 PM to call with information on the money. When Brendel did not call and he did not answer our calls, it was felt he would run. And it was decided he best be eliminated. Around 1 AM Sunday, we broke into the garage through a back window. The next several hours were spent purging the files in the garage. We were hiding in the horse stalls when

Hightower entered the garage around 6:45. He would have been killed had he seen us."

It remained unexplained why Hightower would enter the garage at 6:45 A.M. while the killers were hiding in the horse stalls, since Brendel had supposedly let him in the house the night before to spend the night when he was thrown out of his own home by the restraining order. The more the "Lynx" tried to clear up the story, the more confused it became.

M. STONE: (Reading) "When he left on the bicycle we entered the house and took the Brendels hostage. Brendel's wife made a phone call to cancel weekend plans. A corner of the garage had things belonging to Hightower. A black cap was taken and worn by the one chosen to beat Brendel. Any blood splatters would get on the cap. Brendel was put in the car to keep noise down and beat with a black pry bar. He would not give up the money. He was taken out of the car and shot in the right rear buttocks [sic] then in the left shoulder. Still no money. His wife was called out and strangled in front of him. He agreed to give up the money but it was too late. Brendel was shot in the chest and questioned more about the money location. When he was not convincing he was shot in the chest again. When he fell he was shot in the head."

The letter implied they shot Brendel with a crossbow before he revealed the location of the two million dollars because it was too late. Too late for what?

M. STONE: (Reading) "Five arrows. Five shots. The child was then strangled. The bodies were put in the trunk. The rest of the afternoon was spent searching the house. Everyone wore gloves and skin tight [sic] hoods. You won't find any prints or hair. During the search, the letter Brendel wrote for Hightower was found in the checkbook. It was placed so Hightower could find it. Saturday night the bodies were buried at the grave site. Brendel had no shoes or socks. Wife, pantyhose [sic], no shoes. Child, shoes and socks on.

Because of Brendel's greed and stupidity, his family was killed. Hightower was set up because he was at the wrong place at the wrong time."

The letter stated that even though they left Brendel's letter withdrawing his complaint to the CFTC for Hightower to find, Hightower was nevertheless set up to take the fall for the murders.

M. STONE: (Reading) "We followed Hightower on Sunday and Monday. He did everything exactly like he was told to do. Sunday morning around 4 AM, we entered the Brendel car and took the piece of lime bag out. It was then buried at the gravesite. There are several things I don't understand. Why did you say three arrows wounds instead of five? Hightower said he got a phone call when he received a ransom note which was part of the set up. And why was the ransom for only $200,000? We had asked for $300,000. I told you this because they killed the child. When I have the main name, I will reveal every one and everything. . . . Lynx."

The letters were both written after the bodies were found and a bail hearing had been set for Hightower. There was a long silence in the room before Hightower broke it with a feeble explanation of some of the inconsistencies raised by the letters.

HIGHTOWER: I testified three arrows because that's all I saw. But then the medical examiner said five. The black pry bar used was the same one found in my briefcase. I had no idea the pry bar was in there.
M. STONE: What about Ernie not having shoes and socks on? Are you telling me you heard about that at a bail hearing?
HIGHTOWER: Either that or the fact that I was there when the bodies were buried.
M. STONE: Oh, you were there when the bodies were buried! You said you just dug the graves and after you dug the graves they put a hood on your head and took you away!
HIGHTOWER: I thought I said I was there.
M. STONE: But how would you know that at the grave site?

You testified it was dark out. Only moonlight! Was Emily
wearing a jacket when she was killed!
HIGHTOWER: No.
M. STONE: You saw her when she was killed. Was she
wearing a jacket when she was buried?
HIGHTOWER: No.

Stone grabbed another letter from the folder in front of him.
His voice was edged with undisguised anger as he read aloud
from another note from "Lynx." Although it was confiscated
before it could reach her, this one was for Susan.

M. STONE: Another note! "You have 24 hours to speak
with your husband in reconciling your differences. Five
days to withdraw your divorce. If you don't, we will kill
your parents and children leaving you alive only. If you
discuss this with anyone, then we will still kill your parents
and children just for the challenge of beating the cops. To
show you we're not kidding, your sisters [sic] body can be
found . . . (three dashes)." Is this what you call getting more
aggressive in your letters?
HIGHTOWER: Yes.

Another note, this time detailing for the assassins he was trying to hire the habits and routes of two of the intended victims
was read.

M. STONE: Another note: "Kathy Slicker: Apartment at
East Providence and Riverside. Drives a dark blue Ford
Escort, 1989. Handbell practice, Tuesday, 7:00 to 8:00 at
church. Works at Old Stone Trust in Providence. . . . Clyde
Slicker: Teacher, Rhode Island College. Tennis on Tues-
days at tennis club behind Grossmans on Rt 114 (?) in
Riverside. No set pattern on trips to New Hampshire. Al-
ways leaves on a Friday afternoon. Drives light blue or
grey Ford escort [sic]. License plate [—]."
Did you write that?

Chris did not deny it.

HIGHTOWER: Yes.

M. STONE: Another letter: Dated 11/6/91, the day before the bodies were found . . . "Dear Mr. Hardiman . . . On three separate occasions we sent ransom letters to the Sc— at Colonial Way to give you a final opportunity to secure the release of the Brendel family.

(NOTE: "Sc—" was the way Scriabines were referred to in the letters.)

They again involved the FBI against our specific instructions not to. As a result of their stupidity we have cut up, burned and buried the remains of Alice and Ernie in the Vermont mountains. Our prior contact has informed us that Emily has been effectively sold into slavery into South America for $50,000. Yes, we are being very smug and confident. We are sending you this note because we left no clues and we know they'll never be found. Our people are the best. You will hear from us again. You're [sic] client is innocent. Brendel is dead because he stole money from us and his sister was stupid. Hightower is financially ruined because he refused to cooperate with us. The Sc— and the FBI are embarrassed [sic] because they . . ." (blanked) And you wrote this one? The day before the bodies were found?

HIGHTOWER: Yes. But I don't know if I wrote the date on there. I wrote that after Mr. Giroux involved himself with those three previous letters. That was the first letter I wrote to give Mr. Giroux.

M. STONE: Another note. So you never gave that first "ransom note" to Mr. Giroux?

HIGHTOWER: No. It was just notes.

M. STONE: Notes! You made phone calls from the ACI?

HIGHTOWER: Yes. Rose Amadeo. The assistant pastor there. She accepted my collect phone call at the White Church.

M. STONE: You also spoke to a Mr. Coombs? And your attorney?

HIGHTOWER: But my wife wouldn't talk to me.

M. STONE: Well, why didn't you tell one of these people who spoke to you, to warn your wife that she was in danger?

HIGHTOWER: I don't know.

M. STONE: Another letter from "Lynx" to your ex-wife: "246-0111 (White Church number) 8:40 AM I am a professional assassin and have been told to kill your boys, then parents, then sister if you don't reconcile with your husband immediately. The cops can't help you forever." When did you write this note?

HIGHTOWER: I don't recall the date.

M. STONE: And yet another letter. "Have you ever considered reconciling with your husband? That's too bad because I'm going to kill your boys, parents and sister when your divorce is final. Go to your husband now before your kids become the first to die." You wrote this too?

HIGHTOWER: Yes sir. But I don't remember the date. I do recall that Mr. Giroux looked at the first one and told me I should rephrase it.

By the end of the day's session, Michael Stone had finished reading to the court the letters attributed to Lynx, which Christopher Jemire Hightower admitted to writing himself.

April 8, 1993

The cross-examination was almost over. There would only be a morning session.

M. STONE: You testified that at some point in time you became much more aggressive with these letters.

HIGHTOWER: Yes.

M. STONE: At some point in time did you enter into any agreement with your fellow inmate, Michael Giroux, regarding any book or movie rights you might get.

HIGHTOWER: Yes.

M. STONE: When was that?

HIGHTOWER: I don't remember a specific time.

M. STONE: You testified yesterday that it wasn't long after

you entered into the original agreement of him continuing these letters that you learned he was actually forwarding this information to the state police.

HIGHTOWER: Yes. It was before I entered into the agreement. In order to get Mr. Giroux to continue to send those notes he insisted on having some type of information that I was, in actuality, going to pay him for what he was doing.

M. STONE: You said it was shortly after you were incarcerated that Mr. Giroux started sending out these ransom letters. And right after that you figured as long as he had done that, you would become more aggressive and have him start sending threatening letters.

HIGHTOWER: No, it wasn't decided specifically that way. The original situation was the fact that Mr. Giroux sent these first three letters out without my knowledge. Then I agreed to a fourth letter with him saying that the Brendels were dead and that I didn't want any more involvement with the police. At that point Mr. Giroux became extremely apologetic and apologized for his interference because of the comments I had made that there was Chinese Mafia involved in this and at that point we talked about him and his friends on the outside assisting in providing protection for my family since I had received no help or protection from the police department.

M. STONE: Then you became aware that he was sending these letters to the state police?

HIGHTOWER: Shortly after that, but before the bodies were located.

M. STONE: Before the bodies were located you found out that Mr. Giroux was turning these letters over to the state police. You say it was before that you discussed the book and movie rights?

HIGHTOWER: I don't remember that.

M. STONE: If you knew that Michael Giroux was passing this on to the state police, then there would have been no reason to enter into any agreement with him, would there?

HIGHTOWER: If I didn't do it, then Mr. Giroux would stop doing what he was doing and I wanted to do anything I could to protect my family. Some letters were written to inform them where their activities were, where their homes were. I tried calling the church. I spoke with the associate minister, Rose Amadeo. I spoke with Tom Coombs. I asked him to do some things for me, like get my glasses, which he did. When he (Giroux) started insisting, somewhere along the line, on being paid, that's when I entered into the book and movie rights agreement.

M. STONE: Mr. Hightower, isn't it the truth that you had no idea that Mr. Giroux was not sending these notes out but giving them to the state police instead?

HIGHTOWER: I knew he was giving them to the state police.

M. STONE: Isn't it a fact that you had no idea that from the start he was handing these notes over to the state police. Not because you wanted to watch those people on the outside, but actually kill those people and that you offered him fifty percent of book or movie rights that you would accrue on this case?

HIGHTOWER: No.

M. STONE: What is this, Mr. Hightower?

HIGHTOWER: That's the note to give the movie rights to Mr. Giroux. Dated 12/20/91.

M. STONE: What is this?

HIGHTOWER: Basically the same note.

M. STONE: When did you give him that one?

HIGHTOWER: I don't remember. I guess in January.

M. STONE: Why was it necessary to give him two agreements?

HIGHTOWER: He told me that he had mailed the first agreement out to his people and that it got lost.

M. STONE: You said you knew he was giving these to the state police, why would you believe one got lost?

HIGHTOWER: Well, he wanted another one; it didn't matter, so I gave it to him.

M. STONE: (Reading) "To Mike Giroux from Christopher Hightower" 12/20/91. . . . Dear Mike, Please find this note short and self explanatory [sic]. I Christopher Hightower hereby of sound body and mind agree to divide any profits from movie or book rights related to my case. The division will be equally shared, 50/50. Sincerely, Christopher Hightower."

A second note from Christopher Hightower to Mike Giroux:

"I Christopher Hightower, being of sound mind and body do hereby agree to equally share 50 percent of the proceeds that arise from book and movie rights that arise in my case to one Mike Giroux. This is a legally binding contract. . . . Christopher Hightower."

Isn't it true, Mr. Hightower, that the reason you were agreeing to sign off everything you might accrue from anything was because you wanted Mr. Giroux to hire people on the outside, not to protect your family, but to actually kill them.

HIGHTOWER: No. There is nothing in relationship in that to the Lynx letters that were passed out.

Stone held up yet another letter close to Chris's face for him to see.

M. STONE: Do you recognize this.

HIGHTOWER: Yes, it's my writing.

M. STONE: "December 23, 1991 8:40 AM" It says: "Divorce you. Death. Hightower did not kill the Brendels. I know because I was there and when I have evidence to convict the other three, I will turn myself in." Then it says, "Call them D.A. and D.D. go to a public place together. Set up a certain date and time because you don't trust either one alone. Call them and tell them who you are and where you are and be ready to turn yourself in with the evidence to exonerate Hightower."

Michael Stone would not let up. An impatient, angry note crept into his voice.

M. STONE: Isn't it a fact you didn't know Mr. Giroux was giving these letters to the state police! You thought he was sending them to the people you had agreed to contract to

have some people killed to make it look like they committed the crimes to save you.
HIGHTOWER: No.
M. STONE: Isn't what I've just read a set of instructions?
HIGHTOWER: Yes it is.
M. STONE: Is this your writing?
HIGHTOWER: Yes it is.

As Stone continued to read, it was obvious the prosecutor was angry and he could barely hide it any longer.

M. STONE: "The system is looking for the passing of letters through the mail. That we know. So be careful. You might want to arrange to send a letter out with a name in code so the letter will not be opened by the addressee but for whom the letter is really for. This could be arranged either via the telephone or letter. I'm glad to see the schedule of events. The ones closest to me are in the lead as primary subjects. . . .

The secondary subjects should not be discussed until next week unless all the details can be worked out. A phone call needs to be made. You will revel in its madness and beauty. Make sure you destroy this and envelope. I just received my mail. I go to court on Jan 21, 1992. Arrange subject one, (bowling) on Monday night before the court hearing if possible." (subject #1 being Susan?)

The letters demonstrated beyond any reasonable doubt that, while he was plotting murders from inside prison, he was egocentrically characterizing the beauty of his own madness.
Stone turned to him, held up another letter, and roared:

M. STONE: Did you write this!
HIGHTOWER: Yes.
M. STONE: (Reading) And this! "The parable of life is that all things on earth have a beginning, a middle and an end. Death. The process of this biotic biosphere are all relative. Thus sometimes, the parable is interrupted prematurely. The story is inconsequential. They require no detailed planning

or writing. The results are all that really matters, achieved through a sadistic nature.

Another story at another time would certainly require more planning. As you know the cops think I am an associate with writing letters to the outside. This can't be so because my attorney told me not to write anything. I personally believe that if anybody from the outside is writing anything, they will continue because they know what to say and they have paper, envelopes and stamps. Why waste the money on telephone calls when you can write? That way Ma Bell won't get rich. So perhaps one telephone call to make sure there is no mis-understanding would be appropriate. I need you to believe that I have been put into a cell by myself so I can be watched to make sure I am not mailing anything out. How do you think they can explain the arrival of your mail. You can bet your ass I'm not writing anything. Whoever is out there I'm sure will send one more piece of mail. Obviously there are two stories to this episode. Hopefully one can be told now and the other planned out a little more. Thanks for listening to my babble. You can probably teach a dog to write as well as that, but then again, what are friends for? I know, I know. Yeah. But in my case it must be female. See you later."

It was all so damning and exhausting that it almost was not nec-essary for Stone to go after him any further. Brilliant though the prosecution had been, the defendant had condemned himself with almost every word out of his mouth and every word he had put to paper. Now it was time to close in for the finale and re-create for the jury, in abbreviated form, the events as they really happened.

M. STONE: Mr. Hightower, isn't it a fact that you knew Mr. Brendel would never, ever withdraw that letter he sent to the NFA and the CFTC?

HIGHTOWER: No sir, that is not true.

M. STONE: Isn't it a fact that you went to Middle Highway on that Thursday night with that crossbow with a plan to kill Mr. Brendel?

HIGHTOWER: No.

M. STONE: And that at some time around ten-thirty or so you tried to break in the back door with that pry bar that was found in your briefcase but you sounded off the alarm so you panicked and went back out into the woods, and you waited there in the rain and in the mud to see if anybody came, and when nobody came, you went into the garage and spent the rest of the night?

HIGHTOWER: No.

M. STONE: And when Mr. Brendel came into the garage after taking Alice to work the next day, you killed him with the crossbow?

HIGHTOWER: No.

M. STONE: And then you killed Alice and Emily. . . .

HIGHTOWER: No.

M. STONE: And your plans became interrupted. . . .

HIGHTOWER: No.

M. STONE: And then you disposed of those bodies in shallow graves.

HIGHTOWER: I had no idea where the graves were located.

M. STONE: And when there was not enough money in the house and in the bank accounts you got greedy and went to the Scriabines to get money out of them, didn't you!

HIGHTOWER: No.

M. STONE: And then you called them back because you were afraid they would call the FBI.

HIGHTOWER: I called them back but not because I was afraid they would call the FBI.

M. STONE: You lied to the Scriabines, you lied to the police, and now you are lying to this jury!

Hightower reiterated what he had maintained all along despite all apparent indications to the contrary.

HIGHTOWER: I did what I was told. Since I've been here to the best of my recollection I have told the jury the truth.

Of all the bold-faced lies that had strained the patience of the court, perhaps this last was the most audacious of all. Tragically for all concerned, Hightower's biggest con was on himself.

The attitude in the courtroom seemed guarded and even hostile toward Hightower. By the time Defense Attorney Robert George stood up to attempt some damage control in redirect, Hightower sensed he had not done a complete job in convincing the court of his truthfulness. He did not want to admit to himself how the prosecution had caught him on every point. Perhaps he should have listened to Robert George in the first place. Perhaps he should not have testified after all.

His attorney's face seemed calm as they faced one another again across the barrier of the witness stand, but underneath the facade, Hightower sensed he was grim. He knew George would try to buffer some of the damage of the prosecution's questioning. Under George's redirect, he positioned his body to face the jury in an attempt to help. During cross-examination, he had only glanced at the jury, periodically darting his eyes toward them. Now answering George's questions, he looked directly at them. It was good strategy to make eye contact. To those in the courtroom he seemed more comfortable and relaxed with a friendly attorney questioning him again.

George started the redirect by trying to defuse the importance of the forged school transcripts, suggesting that all Hightower had wanted to do was get accepted; once in school he had been certain he would do well, and he had done well to some extent, so he had really harmed no one. Down deep, all he cared about was the welfare of his family.

R. GEORGE: Did you write those letters of recommendation to go along with your application to Wright State.
HIGHTOWER: Yes. The transcripts were forged also. I wanted to be able to provide better support, a better life for my family.
R. GEORGE: Didn't you consider just getting better grades.
HIGHTOWER: Yes, but I figured if I didn't earn the grades once I was in, I would flunk out, so what's the difference? I was hurting no one but myself.

R. GEORGE: Was it ever discovered at Wright State that the documents were forged?
HIGHTOWER: I have no idea. But I did receive my degree. In the master's, my overall GPA was a 3.86 and when I left the Ph.D. program the combined masters and Ph.D. GPA was 3.76. These were real grades. I never completed the Ph.D. program.

In trying to defuse the money loss of the Investors Guild of Dayton, Ohio, George suggested his client had simply made an honest error in business judgment from lack of experience, and had tried to make restitution; he had never kept any of the lost funds for himself.

R. GEORGE: This investment club of Ohio . . . $102,000 down to around $8,800 or $9,000. Were you using those funds for your own personal use?
HIGHTOWER: No. I reimbursed those people by selling the house and returning the proceeds to the investors. I was never charged with wrongdoing as a result of that. I became registered after the Ohio investors incident.

As for the gun he took with him to Connecticut, what was the significance? It hadn't been used, it was legal, and it was never a secret.

R. GEORGE: Do you recall testifying about the arrowhead?
HIGHTOWER: Yes. I test-fired the crossbow into the bag of peat moss and the arrowhead broke off when I tried to remove the arrow from the wall, the bag of peat moss was against the wall. A total of six arrows had been purchased and when we left the garage five arrows were placed with the crossbow.
R. GEORGE: And you did tell the police about the gun you had from the beginning, didn't you?
HIGHTOWER: Yes.

Hightower could not understand why they would not believe him when he testified he had been followed the whole weekend. He had told that to the police early in their interrogation of him.

HIGHTOWER: I told the police that Monday morning I was aware of two cars following me. One of them had a license plate with a number of sixteen or nineteen and I believe it was a blue Pontiac. The second car was a white Camaro or Firebird and the license plate number [—] or something. I told the police I had written the numbers down on a piece of paper that was in my office on my filing cabinet.

Finally, George tried to defuse the prosecution's suggested motive for murder. Ernie's letter of complaint to the CFTC was essentially unimportant to his future. It had nothing to do with his continuance as an investment broker.

R. GEORGE: If you had lost your license, could you have continued to work as a broker?
HIGHTOWER: Yes. The only time you need to be licensed by the industry is if you are providing trading recommendations to the general public where you have more than fifteen clients involved. Since I only had three or four accounts throughout my entire career, I was not totally concerned with that situation whatsoever.

It didn't work.

Chapter 30

The Verdict

The jury deliberated only one full day. The only thing they asked for was the legal definition of kidnapping. Hightower tried to make eye contact. He looked at the jurors expectantly as they reentered the courtroom. This time, no one said "Good morning, Mr. Hightower" as they returned to their seats in the jury box.

Once seated, Judge Sheehan turned to them.

JUDGE SHEEHAN: Has the jury reached a verdict?
FOREMAN: We have.
JUDGE SHEEHAN: As to count one as to the charge that the defendant, Christopher Hightower murdered Ernest Brendel, how do you find the defendant?
FOREMAN: Guilty.

It was all over. Hightower did not flinch.

JUDGE SHEEHAN: As to count two, as to the charge that the defendant Christopher Hightower murdered Alice Brendel, how do you find the defendant?
FOREMAN: Guilty.
JUDGE SHEEHAN: Count 3, as to the charge that the defendant Christopher Hightower kidnapped Emily Brendel, how do you find the defendant?
FOREMAN: Guilty
JUDGE SHEEHAN: Count four, as to the charge that the defendant murdered Emily Brendel, how do you find the defendant?
FOREMAN: Guilty.
JUDGE SHEEHAN: Count five, as to the charge that the defendant Christopher Hightower broke and entered the Brendel garage, how do you find the defendant?
FOREMAN: Guilty.
JUDGE SHEEHAN: Count six, as to the charge that the defendant Christopher Hightower entered the Brendel home with the intent to commit a larceny therein, how do you find the defendant?
FOREMAN: Guilty.
JUDGE SHEEHAN: Count seven, as to the charge that the defendant Christopher Hightower negotiated a false instrument in the amount of $2,700 with the intent to defraud the Rhode Island Hospital Trust National Bank, how do you find the defendant?
FOREMAN: Guilty.

JUDGE SHEEHAN: Count eight, as to the charge that the defendant Christopher Hightower negotiated a false instrument in the amount of $1,500 with the intent to defraud the Rhode Island Hospital Trust National Bank, how do you find the defendant?

FOREMAN: Guilty.

JUDGE SHEEHAN: Count nine, as to the charge that the defendant Christopher Hightower buried Ernest Brendel in violation of the law, how do you find the defendant.

FOREMAN: Guilty.

JUDGE SHEEHAN: Count 10, as to the charge that the defendant Christopher Hightower buried Emily Brendel in violation of the law, how do you find the defendant?

FOREMAN: Guilty.

JUDGE SHEEHAN: Count eleven, as to the charge that the defendant Christopher Hightower buried Alice Brendel in violation of the law, how do you find the defendant?

FOREMAN: Guilty.

JUDGE SHEEHAN: Mr. Foreman, is this your true verdict?

FOREMAN: Yes it is.

The defense attorney asked for each juror to be polled individually as to each count.

There was very little emotion from Hightower during the reading of the verdicts. Occasionally, he looked at his attorney. To his surprise, they had not believed a word he told them.

Susan: *I heard all this part on the radio at work. Each guilty lifted my heart a step up and out of the refrigerator in which it had been residing for two years.*

The Sentence

In 1979, the death penalty was declared unconstitutional in Rhode Island. Rhode Island's Attorney General Jeffrey Pine had instituted legal proceedings in an attempt to reinstitute it. At the time of Christopher Hightower's sentencing, the maximum penalty permitted by law was life in prison without benefit of parole.

"Do you have anything to say before sentence is imposed?"

Hightower showed no remorse. He continued to stick to his story. "I am a victim," he declared self-righteously. "Rather than search for the truth, someone had to be found guilty of these crimes, crimes that I didn't commit!"

The gentle touch of levity in Judge Sheehan's demeanor that appeared from time to time during the trial was no longer present as he proceeded to impose sentence.

"I've been on the bench for twenty-eight years," Judge Sheehan began slowly. "In those twenty-eight years, the first fifteen were devoted to defending persons charged with crimes. Many were charged with murder and many were charged with multiple murders. I have never in my entire career, either cases that I have tried or cases that I became aware of, seen such a horrible evil crime as this. To hold those two women, the little girl and her mother in that house while their father was dead, and they knowing it, and causing the mother to make a phone call to cover up is probably the most basic evil that I have ever seen in my entire career and hope I never see it again. You deserve life without parole, and I intend to give you, sentence you, to life without parole.

"As to count one, charging you with the murder of Ernest Brendel, wherein the jury has found not only did you murder Ernest Brendel by torture but they have also added in their own hands, that aggravated battery, I sentence you to life, without benefit of parole."

After the first life sentence was imposed, Hightower turned to his attorney and whispered in his ear, but other than that, he showed no emotion. He sat stoically through much of the reading of the sentences, feeling deeply that he was being treated with gross unfairness.

"As to count two charging you with murder of Alice Brendel," Judge Sheehan continued in a strong, firm voice, "I sentence you to mandatory life, that sentence will be consecutive with count one.

"As to count three, I sentence you on the kidnapping charge of a girl, a child under the age of sixteen, namely Emily Brendel, I sentence you to life imprisonment. That will be consecutive with counts one and two.

"As to count four, I sentence you to life without parole. That will be consecutive to counts one and two and concurrent with count three.

"As to count five, I sentence you to ten years in the Adult Correctional Institute.

"As to count six, I sentence you to ten years in the Adult Correctional Institute.

"As to count seven I sentence you to ten years in the Adult Correctional Institute.

"As to count eight I sentence you to ten years in the Adult Correctional Institute.

"As to count nine I sentence you to five years in the Adult Correctional Institute and impose a fine of $10,000. That is consecutive with counts one, two, three and four.

"As to count ten, I sentence you to five years in the Adult Correctional Institute and fine you the sum of $10,000. That is consecutive to counts one, two, three, and four and count nine.

"As to count eleven, I sentence you to five years in the Adult Correctional Institute and fine you the sum of $10,000. That is consecutive with counts one, two, three, four, nine, and ten."

Judge Sheehan looked directly at the convicted murderer, paused for a moment, and then spoke words that resonated, not only for himself, but for the entire room. "And I might, for the record, add the reason of making these sentences consecutive. For seven weeks you caused major law enforcement, both federal and state to search for the bodies of Emily, Ernest, and Alice Brendel. It is this court's opinion you knew exactly where they were from day one, notwithstanding your testimony. I also would ask the clerk to take the letters that I detached from one of the presentence reports along with the pictures of the late Emily Brendel and Alice and put them in the record.

"I wish to inform you, Mr. Hightower, that you have a right of appeal. If you cannot afford an appeal, you can apply for a public defender or you can prosecute the appeal yourself. You have a statutory period which I'll ask you, Mr. George, to inform him of the time for the appeal. . . ."

During their closing statements, the prosecutors had asked for the maximum penalty, the defense had asked for fairness. He received both. Rhode Island had imposed its harshest sentence for the seventh time since it abolishment of the death penalty. Hightower would never again see the free light of day.

"This court will be in recess."

The gavel slammed down as decisively as the blade of a guillotine!

Epilogue

Hightower was convicted of "murder by torture."

He had always wanted to be important. To do something big. But instead of finding a cure for hypertension, he became a murderer. The Brendel murder case is considered a benchmark case in the state of Rhode Island.

Hightower had finally made an impact on the world.

He was not a "serial killer" in the traditional sense of the word—like a Ted Bundy, or a Henry Lee Lucas, or a Wayne Gacy—men who commit a series of random lust killings usually fueled by an explicit fantasy world, with a cooling off period in between, only to kill again in repetitive, ritualistic manners.

He was not a traditional "mass murderer" either, like a man who "goes crazy" and walks into a post office, or an elementary school, or a McDonald's, or to the top of a tower and shoots everyone who happens to fall within his range.

He was not a paranoid schizophrenic; he did not "hear voices" like the Son of Sam, or like Ed Kemper who heard voices telling him to kill in order to prevent the "great earthquake" in San Francisco.

Although Chris Hightower killed three people, his behavior did not fall into any of these mass-murder patterns. It seems as though Hightower was an old-fashioned murderer, the kind who commits a crime to cover up fraud and to get revenge on a world he felt was against him.

The man who had never earned a living during the ten years

he and Susan were married, would never have to worry about earning a living again. Now he would live off the state of Rhode Island for the rest of his life at the expense of the taxpayers.

Why couldn't Christopher reach out for help or admit his difficulties.

That is a question that would haunt Susan for many years to come.

This has been a tragedy for Susan and her family as well as for the Brendel family. Feeling terribly victimized by the situation, she has had to call upon all her resources to survive the nightmarish ordeal.

She knew that she would have to change her name. Legally. Not only for herself but for her sons so that they would not have to carry the stigma of the "Hightower" name for the rest of their lives. The boys' birth certificates show "Hightower" as their last name—always an issue when signing up for activities, such as sports.

Before the trial, I decided to have our last name changed. The boys were embarrassed to be called "Hightower" as boys are wont to use last names only when hollering for each other. I also wanted to protect them from the daily association the name would bring. We were the only Hightowers in the state. My name change was very easy— one appearance in Barrington Probate Court. Unfortunately, the judge did not see fit to allow the change for the children since, at the time, their father had not yet been tried. Instead, someone called the local TV station to make a public spectacle and my request for them was denied. Not to be undone, I took my plea to R.I. Family Court where the judge granted my request despite the objections of Bob George, Chris's lawyer. Those records, with our new name, are now sealed from the public.

At home, on Jones Circle, efforts had been made to keep everything as super normal as possible for the boys. Sporting events, offset by quiet evenings at home, continued. Hands held and prayers said around the dinner table. Grandpa's elaborate train set meticulously laid out by Mitch under the baby grand in the living room, with Mitch demonstrating remarkable patience and control, a welcome legacy from his grandfather, when his younger brother, occasionally got in the way.

At first, plagued by self-doubt, a growing cynicism, even hatred for the man who had so deceived her, Susan managed, step by step, to unshackle herself from the overwhelming grief and pain she felt.

She would have to struggle to turn around the circumstances of her life, but defying all expectations, she was determined to win and to survive. Fortunately she had unconditional love from her parents and the willingness to seek help and support. No more passive acceptance. She would face it head on, with a hardiness she did not know she possessed. She was no longer blaming herself or personalizing the abuse.

People who meet me today can't believe I'm the person who was married to Christopher Hightower. Once they get over their initial shock and disbelief, they ask me all sorts of questions. Until recently, I didn't have many answers.

One frequent question was, how could I have fallen in love with him?

I thought about that one a lot.

I was nineteen. He was a charming, older, worldly man and I loved the dream I had of marriage. I think I loved the dream of what I thought was going to be, of what it could be, and I didn't want to face the reality that it wasn't there and was never going to be there. It was all a pipe dream. He talked me into this dream about how wonderful life was going to be, and how much money he was going to have, and how many things we would do together and with our children. I think he wanted to believe it. I think he really wanted to change what he had been and where he had come from and didn't want to go back to that. That was part of the reason he didn't communicate frequently with his family in Florida. I don't think he wanted to associate himself with his former lifestyle anymore. In retrospect, I came to believe that was one of the reasons he was interested in me, because I came from an area where he wanted to be.

And then, when things started going badly, I couldn't find enough legitimate reason to get out of it because there was no physical abuse.

I still had much to learn.

On a conscious level, I stayed with him as long as I did because I was afraid of his hurting me, taking my children, stalking me. Chris had so brainwashed me that I didn't believe I was capable of making an independent decision. I believed him when he said I wasn't smart even though the grades always were right there. It didn't dawn on me until years later that I was the one doing all the work and making all the good decisions in the family, not him.

On a subconscious level, one of the reasons I remained with him for so many years was the insidious fear of being abandoned for making an unpopular decision—to divorce Chris. With my family so supportive, where did this fear originate? It was a question I thought about long and hard: what wasn't I getting from my own family that was making me so fearful?

My parents would always say, "Just do your best," but I would translate that into never doing well enough for them. So many times I felt they expected more of me, which translated into a sense of being unworthy.

Another reason I stayed with Chris was because to leave him would have been a failure. I rarely failed at anything. I learned easily, I'm coordinated, I'm outgoing, I don't fail much. I don't believe my parents gave me much of a chance to fall on my face. So when I came face to face with big time failure—a divorce—it was hard to accept that I had made such a mistake.

That is also a legacy adopted from my family's philosophy. "You don't give up on something."

For years I couldn't accept that I had made a mistake. I simply thought I had to try harder and *make* things work. I now understand that it takes two to make or break a relationship and that if one person is unwilling to try, the relationship already has failed.

Most troubling of all was the ever-persistent question, whether asked directly or not: "Why did he do it?"

She always struggled with the "why." Why did this man resort to such a horrifying solution to his financial problems?

When the Brendels first disappeared, part of Susan vainly hoped Chris had not killed them. The fact that it would leave a difficult and painful legacy for their sons to work through for the rest of their lives was enough to intensify the wish. Although the signs of potential violence were present in Chris's persistent abuse of his own family, even in retrospect, it was almost impossible to believe he was capable of such brutality. But down deep, Susan always knew it was true.

Repeatedly, people asked Susan, "Did he snap?"

I keep saying, no, he didn't snap. He planned the crime carefully, thinking it out over a period of months. And the more I heard from the police at the time, the more it fit. He had been working towards these murders at least since April—the time he bought the first crossbow.

I believe he ran into a wall everywhere he turned. He ran out of options. Everything was closing in: Ernie filing complaints; bill collectors calling; pressure from his family for money; repossession of computer equipment; threatened loss of his trading license; eviction from his office; his first wife taking him back to court for child support; an audit by the CFTC; and finally, my decision to divorce him.

Everything.

Except for the divorce, each was a separate event I knew very little about at the time, but when linked together, the noose tightened. And it became very tight.

He had nothing left and nothing to lose. He decided to take care of himself by trying to keep the one thing that was all his: the trading license. If that didn't work, he also decided to go out in a blaze of infamy, taking with him as many people as he could whom he believed had "crossed him," and then leaving the rest of his life to fate.

I sense that filing for divorce put a major kink in his plans. My serving him with a restraining order was the singular event that set his fantasies in motion. Everything changed for him at that moment. Under pressure and suddenly without the use of a vehicle, he made a lot of stupid decisions.

For a while my heart was heavy with blame, but after thinking about that point carefully, no, I couldn't feel guilt about my timing to divorce him. I had done it independently and with total unawareness of everything else that was going on in his mind.

Susan's growth and determination to move on with life was determined not only by the death of the Brendels, but by the knowledge that Chris had intended to "eliminate" her, her sons, her entire family, his first wife, and their two daughters as well.

Of all the "Whys?" this was the most troubling of all.

It was the "Why?" that would never be adequately answered, but the one, in a way, that gave her the most strength. She had made the right move.

Looking at it from Chris's warped point of view, she could almost understand, even rationalize all of his answers except the one that called for the elimination of the children. Did he really think he could get away with it? Knowing him, he probably did.

I'm not sure he was prepared to get caught. Chris had managed to get away with so many other con jobs in his life, he believed himself outside the law and was very surprised when he was caught and his smokescreen of fabrications was not believed.

In particular, I don't think he knew he was going to get caught the way he did.

I spent days in his brain during that long period when they were trying to find the Brendels. The police came up to New Hampshire and spent a day with me going over maps of the area, trying to come up with something he liked to do or used to do. Part of me thinks he wanted to get caught; maybe the guilt from whatever he had done long ago had finally caught up to him. I don't know. The other theory is he got trapped in a tight spot, screwed up royally, and made stupid moves because he was under the gun.

Chris always believed that if he thought something, then it was true. That sounds crazy, but it's not, not really. I never believed the defense would make it on an insanity plea. They kept a suicide watch on him at the beginning, and again, when they found the bodies. He was held in an area reserved for the most notorious of people. Malocone, the fellow who ruined the Savings and Loan was in that area with him. Child killers and child molesters are in a separate area. He spent a fair amount of time in solitary for acting up a couple of times, lost a lot of privileges by getting into fights or not following rules.

Typical Chris . . .

When Chris took the stand and began to tell his twisted tale, I knew it was over. He was sane enough to lie and provide structure for all the hard evidence presented. I was not surprised when he claimed the Mafia framed him for these murders, and that the Mafia set him up to take the fall, but embellishing it with drugs and the Mafia made him look desperate, not insane.

He was paranoid about the Mafia coming after him. To me, the claim was always out of left field, but I was not surprised. Prior to the murders he wrote a letter naming Mafia people that he claimed were after him. The people he named were real. He made up a whopper of a story. He wrote down the names, signed the letter, sealed it in an envelope, touching it only where he'd folded it, and had my sister put it in her safety deposit box. (This is the letter Kathy later gave to the police.)

He was fascinated with the Mafia. He loved watching shows like *Hard Copy* and *Inside Edition*. I think he liked

The Godfather and *Goodfellas*. I have material from the time he went to the Providence Library and got them to run through all the *Providence Journal* newspaper articles in which a few of these Mafia names showed up. I have the articles and they've got the yellow highlighter he had put on the names. I believe this is where he got the names.

It seemed that everything about him was a fake! Everything!

I was such a naive kid!

Susan ultimately dealt with the truth about her husband, not only in her own heart but with her two young sons as well. It was Rev. Dye who said he had never seen anyone who demonstrated as much courage as Susan did when she decided to tell her two young sons exactly what had happened. Mitch and Paul were old enough to understand what their father had done. It took a great deal of strength to deal honestly with their feelings about their father.

Explaining to the Boys

Like me, the boys have struggled to understand it all. There were so many things to explain and comprehend—feelings of rage and sadness, confusion over what was happening and why, concern about how others would treat them, and how they felt about themselves.

One difficult task was to explain the U.S. system of justice to them on a level they could understand. That the police thought Dad had killed the Brendels and that a judge had decided there was enough evidence for a trial. Then I explained that a trial was something like a football or soccer game. There are two sides with people "cheering" for each side. The judge's job was to be the "umpire" and make sure Dad got a fair trial—that all the lawyers played by the rules; that the jury was made of 12 people who would listen carefully to both sides of the argument and they would, based on the laws of Rhode Island, make a decision. I told them the trial would go on for a long time and there would be lots of people talking about it and about Dad. Additionally, I told them that Grandpa and I had to testify, telling the court what we saw, and that Grandma would be going to the trial every day so we all could know what was going on.

The boys couldn't understand why so many of their friends had to testify—their buddy who runs the gas station, the UPS man, Paul's soccer coach, David, who taught them about telescopes, Laura and Christina's mom, etc.

I only gave them sketchy details of the actual trial as it progressed; it was more than they could understand or cope with, and Mitch told me he didn't want to know more.

Finally, on the day of the verdict I sat them down in the living room.

In the same way I had sat them down 21 months before, I told them that the jury had listened to all the evidence, the people had thought about all of it for several days and decided that Dad did kill the Brendels.

Paul asked if this meant Dad was coming home now, and I had the heartwrenching task of telling him, "no." That it meant he would stay in jail for the rest of his life and he would no longer have a father to do things with him. He was heartbroken.

Mitch, on the other hand, was relieved. He had no tears left. Now Grandma would be home every day instead of being at the trial when they came home from school and they could get on with their lives.

But the haunting question for Mitch was still, why did Dad have to go and do this and mess up their lives? It remained unanswered.

There were two things vital to the boys' positive adaptation.

First, I always told them the truth. That way, they were never caught off guard by other children, adults, or the media spreading rumors about what had happened. I believe it is absolutely necessary to be straightforward with your children, even when it's something they'd rather not hear. You don't do anyone any favors by hiding family problems in the name of protecting the children. It only causes them greater distress about what might be wrong. They begin to believe they're responsible for the problem and then don't trust you as their parent because you haven't been honest. Kids are very bright and sensitive (along with having big ears!). They pick up on feelings and bits of conversation and turn them into their own personal nightmares.

The second key was taking care of myself. There was no way I could be a good parent if emotionally and physically I was a wreck. That meant lots of sleep, exercise, and down time spent at the beach or in the garden. Emotional support came in the form of journal writing, talking with my friends and family, and regular therapy sessions. With those supports in place (along with copious amounts of help with the kids from my family), I was able to be a supportive mother and role model for my sons.

To watch the boys today you would never know what had transpired. They are very social, well-adjusted kids. Occasionally, they will bring up their father in general conversation, e.g., "My dad had glasses, too," but it is always in the past tense. For them, it's more like a death. Dad had been taken away without a chance to say "goodbye," never to be seen again. We've all been through the mourning process and they accept the truth.

There are periodic flashes of anger at what he did to them and sadness at broken promises Chris made. I believe that breaks my heart the most. He broke promises he had made to both of them and was arrested instead. To hear, "I'm sad because Dad promised to take me bowling but then he got arrested and broke his promise!" is worse than all the promises he broke to me. Their loss of innocence at such a young age is difficult to swallow. And like all kids who live in families run by moms, they wish for a father, to have a "complete" family again. When they are adults, I hope they'll understand how uniquely wonderful it is to live in a three generation household, that a family is defined by those who love each other, not by their blood relationships. I know my sons have come through this so well because of my family, and for that am forever grateful.

Recovery

People who meet me for the first time still find it hard to believe that I was Susan Hightower.

"I can't believe you're so positive about life. How did you survive?" they always ask.

I tell them you have to work yourself through it, accept it as part of your past and then move on. You can't let it run your life or it will ruin it. Learn what you can, count your blessings, and go on to better things. I survived by the grace of God, a loving honest family, supportive community, and a sense of humor (no matter how warped). When out gardening, I took to waving at the sightseers who would drive past the house to see where "he" lived. We joked about who would play each of us in the made-for-TV movie. And we laughed over Mom's piano bench cover that she needle-pointed throughout the trial. So many people asked us what it was and how it was going that we almost put a notice in the newspaper when she finally finished it—one year exactly after the conclusion of the trial.

I feel like my life has been returned to me, as if I've gone back ten years and have them to live over again. What a gift! If I can handle the hell life threw at me, I know I can handle anything. I know that if I had hidden from the horror, Chris would still be controlling my life. Instead, I've learned what I'm really made of. I can do anything I have to do and anything I want to do. I've done more new things in the last three years than in the previous ten, and it feels great! I've begun to dream again and build a future for myself and my children, but I do feel a tremendous sense of obligation to have them turn out better than their father.

I have learned to appreciate all the little things in life and how vital relationships are to surviving in the world today.

I truly comprehend how important it is to be a part of a caring community. There are advantages to living in a small town—everyone knows you, and disadvantages of living in a small town—everyone knows you. But they all still look out after me and the boys.

But along with my joy there is a sense of sadness—not as pervasive and prevalent as years ago, but always with me.

I question parent-child struggles with the boys; are they normal growing pains or related to their own struggle with their father's deeds?

I'm still startled by people who look and act like him.

I deeply regret the suffering of the children (and adults) of the town caused by the violence and loss of trust.

His family persists in trying to contact us.

Periodic publicity still surfaces.

Most of my anger is gone, but when I hear someone talk to their spouse the way Chris used to talk to me, my back goes up immediately. I want to let people know, both men and women, that abuse is so much more than being physically harmed. Only through a women's support group did I learn that abuse comes in all forms. I refused to believe I was abused because he never physically assaulted me. I had to learn about other, insidious types of abuse: emotional, social, economic, sexual intimidation, isolation, threats, using the children and using male privilege to get his way. Broken bones heal, but the scars of emotional abuse are deep and long-lasting. I had to learn and believe that I was worthy of respect and better treatment than I was receiving. And I finally had to learn to be strong enough to get out of the situation.

Although I stopped attending Al-Anon about two years before it all blew up, what I learned in Al-Anon was the foundation for my courage to finally divorce him and the tools to *cope* with each day of the hell my family and I endured. God never let me down and Al-Anon's principles of letting go, taking things one day at a time, adopting an attitude of gratitude, and trying to live the Serenity Prayer carried me through to the other side and a new life.

Moving On

The family is doing remarkably well considering the circumstances. My sister Kathy has found she's more wary of people she doesn't know. She (in fact we all) used to assume people were always telling the truth about themselves and their circumstances. Now, she questions their integrity: how long have we known them? What frame of reference do we have about them? Do they have other qualities that would lead us to believe they are honest? My parents, too, are more wary of new people, especially those trying to influence them in a particular direction.

Otherwise, life has returned to normal. We still see things that remind us of Chris: pictures, tools, a type of candybar. But we have let go of the past as much as possible.

Dad believes the family has become stronger as a unit as a result. We can talk with each other more freely and not hide anything or worry about each other's feelings when expressing our own.

Thinking of Chris

I think it is possible, deep down, he wanted to get caught. That way, he could continue to claim himself an innocent victim of the society and background in which he was raised. Chris wanted complete freedom from all responsibilities. He has that now—no bills to pay, food to prepare, yard to maintain, kids to raise. He doesn't have to think about anyone but himself. But what a price to pay! I do have moments of feeling sorry for Chris—a human being gone bad. What a waste of a human life! He had the potential to do so much good as a father, husband, community volunteer, but instead chose the other path. There are times when I'm enjoying something I take for granted and realize he'll never again get to do those things he loved: drive a sports car around Ocean Drive, rummage through the kitchen to find a snack, take a shower when and as long as he liked, grab a beer and watch the game on Sunday afternoon.

But I must not think of him too often.

Chris Hightower almost killed my spirit, something he claimed he'd never do to a dog. Yet he horribly abused me and used all other people who tried to get close to him to help him. My best friend, Emily, sitting next to me at Chris's sentencing, was the first to rejoice and celebrate with me when I finally decided to get rid of Chris. I will never forget her words the day I told her I had made my decision. She said, "Welcome back! The real you has been gone a very long time and I've missed you."

When I do bring up the past, I remind myself of all the good that came out of such evil: wonderful children, abilities and strengths never before tapped, a reverence for life itself, an understanding of how deeply I am loved by so many, and just how many truly caring folks there are in the world. Most importantly, it deepened my faith in God to take care of me through good and bad.

I married Christopher Hightower as a child, still unformed and naive.

Since the murders, I have struggled to discover the adult Susan Hightower, to think and act independently of others' and society's conventions. To determine, for me and my boys, what is really important. I still believe people are basically good. I trust them, and no, I don't hate all men. I got one in a million in Chris Hightower. Now, I see the red flags coming. I've learned how to gauge other people, to trust and be comfortable with the imperfect, fallible me. I have a few gray hairs, but I'm proud to say I've earned each one.

Don't get me wrong. This entire process was terribly exhausting work. There are days I have to force myself out of bed and into a positive frame of mind. Like any new habit, it takes long practice to think in new and different ways, and like any old habit, my reactions to situations that were previously threatening take a long time to break. Being a growing, learning human being is never easy, but it is well worth the effort.

Working through her grief and her feelings of victimization, there is an intensely inspirational quality in Susan's ability to ultimately cast aside the bitterness, reach out to the God in whom she believes so deeply, and move on to a new life.

Today, she writes:

I'm reminded daily of these hidden gifts from God in the presence of my new husband. He was an unseen opportunity, but I had to stand on my feet before I saw him. His insight and acceptance have allowed me to be myself and love that self in a relationship with him. He has taught me how to dream myself into a reality-based future with unlimited possibilities. We have an equal partnership of interdependence that will sustain us for all of our days. And I know in my heart he is the only man I have found that I trust to help raise my boys into responsible, loving adult human beings.

All this is more than, in my darkest moments, I'd ever dreamed would come to me.

I have learned the hard way, never to say, "never," and never to settle for second best.

Police Sgt. Doug Badger had once said to this author: "I feel that Hightower's answer to everything would be murder. A habitual liar, he thought he could stand there on the stand and lie. He will continue to harass the system until he dies."

Sgt. Badger's prediction came true. Hightower would not give up. He persisted in the claim that he was innocent. From jail, he wrote letter after letter to that effect.

He wrote to Susan's attorney, Arthur M. Reed, warning him that he had already contacted the Department of Justice regarding what "they have done." The "they" referred to Susan and Clyde and the testimony they gave during the trial, which he insisted were lies. He claimed, in his letter, that he did not want to contact them or "scare" them but they "know what happened and what they have done."

He continued to assert that although their "safety" was "still of concern" to him, it was no longer in his hands. He had done all he could to warn the system of their impending danger at the hands of the true perpetrators of the Brendel murders.

It addition, he wanted everyone who had been involved in the case to be indicted for conspiracy.

In his letter to Deborah Westbrook of the U.S. Department of Justice, he demanded an investigation of his allegations that new evidence was available that would prove many of the witnesses against him had "knowingly made false statements" on the witness stand, "thereby committing perjury." He also insisted that the prosecutors were fully aware that their statements were false, thereby "suborning the perjury." He claimed that it was all a planned and concerted effort on the part of the prosecution team to "secure an innocent person's conviction and incarceration."

On his list of official culprits in the conspiracy against him were District Attorneys Michael Stone and Patrick Youngs, Police Officer John Lazzaro, Jack McGraw, Louise James and Keven Ray Eaton of the FBI, Medical Examiner Richard Evans, and Sociologist for the DOC, Alan Feinstein.

Also on the hit list of conspirators were Ernie's sister, Christine Scriabine, his "former father-in-law," Clyde Slicker, and his former wife, Susan Hightower. Although he accused them all of lying on the witness stand, he magnanimously requested that Christine, Clyde, and Susan be provided with immunity from prosecution, provided that they "come to you and detail their parts in the conspiracy and perjury." If they refused to admit their part in the conspiracy against him, he demanded that they be "prosecuted to the fullest extent permissible by law."

Sgt. Badger was indeed right.

With so much time on his hands and always a willing, if not successful, student, Hightower spent many days in the prison library, during which time he had, in essence, become a jailhouse lawyer. His letters to the Department of Justice were diffused with one case reference after another to support his charges of:

". . . bad faith, harassment, or any other unusual circumstance" that would call for equitable relief. (Id. 401 U.S. at 54, 91 5. Ct. at 755,)" and the "reprehensible conduct of the prosecutors that had abridged their professional discipline and the ABA Code of Professional Responsibility, Sections 7-13. See generally ABA Standards, Section 1.1 (c), (e), and Commentary, pp. 44-45," etc.

All of which he righteously claimed led to the "willful" deprivation of his constitutional rights "as demonstrated by the mere number of conspirators" that had aligned themselves against him, Christopher Jemire Hightower, an innocent man.

It seems that the con artist in Convict #B-51024 never slept.

About the Author

Mary S. Ryzuk is the author of *Thou Shalt Not Kill: The John Emil List Story,* which was a selection of The Literary Guild, and of *The Gainesville Ripper,* which was a main selection of True Crime Book Club. She makes her home in Boonton, New Jersey.